PRAISE FOR *Wild Rose*

"[Rose Greenhow] was one of the most interesting characters in Washington during the Civil War. . . . Blackman is the first biographer to have access to her diary, and she has made thorough use of papers that other writers have overlooked. The result is probably as close to a definitive biography as we'll get. . . . Her research is solid and her judgments about her subject [are] sound." —*The Washington Post*

"There were spies aplenty on both sides in the Civil War, most of them dedicated amateurs. Only one could claim to have influenced the outcome of an important battle, and that was Maryland-born Rose O'Neale Greenhow, the subject of a fine new biography. . . . Blackman has written an excellent book, one that tells Greenhow's story without romanticizing a legendary female spy." —*The Washington Times*

"Readers will become engrossed in Blackman's able portrait, which summons the zeitgeist of the entire era through one woman's adventurous life." —*Booklist*

"Tales of Civil War spies are often full of embellished and romanticized derring-do. Not so with Ann Blackman's thoroughly researched biography of Rose O'Neale Greenhow, whose remarkable life needs no embellishment. The story of Rebel Rose, told here with great skill and lucidity, illustrates yet again that truth is stranger than fiction."

—JAMES MCPHERSON,
Pulitzer Prize–winning author of *Battle Cry of Freedom*

"This is a fascinating tale of intrigue and suspense. Blackman has discovered some truly remarkable, never-before-published papers that reveal how deeply involved Rose Greenhow was in the Confederate cause."

—COKIE ROBERTS,
National Public Radio commentator, author of *Founding Mothers*

Seasons of Her Life:
A Biography of Madeleine Korbel Albright

The Spy Next Door:
The Extraordinary Secret Life of Robert Philip Hanssen,
the Most Damaging FBI Agent in U.S. History
(with Elaine Shannon)

Wild Rose: The True Story of a Civil War Spy

Off to Save the World:
How Julia Taft Made a Difference

Wild Rose

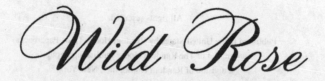

Wild Rose

THE TRUE STORY OF A

CIVIL WAR SPY

ANN
BLACKMAN

RANDOM HOUSE TRADE PAPERBACKS · NEW YORK

2006 Random House Trade Paperback Edition

Published in the United States by Random House Trade Paperbacks,
an imprint of The Random House Publishing Group,
a division of Random House, Inc., New York.

RANDOM HOUSE TRADE PAPERBACKS and colophon are trademarks
of Random House, Inc.

Originally published in hardcover in the United States by Random House,
an imprint of The Random House Publishing Group, a division of
Random House, Inc., in 2005.

Frontispiece photograph of Rose O'Neale Greenhow
courtesy of the Virginia Historical Society

LIBRARY OF CONGRESS CATALOGING-IN-PUBLICATION DATA
Blackman, Ann.
Wild Rose: The True Story of a Civil War spy/Ann Blackman.
p.   cm.
Includes bibliographical references and index.
ISBN 978-0-8129-7045-6
1. Greenhow, Rose O'Neale, 1813–1864.   2. Women spies—Confederate States of
America—Biography.   3. Spies—Confederate States of America—Biography.
4. United States—History—Civil War, 1861–1865—Biography.   5. United States—
History—Civil War, 1861–1865—Secret Service.   6. United States—History—Civil
War, 1861–1865—Women.   7. Washington (D.C.)—Biography.
8. Washington (D.C.)—History—Civil War, 1861–1865.   I. Title.
E608.G83B53 2005   973.7'86'092—dc22   2004061433

www.atrandom.com

Printed in the United States of America

13

Book design by Victoria Wong

To Mike,

with my thanks and love

PREFACE

Searching for Rose

IN AN ODD way, my search for Rose O'Neale Greenhow began as I was
finishing a biography of a contemporary woman from a different political
universe: Madeleine Korbel Albright. Secretary of State Albright had finally granted me an interview only days before the final manuscript was
due. As we shook hands, Albright said to me with an impish grin: "So,
Ann, whom are you going to write about next?"

"Madam Secretary, I have no idea," I replied, returning her smile, "but
she will be long dead."

We laughed, not knowing the secretary had planted a seed. Soon, I had
become fascinated by another prominent Washington woman who, like
Albright, had lived a rich and compelling life in the nation's capital and
had done things few women in history even dreamed of.

Rose Greenhow was little more than a footnote in history, a woman who
spied for the Confederacy, was jailed by President Lincoln, then was exiled to the South and died a dramatic death at sea. Yet as I dug deeper and
deeper, piecing together the puzzle of Rose's life, a fascinating figure
began to emerge, a person of nuance and complexity, with resilience and
power, insecurities and vulnerabilities; a devoted wife who helped her husband negotiate Washington's backbiting bureaucracy, and a loving mother
who named three of her many children Rose until one survived to carry the
name after her. She was a socialite who lived within sight of the White
House and presided over elegant dinner parties, a savvy political strategist

who played the odds on several presidential candidates, a handsome woman comfortable in the company of powerful men—a lady not unlike Madeleine Albright, but one who lived in a time of bitter struggle that ended in civil war. Rose was a strong and independent woman who had a visceral understanding of how Washington operates, a capital obsessed with power.

For more than three decades, spanning ten presidential administrations, Rose Greenhow worked Washington society, as a hostess, a lobbyist, strategist, presidential confidante, and spy. She helped the South win the first major battle of the Civil War and thereby helped to turn an insurrection into the bloodiest conflict in American history. The secret code she used to get information to Confederate generals and the diary she kept in Europe, previously unpublished, fascinated me. Shreds of letters she tried to destroy and hints of passionate affairs with powerful men led me on a hunt through dusty archives and long-forgotten diaries. She was considered dangerous enough to have been arrested at her home by the famous detective Allan Pinkerton himself. President Lincoln had her thrown into jail. And she was probably the first American-born woman to represent a government (in this case, the Confederacy) on foreign soil.

Raised from her teenage years in a Washington boardinghouse that served as a temporary home to lawmakers when Congress was in session, Rose witnessed the unfolding of the American Republic and the growth of its young capital. Like few women of her time, she participated in the nation's divisive struggles over slavery, westward expansion, and the war with Mexico. She went to California for the Gold Rush and came home through the jungles of Panama. During the Civil War, she railed against the Yankees who imprisoned her for sneaking vital military secrets to Confederate generals. President Lincoln exiled her to the South, forbidding her to return to Washington until the war was over.

In the summer of 1863, with the South desperate for help, Confederate president Jefferson Davis tapped Rose Greenhow as his personal emissary to Europe, hoping in vain to persuade the British and French to recognize the Confederate government. Rose negotiated with Napoleon III and fought for recognition of the Confederacy at the highest levels of British aristocracy and government. Prone to debilitating seasickness, she nonetheless traveled thousands of miles by ship and moved back and forth between London and Paris, talking to anyone she thought might advance the Confederate cause.

She was also a slave owner, a social climber, an elitist, and a snob.

Clever, beautiful, articulate, and outspoken, Rose circulated in a society whose members, even today, are remembered as she has not been: her hero John C. Calhoun; Senators Daniel Webster, Stephen A. Douglas, and Thomas Hart Benton; Dolley Madison; Chief Justice Roger Brooke Taney; John and Jessie Benton Frémont; diarist Mary Boykin Chesnut; Presidents Martin Van Buren, John Tyler, James Polk, and James Buchanan; and her Confederate correspondents Jefferson Davis and General Pierre Gustave Toutant Beauregard.

"She was a clever woman, much more clever than was ever admitted by her associates," wrote Confederate navy secretary Stephen R. Mallory after her death. "She started early in life into the great world, and found in it many wild beasts; but only one to which she devoted special pursuit, and thereafter she hunted man with that resistless zeal and unfailing instinct. . . . She was equally at home with Ministers of State or their door-keepers, with leaders and the led, and she had a shaft in her quiver for every defense which game might attempt and to which he was sure to succumb."[1]

Some of Rose's contemporaries—especially the women—snickered or sneered at her behavior. They whispered among themselves that her way with men passed through the bedroom. Rose chose not to write about her romantic life. She was, after all, a woman of tantalizing secrets, alluring if not discreet. Men loved her—married men. They said so in breathless, passionate letters, and they undoubtedly said so when they were alone in her house, wrapped in a tight embrace long after the sun had set. And as Mallory wrote, some probably did succumb.

But there was more to Rose's life than illicit love affairs. Men valued her counsel, as was evident from her correspondence with James Buchanan and the trust put in her by General Beauregard and Jefferson Davis. Few men, however, gave her more than a mention in their official papers, a familiar pattern now recognized by historians seeking to know more about the lives of women. When war came, she burned what letters and papers she had to keep them away from the Yankees.

Born on a small plantation in Montgomery County, Maryland, when the region was an integral part of the South, Rose knew heartbreak and hardship from early childhood. Her father died a violent death when she was barely old enough to know him, and his slave was arrested, convicted of his murder, and hanged. Rose and her sisters were separated and sent to live with relatives.

Like most women of that time, she had no career other than wife and mother and contented herself for years with engineering her husband's success and giving birth to a child every couple of years.

A few remarkable samples of her voice survive. She returned to California in 1857 for a celebrated fraud trial, and her testimony shows she was an exacting witness, undaunted by her male inquisitors. When she was summoned from the Union prison in Washington in 1862 by a federal commission to determine whether to try her for treason or send her south into exile, she used the hearing to blast the enemy for trampling her constitutional rights. She battled the commissioners to a verbal standstill—all without a lawyer. Rose's memoir of her imprisonment in Washington, published in England in 1863, lambastes her captors as murderous tyrants in her characteristic rhetorical hyperbole, but her reporting of life behind bars—with her child—is remarkably consistent with official records.

As I collected pieces of Rose's life, her year as President Davis's emissary campaigning for the Confederacy in Europe remained a mystery. Almost nothing was known about it. In the summer of 2003, I learned that the North Carolina State Archives had a diary that Rose was believed to have kept in Europe. When I received a copy, I couldn't read the handwriting; it was almost illegible. Several people told me it was written in code. Deciphering the diary became a detective story in itself.

I learned that Haskell M. Monroe Jr., the first editor of the Jefferson Davis Papers, had an interest in Rose Greenhow, and I gave him a call. Dr. Monroe, now chancellor emeritus of the University of Missouri, referred me to Professor H. G. Jones, former state archivist and curator emeritus of the North Carolina Collection at the University of North Carolina at Chapel Hill.

Dr. Jones told me he had found the journal among the voluminous papers of David L. Swain, a state supreme court judge, governor of North Carolina, and president of the University of North Carolina, who died in 1868, four years after Rose. The 128-page diary, probably left in Rose's trunk on the blockade runner *Condor* when it ran aground, had been buried in Swain's collection of North Caroliniana for more than a century.

On November 17, 1965, Dr. Jones made an entry in his own journal: "I found the diary of Rebel Spy Rose O'Neil Greenhow in the archives unidentified. Apparently never used." Struck by the unusual bold, black script, and curious about the origin of the unsigned, untitled document, Dr. Jones set about transcribing it, which took years.

"There is no handwriting I had ever seen like hers," he told me.

Dr. Jones thinks Judge Swain acquired the diary from William A.

Wright, the lawyer in charge of auctioning off Rose Greenhow's estate. Dr. Jones shared his remarkable discovery with only one other person—Haskell Monroe. Dr. Jones expected they would publish it together, when it was properly annotated. Circumstances intervened, and they never did. "It was our secret," Dr. Jones said.[2]

Dr. Jones's transcript, which he lent to me, is a treasure, revealing a diplomatic period in Rose's life that we knew nothing about. Through her own words—and with scenes verified in the official papers of others—we see Rose operating in a strange new land, fighting for her cause, undaunted by the haughty powers of emperor and prime minister. We also see a proud mother, a lonely widow, and a daring adventurer who never gave up, no matter the odds. We see how she thought and wrote, the words she chose.

Rose's first entry in the diary is on August 5, 1863, after she and her ten-year-old daughter had boarded the blockade runner *Phantom* for a dangerous race to Europe under fire from Union ships. She made the last entry one year later, just before she boarded another blockade runner for a fateful journey home.

I pieced together her life from letters and baptismal and marriage books; from court, estate, land, and tax records; from passenger ship lists and navy logs; from boarding school archives, old maps, newspapers, and correspondence seized from her house after her arrest. There was rich material in a previously unpublished travel diary kept by her husband and details of her everyday life in an early diary kept by her sister-in-law, Mary Greenhow Lee, who lived with Rose and Robert in Washington when they were first married.

I plunged into the correspondence and papers of Rose's better-known friends and acquaintances, including Calhoun, Buchanan, Confederate minister to England John M. Mason, and Confederate president Jefferson Davis. I found many unpublished diaries and letters buried in the collections of individual libraries, but I also discovered the World Wide Web was an invaluable resource. Cornell University has put all 128 volumes of the Official Records of the War of the Rebellion at a researcher's fingertips. The University of North Carolina at Chapel Hill has Rose's memoir, the now rare *My Imprisonment, and the First Year of Abolition Rule at Washington,* available online. Duke University has some of her letters in its Digital Scriptorium. The Library of Congress has posted images of Robert Greenhow's correspondence with Thomas Jefferson. The daily life of soldiers is described in their own letters home at www.letterscivilwar.com, founded by Tom Hayes of Winthrop, Massachusetts, and key editions of

Confederate newspapers are searchable at www.civilwarrichmond.com, run by Michael Gorman. There are countless gems in small repositories that I would never have tracked down without Google.

Because this is inevitably a story of the tumultuous time in which Rose lived and the city where she grew up, I am indebted to the many historians who have chronicled the period and described the places she resided and the battles she witnessed. I hope that, in their lights, I have got it right.

A biography, particularly one written 140 years after the death of a subject who left too few tracks, is by necessity an incomplete mosaic. Frustrating gaps remain. I still don't know Rose's birth date or just when she first arrived in Washington or how she was educated. Her maiden name, O'Neale, has been spelled in a variety of ways throughout the years. After she married, she usually signed her name Rose O'N. Greenhow. On the typed book contract she signed in England in 1863, the name of the author, Rose O'Neale Greenhow, was written in script. "O'Neale" was crossed out.[3] And I can only imagine what correspondence she destroyed before her arrest.[4]

To portray Rose Greenhow as I found her, I have preserved her language as she used it. When I quote from her letters, prison memoir, and European diary, her spelling and punctuation, which don't follow the rules as we know them, are unedited unless that would lead to misunderstanding. I have tried to follow the same guide with other primary sources. Rose's views on race and slavery will be abhorrent to many readers, as they were to me. That they were shared by her compatriots on both sides of the Atlantic is illuminating and horrifying. It is part of the historical record of the United States of America.

One aspect of my research that I enjoyed most was learning about the history of Washington, D.C., where I have lived and worked for more than three decades. The city is in the midst of a magnificent revitalization. Historic buildings are being restored; museums, galleries, restaurants, theaters, and street life have returned to downtown. Just off Pennsylvania Avenue, one can spot the studio of Mathew Brady, photographer of the Civil War, who photographed Rose and her daughter in prison. There is even an international spy museum in the center of Rose's old neighborhood. It is now not only safe but exhilarating to stroll from Capitol Hill to the White House, imagining what the broad, unpaved avenues and back alleys looked and felt like in her day.

As I write, the capital is once again divided by another controversial war. Washington is polarized as it was in 1860, torn by problems of race, religion, region, class, and party. Bitter rivalries alienate families and friends. In the nation's third century, the issues at the heart of the struggle that brought civil war—liberty, equality, and justice—have yet to be resolved.

Rose was on the wrong side of that struggle. She was, as she said herself, "a Southern woman, born with revolutionary blood in my veins."[5] Yet even those of us who could never accept her politics cannot help but be amazed at her resilience and zeal. Rose Greenhow was a woman of courage, imagination, and conviction, who took risks, enormous risks, for the Confederate cause, in a war for which she was willing to give her life—and did.

Contents

Part One

WASHINGTON
AT WAR

CHAPTER I

Rose's Game

THE SUMMER SUN beat down on a wooden milk cart rumbling along a dirt road that stretched up the Washington side of the Potomac River. A long, lazy cloud of yellow dust trailed from the wheels and hung in the heavy summer air. The driver, wearing a frayed gray frock, passed one sprawling Union army encampment after another. To soldiers moving supply wagons upriver to reinforce newly dug-in positions, the slender figure seemed but a simple farm girl returning home from a morning of selling sweet cream and buttermilk at the city market.

She was, in fact, not a country girl at all, but a beautiful, well-bred sixteen-year-old named Bettie Duvall, on a secret mission to Confederate territory. It was Tuesday, July 9, 1861, and the untested troops of North and South were spoiling for their first real fight.

Heading out of the Federal City through Georgetown, Miss Duvall rode by Camp Banks at Georgetown Heights, headquarters of the First Massachusetts Infantry. Some of the soldiers had left that morning, trudging up the road to Great Falls to relieve another unit that had lost two men, shot by rebels from across the river. The two were among the first casualties of war, and the city was in mourning. The Union troops occupied themselves as best they could. "We have received some new pants today, dark blue," one wrote in his diary. "Are to have blue jackets, I believe."[1] When he was hungry, the soldier sneaked out of camp to look for apples, gooseberries, and currants. He also picked a rose from the garden of a departed secessionist and sent it to his parents.² A few soldiers beat the heat by taking a dip in the river. They had been told to be ready to march at a moment's notice.³

All around camp, thin wisps of dark smoke curled up from cooking fires, carrying the smell of burnt sugar to hungry soldiers. Boiled rice with sugar sauce was being prepared for dinner.⁴ It was a simple meal, but the men liked the sweet taste, and it was certainly a step up from skillygalee, hard bread soaked in cold water and fried brown in pork fat. "I must say that Uncle Sam don't feed his soldiers as he ought," wrote a soldier who signed his letter "C.B.L." "Hard crackers and salt junk is not the thing for a man to fight on."⁵

Farther up the road, the cart passed Camp Winfield Scott, headquarters of the Second Michigan Infantry, "Richardson's Brigade." It was, in the words of soldier Charles B. Haydon, "a beautiful location," that rose "almost to the dignity of mountains."⁶ There had been some fighting upriver two days before, and the infantrymen were eager for more action. "I for one am ready to work & give if need be all I am worth which is very little, til the last secessionist is dead or subdued," Haydon wrote.⁷

The men's provisions were poor, and theft was a problem. Disease was worse. Measles had broken out, and the sick list lengthened daily. Many were also suffering from severe diarrhea and bloody flux, or dysentery, the result of their insufficient diet. When the surgeon expressed bafflement about how to cure it, some men took to doctoring themselves by drinking the juice of boiled blackberry root. They knew they had to get better quickly, because they had been ordered to pack their knapsacks and expected to move out that night.⁸

A mile beyond the camp, the cart turned sharply left and rattled onto the loose old boards of Chain Bridge. Union artillerymen at Battery Martin Scott, a new, two-tiered stone-and-turf fortification overlooking the bridge, could see the cart and driver from their outpost with its commanding, panoramic view of the Potomac. Twelve-pounder guns mounted at the end of the bridge could sweep the span, and one hundred feet up the hill, three big forty-two-pounders could rake not just the bridge, but the heights beyond. The Union cannoneers used an old stone mill on the opposite side of the Potomac to get their range. But the cart made its way peacefully across. No one stopped the driver.

Bettie Duvall continued up the road. She had left the city hours earlier and had not even gone halfway to her uncertain destination.

Despite regular reports of Confederate soldiers lurking around their camps, Union troops controlled both banks of the river, including the northern edge of Virginia from Alexandria below the capital to encampments all along Arlington Heights and up to Chain Bridge. Colonel William Tecumseh Sherman had command of the three New York regiments and the Second Wisconsin Infantry assigned to protect the far side of the river.[9]

The weather had been intensely hot, interrupted only by severe afternoon thunderstorms. During those brief, violent downpours, water rushed through the soldiers' tents like a river, soaking knapsacks and forcing them to sleep on raised boards. Confederate patrols fired across the river at Union encampments at night, and the Union forces returned fire, reporting some casualties. Everyone was on edge.[10]

Bettie Duvall drove her cart up a steep hill into the Virginia countryside. The road was narrow and badly cut by wagon wheels, slowing her progress. While most of the Union wagons and artillery were behind her, the young Southerner had to look out for Yankee scouts and pickets.

Not wanting to travel after nightfall, which would increase the danger, she stopped at Sharon, a plantation on the Georgetown & Leesburg Road[11] just west of the village of Langley. It was owned by the family of her friend Lieutenant Catesby R. Jones. Jones had resigned his post as an officer in the United States Navy and left to join the Confederate navy[12] when Virginia seceded from the Union three months earlier, but the family still lived in the ancestral home. The next morning, Miss Duvall changed into a stylish riding habit, abandoned her humble cart, borrowed a saddle horse, and cantered off in the direction of Lewinsville and Tyson Cross roads, where travelers sometimes stopped in a peach grove to rest.

The dirt road took her past deserted wooden houses and farms with weathered ox fences and through undulating fields of ripening wheat and Indian corn.[13] She headed for the village of Fairfax Court House, some twenty miles west of Washington and only ten miles north of Manassas Junction, the Confederate headquarters of General Pierre Gustave Toutant Beauregard. The Louisiana native, hero of Fort Sumter, had just arrived at Manassas from Charleston to take command of the Confederate Army of the Potomac.

Near Vienna, Miss Duvall came upon a Confederate outpost and was ordered to halt. The Confederate soldiers, whose gray jackets had already faded to butternut by the relentless sun and yellow dust, had dug trenches in the road and felled thick trees to slow the Union army's expected advance.[14] At last, she had reached friendly territory.

Miss Duvall told the pickets she had come to see Brigadier General Milledge Luke Bonham, a South Carolina politician who days before had been ordered to relinquish his command of the army to Beauregard, a professional soldier. Bonham, who remained as the general's top aide, was at Fairfax Court House, about five miles to the south. The soldiers escorted their charge to Bonham's headquarters, where she tied her horse to the bough of a tree. But when the general learned of his visitor, he at first refused to see her, fearing she was yet another lady spy dispatched by the Federals to assess the strength of the Confederate army. Told that the young woman was prepared to take her message to Beauregard herself and also, perhaps more important, that she was "very pretty," Bonham relented. "I was very much startled," he wrote, "at recognizing the face of a beautiful young lady, a brunette, with sparkling black eyes, perfect features, glossy black hair." Bonham, who seven months before had been a congressman from South Carolina, remembered seeing Bettie Duvall in the spectator gallery of the House of Representatives, a frequent gathering spot for Southern ladies.

When she told him the content of her message and he agreed to forward it to his commander, Miss Duvall reached back, took a tuck comb from a chignon of long, silky hair that had been wound gracefully around her head, and shook loose her locks. Bonham watched spellbound as a tiny bag fell out. It was not larger than a silver dollar and had been carefully stitched out of a torn piece of glossy black silk, the kind used in the finest of mourning clothes. The purse contained a slip of white paper with a combination of numbers and letters written in bold handwriting with black ink: 054 I 7 3. It was code for "Beauregard."[15] With it was a ten-word message, also in code, with information Beauregard would find critical: "McDowell has certainly been ordered to advance on the sixteenth. ROG."[16]

Bettie Duvall's mission was complete. The Confederates now knew that Brigadier General Irvin McDowell, commander of the Union forces around Washington, would march out to attack them in less than one week.

The initials ROG belonged to Rose O'Neale Greenhow, a ravishing and fearless Southerner and grande dame of Washington society. She operated a Confederate spy ring in the nation's capital, and Bettie Duvall was one of her scouts. An engaging widow with three daughters, including an eight-year-old who carried her mother's name, Rose was the heart and soul of the operation.

She had a passion for politics and many friends, both Democrats and Republicans. She also had an almost reckless disregard for danger and a fiercely independent streak. She could be manipulative and headstrong at one moment, dripping warm Southern *cha-arm* the next, each syllable melting slowly from her lips like delicate drops of dew.

Now in middle age, Rose was a handsome woman who carried herself with an air of elegance. While lines creased the corners of her dark, deep-set eyes and her waist had thickened slightly—she had given birth to eight children, five of whom died young—Rose radiated sensuality. In late evening, when she let down her luxuriant dark hair, it fell below her waist.[17]

Rose also exuded a hint of vulnerability that men found irresistible. And unlike most well-bred Southern women in an increasingly partisan capital, she entertained Union and secessionist friends not only at her table—but, it was whispered, on late night calls as well. Senator Henry D. Wilson of Massachusetts, an abolitionist Republican, was a frequent visitor. So was Senator Joe Lane of Oregon, a Democrat. Both entertained thoughts of higher office.

Rose captivated the hearts of even the most proper gentlemen, usually to their regret and sometimes to their dismay. With flattery and the finest of feminine wiles, she cajoled military secrets from Union sympathizers, whose inflated egos blinded them to her clever ways and loosened their tongues. Skilled at the art of gathering information from normally tight-lipped officials, she entertained statesmen and diplomats and charmed their lesser-ranked clerks and aides as well. Some may have had unimpressive titles, but their access to paperwork, including military maps, made them vital contacts.

But as with many players on the Washington stage, Rose's graceful manner and keen sense of style masked a nagging secret. Since the accidental death seven years before of her husband, Robert Greenhow, who had been a high-ranking official at the State Department, she had no regular source of income and was later forced to rely on a son-in-law for financial support.[18] That's never easy, especially for a proud woman like Rose Greenhow, but over the years it forced her to be resourceful. She had become a skilled seamstress and could make the fine black silk dresses with a decorative thread of white lace down the arm that she wore for years as a sign of mourning. She would have had no trouble stitching the small black purse Bettie Duvall had concealed in her hair.

Rose Greenhow was a sophisticated lady of many talents, many passions. When James Buchanan was inaugurated in March 1857, she became one of the capital's most prominent and influential women, a close friend and confidante of the president, whom she had known for years. Although Buchanan was a lifelong bachelor, there was no suggestion that he and Rose ever had a romantic involvement, none whatsoever. In fact, historians have long thought he was asexual.[19]

Yet Rose basked in the glow of her friendship with the president. It offered her entrée to the highest levels of Washington society—to the White House, the embassies, and the most exclusive salons, where political gossip was traded over fine Madeira and old port. It also gave Rose a measure of influence, which in Washington is the coin of the realm.

There were other men in her life, powerful men of equally great ambition. They pursued her; she pursued them. It was a game, Rose's game, and she didn't give a damn what anyone thought.

CHAPTER 2

Grande Dame

THREE YEARS BEFORE — April 1858 — Rose stood out like a "diamond" at an elegant masquerade ball that eclipsed every social event the young capital had ever known. "All Washington was agog," wrote Virginia Clay, wife of Alabama senator Clement Claiborne Clay.[1] But the pomp and pageantry at the Federal-style mansion of California senator William Gwin and his wife, Mary, masked a certain tension in the air. Washington had always been a city where political opponents jostled by day, vying to register their views for the public record. After sundown, however, they generally put aside partisan politics. But now the struggle over slavery was dividing the country into ever more passionate camps, and social life showed the strain. Even old friends had begun to circle one another cautiously.

Rose Greenhow was the exception. Disguised as "A Housekeeper of the Old School," the distinguished widow sparkled as she floated from one group of politicians to another, mixing easily with Democrats and Republicans, flirting with the men, fully aware that their eyes followed her eagerly—appraisingly—taking in every detail as she made her way across the room. "Although the costume was not as showy as some," gushed *The New York Times* in a front-page story, "the esprit of the wearer made her glorious as a diamond richly set." Rose's daughter, Little Rose, who had just turned five, was at her mother's side, as always. The child "appeared to great advantage as the 'White Lady of Avenel,' "² a shadowy beauty in Sir Walter Scott's romance *The Monastery.*

President Buchanan was there, having traveled only four blocks by black horse-drawn carriage from the White House to the corner of 19th and I streets, just off Pennsylvania Avenue. Members of the president's cabinet, many prominent senators and congressmen, diplomats—the cream of Washington society—and a handful of newspaper reporters were on hand. Among the journalists was Ben: Perley Poore, a longtime Boston correspondent, who was disguised as "the Merry Monarch." The ballroom was lined with floor-to-ceiling mirrors, and the richly furnished drawing rooms on the other side of the entrance hall were filled with flowers from the White House conservatories.[3]

Mary Gwin greeted her guests at the door with President Buchanan beside her.[4] Senator Gwin considered the elaborate garb his wife dictated for the occasion undignified and decreed that the president and top officials could wear "citizen's dress."[5] For the rest, costumes were obligatory. The senator's wife was disguised as "a Lady of the Court of Louis Quatorze" with a skirt of white *moire antique* and trailing a train of cherry satin. The Gwins' daughter wore a "Greek Girl" costume that consisted of a white satin skirt with full white satin pantalets. Her hair was plaited with pearls.[6] Mrs. George H. Pendleton, daughter of Francis Scott Key, came as "the Star-Spangled Banner." "She was robed in a white satin gown of dancing length, over which were rare lace flounces," wrote Mrs. Clay. "A golden eagle with wings outstretched covered her corsage, and from her left shoulder floated a long tricolour sash on which, in silver letters, were the words 'E Pluribus Unum.' A crown of thirteen flashing stars was set upon her well-poised head."[7]

Rose Greenhow's tall, beautiful niece and namesake, Rose Adele Cutts—known as Adie and now the wife of Illinois senator Stephen A. Douglas—was "radiant in pale tints of the morning,"[8] disguised as "Aurora," a vision of dawn; the wife of Ohio senator George Ellis Pugh represented "Night." The minister of the Court of St. James's, Lord Napier, who lived on the next block in a building that had served as the residence of President Monroe after the British burned the White House, wore his court clothes. Lady Napier, dressed all in white with a headdress of scarlet honeysuckles,[9] was disguised as "a Lady of the Olden Times."[10] Varina Davis, the controversial wife of Mississippi senator Jefferson Davis, came as eighteenth-century French *femme de lettres* Madame de Staël, speaking "caustic repartee" in French and broken English.[11] "We galoped wildly over Mrs. Gwin's wonderfully waxed floors," wrote Mrs. Clay. "The galop, I may add in passing, was but just introduced in Washington, and its popularity was wonderful."[12]

Despite the Gwins' Southern sympathies, they invited many Northerners to their party, including New York senator William Henry Seward, an ardent opponent of slavery, who a month earlier had denounced the Supreme Court for ruling in the Dred Scott case that blacks—whether slave or free—would never share equal rights with whites. Seward's speech accused the High Court of conspiring with Buchanan "to fasten slavery upon the United States for all time"[13] The New York senator was bitterly attacked, not only by Southerners for his well-known abolitionist views, but by some Northerners, who said only a deranged person would attack the Supreme Court of the United States in such disrespectful terms.

Rose Greenhow was at ease among these preening power brokers. She knew their vulnerabilities, when to flatter, when to listen, and how to discreetly share tidbits of information to elicit more. Democrats had been in power for many of the last thirty years, and Rose, who had lived in the city for most of that time, enjoyed the attention she won as "a wealthy and brilliant woman of the capital," as Mrs. Clay described her. "In the days of Presidents Pierce and Buchanan, Washington was a city of statesmen, and in the foreground . . . were fashion and mirth, beauty and wit."[14]

By 1858, Washington was a city of growing sophistication, and the Gwins' grand ball helped establish that. Many of the guests later dressed up again in their fancy costumes to have their pictures taken by Mathew Brady, a New Yorker who was making a name for himself doing photographic portraits of famous people. A collection of his work had been published the previous year in *Harper's Weekly,* and Brady had just opened what he called the National Photographic Art Gallery at 350–352 Pennsylvania Avenue, at the foot of Capitol Hill. Like the Gwins' party, Brady's gallery assembled images of Northerners and Southerners alike, despite the gathering clouds of war.

Rose Greenhow and her Southern friends were spending large sums on their homes and adding the latest time-saving conveniences, such as Hamilton Smith's brand-new invention, the rotary washing machine, and I. M. Singer's new "Grasshopper" sewing machine. They purchased fine silver from Galt's jewelry store on Pennsylvania Avenue and expensive chocolates from a little sweetshop called Gautier. Rose bought good lace from Harper's, known for its dainty salesmen, and stylish hats from Madame Delarue, who sold her wares with a snarl. She probably had her hair styled by François, who made house calls and used pomades and dyes and "rats" to thicken thin hair that was worn *à la Grecque*, tightly braided and fastened on top with a decorative dagger or sword and sometimes crowned with a tiara. President Buchanan's niece Harriet Lane, who acted as his White House hostess, appeared at a party sporting a dress with a low neckline to show off her ample bosom, shocking many Washingtonians with her risqué display of flesh—but setting a new fashion.[15]

Rose loved being part of the city's social life and lived quite comfortably for a time, having received a substantial settlement after her husband Robert's accidental death in 1854. She moved into Brown's Hotel, a fashionable hostelry on Pennsylvania Avenue that was popular with Southerners, but it appears she either spent lavishly or lost money speculating in stocks. Less than three years later, she was forced to put up her furniture as collateral to borrow the $260 that enabled her to rent a small house at 206 G Street, between 18th and 19th streets.[16] The arrangement allowed her to keep the furnishings, which included a ten-piece parlor suite covered in plush green material, a rosewood table with a marble top, an oak dining room table with six chairs with wooden seats, and two kitchen tables. There was also a walnut bedstead with a husk-and-cotton mattress, a comforter and feather pillows, a walnut wardrobe, a washstand with a marble top, and a clotheshorse.[17] Sometime after the Gwins' ball, Rose moved a few blocks to a fashionable neighborhood near St. John's Episcopal Church, "the Church of Presidents." Her home, at 398 West 16th Street, was within sight of the White House.[18]

Despite her precarious finances, Rose kept up appearances and was not a woman to brood over her circumstances. Just the opposite. She had a quick wit that put people immediately at ease, liked to make men laugh, and often did. But other prominent women, especially the wives of important officials, neither liked nor trusted her. At a time when women were expected to defer to their husbands' view in matters of politics, Rose was outspoken and blunt. She also had a reputation as a woman who would do anything—yes, *anything*—to get ahead. She was *ambitious*, other women said, gossiping among themselves. That may have been fine for a man, but not for a Southern woman of their breeding.

But it wasn't just ambition that drove her. Since Robert's death, Rose was often alone, cut off from the familiar banter of family and friends. Daughter Florence had married S. Tredwell Moore, who became a prosperous miner in the far West. Gertrude and Leila were in boarding school. Little Rose was her mother's only constant companion.

Rose's days were generally filled with chores and activities—shopping, sewing, social calls to other women, which could be exceedingly tedious, and, of course, visits to Capitol Hill to listen to debates from the congressional galleries and attend the Supreme Court. But the evenings were long and empty, and it was in the evening that the widow let her thoughts drift back to happier times, when she longed to be held by someone she loved, someone who could finish her sentences and love her in return. In the evening, Rose wrote poetry.

Since the Gwins' ball, many Southerners had begun socializing strictly among themselves. Rose's unapologetic support for the South was well known, but she was one of the few women in town who continued to invite Northerners to her gatherings.

One guest was Colonel Erasmus Darwin Keyes, a handsome, witty widower whom she had met years before, probably in San Francisco. Born in Massachusetts, Keyes was a West Pointer who taught at the Military Academy before being sent west during the Indian wars. He came to Washington in January 1860 as military secretary to the commanding general of the army, Major General Winfield Scott, whom he had previously served as an aide-de-camp. Keyes loved the Washington social life and prided himself on knowing the important players. He lost no time looking up Rose Greenhow, who even in her late forties knew how to gaze into a man's eyes and pierce his heart.

By his own admission long after the war, Keyes had a weakness for Southern damsels and "even with some of the matrons, not withstanding the incandescence of their treason." In his view, "beautiful women ought to be considered as contraband of war, and captured whenever found, and detained till after the fight under guard of a person of their own sex."[19]

Recalling one dinner at Rose's home, he described his hostess as "one of the most persuasive women that was ever known in Washington." Always charming on such occasions, Rose spent the evening trying to convince him not to take part in the war they both saw coming. "Among an assortment of arguments, she dwelt upon the sickliness of the Southern coasts in the summer," Keyes wrote in his memoir. "But she showed her women's weakness by prescribing to me remedies against the deadly miasmas." Keyes claimed he was never in danger of being co-opted, but "I well remember how often I was lured to the brink of the precipice."[20]

Rose's longtime rival Jessie Benton Frémont, the wife of explorer John C. Frémont, alleged years later that Rose seduced Keyes to obtain classified information from him and tried to sell love letters from him found in her house. "As a U.S. officer, she found him valuable for information—their old relations being 'confidential,' " Mrs. Frémont wrote.[21]

Senator Seward, a neighbor who lived on Lafayette Square, was another frequent guest, at least for a time. Rose found he became quite talkative after dinner, when he would light up his favorite Cuban cigars and indulge in a bit of her fine old whiskey. He was "in the morning . . . the most reticent of men in the world . . . and after supper and under the influence of the generous gifts which the gods provide, the most genial and confidential of men," she recalled. "I have often had occasion to admire the confidingness of his nature on these occasions and wondered if the judgment of the world was correct in ascribing to him the character of a subtle schemer and tortuous intriguer."[22]

One evening in the winter of 1860, when Seward was regarded as the front-runner for the Republican presidential nomination, Rose invited him to a dinner party at her new home on 16th Street. Another guest was powerful Massachusetts congressman Charles Francis Adams, the son of John Quincy Adams, and young Adams's wife, Abigail.

Politics had become so volatile that it was generally not discussed in mixed company. But that night over dinner, someone made a tactless allusion to antislavery fanatic John Brown, who had led a bloody raid on the federal arsenal in Harper's Ferry sixty-five miles northwest of Washington, hoping to seize the arsenal's guns and start a slave rebellion. Brown was captured, convicted of murder, treason, and inciting a slave insurrection, and hanged on December 2, 1859. The South rejoiced that justice was done, but in the North, he was proclaimed a hero. Throughout New England, church bells tolled, and minute guns were fired in his honor.[23]

When Brown's name was mentioned during dinner, Abigail Adams looked straight across the dining room table at her hostess and called him a "holy saint and martyr."

"I have no sympathy for John Brown," Rose replied in a soft, clear voice that silenced the table. "He was a traitor and met a traitor's doom." Then, turning to Seward, she referred to a conciliatory speech he had made on the Senate floor that week: "I think you evinced very good taste in repudiating all connection with John Brown in your speech a few days since in the Senate."

"I met him once, and but once only," Seward said. "He called on me about some matter of business, the nature of which I don't now recollect. He struck me as a wild and visionary man, erratic in his ways, and singularly striking in his appearance. But, at the same time, in our brief interview, he impressed me with the conviction that he was a bold, truthful, and honest man, but eccentric to a degree bordering on an unsettled state of mind." Mrs. Adams held her tongue, as did Rose, and an unpleasant awkwardness hung over the table until Seward diplomatically changed the subject.[24]

The incident quickly became the talk of the town. The next time Rose saw President Buchanan, he questioned her about it in a manner that might be called kidding on the level, and it put Rose on the defensive. "Do you keep spies in my household?" she snapped, embarrassed. "I should have shrunk from the most distant allusion to these incidents, had they not become matters of public notoriety. I had hoped that the social gatherings of so humble an individual as myself would have escaped observation."

Buchanan laughed. "How you talk!" he said, by Rose's later account. "I have heard it spoken of by five or six persons, who all greatly commended your spirit and independence. And you have my most hearty approval."[25]

Senator Henry Wilson of Massachusetts told Rose that the Republicans regarded Mrs. Adams's outburst as "very ill-timed." He, like Seward, had distanced himself from the raid because of his uneasiness with Northern extremists.[26] He did nothing, however, to distance himself from Rose, whose attentions he appears to have found flattering.

Several days later, Rose ran into Seward on the street, and he greeted her effusively: "I have just been writing to our friend Lady N[apier] and have told her that in all Washington, you are the only person who had the independence to give a mixed dinner party." Embarrassed that she was still the subject of Washington chatter, Rose replied: "You may also add, that I am so well satisfied with the result of that experiment that I shall not try it again."[27]

What she did not say was that if Seward had understood her real motive—studying those she expected would soon be her enemies—he would not have been so gracious.[28] In Washington, where information is power, Rose realized that her effectiveness lay in knowing what each side was thinking.

Rose cultivated the friendship of Democrats with presidential ambitions as well as Republicans. In late March, she gave a dinner at her house in honor of Senator Joe Lane from the new state of Oregon. Lane, a Southerner by birth who had been a general in the Mexican War, was a pro-slavery Democrat, a member of the Military Affairs Committee, and a likely candidate for president. Buchanan, who was not running for reelection, was said to favor Lane to succeed him, but the Democrats were growing more fractious by the day. Lane had a wife and eight children back in Oregon.

The evening of Rose's dinner party, twelve guests sat around her circular dining room table, with Lane seated to the hostess's right and California senator Milton S. Latham at her left. Other guests included Governor William Smith of Virginia; Judge Alfred Iverson of Georgia; former attorney general Caleb Cushing of Massachusetts, who would preside over the deadlocked Democratic National Convention the next month; and Rose's attorney, Edward J. Pringle of California, who represented her in a complicated California land deal that had involved her late husband. Rose's auburn-haired daughter Gertrude, radiant at twenty-one, joined them. "This was a diplomatic dinner given to advance the stock of Joe Lane of Oregon who is said to be exceedingly sweet upon the giver," Senator Latham wrote that night in his diary.[29]

Several of Lane's letters, which he signed using only his last name, found later in Rose's house, suggest that while Lane was indeed sweet on Rose, *she* may have been pursuing *him* as well. "I have had the pleasure of receiving your note," Lane wrote one day, "and would go up and see you this morning, but I am obliged to be with the Committee on Military Affairs, at 10, this morning and may not be able to leave the Senate until late this afternoon, and of evenings, you are crowded with company." Lane expressed disappointment that Rose had not been home the previous night when he called on her. "I hardly expected to find you at home last eve. It was only a quarter after 10 when I left. I could not sit long alone naturally impatient, restless and almost reckless. How could I stay alone? I will see you before many days shall pass by. Very truly, Lane."[30]

In another letter, he told her he was feeling very feeble but would visit her if she insisted. "Believe me, my dear, I am not able to move as a young man should," he wrote. "Please answer."[31] He frequently noted he was busy in the Senate but would like to see her when he could.

On Thursday, April 24, Lane and Stephen Douglas, who was Rose's nephew, were being discussed as presidential candidates at the Democratic National Convention in Charleston, but both senators remained in Washington during the deliberations. Lane wrote Rose that night, "I have no news except that the minority platform has been adopted [by a] vote [of] 165–138. I will try and come up tonight."

The convention deadlocked over slavery, and the party fractured, with the opposing camps leaving Charleston to regroup in separate cities. On

May 22, nearly a month into the crisis with no resolution in sight, Lane wrote to Rose from the Senate chamber, suggesting that she was putting too much pressure on him to call on her: "Your note has been recd," he wrote. "I would be glad to see you but you must bear in mind that the Senate meets at 11. Committees meet at 9. And of an evening, you [are] surrounded by admirers and to meet them afford me no pleasure, and besides, I have no desire to be in the way of anyone. I have no complaint to make but don't like to meet those above referred to. I may however call and see you at 9 this evening. (not certain however.) Very truly your friend, Lane."[32]

The political parties were increasingly torn. Four days before, the Republicans had bypassed Seward on the third ballot in favor of an Illinois lawyer named Abraham Lincoln, whom Stephen Douglas had defeated for a Senate seat two years before. Rumbling began in South Carolina, home of Rose's late hero John C. Calhoun, the champion of states' rights, that if the Republicans won, South Carolina would leave the Union.

The next month, Douglas was nominated for president by the Northern Democrats at their convention in Baltimore, and the Southern wing picked Vice President John C. Breckinridge of Kentucky to head its ticket, with Lane nominated for vice president. Rumors of insurrection were rampant. Buchanan received a warning to fortify the military's small, weak forts in Charleston harbor.

If Douglas succeeded, Rose would be aunt of the new first lady and, it would seem, an intimate friend of the vice president if Breckinridge won. But instead of a rush of anticipation, she felt a deep sense of foreboding. One evening she put her thoughts into verse and wrote them on stationery embossed with her monogram, ROG:

PRESENTIMENTS

There is a feeling of the heart
A dreary sense of coming evil
That bids all mirthful thoughts depart
And sends enjoyment to the d——l

A cloud that bodes the coming storm
And partly wraps the heart in sorrow
And bids our feelings bright and warm
Prepare a shroud upon the morrow

When all is sunshine to the soul
It turns its brightest hour to sadness
And grief with misty clouds will roll
Above the sunniest scenes of gladness.

Rose, who had already known more than her share of hardship, scribbled two lines under the poem that suggest how frightened she was by "the coming storm": "No misfortune of my life has been foreshadowed by a presentiment," she wrote. "Its warnings oft times disregard but ever-recurring when the thunderbolt has fallen."[33]

It was the summer of 1860, and the thunderbolt was closer than she knew.

CHAPTER 3

"The Coming Storm"

THE ELECTION OF Abraham Lincoln as president in November 1860 spelled the end of almost three decades of Democratic rule, the sudden eclipse of Rose Greenhow as a grande dame of Washington society, and the breakdown of civility in the nation's long struggle over slavery. Hope of compromise faded, and the Union teetered. The soft-spoken lawyer from Illinois won without a single electoral vote from a Southern state. Rose's nephew Stephen A. Douglas ran a dismal fourth in the presidential race, and the Breckinridge-Lane ticket's second-place showing garnered only 72 electoral votes compared with Lincoln's absolute majority of 180. Talk of secession in the South rose from idle threat to serious business, and within weeks—well before the president-elect left Illinois for the capital—the union that had held together in the long war for independence from the British and the formation of a means of self-government began to break down.

A few days before Christmas, President Buchanan was seated at a fashionable wedding when a great ruckus erupted in another room.

"Madam," he said to a fellow guest, "do you suppose the house is on fire?" Just then a congressman from South Carolina burst into the room.

"Thank God, thank God," he cried, brandishing a telegram in the air. "South Carolina has seceded!" The president, stunned, left immediately for the White House. Several of his cabinet officers from the South resigned almost immediately to return to their home states.[1]

On New Year's Day 1861, Senator Douglas and his wife, Adie, a grand-niece of Dolley Madison, threw an elegant reception at their home. His Senate colleagues, William Seward of New York and Lyman Trumbull of Illinois, were among dozens of guests, and the gaiety of the party belied the anxiety and gloom that was settling over the city that winter.[2] "Senator Douglas probably received more calls than anyone except the President, and his palatial mansion was crowded all day," said a report in *Frank Leslie's Illustrated Newspaper.* "In the dining room was a sumptuous spread . . . with eggnog, apple toddy, wine and confectionary. At this hospitable board the North and South mingled fraternally and even such secessionists as [Virginia editor and congressman Roger A.] Pryor could not decline to drink to the standing toast, 'The Union.' "[3]

Much of the South, however, did not feel so magnanimous. That same day, South Carolina began seizing Federal property around Charleston harbor, and Buchanan ordered General Scott to quietly reinforce the small Federal garrison at Fort Sumter, an unfinished pentagonal fortress on a man-made island at the entrance to the harbor. The order leaked, embarrassing Buchanan, and other Southern states began to fall away. Mississippi followed South Carolina, then Florida and Alabama, one each day. Georgia, Louisiana, and Texas went next. The seceding states took Federal property with them: forts, vessels, custom houses, mints, arsenals.

The Buchanan government, for the most part, remained passive and uncertain, but Treasury secretary John Adams Dix signaled he had no patience for rebellion. A few days after Dix took office, the captain of a Treasury Department revenue cutter in New Orleans refused an order to bring his vessel to New York. Dix telegraphed the ship's second in command to take control of the vessel, arrest the captain, and bring the ship north. "If anyone attempts to haul down the American flag," he famously added, "shoot him on the spot."[4]

On Monday, January 21, Senator Jefferson Davis of Mississippi took the floor to bid his colleagues farewell. The gallery was packed with Southern women eager to witness the emotional scene. Rose, a friend of Davis and his wife, would have made every effort to be there.

As he stood to address the chamber, Davis, always in frail health and recently unable to sleep, felt a wave of nausea wash over him. He paused, regained his composure, and in an emotional voice paid tribute to another Southern patriot, John C. Calhoun: "It was because of his deep-seated at-

tachment to the Union—his determination to find some remedy for existing ills short of a severance of the ties which bound South Carolina to the
other States—that Mr. Calhoun advocated the doctrine of nullification,
which he proclaimed to be peaceful, to be within the limits of State power,
not to disturb the Union, but only to be a means of bringing the agent before the tribunal of the States for their judgment."

For Rose, who had known Calhoun for years and thought of him as a
mentor, the sentiment would have been like a balm for pain. "Secession
belongs to a different class of remedies," Davis continued. "It is to be justified upon the basis that the states are sovereign. I am sure I feel no hostility toward you, Senators from the North. I am sure there is not one of
you, whatever sharp discussion there may have been between us, to whom
I cannot now say, in the presence of my God, I wish you well. . . . Mr.
President and Senators, having made the announcement which the occasion seemed to me to require, it only remains for me to bid you a final
adieu."[5]

With that, Davis turned and left the Senate chamber.

Rose's sympathies remained with the South, but she began focusing her
attention on a potentially useful Northerner, a powerful Massachusetts
senator named Henry D. Wilson. Wilson was not an obvious playboy.
Brought up to be a farmer, he was a stocky man with a large paunch and a
permanent scowl who lived with his ailing wife, Harriet, in one of Washington's boardinghouses for congressmen.[6] Wilson learned the cobbler's
trade, manufactured shoes, owned a newspaper, and ran unsuccessfully for
several offices in Massachusetts before his election to the Senate. He was
regarded as having few social skills. But in Washington, where power
opens doors and hearts at least as effectively as suave good looks, his title
as chairman of the Committee on Military Affairs made him an attractive
dinner guest. Wilson's committee would play a critical role in raising
Union forces after the outbreak of war and in assessing the strength of the
army and navy. Rose knew the senator had access to the military's plans,
deployments, and operations—information that could be extremely valuable to her Confederate friends.

Wilson was a driven man and spent long days in the Senate. But after
hours, in the privacy of his Senate office, he penned steamy love letters to
Rose that he signed simply "H." At least, that is how Rose made it appear.

There was an urgency to the letters, a breathless, passionate, and sometimes apologetic tone that implied the writer had a relationship with Rose

far beyond a few scones and a cup of tea. "Your note caused me great pain because when I read it, I realized you had suffered," "H" wrote at one point. "You wish me to say whether or not I will be with you tonight and also to say that I love you. I do say both. I am thankful to you for not doubting me. I am sick and suffering. Yours, H."

The hastily scrawled notes seem to respond to repeated requests by Rose for reassurance and more frequent visits. While her letters to Wilson are long lost, probably burned, some liked to imagine her enticing him into her boudoir with perfume and enough brandy that he would fall asleep after a tumble in the sheets, giving her time to rifle through his briefcase for classified documents.

One letter, written on congressional stationery on a day that Wilson was leading the debate about organizing a militia for the District of Columbia,[7] offered an apology, a promise, and a hint of danger:

United States of America
Thirty-Sixth Congress

30 JANY 1861

Your note is recd. Believe me or not, you cannot be more wretched than I am. I cannot complain. Let it suffice until we meet that for the last few days every moment and act of mine have been watched with Hawkeyed vigilance. For your sake more than my own I have been compelled to be cautious. But tomorrow at 10 A M I will see you at all hazzards.

Yours ever,
"H"

There was no war yet, and it's not clear who was watching "H." A suspicious wife? A political rival? Why would he say his caution was more for her sake than his?

Other letters offered illness as an excuse for not visiting:

I am in receipt of your note. If you knew how I suffered last night, and am still suffering. You could find it in your heart to forgive me. I had a burning fever the whole night. I am now only able to sit up because I must be with you tonight.

But sick or well, I will be with you tonight—and then I will tell you
again and again that I love you; as I now do and that too most truthfully.

Ever your
"H"

"You know that I <u>do love</u> you," said another. "I am suffering this morning in fact I am sick physically and mentally and know nothing that would
soothe me so much as an hour with you. And tonight at whatever cost I
will see you."

Her busy lover sometimes blamed his work:

If fate is not against you, I will be with you this night. I long for your sympathy for I need it. I have been labouring hard and incessantly.

My love is all.

Yours and only yours
"H"[8]

Rose kept the love letters, thirteen in all, tied in a bundle with yellow
ribbon. They were found in her house after she was arrested. Yet if she
thought they were incriminating, she could have burned them, as she did
much of her own correspondence—unless she was setting up Wilson for a
lover's revenge or trying to punish him for siding with the Union.

Scholars have wondered for more than a century whether Rose whee-
dled strategically important information from Wilson, inflated the quality
of her information by using his name—or framed the ambitious abolitionist. Whatever may have been discussed over dinner or in the bedroom, the
"H" letters contained no breach of national security. At least two historians who compared Wilson's handwriting with the penmanship in the letters insist the senator didn't write them. Ernest McKay wrote that the
official clerk of the Military Affairs Committee was a young man with the
initials "H.W."—Horace White—and that his handwriting "strongly resembled" the penmanship in the love letters. John Myers, a Wilson biographer and professor of history at the State University of New York,
Plattsburgh, adds that Wilson was devoted to his wife, which made it un-
likely that he had an affair with Rose.[9]

Hamilton Fish, who served with Wilson in the Senate before the war and was Grant's secretary of state when Wilson was his vice president, was among those who said years later that Rose and Wilson had an intimate affair. He did not, however, claim to have firsthand knowledge of the relationship.[10]

If Wilson was the "H" who signed the letters and did have a liaison with Rose, he paid no penalty. Allan Pinkerton, founder of the Chicago detective agency that bore his name, never mentioned the "H" letters in his official reports after he arrested Rose and directed the search of her home. But the exclusive club known as the United States Senate has a long history of taking care of its own. Some papers—quite possibly those letters—were taken from Rose's house after her arrest and slipped to the secretary of the Senate for safekeeping. When a special commission was considering what to do with Rose after she had spent nearly a year in prison without trial, the commissioners wrote the secretary of the Senate, saying they had found a note revealing that "you have some of the papers taken from her house at the time she was arrested." The commissioners asked that the materials be turned over to the investigating panel, but whether or not they were—and just what they contained—remained a mystery.[11] Wilson remained as chairman of the Senate Military Committee throughout the war and was elected vice president of the United States in 1872 on a ticket with Ulysses S. Grant.

The "H" letters themselves are stored in the National Archives with other correspondence seized from Rose's home and carry an archivist's notation: "Supposed to have been written to Rose Greenhow by Henry Wilson, U.S. Senator from Massachusetts." Other letters and Rose's own memoir of the war years show she was trying to get information from Wilson—and at one point she cited him as a source—but the nature of their personal relationship was not spelled out in the correspondence.[12]

In February 1861, the first seven departed states met in Montgomery, Alabama, to form the Confederate States of America and elected Davis as their president. A West Point graduate and hero of the Mexican War, as well as a former congressman, secretary of war, and two-term senator, Davis had a résumé that made him appear better qualified to be a president than Lincoln.[13]

Longtime Washington residents worried that if Maryland and Virginia seceded, the District of Columbia would be surrounded by Southern states and designated the capital of the Confederacy. If war broke out, they would be the first targets. Many of Rose's friends and neighbors quickly abandoned the city. Washington banker and philanthropist William Wilson

Corcoran, who lived across the street, was among those who packed up and left town. He spent the war in Paris and London. Southern members of Congress resigned their positions to return home, and military officers from the South switched sides and rode off to defend their states and the new country forming below the Potomac.

"Imagination can scarcely conjure up an atmosphere at once so ominous and so sad," wrote Virginia Clay of Alabama, wife of one of the departing senators. "Carriages and messengers dashed through the streets excitedly. Farewells were to be spoken, and many, we knew, would be final. Vehicles lumbered on their way to wharf or station filled with the baggage of departing Senators and Members."[14]

Almost overnight, the character of the city changed. "How shall I commence my letter to you?" Eugenia Phillips wrote her friend Mrs. Clay after the Clays had left Washington. "What can I tell you, but of despair, of broken hearts, of ruined fortunes, the sobs of women, and sighs of men! . . . I am still in this horrible city. . . . The Gwins are the only ones left of our intimates, and Mrs. G- is packed up ready to leave. Poor thing! Her eyes are never without tears." Eugenia Phillips stayed behind and joined the Confederate spy ring that Rose organized, much to the consternation of her husband, Philip Phillips, an Alabama congressman who opposed secession and sided with the North.

Rose had no intention of leaving, nor could she. Her beautiful daughter Gertrude, the third eldest, had contracted typhoid fever and was too ill to be moved. "Gertie," as she was known, had been sick for months with the characteristic high fever, weakness, and loss of appetite that accompany the disease. Rose's sister-in-law and longtime dear friend, Mary Greenhow Lee, wrote from Winchester, Virginia, to commiserate about Gertrude's health.

In a letter dated January 14, 1861, Mary said that typhoid was "considered so dangerous a disease in our climate and so infectious that I have been still more uneasy at your long silence." She allowed that she looked to God for help and hoped Rose would, too. "I still believe we will be spared the horrors of civil war & and I do not think it is religious enthusiasm that makes me take the first gleam of hope from the day God's people implored him to avert a dreadful calamity," Mary wrote. "The Secession spirit is certainly gaining ground in Virginia, even here which I consider one of the most disaffected portions of our local State."

Mary had a strong Episcopal faith and counseled Rose to take her Catholicism more seriously. It is the first suggestion Rose may have been

so weighed down by tragedy that she let her faith lapse. "Dear Sister,"
Mary asked, "why will you not trust in the same God who has inspired me
with perfect trust in his Providence? I place myself in his hands and I rest
with perfect peace."[15]

Gertrude continued to fail throughout the winter, distressing Rose,
while her Southern compatriots went about establishing a new government
and, in some cases, preparing for war.

Lincoln was scheduled to travel to Washington by train in time for his
inauguration, set for March 4, but Allan Pinkerton, the railroad detective,
picked up word that a band of secessionist fanatics intended to assassinate
him before he reached the capital. Pinkerton, who had made a name for
himself tracking down embezzlers, bank and train robbers, counterfeiters,
and murderers throughout the country, learned of the supposed assassina-
tion plot while working for the Baltimore, Wilmington & Philadelphia
Rail Road, which believed its tracks and bridges were threatened by secessionist saboteurs. Pinkerton infiltrated the conspiracy and persuaded the
president-elect to enter Washington incognito.

Armed with knives and pistols and backed up by several of his private
security agents, the Chicago detective accompanied Lincoln through
Maryland. The president-elect slumped in the last berth of a Baltimore
train, draped in an old overcoat with a wool cap pulled over his head, mas-
querading as a sick man. One of Pinkerton's operatives, Mrs. Kate Warne,
sat with him and told the conductor she was caring for her "invalid
brother." The train pulled into the Baltimore & Ohio station in Washington
before dawn, and Lincoln slipped into the city and holed up in a second-
floor suite at the Willard Hotel on Pennsylvania Avenue until his oath taking.[16]

When the ruse became known, Northerners were embarrassed by Lincoln's deception, Southerners delighted at what they took as a show of
cowardice. In the hands of political cartoonists, Lincoln's overcoat grew
into a long cloak, and his wool hat became a Scottish tam-o'-shanter.[17]

Inauguration Day dawned raw and windy.[18] An armed cavalry troop escorted the president-elect down Pennsylvania Avenue to the Capitol. Soldiers lined the parade route that was crowded with onlookers but
uncommonly quiet. Riflemen stood poised at every window. Rose's family
friend Chief Justice Roger Brooke Taney, well into his eighties and looking even weaker than he had stumbling through the Dred Scott decision
four years earlier, held the Bible and administered the oath as Lincoln
raised his hand and swore to "preserve, protect, and defend the Constitu-

tion of the United States." The crowd in front of the Capitol barely listened as the tall, lanky president promised not to interfere with slavery in states where it was lawful but warned that he did not recognize the right of secession. "In *your* hands, my dissatisfied fellow-countrymen, and not in *mine,* is the momentous issue of civil war," he said. "The Government will not assail *you.* You can have no conflict without being yourselves the aggressors."

The seven states of the Deep South had already left the Union. Lincoln could do little to hold the four states of the "Upper South"—Virginia, North Carolina, Tennessee, and Arkansas—but he was determined to keep the remaining slaves states of Maryland, Missouri, and Kentucky from joining the others.

Even Rose conceded that Buchanan had been "unfit to grapple with the terrible events." He had, she later wrote, "grown old in the service of his country . . . and would, I believe, have sacrificed his own life to have averted the doom of disruption, and sought, at least by a negative policy, to stay its progress. By a fatality of birth, he was thrown on the wrong side when the sectional divide came."[19]

Rose had nothing but disdain for Lincoln, whom she referred to derisively as "Beanpole," but she was preoccupied by Gertie's deteriorating condition. The young woman's body lost its ability to resist the dreadful wasting disease that had sapped her strength for months. On Sunday, March 17, less than two weeks after the inauguration, Gertrude died.

In the twenty-six years since Rose had married, she had given birth to eight children. Gertrude, the child who most resembled her mother, was the fifth to die. Rose spared no expense for the funeral service, held at her house,[20] with eight carriages to take mourners to the cemetery following the hearse. The bill came to $105, including $50 for the coffin, $5 for ten pairs of gloves, and $3 to open the grave.[21]

The long, tragic spring was made sadder still by increasing political strain in Rose's family. Loved ones were choosing sides. James Madison Cutts, husband of Rose's sister Ellen, had been named second comptroller of the Treasury by Buchanan, but he was siding more and more with the North. Rose's niece Adie and her husband, Senator Douglas, became intimates of the Lincolns. During the president's inaugural address, his one-time political opponent from Illinois literally held Lincoln's hat.[22] Rose's son-in-law, S. Tredwell Moore, the husband of Florence, had made captain in the Union army and was back in Nevada in charge of supplies at Fort Churchill. Florence, whose three-year-old son had died in Rose's home two years earlier, was expecting again but confined at Fort Churchill with a difficult pregnancy.²³ She had little enthusiasm for her husband fighting with the Yankees, if it came to that. But like most professional officers, he saw the war as a career opportunity.

Moore, as the family called him, was an Ohio native and had been a prosperous miner in California when he married Florence. The young man had great respect for his mother-in-law, if not for her politics, and he repeatedly asked her to use her influence, first to help him move back to the Presidio in San Francisco and then to obtain a commission as a colonel in an Ohio volunteer regiment in order to get him into the war. On March 11, Moore wrote Rose saying he had heard John C. Frémont would be appointed secretary of war. Frémont, the controversial "Pathfinder" who had explored California and been cashiered from the army for insubordination, was a longtime rival of Rose's husband, Robert Greenhow. Rose and Frémont's wife, Jessie Benton Frémont, were not even on speaking terms.²⁴

"If he should receive the appointment," Moore fretted, "good-by to any influence you may have—with the love that Mrs. Frémont bears you. I hope it is a false rumor. . . ." (It was.) Moore told his mother-in-law he thought of her as his own mother. He had paid off his debts, his mines were doing well, and he had a few thousand dollars in the bank. "Should the mines turn out as I expect, I will be well enough off to permit us to live comfortable 'Union or no Union,' " he confided. "This is of course for yourself and should not be repeated."²⁵

Rose had no desire to have her only son-in-law fighting for the North, but she respected the officer's wishes and felt it her duty to honor them. She wrote Seward, whom Lincoln had appointed secretary of state, asking that Moore be transferred to the Presidio. "Capt. Moore is a strong Union man and holds himself ready to obey the orders of the Federal Gov," Rose wrote, avoiding any reference to her own political views. Then she added a line she knew would appeal to Seward's vanity: "His wife is, as you know, a Sewardite.

"My good friend, I have this very much at heart, and will hold myself greatly in your debt if it is accomplished. Very truly yours, R. Greenhow."²⁶

War drew closer by the day. In Charleston harbor, Fort Sumter ran out of food for its small garrison of Federal troops, and Confederates with guns turned back an unarmed merchant ship that attempted to resupply it. Lincoln was being advised to abandon the fort before the men starved or send an armed naval force to take them food and supplies.

Brigadier General Pierre G. T. Beauregard, one of the first West Pointers to resign his commission in the Union army to accept appointment in the new Confederate forces, had been put in command of Confederate forces in Charleston. When President Davis learned Lincoln planned to resupply Sumter, he ordered Beauregard to demand that the fort's commander surrender. Major Robert Anderson, who had taught Beauregard gunnery at West Point and now had charge of the small, hungry garrison behind the thick walls of the fort, refused his former student's demand. Both men knew the South was ready to force the issue.

At 4:30 A.M. on April 12, the Confederate battery at Cummings Point opened fire on Fort Sumter, and after forty hours of pounding by heavy artillery, the Union commander surrendered without having lost a man. The divided nation was at war with itself.

From the North and West, green militia began pouring into Washington in response to President Lincoln's call to arms to put down the insurrection. The new president, in office barely six weeks, sought 75,000 volunteers. By the end of June, 52,700 recruits were drilling and getting ready for battle. Their numbers nearly doubled the size of the young federal capital, surrounded as it was by secessionist Virginia to the south and the proslavery state of Maryland to the north, still tenuously part of the Union, but who knew for how long. As each company arrived, its men paraded past the White House to pay their respects to President Lincoln, who often went out to the gate and greeted the soldiers personally.

The normally quiet city was bustling with dress parades, flag raisings, and regimental concerts as the armies made ready for war. Lincoln hosted a concert for volunteers at the White House on Wednesday and Friday afternoons at 5:00 P.M.[27] All along the streets, marching bands played "Yankee Doodle," filling the air with the shrill whistle of fife tunes and the beat of marching drums. Most of the men conducted themselves with proper decorum, but a few caroused through the streets, shooting their muskets in the air. Citizens brave enough to venture outdoors offered sweets and Bibles to the troops.[28] Rose would have preferred they starve.

The rebellion grew. Virginia seceded, followed by Arkansas, Tennessee, and North Carolina. Rose's nephew James Madison Cutts Jr., Adie's brother, joined the First Rhode Island Volunteers. Another Yankee soldier in the family.[29]

Rose's son-in-law, Tredwell Moore, was desperate to get into the fray. On April 20, he wrote Rose again from Fort Churchill: "I hope that something can be done to prevent civil war, but if it must come, I think I am on the winning side, as we have the money and the numbers to prosecute a vigorous war." Moore also told Rose that he hoped she would be able to remain in Washington for at least a short while, "as events are now crowding on so rapidly that you may be of great service to me there."[30] Florence wrote to her mother a week later. She was worried about Rose's safety in Washington and asked that she come stay with them in Nevada. "I am so uneasy about you being in Washington," Florence wrote. "If we are to remain here, dear mama, had you not better come to us. It seems to me that Washington will be the center of the fight, and I so much wish that you were safely out of it." Florence told her mother that Moore had still not received the Ohio command he had requested: "Oh, I hope he may not get it. I so much dread his going to the wars. Moore is so tired of this inactive life. He is ready for any wild scheme that offers."[31]

In May, the Confederate capital moved from Montgomery, Alabama, to Richmond, putting the opposing governments barely one hundred miles apart. Washington was now on the southern edge of the Union, with Virginia, the heart of the Confederacy, at its front, just across the Potomac River. Maryland, a stronghold of Confederate sympathy, was at its back. In Baltimore, forty miles northeast of Washington, the mayor and police chief led a raid to blow up the railroad bridges and stop trains from bringing Union troops from up north through Maryland to protect the capital. Lincoln put the city under martial law and suspended the right of habeas corpus.[32]

Northerners cheered as their volunteers headed toward Washington. "From Maine to Maryland, it was a continual ovation," wrote a soldier named Hal with the First Maine regiment. "We were feted and toasted, presented with flags by the men and kissed by the women. In New York we were served with a splendid 'Fete champetre.' At New Brunswick [New Jersey], an old lady hobbled out to her door-step as we passed and flourishing her crutch, cried, 'Go it.' "[33]

Throughout the spring and summer, Northern soldiers poured into the capital. The streets filled with the noisy clatter of army wagons. Members of the Fifth New York Regiment set up camp on Pennsylvania Avenue and dug narrow trenches in the muddy street for their camp kettles. When they cooked dinner, ladies in sweeping crinoline stood by and watched them eat.[34] Rations generally consisted of salt meat, potatoes, rice, and crackers. Blacks, slave and free, came by to sell them corn cake, eggs, milk, and pies.[35]

Regiments camped in every building and on every block. Steamers and schooners filled with blankets, coal, and hard bread jammed the Washington Navy Yard. Warehouses grew so full that the army began storing barrels of flour in the main entrance of the Treasury building.[36] A herd of cattle grazed on the grounds surrounding the half-built Washington Monument, waiting to be slaughtered and turned into beefsteaks for hungry soldiers. The putrid smells of offal, as well as fumes from the nearby city dump and the filthy canal, hung in the heavy air like foul breath, attracting swarms of mosquitoes.

The Eighth Massachusetts made its home in the marble halls beneath the Rotunda of the Capitol, with soldiers from the Sixth and Seventh New York regiments. They built six large ovens in the basement to bake bread and set up large ranges for making coffee and cooking soup.[37] When not practicing drills in the park outside the Capitol, they held mock sessions of Congress and amused themselves by offering up pompous speeches. Some sat at the lawmakers' desks and wrote letters home on the official stationery of the House and Senate. The Fifth Massachusetts took over the Treasury building, sleeping on the floor with only a blanket as cover and cooking meals in the courtyard.[38]

The New York Fire Zouaves, a wild and brawny regiment recruited from volunteer fire departments, marched up Pennsylvania Avenue, conspicuous in their billowing pantaloons, short jackets, and snug red caps with gold tassels. A few broke away to catch a wandering pig, cut it up with their huge bowie knives, and ate it.

In May, a tailor shop next to the Willard Hotel caught fire at 2:00 A.M., putting the hotel in imminent danger, and the Zouaves put out the flames. The exotically uniformed soldiers, commanded by Colonel Elmer E. Ellsworth, who had worked for Lincoln in his law office in Illinois, were invited by the Willard's grateful owners to join the hotel's guests for breakfast.

Professor Thaddeus Sobieski Coulincourt Lowe, the aeronaut from Cincinnati, Ohio, busied himself with demonstrations of a huge, gas-filled balloon that he launched one thousand feet in the air from the Smithsonian Institution and the grounds of the Executive Mansion. Few people had seen anything like it. Telegraph wires were strung from the ground to his platform beneath the silk balloon, named *Enterprise*. Lowe hoped to persuade Lincoln that the balloon could be used to soar over the Virginia countryside, spot enemy forces from the air, and report their positions and strength to commanders on the ground.[39] Like many technological innovations sweeping the country, the concept of aerial reconnaissance struck many military commanders as ridiculous. But Lincoln, who had a fondness for inventions, was intrigued.[40]

Standing on the Washington side of the Potomac, Union officers could see a Confederate flag—the Stars and Bars—flying above Marshall House, a tavern in Alexandria owned by well-known secessionist James Jackson. The irksome flag showed just how close the enemy was. Every evening at 9:30 P.M., the draws at Long Bridge and Chain Bridge were hoisted to block passage between Washington and Virginia.[41]

At 2:00 A.M. on Friday, May 23, hundreds of green troops from the Michigan Regiment and the New York Seventh and Twelfth marched quietly through the streets of Washington and across Long Bridge into Virginia to secure Arlington Heights, the high ground opposite the capital. Their path was illuminated by a round moon hanging in the cloudless sky. The Zouaves embarked in two steamers for Alexandria, just downriver on the opposite bank, and reached the wharf at 4:00 A.M. Confederate sentries fired a few shots to warn the populace, then ran away.

Colonel Ellsworth marched his firemen up Main Street to the center of town, where the secessionists surrendered. At Marshall House, Ellsworth climbed the stairs to the roof, tore down the Confederate flag, and stomped on it. James Jackson, the enraged tavern owner, pointed his double-barrel shotgun at Ellsworth and shot him at point-blank range. The president's friend was the first Union officer to die in the war. Corporal Francis Brownell, a handsome soldier in Ellsworth's unit, fired his musket into Jackson's brain, killing the rebel innkeeper on the spot. The soldier sank his bayonet into Jackson's body as it fell.[42]

All over Washington, bells tolled and flags flew at half-staff. President Lincoln had Ellsworth's body brought to the Washington Navy Yard the next day, and a solemn cortege wound through the streets of the capital to bring the officer's body to the White House. Crowds of citizens and soldiers lined the streets, eager to catch a glimpse of the sad spectacle.

"The papers still breathing vengeance," Elizabeth Lindsay Lomax wrote in her diary.[43] When the carriage bearing Lincoln and Secretary Seward stopped in front of the Treasury building, Corporal Brownell stepped forward and presented the president with the flag captured by Ellsworth and stained with his blood.[44] The cortege continued on to the Executive Mansion, where Ellsworth lay in state in the East Room until the funeral.

As Lincoln was exchanging a few words with the soldiers, an officer dashed up Pennsylvania Avenue to announce that secessionist forces had attacked Union troops on the Virginia side of the river. General Joseph Mansfield, who was part of the procession, stepped out of line and gave an order to prepare for immediate action. Citizens climbed to the tops of houses and public buildings to watch the Union troops march across Long Bridge to meet the enemy. It was a false alarm.[45]

In June, after the Zouaves seized the Virginia side of the river, they emptied the slave pens in Alexandria owned by dealers Price & Britch. "I need not tell you that these dens are a disgrace to the civilized world," wrote a Massachusetts soldier who called himself Bunker Hill. "I brought away an iron door fastening, of two pounds weight, as a specimen of the 'Jewels of Slavery.' "[46]

Almost every town and hamlet in the North could boast a representative in the capital as volunteers flooded the city. During a dress parade, a member of a Michigan regiment turned to President Lincoln as he passed the White House gate and asked the commander in chief for a dollar. "My dear young Sir," replied Lincoln, dressed in a white linen coat, "I have not a dollar with me. If I had twenty I would give them to you." A soldier with the Washington Light Guard who observed the scene wrote home: "The president is situated as many of his troops are, dead broke."[47]

Many of the arriving soldiers were disappointed to find their national capital lacked the refinement of New York or Boston, that it was filthy and most of the streets were unpaved. "My opinion regarding the city of Washington is not a favorable one," wrote a Massachusetts soldier, a member of the Roxbury City Guards who signed his letter "J.L.B." "It is a dirty, low place filled with pigs and niggers and you would laugh to hear the people talk."[48] Another soldier was similarly unimpressed: "When at home, we are not accustomed to see hogs running at large in the principal streets, or the carcasses of dead dogs and goats left to decay in the heart of the city, as is the case here, much to the disgust of our nasal organs."[49]

Florence Moore followed the activity from faraway Nevada, relieved for her mother that the defenses seemed strong but torn by her inbred sympathy for the South and sense of loyalty to the Union: "What a state of excitement you must all be in in Washington," she wrote. "But I think the Union men are concentrating so many soldiers near there that the Southern Army will not approach it. Poor Moore is almost beside himself at having to remain here inactive whilst so many are earning laurels. But I thank God for it. Of course he will fight for the Union. And although of course, dear mama, all my earnest feelings are enlisted for the Southerners rather than the Yankees, still I do think the Union should be before all mere State feeling, and do think the Secessionists a little like traitors. Still, I honestly pray that Moore may not be engaged in this horrible civil war."[50]

Moore appealed to Rose again, asking that she contact the new secretary of the Treasury, Salmon Portland Chase, former governor of Moore's native Ohio, whom Moore knew. "I think, dear mama, that the present crisis opens an opportunity for us young men that should not be neglected," Moore wrote, adding he had sent her $750 in drafts since January 1 and was surprised that she had not received the money.[51] Moore later claimed he sent Rose more than $10,000 over the years to keep her afloat, loans he sought unsuccessfully to recover from her estate.[52]

Rose wrote to Chase, an ardent abolitionist, who as Treasury secretary was in charge of finding funding for the Union army. She requested that the young man be transferred to Ohio to head a volunteer regiment. It was the classic conflict. Rose was bowing to family loyalty, asking a favor of a political opponent for a son-in-law in an army she despised. She may have felt under obligation to Moore for his repeated generosity. "I make this application as a matter of duty to him," she wrote Chase, "and can have no feeling but that of sorrow even if through your goodness he obtains his wishes, for I feel that no laurels can be won against our kindred and friends."[53]

Chase answered, promising to have Moore promoted, but he could not resist scolding Rose for her characterization of the war. "I regret to observe that you regard the war as 'a war against our kindred and friends,' " Chase wrote. "It seems to me rather a war for the rescue of kindred and friends and of our country."[54]

Mary Greenhow Lee, now separated from Rose by enemy lines, had a trusted slave smuggle a letter to her sister-in-law telling of the aid she was giving Confederate soldiers and the resistance she put up when Yankees came to her door in Winchester, at the northern end of the strategic Shenandoah Valley in Virginia. Mary Lee, who had lost her husband about the same time Rose was widowed, opened her home to soldiers from Alabama[55] and the slaves who accompanied them, she said. She also expressed disapproval over Moore's efforts to find a more active post than his quartermaster's job out west, where there wasn't likely to be much fighting: "If he is willing and anxious to take up arms and absolutely fight the South, I fear my opinion of him will be less favorable than it has been up to the present time." Mary closed her letter with the suggestion that Rose and the girls come stay with her: "I will be ready for you at a day's notice."[56]

The cross-country correspondence continued. Florence worried her mother's Southern sympathies would get her in trouble in Washington and warned her not to associate with secessionists. On June 23, the young woman begged Rose to be careful. "I am so worried about the news from Washington," Florence wrote. "They say some ladies have been taken up as spies. I so dread to hear of some of my friends. Dear mama, please keep as clear of all secessionists as you possibly can. I so much fear everything to you all alone there. Oh dear, when will this dreadful war end. I thank God for every moment that Moore is kept out of it. Do not, dear mama, say anything for the South for I really think he believes all Southern men should be hung."

Moore attached his own brief greeting—and advice—to the same sheet of paper: "Keep a bright lookout to my interests and do not, even should your inclinations be for the South, do anything which would for an instant compromise you. Nothing could be gained by it, and I feel sure your feeling must be for the preservation of our glorious confederacy."[57]

Their warnings came too late.

CHAPTER FOUR

The Making of a Spy

SOMETIME IN THE spring of 1861, Captain Thomas Jordan, a West Pointer and quartermaster in the U.S. Army, visited Rose in Washington and let her know he intended to switch sides to fight for his native Virginia. He asked her to help him organize an espionage ring in the capital. Jordan knew Rose's social position and political savvy gave her access to top political and military officials, and he needed someone who would remain behind to funnel intelligence to the South.

Years later, Hamilton Fish would claim Jordan learned Rose was having an affair with his old colleague Senator Henry Wilson and established "the same kind of intimacy" with her to learn what secrets Wilson may have spilled.[1] Such salacious, thirdhand Yankee gossip swirled around Rose throughout her life and until long after she died, but it did not stop her from accepting Jordan's proposition that she aid the Confederacy.

Jordan taught her a rudimentary cipher she would use to send her secret dispatches and directed that she address them to his alias, Thomas J. Rayford.[2] The code was quite simple, but Union counterintelligence would have had to intercept at least half a dozen messages for decoders to break it.[3] One letter or number or symbol stood for a different letter or number or for a word, such as "Lincoln," "infantry," or "Pen Avenue."[4]

Rose turned her stately residence on 16th Street into the unofficial headquarters for the South's secessionists, many of whom in those early days of the breakup still held important jobs in the executive branch, despite the

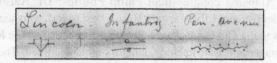

new administration.[5] Located near Lafayette Square, where residents often gathered to exchange the latest news, Rose's three-story house became a convenient meeting place and a hotbed of activity. .

After organizing his recruiting ring, Jordan resigned his commission on May 21, went south, and signed on as a lieutenant colonel in the Confederate army, where he was immediately appointed adjutant general of the forces headquartered at Manassas Junction. Only twenty-six miles from the enemy capital, he was in an ideal position to communicate with the spy network he had established.[6]

With Lincoln and his Republicans in power, Rose was no longer a member of the president's inner circle. The power and prestige she had enjoyed during the Buchanan years ended abruptly with the change in administrations. But Rose knew Washington and still had connections. She determined to use them for the cause. Reared on the pro-slavery, pro–states' rights principles espoused by her hero Senator John C. Calhoun, Rose was now seized by a deep sense of nationalism and a burning anger that made her want to fight for the South—her land, her people, her way of life. Isolated in her own city by the threatening new forces of the North, she was willing to risk everything.

Gertrude's death had plunged her again into mourning, and with the departure of so many friends, she had less support than ever. But for the company of Leila, who was away at boarding school much of the time, and Little Rose, now eight years old, she was alone, a Southern widow in a Northern town.

For hours at a time, Rose practiced writing the strange, awkward symbols Jordan had given her, carefully tracing the lines and curves and dots until she got them right. The cipher was central to her secret mission, and she knew her Southern comrades were counting on her. She was determined not to fail them.

Rose assembled a band of accomplices, both men and women, who kept watch on military movements around the district and tapped official sources for useful intelligence. She organized a small circle of Southerners who began meeting regularly—and openly—at her home, often arriving late at night. The group included the clever Eugenia Phillips, wife of former Alabama congressman Philip Phillips; Dr. Aaron Van Camp, Rose's dentist; and Lily Mackall, Rose's best friend, who accompanied her on visits to the Old Capitol, once the boardinghouse where Rose had lived as a teenager and later nursed Calhoun on his deathbed. The building had been abandoned, but after war broke out, iron bars were added to the windows, and it was converted for use as a military prison. The women took food, clothes, and bandages to Confederate soldiers being held as prisoners of war.

On one visit, Rose caught sight of the prison superintendent, William P. Wood, who had worked for Lincoln as commissioner for public buildings before falling into disfavor. Dressed entirely in black but for a white scarf tied around his neck, Wood was haranguing prisoners, "trying to persuade them that they would all be hanged unless they took the oath of allegiance to the Abolition Government," Rose wrote in her memoir. She interrupted the prison chief to reassure the soldiers "that our Government would fearfully retaliate [against] any violence against them." Several days later, military authorities barred her from the prison.[7] "Mrs. Greenhow is at liberty to leave clothes at the entrance of the Old Capitol Prison for the prisoners, but will not be admitted beyond that," specified the order. It was signed by Brigadier General Joseph K. F. Mansfield, then commanding the city of Washington.[8]

One of Rose's fellow conspirators was Edward Jenkins Pringle, her lawyer and friend who kept in close touch with her during the winter and spring of 1861. She had met Pringle in San Francisco in the early 1850s. After Robert Greenhow died there, Pringle represented Rose's interests in a contentious land deal battle that had involved her husband, a specialist in land claims. Pringle also kept an account of Rose's finances and sent her occasional dividend checks from railroad stock she owned.

An uncompromising critic of Lincoln's Republicans, he told Rose in a letter dated January 10, 1861—nearly two months before Lincoln took office—"The new administration is a farce."[9]

A series of letters from Pringle to Rose shows he had high regard for her political skills and indicates he helped her woo Senator Wilson to glean secrets from the Committee on Military Affairs to pass along to the South. "I left you yesterday from motives of delicacy not liking to interfere with an agreeable tête-à-tête," Pringle wrote in one undated letter. "I am glad it so happened that I missed your distinguished Black Rep friend. . . . We must press on. If you will write a note to Wilson and enclose a document, I will make William carry it to him."[10]

In another letter, undated but written before Jefferson Davis resigned from the Senate on January 21, Pringle wrote: "Do send me the map. I just met [former Buchanan attorney general Jeremiah S.] Black (my route to Jeff Davis) and had a long and rather satisfactory talk. You had better not try him today. Jeff Davis not in. Gone to Senate. I am going after him at once."[11]

Correspondence after the war broke out betrayed a clear military purpose. At one point, Pringle told Rose to look among her papers "for a letter from The Engineer Department to the War Department which gives the description of the Govt reserves. We will take that letter and the map (which I believe you have) with us at 6 o'clock."[12] The letter does not disclose the identity of their liaison.

When Pringle visited Washington that summer, Rose invited him to stay with her on 16th Street, but the lawyer declined, perhaps out of an abundance of caution because it had become a gathering place for secessionists, perhaps out of a sense of discretion. "I am much obliged for your offer of a room at 398, but my bachelor habits would not suit your abode,"[13] he wrote politely in a letter dated June 21. By that time, Rose was consumed by her mission and sending regular messages to military leaders in the South.

The buildup had begun. The capital was teeming with Union recruits, and Confederate forces were digging in at Manassas Junction for what generals and soldiers alike expected to be the first real battle of the war.

Rose's July 9, 1861, message carried by Bettie Duvall informed Beauregard that the Union's Army of Northeastern Virginia was about to move. He must prepare for battle.[14]

On July 15, five days after Miss Duvall's mission and a day before the advance predicted, Beauregard secretly sent a man to call on Rose for confirmation. The courier, a Washington native named George Donnellan, crossed the Potomac River by ferry below Alexandria and made his way into the city with instructions to go to Rose's home, which Beauregard said was "within easy rifle range of the White House."[15] Donnellan had once worked as a clerk at the Department of the Interior, and Rose knew him well.[16] His orders were to deliver a message to the lady of the house and to present it only to her.

In the early morning of July 16, just after first light, the courier arrived on Rose's doorstep and handed her a scrap of paper. It contained only two words, written in Jordan's code: "Trust bearer."[17] The elegant widow hurriedly scribbled a note in the same cipher that confirmed her intelligence sent a week earlier. "Order issued for McDowell to march upon Manassas tonight," she wrote. Rose later said she got the information from a reliable source who claimed to have a copy of the order sent to General McDowell.[18]

The messenger gobbled down a quick breakfast, hid Rose's encoded note in the hollowed-out heel of his boot, and set out to get the message back to Confederate territory. He traveled first by buggy, then by horseback, down the eastern shore of the Potomac to a ferry in Charles County, Maryland, where he crossed into Virginia and handed the message to a Confederate cavalry officer, Colonel Daniel Ruggles, with the following instruction: "This must go thro' by a lightning express to Beauregard. Incur any expense upon authority of my instructions and I'll certify to the bills when I return. G. Donnellan."[19] Ruggles relayed it by fast horsemen to Manassas, eighteen miles to the west. At 8:00 P.M., the message was delivered to Beauregard, and within thirty minutes,[20] the code had been deciphered: The enemy, "55,000 strong," would begin their march that day from Arlington Heights and Alexandria, then move on to Manassas, via Fairfax Court House and Centreville.

According to Beauregard, he telegraphed the information to President Jefferson Davis in Richmond, the new capital of the Confederacy,[21] asking Davis to rush reinforcements from General Joseph E. Johnston's twelve-thousand-man army posted sixty miles northwest, protecting the Shenandoah Valley. Johnston loaded his army onto trains, a first-time use of the railroad to rush to a battlefield, and hurried to Beauregard's aid, assuring that not one army but two would fight the Union at Manassas.[22] Jordan rewarded Rose with a message the next day: "Yours was received at eight o'clock at night. Let them come: we are ready for them. We rely upon you for precise information. Be particular as to description and destination of forces, quantity of artillery, &c. (Signed) THOS. JORDAN. Adjutant-General."[23]

As Rose had predicted, General McDowell ordered his army to march toward Manassas on the afternoon of July 16. Wagons bearing their provisions were to follow the next day. As the soldiers crossed Chain Bridge, the band played "Yankee Doodle." The men marched until 10:30 that night, halted outside Vienna, and started again at 5:00 the next morning. They passed burning buildings set afire by small units of Confederates retreating toward their main defenses.[24] Marching at double-quick time, the Union advance was still several miles short of Manassas on the morning of July 18.

The troops met no resistance from the Confederates, who had taken up positions behind Bull Run, a steeply banked stream that wound through the rolling hills and flat plains of the Virginia countryside. After a brief rest, the Union men were ordered to fall in and resume their march.[25] Their division commander had orders to keep up the impression the army was moving directly on Manassas but not to bring on a general engagement while General McDowell contemplated a flanking maneuver. However, as they approached Blackburn's Ford on Bull Run, Union officers sensed an opportunity and directed their troops forward to take the ford. General James Longstreet's Confederate brigade was ready and waiting under cover of the woods along the stream. They inflicted a stinging blow to the Federals, who were compelled to fall back. It was a brief encounter, but a major boost to Southern morale. McDowell ultimately had to adjust his plans.

The balance of the Union army halted to wait for its supplies to catch up. The still-raw regiments, "not soldiers, but civilians in uniform, unused to marching, hot, weary, and footsore, dropped down as they had halted and bivouacked on the roads about Centreville,"[26] wrote James B. Fry, an aide to McDowell. McDowell would wait until Sunday, July 21, to send his army into the field to meet Beauregard, his West Point classmate. It would be the first major battle of the Civil War.

The Federal City teemed with soldiers and talk of war. On Saturday, July 20, 1861, dawn brought relative calm. Yet by midmorning, as troops and wagons rumbled across the Potomac, the heat was already oppressive, and suspense and excitement awakened the capital. So confident were the Republicans of Union success that there was almost a holiday spirit. Throughout the day, hundreds of Washingtonians, congressmen and senators, businessmen, ladies, and even ordinary citizens, obtained passes to Virginia from the headquarters of Major General Winfield Scott, the venerable commanding general of the Army of the United States, a hero of the Mexican War. They wanted to see the battle unfold with their own eyes.

The next morning, a Sunday, people rode in elegant black carriages through the streets of Georgetown and across Aqueduct Bridge toward the town of Manassas and Bull Run. Secretary of War Simon Cameron had been among the visitors to McDowell's army the day before the battle. Other notables, including Senators Henry Wilson, Benjamin Wade, James Lane, and Lafayette Foster, came as spectators, eager to witness the fighting that Sunday.[27] Wearing a straw hat, Mathew Brady, photographer of the famous, carried a large camera and plate holder in his wagon, covered in black cloth and filled with chemicals. He was determined to become the first person to take photographs of a battlefield.[28] On their way, some spectators stopped at the corner of M and 1st streets, where Crandall's store was selling spyglasses as well as clever canes that opened into a seat. Thomas's bookshop sold battle maps for five cents.[29]

The twenty-five-mile ride from Washington to Centreville by carriage normally took about six hours, and most people packed meals to sustain them along the way. William Howard Russell, a British dandy who served as correspondent for *The Times* (London), reported that spectators were so confident of Union success that there was a great demand for luxury picnics packed with cigars, bottles of fine wine, and silver flasks filled with bourbon. "The French cooks and hotel keepers, by some occult process of reasoning, have arrived at the conclusion that they must treble the prices of their wines and of the hampers of provisions which the Washington people are ordering to comfort themselves at their bloody Derby," Russell wrote.[30] Near Centreville, he described running into an officer galloping fast and shouting loudly, "We've whipped them on all points. We have taken all their batteries. They are retreating as fast as they can, and we are after them." As the crowd cheered, congressmen shook hands with one another and cried out, "Bully for us. Bravo!"[31]

Those who left the scene early arrived back in the capital with reports of a Federal victory. Crowds congregated at the Willard Hotel, a gathering spot on Pennsylvania Avenue for Union supporters, and they awaited news bulletins from the battlefront. But when there was no news, rumors of trouble began to circulate. It wasn't until 6:00 P.M. that President Lincoln received word in the White House from a haggard Secretary Seward: "The battle is lost. The telegraph says that McDowell is in full retreat and calls on General Scott to save the capital. . . ."[32]

As panicked Union soldiers retreated, they abandoned wagons, horses, cannons, provisions, and knapsacks. "Dear Mother," wrote a Rhode Island soldier the next day: "The balls whistled around my head like hailstones. The scene was terrible. Shells were exploding and cannon roaring that the cry of the wounded could not be heard. Cavalry, infantry and artillery, in one confused mass, hurried away as fast as possible. I leaped over a fence and had hardly done so when I heard a loud crash and looking back, I beheld the upper half of a soldier's body flying up the hill. He had been cut in twain by a solid ball. A cry of mortal terror arose from the flying soldiers and they followed me into the wood."[33] Leonard C. Belding of Company K with the Second Rhode Island found himself surrounded. "Three of my most intimate friends were shot down by my side," he wrote to his parents on July 24. "Another had his leg taken entirely off, the blood flying in my face. I felt so badly that I almost fainted, but I rallied immediately, and clenching my teeth, went in and every shot that I fired made it. I can assure you that I saw five of the rebels fall dead, and I thought the death of my friends avenged. I had several bullet holes in my clothes and thought some of the time that I should never see home again."[34]

As the soldiers fled, they threw their muskets in a creek. Famished and parched from thirst, some drank dirty water from the road. "It was hardly fit to drink but yet it was water," Allen, of the First Massachusetts, wrote to his parents.[35] A team of horses ran straight into terrorized crowds of civilian spectators who had expected to be celebrating victory.[36] Dead bodies and severed limbs littered the bridges and countryside. One Union senator threatened the retreating soldiers with his rifle. *How dare they retreat!* Another lawmaker tried to block their path with his carriage. Mathew Brady abandoned his wagon and camera and got lost in the woods. Senator Wilson, who was fired on by a Confederate soldier, rode back into Washington on an army mule. "All is lost," wrote a soldier named George, from Massachusetts.[37]

Frederick and Henry Hubbard, two brothers who had not seen each other for four years and were fighting on opposite sides, were astounded to meet each other in a stable on the battlefield. Both were wounded. Frederick had been fighting with the New Orleans Washington Artillery, Henry with the First Minnesota Infantry. "By the merest chance, I learned he was here wounded and sought him out to nurse and attend him," explained Henry in a letter home.[38]

Professor Lowe, the plucky aeronaut from Cincinnati, was having his own problems. When he arrived at the city gasworks to pump up his balloon, a competitor was already there, pumping up his. Lowe was delayed and didn't get his balloon inflated until Sunday afternoon. Then he loaded it onto a wagon, found a few dozen soldiers to accompany him, and set out for Manassas. But he was too late. "Unfortunately, when we arrived at Falls Church I was informed of the retreat of the [Union] army, and thinking it useless to attempt to go farther, I concluded to remain there," Lowe reported, "even after all the troops had passed by." It was in the midst of a drenching rain, but he still hoped he might get his balloon into the air to report on the Confederates' expected advance on the capital. But as the

Northerners withdrew their troops, right down to the last picket, Lowe thought better of it and hauled his equipment back to Fort Corcoran, the wind and rain fighting him all the way.[39]

In Washington, there was great celebration among the secessionists, who predicted that in twenty-four hours, they would rule the capital.

Rose Greenhow, however, was not there to join them. She had spent the weekend in New York, where she heard the news of the Yankee defeat from strangers buzzing about it on the street. Manhattan was filled with anxiety and a sense of looming danger. "The whole city seemed paralyzed by fear," she wrote in her memoir, "and I verily believe that a thousand men could have marched from Central Park to the Battery without resistance, for their depression now was commensurate with the wild exultation of a few days before."[40]

Rose had escorted her daughter Leila, who was almost twenty-three, to New York to put her aboard the steamship *Champion*, which left on July 22, bound for the port of Aspinwall in the Caribbean. There Leila would take a rickety, single-track train ride over forty-seven miles of dense forest and deep gorges across the Isthmus of Panama to Panama City on the Pacific, where she would wait for another steamship to take her to San Francisco.[41] From there, she would travel, probably by stagecoach, to the home of her older sister, Florence, who was now living in Utah Territory. Moore had become a captain in the Union army at the outbreak of war and was stationed at Fort Churchill in Nevada.

It is hard to imagine which situation was more hazardous for a beautiful young woman—wartime Washington, with a regiment of motley, nervous soldiers camped on every block, or a long voyage over perilous seas to San Francisco and on to Utah. For a mother, it was an unbearable choice.

Rose did not send her youngest daughter, Little Rose, on the trip. The child was only eight, and her mother may have felt her too young for such an arduous voyage, or perhaps the heartache of parting with all three children so recently after the death of Gertrude was too much to bear.

Rose returned to Washington by overnight train. Throughout the trip, she was forced to listen to a passenger from New York, who loudly denounced the South. In Philadelphia, she watched as most of the women left the train, terrified that rebels would attack before they reached Washington. Lieutenant Wise, a handsome young Union officer, drew close to Rose and advised her to disembark with him. "I have no fears," she replied laughingly. "These rebels are of my faith. Besides, even now I shall not be in time to welcome our president, Mr. Davis, and the glorious Beauregard."

"I should probably see those gentlemen there in irons," Wise replied with a sneer as he and others got off the train and joined the women. "Discretion is the better part of valor." The New York passengers disembarked prematurely. When the train arrived in Baltimore, the city was filled with Union soldiers. Southern sympathizers, of whom there were many, pelted passing soldiers with bottles and stones. "It was even difficult to thread one's way to the train on account of the military," Rose wrote. When she finally reached the capital at 6:00 A.M., she was immediately surrounded by dozens more soldiers crowding the depot and the streets. The battle had taken its toll. The men were so panic-stricken, she wrote, "that they startled at the clank of their own muskets."[42]

When Rose arrived home, she found a secret message awaiting her from Manassas: "Our President and our General direct me to thank you. We rely upon you for further information. The Confederacy owes you a debt. (Signed) JORDAN, Adjutant-General."[43]

After freshening up, Rose went immediately by carriage to Capitol Hill, where she made an appearance in the Senate gallery to take the pulse of the capital. "I saw the crest-fallen leaders who, but a few days before, had vowed 'death and damnation' to our race," she wrote in her memoir. "Several crowded round me, and I could not help saying that, if they had not 'good blood,' they had certainly 'good bottom,' for they ran remarkably well."[44]

Union lawmakers, now on the defensive, did their best to put their own spin on the story. Senator Wilson boasted privately to Rose that it was only as a result of his personal intervention that the entire Union army hadn't fallen pell-mell into the Potomac River. Secretary of State Seward called on her to say she should tell her secessionist friends that on his personal authority, all would be over in sixty days. "Well, sir," the Southern matron replied, "you have enjoyed the first fruits of the 'irrepressible conflict.'" She reminded him that she chose the phrase from a fiery campaign speech about the country's division on slavery that Seward, an unsuccessful Republican candidate for president, delivered three years before.[45]

On Wednesday morning, the weather turned favorable. Professor Lowe's balloon was still inflated, and no Confederate army had arrived to attack the capital. He would take up his balloon for a look. Claiming he ascended to an altitude of about three and one-half miles above Arlington (an almost impossible feat without oxygen and more modern equipment), he "had a distinct view of the encampments of the enemy, and observed them in motion between Manassas Junction and Fairfax."[46] What an enormous relief. The rebels weren't coming after all.

The streets of Washington were jammed with armed and unarmed soldiers, their nerves frayed. Many were drunk and stirring up trouble. Everywhere, chaos reigned. Women stayed inside their houses, afraid of insults and curses. Although wealthy Southerners continued to leave the city and several army officers urged Rose Greenhow to accompany them, she vehemently declined. "I resolved to remain conscious of the great service I could render my country," she wrote, "my position giving me remarkable facilities for obtaining information."[47]

Rose sat in her parlor until late that night, recording her impressions in a small brown leather diary that she would later turn into a memoir. From the window of her house, she could hear the dull rattle of metal chains tied to the legs of captured Confederate soldiers being marched through the mud down Pennsylvania Avenue to the Old Capitol Prison. John B. Tidball, an army artilleryman, wrote in his journal that as rebel prisoners passed the Willard Hotel, angry Fire Zouaves "pelted them with bricks and stones and swore they would kill them."[48] Those assigned to protect the Confederate soldiers shouted that they would shoot anyone who continued the assaults.[49] To a sad and lonely widow, it was a sickening scene, a pitiful precursor of the dreadful days that lay ahead. Rose cried as she watched them pass. It was, she wrote, "like the rumbling of distant thunder presaging the coming storm."[50]

Beauregard never did follow up his victory at Bull Run with an attack on the capital, and perhaps the Confederates lost an opportunity for even greater success. But in the first major battle of the war, they demonstrated that the mischievous rebellion Lincoln thought would be over in ninety days was a far more serious affair. Rose Greenhow's early warning had helped set the stage for four years of bloody conflict that in the end would lay waste to her beloved South.

Rose was convinced of the righteousness of her cause, unwavering in her conviction that slavery was morally sound, protected by the Constitution, essential to the South's economy, and a God-given way of life. But to defend it, she had chosen a dangerous path.

CHAPTER 5

"A Dangerous Character"

ROSE CONSIDERED THE victory at Manassas, known to Northerners as the Battle of Bull Run, a personal triumph and later bragged that "the Southern women of Washington are the cause of the defeat of the grand army. They are entitled to the laurels won by the brave defenders of our soil and institutions. They have told Beauregard when to strike!"[1]

In the weeks after the battle, Rose continued to channel reports to Beauregard. She sent at least nine coded messages, some containing military information from Union sources, others with data gathered from her ring of collaborators and local newspapers. Rose sat at the desk in her library, studying the material, making notes, even writing coded messages into the margins of newspapers. But she was careless. Unlike a professional espionage agent, she kept copies of some reports in her home, including at least one as she first wrote it and as she then encrypted it. That presumably would give anyone who found both versions enough information to break the cipher Jordan taught her, rendering it useless or, as he feared, even dangerous. Union officers apparently attempted to use it later to deliver misleading information to Confederate generals.

"All is activity," Rose reported on July 31, ten days after the battle that sent Union forces reeling back toward Washington. Major General George B. McClellan, whom Lincoln had summoned to take command of the Army of the Potomac after the disastrous setback, "is busy night and day but the panick is great and the attack is hourly expected. They believe that the attack will be made simultaneously from Edwards Ferry and Balti-more. Every effort is being made to find out who gave the alarm." Never one to miss an opportunity to give the men in her life a bit of advice, Rose added, "A troop of cavalry will start from here this morning to Harper's Ferry. Don't give time for re-organizing."

The morning of August 5, Rose told Beauregard her group was plan-ning sabotage as well as intelligence gathering. "If possible their telegraph wires will be simultaneously cut and their guns spiked along the Va. Side," she said. "If information of such character reaches you from the proper source, we trust immediate reliance will be placed."

Later the same day, she offered information about Federal troop move-ments, but her copy of the message was torn to bits, and Federal detec-tives' attempts to reconstruct it were not completely successful:

"There are 45,000 on Va side 15,000 around this City to wit Up the river above Chain Bridge—at Tennleytown, Bladensburg—across Anacostia Branch & commanding every approach to the City. If McClellan can be permitted to prepare he expects to surprise you but now is preparing xx against one. Look out for masxx batteries wherever you go. Their reliance this time is on abundance of artillery—which they have disposed formida-bly. . . . A line of daily communication is now open through Alexandria."[2]

After rushing to the capital from western Virginia to take command of the dispirited Union troops in the wake of their first defeat, General McClellan moved immediately to restore order and discipline in the ranks and rebuild the pride of the young volunteers after their humiliating introduction to war. Supremely confident at thirty-four, "Little Mac" galloped through the city's streets on horseback, sitting straight in the military saddle that bore his name. He visited one encampment after another to watch the soldiers drill and drill until they could function as a single blue formation. The handsome McClellan, dashing with his tightly tailored uniform, wavy auburn hair, arched eyebrows, and thick mustache, was the picture of con-fidence. Genial but demanding, he won the respect of his men, who cheered him as he rode past. If he found soldiers with liquor, he ordered them to spill it on the ground. For regiments that performed well in drill, he offered a $5 prize.[3] "Gen. McClellan is a fine looking officer with an en-ergetic and determined countenance," wrote Massachusetts soldier Charley O'Malley on August 5, after McClellan reviewed his regiment. "He has no beard but a light moustache shades his upper lip. In appearance he is very martial. He is a favorite with the Army."[4]

McClellan, who had studied the armies in Europe and observed the

Crimean War, enjoyed the company of two French noblemen, brothers, who volunteered their services to the Union cause, the Comte de Paris, pretender to the throne of France, and the Duc de Chartres. They were dubbed Captain Parry and Captain Chatters by McClellan's men. The young, energetic officers were also welcomed by President Lincoln, but they didn't impress Rose, who thought them effeminate. "They were amiable ladylike-looking young Frenchmen," she sniffed, "better fitted from their appearance to assist in Mrs. Lincoln's educational scheme" than in McClellan's army.[5]

Rose was equally disdainful of the new circle of elite that now made up Washington society. "The Republican court," she called it disdainfully. "The refinement and grace which had once constituted the charm of Washington life has long since departed."[6]

One afternoon, Rose and some of her Southern lady friends were seated in the Senate gallery listening to a heated discussion about the role of the military committee in reorganizing Northern forces. Rose leaned over to a friend and made a derogatory remark about the Yankees, prompting the young man seated next to her in the blue uniform of a Union lieutenant colonel to turn to her and shout: "That is treason! We will show you that it must be put a stop to. We have a government to maintain."

Rose leaned forward on the bench and replied in her most refined manner, enunciating each syllable softly and slowly: "My remarks were addressed to my companions, and not to you. If I did not discover by your language that you must be ignorant of all the laws of good breeding, I should take the number of your company and report you to your commanding officer to be punished for your impertinence."

Recognizing Rose Greenhow as a regular visitor, the Senate doorkeeper appeared immediately at her side. "Madam," he said, "if he insults you, I will put him out."

"Oh, never mind," Rose replied. "He is too ignorant to know what he has done."[7] She ignored him, but they were destined to meet again.

At that moment, there was much rustling on the Senate floor. A rumor swept the chamber that a battle had begun across the river in Arlington. Rose joined a group of lawmakers gathered on the portico of the Congressional Library, where they could see wisps of smoke rising from campfires across the river. "That is no battle," she said in disgust. "The rebels are cooking their dinners."[8]

Among those McClellan brought with him to Washington that July was the agent of Rose's undoing: famed detective Allan Pinkerton. Operating under the nom de guerre Major E. J. Allen, he set up a secret service for McClellan to gather intelligence in the South and conduct counterespionage operations in Washington and elsewhere.

By summer, Pinkerton had informers behind the rebel lines and was providing McClellan with estimates of enemy troop strength. But Pinkerton was a better detective than he was a military analyst. The inflated figures he gave McClellan helped convince "the Young Napoleon" that his forces were outnumbered by one hundred thousand Confederate soldiers in northern Virginia. McClellan had Washington placed under martial law,[9] and for more than a year, he resisted Lincoln's entreaties to attack the enemy, sure he was facing a superior force.

Yet rumors of an invasion of Washington were rife. On August 7, Colonel Robert Cowdin of Massachusetts startled his troops as they finished a dress parade and were about to head for their tents at Fort Albany in Arlington Heights, just across the river from the capital. The colonel told his men "that Gen. Beauregard and Jeff Davis were on the march to take the Capitol," wrote one soldier in the regiment. "He told us that we must sleep on our arms; that we must be ready to do battle at any moment, that there was no retreat. If they pass, said he, they must pass over my body."[10] The attack, of course, didn't come, but such reports kept everyone on high alert.

To relieve the tension, a Rhode Island soldier strung a tightrope across Pennsylvania Avenue from the roof of the National Hotel to the roof of the Clarendon Hotel and astonished passersby with his daring, high-wire balancing feats. "I saw him on Thursday afternoon and think that he did perform first rate," wrote a Massachusetts fighter named John. "The height from the street, I think, was fifty feet or more."[11]

Encampments around Washington grew increasingly unsanitary with the crowded conditions and units poised in their defensive positions for weeks and months. Disease ravaged some units. Young David Garrison, a private from Port Jervis, New York, wrote his parents that he had received a vaccination for "the small pox," one of the great medical advances of the time. He enclosed lockets to his sisters, Hannah, Mary Jane, and Eliza, as "a sample of a soldier's jewelry."[12] Six months later, he died of typhoid fever at Yorktown.

One of Rose's messages written on her handsome, heavy white stationery with a thin black border, a symbol of mourning, informed her friends on August 9:

During the present, movements of troops and ordnance, xx munitions have been active. Every approach to the Capitol xx been and is being fortified. Great reliance is placed in their future or present plan of battle, to wit, plenty of artillery and cavalry. They are not entirely fortified now but add xuch to their strength and power of resistance . . . there are . . . 10,000 now protecting this city. Every arrival and departure every movement in fact has been noted by eye witnesses placed at the out and inlets for such purpose . . . the papers do still chronicle the movements correctly as have been verified by means mentioned above. . . .

She kept up her reports, trying to specify troop strengths and positions, information of tactical value to Confederate commanders. A few fragments survive of a dispatch dated the next day:

McClellan is very active and very discreet. McDowell moved toward Fairfax yesterday at 9 A.M. with 20,000 men. Every order is being executed without attracting attention. Activity pervades McClellan's forces. It is reliably stated that 45,000 occupy the Va. side and 15,000 the approaches from the District side of the city. McClellan's movements indicate apprehension of an attack. Banks has 35,000 men more or less so the reliable rumour says. It is doubtxxxxxxx a combined force of 100,000 xxxx above mentioned McClellan.

She warned in one note that General Hiram Walbridge, a former New York congressman and friend of Lincoln, was a spy, adding: "This goes by safe hands but do not talk with anyone about news from here as the birds of the air bring back." Showing she was an amateur--and a woman—she told Jordan, "I wish I could see you as I know much that a letter cannot give. Give me some instructions. You know that my soul is in the cause. . . . Tell Beauregard that in my imagination he takes the place of Cid.

"Always yours, R.G."[13]

WASHINGTON WAS TAKING on the appearance of an armed camp. Every broad avenue was guarded, and there were patrols around all public buildings. Sentries paced back and forth in front of the White House, and at 6:00 P.M., the gates were closed. Citizens knew to listen for the sound of three guns fired from the provost marshal's office, a prearranged signal that the capital was under attack. The firing would be followed by tolling of church bells at fifteen-minute intervals.[14] Rose's circle of informers continued to supply her with information, and she sent Beauregard a map with drawings of the guns at Fort Corcoran and Fort Ellsworth.[15] "During this period, I was in almost daily correspondence with Manassas," she wrote.[16]

Rose's pro-Union neighbors were suspicious of her activities and kept an eye on her. They noted that men, some in uniform, visited her house in the late evening. Suspecting that she was seducing Federal officials to get their military secrets, someone reported the activity to Thomas A. Scott, the recently appointed assistant secretary of war.[17] Scott, who had been vice president of the Pennsylvania Rail Road, was in charge of the federal government's railroad and transportation systems and called in Allan Pinkerton.

By his own recollection and official war reports, it was shortly after Pinkerton arrived in Washington that Scott assigned him to look into the situation at Rose Greenhow's home. Pinkerton took two of his detectives to her house and surveyed the scene. It appeared to be empty, the shutters drawn, and Pinkerton concluded no one was home. A light rain was falling as the detectives checked out the various entrances and set up their surveillance operation to check on anyone coming or going. Pinkerton left his detectives and returned to headquarters for more assistance. He selected three of his best men and returned with them to the house after dark. As they approached the front walk, a violent storm erupted, hurling rain in such torrents and blowing so hard that the men's umbrellas turned inside out. The few pedestrians on the street rushed for shelter, paying no attention to Pinkerton and his squad.

From the street, Pinkerton could see that the shutters were still closed, but there was a light on in the parlor. He decided the house must be occupied, but he couldn't see anyone inside from street level. Pinkerton summoned two of his tallest, strongest men and, after removing his boots, climbed onto their shoulders right under a parlor window and peered inside, his eyes barely above the sill. "Noiselessly raising the sash and turning the slats of the blinds, I obtained a full view of the interior of the room," Pinkerton wrote.[18]

As the detective described it, Rose Greenhow's home "was not at all imposing in appearance" but was large, roomy, and "furnished with every consideration for wealth and tasteful refinement." Valuable portraits hung on the walls, and several statues and decorative objects were placed about the room. A portrait of Rose's eldest daughter, Florence Moore, adorned one wall. The front and back parlors were separated by a large drape of red gauze. A rosewood piano with pearl keys stood in the back room.[19] In the hall was a picture of Gertrude, painted a year or so before her death. Her auburn hair and light blue eyes captured more than one observer: "A smile of beauty played around the lips, and the eyes are lighted with a strange fancy, such as is often seen in the eyes of a girl just budding into woman-hood."[20]

But to the detective's disappointment, he could see no one in the front parlor. Just as he was about to voice his disgust, one of the detectives holding him uttered a sharp "Shhh." Someone was approaching the house.

Pinkerton jumped to the ground, and the three men ducked under the stoop. They heard footsteps on the stairs leading over their heads to the front door and listened as the front bell rang. The door opened, and the caller entered the house. Pinkerton, ordering his men back into position, climbed back on his perch and saw a uniformed figure seated in the parlor. "I immediately recognized him as an officer of the regular army," Pinkerton wrote. "I had met him that day for the first time. He was a captain of infantry and was in command of one of the stations of the Provost-Marshal."[21]

Pinkerton noted the tall, handsome man, about forty, had removed his cloak, "and as he sat there in his blue uniform, and in the full glare of the gaslight, he looked a veritable ideal soldier."[22] But the detective thought the officer's face had a troubled, restless look: "He appeared ill at ease and shifted nervously in his chair."[23] In a few moments, Rose Greenhow entered. The man jumped to his feet and gave her a long, courtly bow. "His face lighted up with pleasure as he gazed upon her," according to Pinkerton.[24]

One of Pinkerton's assistants gave another warning as some pedestrians neared the house. The gumshoes dove back under the stoop. When Pinkerton resumed his vantage point, he saw the captain and Rose seated at a table in the back of the room, deep in conversation. Pinkerton strained to hear them, but the heavy rain pounding on the windows drowned their soft voices. He caught only fragments of what they were saying. "I heard enough to convince me that this trusted officer was then and there engaged in betraying his country and furnishing to his treasonably inclined companion such information regarding the disposition of our troops," Pinkerton wrote.[25]

The captain took a map from an inner pocket of his coat and held it up to the light. Pinkerton imagined it showed the fortifications around the city and a plan of attack. He watched intently as the couple talked and referred frequently to the map. But once again, he had to duck under the stoop to avoid a pedestrian. The next time he looked in the window, "the delectable couple had disappeared."

After waiting impatiently more than an hour, Pinkerton saw the captain and Rose stroll back into the parlor, arm in arm, and sit down again. His surveillance was cut short once more by passersby. While the men crouched under the stoop, they heard the front door open and the traitor captain's step above. "With a whispered goodnight and something that sounded very much like a kiss, he descended the steps," Pinkerton wrote.

Soaked to the skin and forgetting his shoes, the intrepid counterspy gave chase "through the blinding mist and pelting storms," as the captain walked hurriedly away from the house at half-past midnight. New to the city, Pinkerton didn't know where he was going but kept his man in sight, creeping "stealthily as a cat" in his drenched stocking feet.[26] The detective imagined he saw a revolver glistening in the officer's hand but kept following. At the corner of Pennsylvania and 15th Street, the captain disappeared abruptly, passed a guard, and vanished into a building. Four armed soldiers lunged out at Pinkerton, their fixed bayonets pointed at his chest. "Halt, or I fire!" yelled the officer of the guard. Pinkerton realized he could not escape and tried to explain he was lost, but the guards seized him and marched him to the guardhouse.

A half hour passed, and Pinkerton was taken upstairs to face the captain of the guard. "I was a sorry figure to look at," Pinkerton wrote, "and as I surveyed my weather-soaked and mud-stained garments and my bare feet, I could scarcely suppress a laugh, although I was deeply angered at the sudden and unexpected turn affairs had taken." To Pinkerton's amazement, the captain was the same man the detective had been spying on all evening and had followed into the building. The officer "was pacing excitedly up and down the floor; stopping immediately in front of me, he glared fiercely at me for some minutes without uttering a word," Pinkerton wrote.

"What is your name?" the captain demanded.

"E. J. Allen," Pinkerton replied, using his pseudonym.

"What is your business?"

"I have nothing further to say," Pinkerton told the captain, "and I decline to answer any further questions."

The captain seemed nervous and fingered two revolvers that were lying on his desk. Turning to a sergeant, he issued an order, "Take this man to the guard-house, but allow no one whatsoever to converse with him." Pinkerton made a deep bow to the captain as he left. The officer swore at him.[27]

Pinkerton found himself behind bars, surrounded by drunken prisoners. Some were lying on the floor, others laughing and singing. One prisoner was cursing the men who arrested him. The cell was cold; Pinkerton's clothes were still wet, and he shivered uncontrollably. "I shook like an aspen and my teeth for a time chattered like castanets," he wrote. A guard brought him a blanket, which he wrapped around his shoulders. "One might more readily imagine that I had been fished out of the Potomac than that I was the chief of the secret service of the government," Pinkerton noted.[28]

Pinkerton thanked the guard and made a few jokes. The guard smiled, and soon the two men were laughing together. Pinkerton asked if the guard would mind delivering a note for him when his duty was over. Not at all, the young man replied. Pinkerton scribbled a few lines to Thomas Scott, the new assistant secretary of war who had put him on the Rose Greenhow case. An hour later, the guard returned and Pinkerton called out, "How's the weather outside?"

"All right, sir," the guard replied with a wink. Pinkerton knew his note had been delivered. Later that evening, the sergeant appeared at the prison door and called for "E. J. Allen." Pinkerton followed the sergeant to the office of the same captain he had observed at Rose's home.

"The secretary of war has been informed of your arrest and you will be conducted to him at once, and then we shall see if you will remain silent any longer," the captain told Pinkerton in his most imperious and commanding manner. As he led Pinkerton down the hall, he laughed at the detective's sorry appearance, and Pinkerton laughed, too, "for a more realistic picture of a 'drowned rat' I never beheld." As soon as Pinkerton was ushered into Scott's private office and the two men were alone, the detective related the events of the previous evening and the captain's visit to Rose Greenhow.

"Mrs. Greenhow must be attended to," the assistant secretary told Pinkerton. "She is becoming a dangerous character. You will therefore maintain your watch on her, and should she be detected in attempting to convey any information outside of the lines, she must be arrested at once."[29]

Scott tapped a bell on his table, and the suspect officer appeared. "Captain," Scott asked, "will you give me the particulars of the arrest of this man?" The captain replied that he had been visiting some friends on the outskirts of the city, and when returning late at night, he noticed that he was being followed. Suspecting a burglar, he had Pinkerton arrested.

"Did you see anyone last night who is inimical to the cause of the government?" Scott asked.

The captain flushed and glanced quickly at Pinkerton. "No, sir, I have seen no person of that character," he replied.

"Are you quite sure of that?" Scott inquired.

"I am, sir."

"In that case, Captain, will you please consider yourself under arrest. Surrender your sword at once."

Pinkerton took a carriage to his office and dispatched replacements for the men who had spent the night on watch at Rose's house, wondering what had become of their boss. He was relieved to learn they had recovered his shoes.[30]

Not long afterward, Martha Elizabeth Wright Morris of Ohio, whose husband had taken a job in Lincoln's State Department, was introduced to Rose by a friend living at Brown's Hotel. Rose confided that "she expected soon to be in Richmond, Va.," Mrs. Morris wrote in her memoir.

" 'Oh,' I said, 'I wish I could send a letter to my sister who can be found near there as she left New Orleans to join her husband, one of the staff officers for General Beauregard, and it is some time since we have heard from her.' "

"I am a personal friend of Beauregard," Rose was said to reply, "and if you bring me a letter, I will see that your sister receives it." Delighted, Mrs. Morris went immediately to her room and began a long, newsy missive. But when her husband, Robert Hunter Morris, an aide to Seward, realized what she was doing, he ordered her to abandon any attempt to communicate with her sister and not to see Rose again.

"I reluctantly gave up," Mrs. Morris wrote in her black, leather-bound memoir.[31]

President Lincoln had ordered a net dropped on the South's most dangerous spy, but even he could not imagine that her career had barely begun.

Where did the audacious Rose Greenhow come from, and how did an independent woman operating in a man's world of power and politics pull off such brazen capers?

Part Two

THE MAKING
OF AN
INDEPENDENT
WOMAN

CHAPTER 6

Death of a Master

ROSE O'NEALE WAS born on a small plantation in Montgomery County, Maryland. Her father, John O'Neale, a planter like his father and grandfather before him, was a Roman Catholic, a slave owner, and a drunk. In the seven years after his New Year's Day marriage to Eliza Henrietta Hamilton in 1810, the couple produced five daughters: Susannah, who was born the same year; Mary Eleanor, to be called Ellen, born a year later; Rose, who came in 1813 or 1814, followed by Mary Ann in 1816; and in 1817, John Eliza, a girl who would be called Liz.[1] But it was Rose who was the high-spirited one, a child with dark eyes, a lithesome gait, and a will of iron, very much like her father.

By 1817, the O'Neales lived on 560 acres of rolling hills and deep hollows in the shadow of Sugar Loaf Mountain on a farm called Conclusion, a name the property deed bears to this day. The land, in a heavily wooded section of western Montgomery County, was near Barnesville, a rural community of about fifteen families, most of them farmers like the O'Neales.[2] "They owned lands and negroes, were hospitable and intelligent and were highly respected," wrote Dr. William Turner Wootton, the son of the family physician.[3]

The O'Neale farm was about thirty-five miles northwest of Washington, the District of Columbia, which was still being rebuilt after the British burned its finest buildings in 1814. Ten Mile Creek, a clear, narrow stream, wound through a thick forest of tall red oaks, black gum trees, and stately tulip poplars, flooding fords during the March thaw. Loose flocks of mockingbirds, singing in flight, floated overhead, and Baltimore orioles with their orange bellies and yellow green plumage, darted from branch to branch, calling out to one another with a clear, flutelike whistle. The earth was rich and red and so moist from the winter melt-off that it seemed to sparkle in the sunlight. A stand of fir trees, when rustled by wind, filled the air with a pungent burst of balsam.

The O'Neale family built a farmhouse in a valley near the confluence of three springs that supplied water for the coldhouse, where milk and cheese were stored.[4] By April, when the weeping willows began to leaf and the lush green hills were covered with a creamy canopy of dogwood blossoms, the fields were ready for planting. As the owner of fifteen slaves and a sizable farm, John O'Neale was a wheat and tobacco planter of modest wealth in his community, where social status was measured by land and slaves. But with five daughters and a wife to support, O'Neale struggled to make ends meet. That hardly interfered with his carousing.

Early in the planting season of 1817, John O'Neale, as was his custom, took his favorite slave, Jacob, with him on one of his regular outings. O'Neale, who was thirty-four years old, had what was generously described as "a fondness for fun and sport,"[5] a taste for horse racing, foxhunting, cockfights, and liquor. He did not lack for companionship in Montgomery County.

His first cousin, a Montgomery County farmer named Isaac Riley, was the owner of Josiah Henson, the slave who became a model for Uncle Tom in Harriet Beecher Stowe's powerful nineteenth-century novel *Uncle Tom's Cabin.* Before writing her controversial book, Stowe interviewed Henson, who described to her his treatment and dramatic escape in painful detail. John O'Neale's handling of his slaves was no different from that of Isaac Riley and many other Southern farmers, and Jacob's role was very similar to the one described by Josiah Henson.

Jacob, then twenty, was among the most valuable of O'Neale's possessions and accompanied his master wherever the gentleman farmer sought his pleasures. It was not unusual to see them trotting along the narrow country paths and through the fields and apple orchards that linked one farmstead to another. The farmer would be perched high on his horse, his slave, like a shadow, running and walking beside him.

Jacob, whom O'Neale called Jake, served at his master's pleasure at all hours of the day and night. He entertained his master's friends with acro-

batic tricks to "add to the frolic" when O'Neale was in the mood to show
him off. Jacob was double-jointed and dazzled audiences with body-
twisting leg- and arm-bending maneuvers that made people gasp. "He
could turn on his hands and feet like a wheel, and perform many athletic
tricks like those seen in a circus," wrote Dr. Wootton.[6] *Uncle Tom's Cabin*,
which was published in 1852, opens with a description of a young male
slave being asked to perform similar acrobatic tricks.[7]

At about midnight on April 22, 1817, O'Neale left Nathan Trail's tavern near Bunkers Hill, not far from his farm, and headed for home. As
usual, Jacob was with him. According to court records, it was dark and
raining, and O'Neale was quite drunk, having spent the whole afternoon
and evening at the tavern. O'Neale's horse had recently been injured, and
its tail was tied up to the saddle in a way that made it painful for the horse
to walk.[8]

Shortly after leaving the tavern, O'Neale decided to return for another
bottle of whiskey, but he couldn't get his horse to step close enough to the
door for the master to take it from Nathan Trail's hand. The obedient Jacob
accepted the whiskey for his owner, and they set off again together.
O'Neale shared enough of his liquor with Jacob to get the young slave
drunk as well. Sheriff Arnold Winsor later testified, supported by Dr.
William Brewer, a physician and friend of the O'Neale family, that at a
certain point on the road home, O'Neale ordered Jacob to go on ahead to
the farm. Jacob, the sheriff said, retraced his path early the next morning
and found his master in the lane, about 150 yards from his house, "thrown
from his horse and lying on the ground, bleeding from the head."

Jacob was still under the influence of alcohol, but he rushed home and
sought help from another slave, named Esther, probably his mother. She
told him, according to Sheriff Winsor, who questioned Jacob later in jail,
that he should go back and finish off O'Neale. In Josiah Henson's memoir,
composed years after escaping to Canada, he told of a similar incident
with his master, Isaac Riley, getting drunk and falling, then blaming his
slave.[9]

According to court records of the O'Neale case, Jacob walked up the
lane where his master was lying, found a sizable stone, and smashed the
man's skull with the rock. Jacob then raced to fetch Dr. Brewer, who went
to the scene to find O'Neale dead on the ground. The bloodied landowner
had three head wounds, Brewer testified, one apparently caused by the
rock and two others, but it was impossible to tell which one had caused the

man's death. In an aside, the court records note Dr. Brewer "discovered an uncommon backwardness on the part of all Oneales negroes to render assistance to him."[10]

When the county court convened at the courthouse in Rockville three months later, on the first Monday of August, Jacob was put on trial for murder. He pleaded not guilty. The court's minute book lists seven witnesses for the prosecution in *State of Maryland vs. Negro Jacob:* William Brewer, Nathan Trail, Arnold T. Winsor, William Chiswell, Negro Harry, Francis Jamison (O'Neale's brother-in-law), and Dennis Lackland. Chiswell and Thomas Sparrow had testified before a grand jury that indicted Jacob. The court gave Chiswell a per diem for sparing two of his slaves, Juda and Margery, to appear in court. Slaves had limited legal rights and were not permitted to testify against white people. Their testimony about other slaves could be used, although anything they said could jeopardize their own safety and that of their families when they went home to their owners.

The sparse remaining records of Jacob's trial show little more than that the jury of twelve white men heard the testimony of the sheriff, the doctor, and the tavern keeper and concluded that O'Neale died from a single wound to the head, despite the doctor's testimony that he could not determine which of the three head injuries caused O'Neale's death.

It was not unusual at the time to force a confession from the accused, especially in the case of a slave, but there is no record that Jacob confessed to the crime. He did give an account to the sheriff while being held in irons at the Rockville jailhouse, but Jacob denied any intention of killing his master. He was, nonetheless, found guilty of first-degree murder before the week was out and sentenced "to be hanged by the neck until he be dead."[11]

In his memoir, Josiah Henson described being blamed for an accident involving his master:

> My master got into a quarrel with his brother's overseer, who was one
> of the party, and in rescuing [him,] I suppose I was a little more
> rough . . . than usual. I remember his falling upon the floor, and very
> likely it was the result of a push from me, or a movement of my elbow. He
> attributed his fall to me, rather than to the whiskey he had drunk, and trea-
> sured up his vengeance for the first favorable opportunity.[12]

Almost immediately after Jacob was found guilty of murder, his court-appointed defense counsel, Benjamin Stoddert Forrest, petitioned Governor Charles Ridgely of Hampton to spare Jacob's life, arguing that Jacob had never confessed to a crime and that there were "strong circumstances" indicating that O'Neale died in the fall from his horse. Jacob, the lawyer said, "has at all times obstinately denied any intention of killing his master but avers that he found him past recovery in a lane, having fallen from his horse; that in this situation he gave him one blow in a moment of intoxication occasioned by the imprudence of his master in furnishing him with a large quantity of whiskey." Forrest urged the governor to show mercy and commute Jacob's death sentence to life imprisonment. "I am convinced," he said in his letter to Ridgely, "that there does not exist in the County the least necessity for such an example as is to be made of Jacob."[13]

As usual, the governor ignored the plea. On Friday, October 10, 1817, less than six months after O'Neale's death, Jacob was taken from his cell in the Rockville jail to the gallows erected in the courtyard and hanged.[14]

The refusal of a pardon or commutation of Jacob's sentence was hardly uncommon. In the half century between 1787 and 1837, Maryland governors considered petitions in forty-three murder cases involving slaves. In twenty-three of those cases, death warrants were issued. Six death sentences were commuted to lesser punishments, nine slaves were ordered sold outside the United States, and five were pardoned. In most of the cases, the victim was another slave; no one convicted of murdering his master escaped the death penalty.[15] O'Neale's widow was credited with $400 for Jacob's loss, as he was considered property she could not sell.

Hangings like Jacob's were public events often requiring tickets and attracting huge crowds. In one notorious case only about fifteen miles from Conclusion, four black men convicted of murdering Edward Owings, a white planter, were hanged in January 1816 near Frederick, Maryland. According to the local papers, six thousand people turned out, more than the entire population of Frederick.[16]

There are no records of how Jacob spent his final months in the county jail, but even as early as 1817, his fellow inmates included a steady flow of runaway slaves caught by bounty hunters in Maryland and incarcerated pending return to their owners or sale. Some belonged to slaveholders in Montgomery County; others were trying to escape from farther south into Pennsylvania and free states to the north, which included New York, New Jersey, Vermont, and Massachusetts. The Montgomery County jail records for one eight-month period after Jacob's execution show owners of seven runaways were charged 30 cents a day for imprisonment of their slaves, $1 for shackling them in irons, and 26⅔ cents for commitment and release. The slave catcher collected a $6 reward from the county for bringing in an escapee and sometimes considerably more from the slave owner.[17]

The death of John O'Neale devastated his widow and five daughters. A fatherless family often fell on hard times, and Eliza O'Neale's situation grew nearly desperate as she struggled to hold on to her farm and keep her family intact. Despite having grown up in a family with substantial land-holdings in the state and being married into a prosperous family, she was unable to pay off her husband's debts from land he had purchased. She managed for only a few years.

The O'Neales were Roman Catholics, originally from Ireland, although John's ancestors apparently settled in Spain before immigrating to America, where Captain James Neale won a land grant from the British crown in 1652.[18] Most of the American colonies were not friendly to Roman Catholics, who were prohibited from openly practicing their religion or holding office, but Maryland was one of the few places where Catholics could be respected members of the community.[19] The second Lord Baltimore, who inherited Maryland from his father in 1632, protected the rights of his fellow Catholics in Maryland and attracted many English and Irish Catholics to the colony by promising them land and even manors, if they brought enough servants to settle and cultivate their land. His Act Concerning Religion, adopted by the Maryland Colonial Legislature in 1649, established the principle of religious toleration and set a ten-shilling fine or whipping for anyone who called another by the name of his religion "in a reproachful manner."[20] That was three years before Captain Neale received his land. The act was abolished less than fifty years later, after Protestants seized the throne in England, but its existence had facilitated the establishment of numerous landholding families of different faiths and villages and towns populated by adherents of an assortment of Christian denominations.

No such tolerance was afforded the growing number of black Africans being imported to Maryland. Fifteen years after adoption of the law to protect all Christians in the colony, Lord Baltimore formally legalized enslavement of blacks to counter the belief of some colonists that blacks could be freed from bondage by accepting Christ. A second law, prompted by a number of marriages between white women and slaves, specified that the children of freeborn Englishwomen who married slaves would inherit their father's status and be slaves for life. This practice was in place for only a short time before it was revised to the usual practice of a child's status following that of the mother, with a provision of long-term service for mulatto children.

In fact, the Catholic Church was not only among the great defenders of slavery in the American South, it was one of the largest slaveholders. The Jesuits and Georgetown College, a Jesuit institution founded in 1789, operated six plantations in Maryland up to the nineteenth century and maintained them with slave labor. About four hundred slaves worked on the Jesuit estates in the mid-nineteenth century, and their owners debated whether or not to standardize their treatment, by barring, for instance, the whipping of pregnant women, and how to promote morality among slaves whose conduct was "a reproach to a Society that taught sanctity to savages."[21]

Catholic slave owners encouraged their slaves to practice Catholicism because they believed their religion inspired them to be obedient, industrious, and honest. "Catholic slaves are preferred to all others, because they are more docile and more faithful to their masters," said the Reverend John Grassi, president of Georgetown College in 1818.[22] Ironically, later in the century, Georgetown University would be headed by the mixed-race son of a Georgia planter and his slave mistress. Father Patrick F. Healy (1834–1910) was reared in the North and passed for white his whole adult life.[23]

After the American Revolution, Maryland's Catholics regained rights they had lost after 1689, including the right to vote and hold office. They were once more permitted to begin building churches and worship publicly.

Upon being appointed the first Catholic bishop in the United States in 1785, John Carroll reported to the church in Rome that the Catholic population in Maryland, where he made his headquarters, was about nine thousand freemen, three thousand children, "and the same number are slaves of all ages, who come from Africa."[24]

The Catholic community around Barnesville, Maryland, built a white frame church in 1808 and named it St. Mary's. John O'Neale and his family were parishioners. Within five years, the parish, which included landowners, lawyers, farmers, and even a few slaves (who sat separately in a small upstairs gallery),[25] had grown to 160. The first pastor, Father James Redmond, came by horseback one Sunday a month to conduct services and listen to confession.[26]

John O'Neale's father, Lawrence O'Neale, had been among the best-known and most successful members of the family in America. Already an established planter and surveyor when he was in his thirties, he was granted the colonial titles of gentleman in 1770 and esquire in 1773, the year he became sheriff of Frederick County. If he was Catholic, which his children were,[27] he may have done what many Catholics did at the time to hold office, which was to outwardly conform to Protestantism.

Lawrence O'Neale appears to have joined the Revolution against the British crown, although his role is not clear. By 1781, he was appointed a recruiter of militia and later a justice for Montgomery County. He was elected to the Maryland House of Delegates from Montgomery County in 1780 and served until 1796. His interest in land speculation appears to have gotten him in trouble with his colleagues toward the end of his public service. In 1794, a resolution was introduced to expel Lawrence O'Neale from the chamber. That failed, but the House did vote to censure him for attempting to register some land claimed by a fellow planter. O'Neale continued to trade and acquire land throughout his career, and at the time of his death in 1815—two years before his son John was killed— he owned about three thousand acres and held forty-one slaves, making his personal property worth more than $31,000,[28] very substantial holdings for a gentleman planter of the time. His older son, Henry O'Neale, inherited the bulk of Lawrence's estate but died before it was settled. John, the younger and wilder brother, had comfortable holdings in land and slaves, but he was in debt to his father's estate, and his widow would find it impossible to keep her farm and family intact.

Like many Southern planters with moderate landholdings, John O'Neale was cash poor, with most of his capital tied up in slaves and land.[29] In his will, which was witnessed by Maryland attorney Roger Brooke Taney, later to become chief justice of the United States Supreme Court, O'Neale left his property to his wife and children.[30] But to pay his debts, including more than $2,000 owed to his father's estate, O'Neale's widow was forced to sell almost everything he had. The inventory included his fifteen slaves, who were each given a dollar value by the appraisers. There were six males over the age of twelve, a couple of ten-year-old boys, two women, and five little girls, who were probably baby-sitters and playmates of the O'Neales' daughters. The names of the slaves and their value were listed in bold script, line by line:

Negro Boy John, 20, $500.
Negro Boy George, 21, $500.
Negro Boy Harry, 25, $450.

Negro Boy Jacob, 20 years	$450.
Negro Boy Austin, 16 years,	$450.
Negro Boy Sigh, 12 years,	$350.
Negro Boy Phillip, 10 years,	$300.
Negro Boy Moses, 10 years,	$300.
One Negro woman, Easter	
[Esther], 45 years,	$150.
Negro Henny and child,	$350.
Negro Girl Alice, 13 years,	$250.
Negro Girl Miriah, 8 years,	$175.
Negro Girl, Verlinda, 6 years,	$150.
Negro Girl Nelly, 3 years,	$100.[31]

It was customary for relatives and friends to help out the bereaved family as much as possible. One way was to purchase slaves and other items they could afford to supply cash for the household. According to O'Neale's estate records, Eliza O'Neale, now head of the family, kept twelve-year-old Sigh for herself. John O'Neale's brother-in-law Francis Jamison bought Austin. Eliza's brother-in-law bought George. Her paternal grandmother bought Phillip. An aunt bought John. Harry, who had testified against Jacob at the trial but was contradicted by white witnesses about Jacob's character, was sold privately, as was Esther, who had been accused of putting Jacob up to murder but wasn't charged.

The rest of O'Neale's personal property included little of value: four featherbeds and a barrel of feathers, appraised at $120; a silver watch and gold chain, $50; seven silver tablespoons, $16; a walnut dining table, $6; several dozen earthen plates, curtains and table linens, various farm tools, and a few books. There were three horses, eight hogs, twelve sheep, and a cow with yearling, plus 436 pounds of bacon in the cold cellar, much of it for feeding the slaves. Even potatoes and oats, still in the field, were counted.[32]

Eliza O'Neale, a widow at twenty-three with four daughters and a fifth child on the way, was not in an enviable position. According to court records, the balance of her husband's estate was down to $2,609.94.[33] The price of both wheat and tobacco was plummeting, sending farmers all over the area into a general depression.[34] She had no sons to help with the land. She was responsible for her daughters' physical well-being, education, religious training, and eventually their dowries. Within a few years, her resources would be drained.

Two years after John's death, the value of the estate had dropped to $1,162.51, according to court records, and within four, it was down to $306.92. Eliza O'Neale struggled to hold on to the farm for five more years, but eventually the court ordered her to sell the family homestead to settle her debts. In January 1825, an auction was held at Mrs. Scholl's Tavern in nearby Clarksburg, and Conclusion was purchased by George C. Washington for an undisclosed price.[35] A survey of the land showed that the farm actually contained fifty fewer acres than Lawrence O'Neale claimed when he bought it in 1804 and later passed it on to his son.[36]

It wasn't unusual for a widow in Eliza O'Neale's circumstances to send a pair of "extra" daughters to live with an aunt,[37] and her sister Maria Ann was living in Washington with her husband, Henry V. Hill, a carpenter[38] who was planning to open a boardinghouse. After several years of struggling financially, Eliza O'Neale selected her second and third children, Ellen and Rose, to live with their aunt Maria in the capital.[39] As there are no remaining records, the date is unknown, but it was probably around 1828, when Rose and Ellen were teenagers.

By the standards of the day, it was not a long journey, not more than a day's trip in any case, but it's never easy to pick up and start a new life, whatever the circumstances, and the city streets of Washington were a world away from the fertile fields and farm life the girls had known. Eliza O'Neale, whose regular visits to her children over the years suggested she was a loving mother, had probably done the best she could for her daughters in the aftermath of their father's tragic death. Perhaps it wasn't always enough, that occasionally one daughter or another felt abandoned and adrift, but sometimes that's all a mother has in her, all she has to give.

No one could have known the choices the O'Neale girls would be forced to make over the next three decades, tumultuous years that would eventually lead one section of the country to rise up against the other in a bloody civil war. As hard as she tried, Eliza O'Neale could never have prepared her daughters for all life's contingencies. At some point, she had to say a prayer, entrust her children into God's hands, and let go. And at some point, that's exactly what she did.

CHAPTER 7

Washington Society

ROSE AND ELLEN traveled to Washington by stagecoach, a twenty-five-mile journey along the Frederick–George Town Road, once an Indian trail, later renamed the Rockville Pike. The stone and gravel roadbed was so rough, the driver frequently had to direct passengers to lean out of the stagecoach, first on one side, then on the other, to prevent it from tipping over. "Pass-en-gers, lean right!" he would bellow over the pounding of the hoofbeats. "Pass-en-gers, lean left!"[1]

Just south of the village of Tennally Town, the driver would bring the horses to a stop at Cookendoffer's Tavern for his passengers to enjoy a meal before continuing on into the city. When they approached High Street, now Wisconsin Avenue, in Georgetown Heights, the sisters could look down a wide, naturally sloping hillside dotted with handsome, red-brick mansions to the Potomac River.[2] Off to their left was the young Federal City.

The stage carrying the O'Neale sisters rumbled through old George-town, once part of Montgomery County and settled fifty years before the government moved to Washington. Connected to the capital by two bridges over a tributary of the Potomac called Rock Creek, Georgetown was a thriving community with lovely houses, good schools, a small, bustling port, and many merchants.[3] O'Donnoghue's Soap and Candle Factory was on the west side of town. John Laird & Son, tobacco merchants, shipped boatloads of tobacco to Europe from the wharves at the foot of Frederick Street.[4] Suter's Tavern, where George Washington had discussed plans for the Federal City, was tucked between Bridge and Water streets,[5] often crowded with ox-drawn farm wagons loaded with fruits, vegetables, and tobacco to be sold in the city markets.

Washington was a natural crossroads for north and south and a central hub of shipping and stagecoach travel. Many of the residents came from the slaveholding states of Maryland and Virginia, as well as from Kentucky, Tennessee, and Georgia, giving the city a distinctly Southern flavor. New Englanders visited on government business and sometimes stayed for months at a time, but they complained that the city was far from a sophisticated metropolis like Boston, New York, or Baltimore.

The main thoroughfare was Pennsylvania Avenue, a rutted road with mud so deep during the wet months that wagon wheels sank up to their hubs.[6] In dry months, it was caked with red dust. Yet the Avenue, as it was called, was the city's central promenade, a place to stroll in pleasant weather, to see and be seen. And almost everyone, Northerner and Southerner, rich and poor, young and old, black and white, shopped at the Center Market on 8th Street, now the site of the National Archives. Selling beef, venison, poultry, fresh oysters, and fish of all varieties, it was the best in town.

When the federal government moved from Philadelphia to Washington in 1800, the established port cities of Alexandria and Georgetown were incorporated as part of the one-hundred-square-mile diamond carved out of Maryland and Virginia that Congress had designated for the District of Columbia. They had been exporting tobacco and developing their own societies for half a century. The new city between them was known as "Washington" or, simply, the Federal City. Designed by the Paris-born Revolutionary War engineer Pierre L'Enfant, it offered long, broad avenues that acted as metaphor for a national capital based on classical roots and soaring ideals.[7]

But Rose and Ellen were arriving in a city that still left much to the imagination. Cattle grazed freely on grassy pastureland that separated the few government buildings, and pigs wandered in search of garbage that residents tossed from their windows. A tidal creek called the Tiber River ran deep into the city, making it necessary to construct houses on the northern side of the Avenue as the south side was often flooded. Store deliveries sometimes had to be made by flatboat.

The girls' destination was Hill's Boarding House, a three-story brick building with tall, arched windows, located at the corner of 1st and

A streets NE, right across the street from the Capitol and now the site of the Supreme Court. The boardinghouse belonged to their mother's sister Maria and her husband, Henry V. Hill, and would be the girls' home until they married.[8] The building had been constructed as a temporary house for Congress after the British burned the Capitol in 1814, and it would serve that purpose until 1819. Known as the Old Brick Capitol, it was used as a school before the Hills opened their rooming house.[9]

Hill's was one of several respectable places where congressmen, Supreme Court justices, and other distinguished visitors could stay while Congress or the Court was in session. Early city directories listed members of Congress by their boardinghouse rather than by state.[10] The establishments were like fraternities, with plenty of banter and ample supplies of liquor. Each had its own identity and regional clientele. Northerners generally roomed with Northerners, Westerners (from west of the Appalachian Mountains) with Westerners. Indian chiefs Red Cloud, White Feather, and Crazy Horse stayed at Mrs. Beveridge's on 3rd Street NW when they came to town to negotiate treaties with the government.[11] Boarders were summoned to breakfast and dinner by a bell and sat together at a long table with no consideration to rank. Congressmen shared a room, sometimes even a bed, making for little privacy. Manners were all but forgotten. Because soap was scarce, Southern women like Rose and Ellen substituted powder—white, pink, or lavender—for bathing.

Hill's was popular with Southern politicians. South Carolina statesman John C. Calhoun, who served as vice president under John Quincy Adams and became an outspoken proponent of slavery, was the Hills' most prestigious boarder and lived there on and off until he died there in 1850.[12] He became a close friend of Rose O'Neale, who worshipped him and stuck by him until his death. Other boarders at Hill's included North Carolina congressmen Abraham Rencher, a Whig, and Henry W. Conner, a Democrat; also Charles A. Wickliffe of Kentucky and Cave Johnson of Tennessee. Rencher and Johnson later served terms as postmaster general.[13]

Only wealthy lawmakers could afford to bring their wives to Washington for congressional sessions, so the boardinghouses were filled with lonely men. The O'Neale sisters would have been popular company. Even as teenagers, they were considered beauties.

Rose was a standout. She had a pale olive complexion and shiny black hair, parted in the middle and pulled tightly back from a face that formed a perfect oval. Her waist was tiny and her breasts full, giving her figure hourglass perfection. Poised and graceful, with deeply set chestnut eyes shaded by dark eyebrows and long lashes, Rose carried herself with a flirtatious air. "She was a celebrated belle and beauty, the admiration of all who knew her," wrote Dr. Wootton.[14]

The sisters would join the men for dinner, where everyone helped themselves, family style, from heaping platters of local specialties: Maryland crab cakes, baked perch from the Chesapeake Bay, roasted duck, venison, fruits, and pie of every variety. Madeira, a sweet, fortified wine imported from the island off Portugal, was in ready supply.

The girls were exposed to a steady stream of political talk and backroom maneuvering, daily lessons in how the patronage system operated, cronyism, and the importance of horse trading in getting bills passed.[15] "Every day or rather evening, I was in company with some of the most distinguished actors in this interesting drama," wrote Margaret Bayard Smith, one of the earliest chroniclers of life in the nation's capital. "I knew the causes of the circumstances and the motives of their actions on which public opinion speculated and so often misinterpreted. It was curious and amusing to compare rumour and truth, and it was highly interesting to watch not only the development of characters, but of events."[16]

Margaret Bayard Smith, by virtue of her marriage to Samuel Harrison Smith, founder of the *Daily National Intelligencer* and president of the Washington branch of the Bank of the United States, was a grande dame of Washington society. She was also an astute observer of the highs and lows of the city's social scene. "I never witnessed such a dullness and gloom as that which pervades society," she wrote in February 1829, just before the inauguration of the recently widowed Andrew Jackson, who had defeated John Quincy Adams. "The party who are withdrawing from office, sad and melancholy, will not mix in society and the private parties given are uninteresting to strangers, because there are no Secretaries or public characters there—Gen. Jackson and his family, being in mourning, decline all company."[17]

By 1830, the city had established its rhythm, coming alive in autumn when Congress convened and all but closing down in the hot, humid months. The marsh behind the Executive Mansion smelled so foul of rot and mosquitoes were so thick that ladies found it too uncomfortable to stroll after supper. Like Congress, many residents simply left town.

Rose and Ellen had an older sister, Susannah, living in Georgetown, and they often took a carriage from Capitol Hill to see her. The trip along the rutted, muddy Avenue could take the better part of an afternoon. Susannah was married to James Peter, a member of one of the city's most prominent and wealthy families. It was quite a coup for a young woman brought up on a small Maryland plantation to marry into a family of such renown.

The wedding was on January 12, 1830, at the O'Neale family parish in Barnesville, Montgomery County.[18] James was a grandson of Robert Peter, the first mayor of Georgetown, and a nephew of Thomas Peter and his wife, Martha Custis Peter, granddaughter of Martha Washington. The Peters were among the city's largest landowners and lived at Tudor Place, a neoclassical mansion overlooking the Potomac in Georgetown Heights. It was designed by Dr. William Thornton, the first architect of the U.S. Capitol.

Susannah's marriage into the Peter family gave Rose and Ellen O'Neale entrée to Washington society, a clubby cadre of lawmakers, diplomats, newspaper publishers, and aristocratic gentry who traced their roots to plantations in the Virginia and Maryland countryside. The first families of Georgetown were often self-made Americans, wealthy from exporting tobacco since the eighteenth century. The O'Neale sisters were invited to buffet receptions, intimate teas, dinners, and candlelit balls given by the Peters,[19] who took pride in opening their drawing rooms and formal gardens to the capital's most important citizens and foreign visitors. Their parties were famous for a potent homemade apple-brandy punch, made with red-streaked apples toasted in front of a fire and soaked in the finest cognac. Guests included the Marquis de Lafayette during his famous trip to the United States in 1824, Andrew Jackson, Daniel Webster of Massachusetts, and John C. Calhoun.[20]

As attractive daughters of an established family of Maryland planters with a sister married into social prominence, Rose and Ellen O'Neale were invited to diplomatic receptions and glittery balls and on long walks up and down the Avenue. They went to the Executive Mansion for parties that the president and first lady gave weekly between Christmas and Lent.[21]

Cave Johnson, who lived at Hill's Boarding House when the House of Representatives was in session, courted Rose, or at least was said to escort her about town.[22] The Tennessee congressman, who had fought Indians with Andrew Jackson before being trained as a lawyer, had only recently come to Washington himself.[23] He was a good twenty years Rose's senior, old enough to be the father she had hardly known. But he would have provided valuable access for a young woman learning the subtleties of etiquette and protocol in a new city and anxious to meet the key players and eligible bachelors.

Like many women new to Washington, Rose knew men who carried the title of congressman or senator. Even if they had sour breath and potbellies, as many did, they were usually well educated, were frequently schooled in the law, and carried themselves with a sense of self-assurance and swagger that impressed a country girl. One can imagine a politician like Cave Johnson with Rose on his arm, strolling past the White House in the early evening, telling her of his own plans to live there one day. There was hardly a man in Congress who didn't think he could—or should—be president. Johnson could be proud of sporting such a young and lithesome companion, a beauty his colleagues would surely notice. He might even have introduced her to his good friend President Jackson. Rose, who seemed to find a sense of security in men her father's age, could not have asked for more.

Johnson was also a good friend of James Buchanan of Pennsylvania, a tall, stiffly formal congressman soon to be named minister to Russia. In later years, when Buchanan became President Polk's secretary of state, then was elected president himself in 1856, Rose was among his confidants.

Rose and Ellen O'Neale were prettier than most of the young, single women in town, but they were not assured of a place in the upper strata of capital social life. There were more and more girls coming into the city, relatives or friends of government officials.[24] All were eager for invitations to the best events.

Unlike the old families of Boston and New York and Philadelphia, few people were born into Washington society. Georgetown and Alexandria had their established hierarchies, and there were wealthy planters in nearby Maryland and Virginia. But the Federal City was generating a celebrity class, a revolving society of officials, influence peddlers, and newspaper owners, whose positions depended on access to power—the power of the White House, Congress, and, to a lesser extent, the courts. A man's status was commonly measured by his proximity to the president, a woman's by her husband's rank and influence. Men worked in the spotlight, while their wives used social activities to build a network of powerful friends.

It did not take long for Rose and Ellen to learn how the social and political spheres of Washington intertwined. Like other women, the girls spent mornings and evenings paying formal visits to friends, neighbors, even strangers—anyone they wished to cultivate or impress in a town governed by politics.[25] An introduction to the wife of an important official often opened doors to other influential individuals.

When weather permitted, they donned pretty bonnets and hailed a carriage to make their rounds.[26] Formal calls began at noon and lasted until three o'clock. If the lady of the house was not dressed to receive guests, or simply not in the mood, she would instruct her servant to announce, "Not at home," which happened more often than anyone would admit.[27]

Like other women in Washington society, the O'Neale sisters kept a list with the names of those they visited and those who left handwritten calling cards at their house.[28] Failure to return a visit was considered an insult, but the call ritual could take up much of their time. "My visiting list is one of the smallest of any lady in Washington," wrote Margaret Bayard Smith in December 1831, "yet to keep up an interchange with only 70 or 80 persons consumes all my morning hours."[29]

Proper etiquette dictated that young women pay the first call on older matrons, especially those who were socially prominent. "I never knew ladies to visit young girls first," Dolley Madison advised her nieces Mary and Dolley Madison Cutts, who were close friends of the O'Neale sisters.[30] "Indeed, I know they made a point of not doing so, and in my humble opinion, they were right. When they or you take a journey, the first call must be made by you."[31]

Dolley Payne Todd Madison, wife of James Madison, the fourth president of the United States, was the most prominent social arbiter in Washington society for almost half a century.[32] She presided over the first inaugural ball when her husband became president in 1809 and remained a respected and much admired presence until she died in 1849. As first lady, she was regal in manner and appearance, yet she opened the doors of the White House to ordinary Americans. She greeted her guests dressed in rich, brightly colored silks and blue feathered turbans[33] and served unusual delicacies, such as ice cream in warm pastry. Her weekly receptions, called "Wednesday drawing rooms," required no invitation and attracted hundreds of callers, causing some to refer to them as "crushes" or "squeezes."

After retiring to Montpelier, the couple's elegant estate in Orange County, Virginia, Mrs. Madison remained an influential figure but was often lonely. Although the couple received many guests, the gregarious Dolley missed the companionship of her Washington friends and relatives and lavished attention on her nieces and nephews. One of them, James Madison Cutts, the brother of Mary and young Dolley, courted Ellen O'Neale and won her hand.

Ellen O'Neale and James Madison Cutts were married on December

17, 1833,[34] and spent their honeymoon at Montpelier. As their carriage approached the mansion, the former president came out, leaning on his faithful servant Paul Jennings, who had been born a slave at Montpelier and served Madison at the White House. At the age of eighty-two, Madison was in failing health and was unable to join the family for dinner. But he stood in the dining room doorway and offered the bride and groom a toast to their good health. Ellen later thanked him with a charming note.[35]

Mrs. Madison was especially close to James Madison Cutts, whom she called Mad. She referred to his wife, Ellen, as "my pet." After the birth of their son, named James after his father and great-uncle, Mrs. Madison doted on him like a grandson, keeping him always at her side, even when she entertained.[36] As Ellen's sister, Rose was accepted into Mrs. Madison's circle and called on the elderly lady at her home in Lafayette Square for many years after she returned to live in Washington following her husband's death in 1836.[37] The Dolley Madison connection gave Rose and Ellen yet another window into the glittery world of Washington society.

It was not unusual for bright women to become interested in the great issues facing the young nation, and part of their education came from making regular visits to Capitol Hill. Ladies wearing heavy dresses with wide hoopskirts crowded into the visitors' gallery of the House or Senate to listen to the great orators of the day: Senators Henry Clay of Kentucky, Daniel Webster of Massachusetts, and John C. Calhoun of South Carolina. Calhoun's daughter Anna Maria, several years younger than Rose, was a regular visitor.[38] Anna was enthralled with politics, and her father doted on her. "I am not one of them, who think your sex ought to have nothing to do with politics," Calhoun wrote her.[39] Women had no vote and few rights, but Rose, at least, came to understand that a Southern belle could play politics in Washington society.

On the dark side of life in Washington, gossip was a brutal weapon. What women whispered in their drawing rooms could empty chairs in the president's cabinet room—and did. About the time the O'Neale sisters arrived in Washington, the newly installed administration of Andrew Jackson was rocked by a scandal involving a woman named Margaret O'Neale Timberlake Eaton. She was no relation to Rose and Ellen O'Neale, but made their surname notorious. As a young woman, Margaret O'Neale had charmed then senator Jackson by playing religious music on the piano when he stayed at her father's boardinghouse. Margaret later married a navy paymaster, John Bowie Timberlake, but their union was not a happy one, and local wags whispered that she cheated on him.

Timberlake died, some said of a broken heart, others that he committed suicide. His widow—she insisted only her enemies called her Peggy, as in the "Peggy Eaton scandal"—moved home to her father's rooming house and took up with John Henry Eaton, a Tennessee senator and close friend and adviser to Jackson. Eaton married her, hoping to quell the gossip, but Washington society was scandalized.[40] Louis McLane, who became secretary of state in Jackson's second administration, cracked that Eaton had "married his mistress—and the mistress of 11-doz. others."[41] Many cabinet wives refused to go to the wedding or allow their husbands to attend.[42]

When the newlyweds paid a call on Floride Calhoun, who as wife of the vice president was the second-highest-ranking woman in Washington, Mrs. Calhoun received the couple but later told her husband that she had no intention of returning the call.[43] The affront was unmistakable.

Jackson not only liked the new Mrs. Eaton and was stubbornly loyal to her husband, but he was convinced that his political enemies were using the Eaton affair to smear him. The president-elect wasn't the type to shrink from a fight or bow to vicious gossip. He was still in mourning for his beloved wife, Rachel, who died of a heart attack shortly after the election. During the campaign, Jackson's detractors had dredged up a forty-year-old charge that Rachel had married Jackson while still wed to her first husband, technically true because her divorce, unknown to her, had never been finalized. Jackson blamed his political enemies for her death and despised scandalmongering.

Ignoring the advice of several advisers, Jackson picked Eaton to be secretary of war, making Margaret Eaton the wife of a cabinet member and one of the highest-ranking women in the Federal City.

The wives of Jackson's other cabinet members, the high priestesses of Washington, refused to accept Margaret Eaton as one of their own, insisting there was a moral issue at stake. They were taking "a stand, a *noble* stand . . . against one who has left her straight and narrow path," wrote Margaret Bayard Smith.[44] When the pastor of the Second Presbyterian Church criticized Margaret Eaton in public, Jackson, a member of the congregation, summoned him to the White House to be rebuked, then abruptly quit the church.

Jackson suspected Henry Clay, his longtime foe from Kentucky, of encouraging the dissension, but he also distrusted Vice President Calhoun, who had supported him in the campaign but was distancing himself from the administration on states' rights issues and preparing his own run for the White House.

The pot simmered for two years until Secretary of State Martin Van Buren, a former governor of New York and a shrewd behind-the-scenes politician, sought a compromise. In April 1831, with Jackson's assent, Van Buren offered to resign and suggested that Eaton step down as well, giving the president an opportunity to ask for resignations from the rest of his cabinet to allow for a thorough reorganization. In a dramatic bow to Jackson that some too hastily interpreted as a government collapse, all gave up their posts.

Despite predictions the scandal would strengthen Clay and Calhoun, it actually set the stage for a showdown between Van Buren and Calhoun that marked the end of the vice president's rise in national politics.

To Calhoun's dismay, Jackson seized the opportunity of appointing a new cabinet to pick replacements from the Van Buren camp[45] and rewarded Van Buren for his loyalty by nominating him to be minister to the Court of St. James's in London, the government's most important diplomatic post. Ambassadors, however, are subject to Senate confirmation, and Calhoun's allies in the Senate attempted to block the president's choice. When the Van Buren nomination deadlocked in January 1832, Vice President Calhoun, as the constitutional president of the Senate, cast the tie-breaking vote to defeat Van Buren. In a flash of bitterness, Calhoun gloated that the president's political embarrassment "will kill him, kill him dead."[46]

But he underestimated Jackson as a gut fighter who knew how to settle a score. Jackson dropped Calhoun as his running mate for reelection, put Van Buren on the ticket instead, and was reelected by a comfortable margin. Calhoun returned to the Senate, where he continued to champion slavery and states' rights. The Eaton scandal cast such a pall on the early years of the Jackson administration that many cabinet wives simply stayed away from the city to avoid Margaret Eaton. The number of social functions dropped precipitately until the Eatons finally left town and the social whirl resumed. In her autobiography, written forty years later, Mrs. Eaton wrote: "God help the woman who must live in Washington."[47]

But Rose O'Neale was young and beautiful and filled with dreams. Washington would become her home.

CHAPTER 8

Slavery in Washington:
"A Tale of Woe"

THE WASHINGTON SOCIETY Rose was growing into was more Southern in its culture and traditions than Northern and open, of course, only to whites. Anyone walking from Capitol Hill to the White House might pass at least six slave pens, foul and filthy cells where black servants were held awaiting auction. Even in daylight, amid the clatter of horse-drawn carriages and shouts of street vendors, passersby could hear the moans and cries of chained slaves emanating from barred basement windows.[1]

The worst was operated by Thomas Williams on the corner of 8th and B streets SW, down near the river, in a house covered with yellow plaster and thick metal bars on the windows. Slaves were handcuffed and chained to the floor.[2] Another was Robey's at 7th Street and Maryland Avenue SW, described by an English traveler as "a wretched hovel, surrounded by a wooden paling fourteen or fifteen feet in height, with posts outside to prevent escape and separated from the building by a space too narrow to admit a free circulation of air."[3] Joseph W. Neal ran another pen on 7th Street.[4] Barred windows leading to the basement of the Charles Hotel on 3rd Street and the Avenue revealed six arched cells thirty feet long, with heavy iron doors and iron rings embedded in the walls.

Slaves were marched up the Avenue, manacled and chained together in a long line. "Traders occasionally staged grotesque parades," writes historian Jennifer Fleischner, "like the trader in 1822 who gave the first pair of slaves violins to play, the second cockaded hats to wear, and the slave in the center, his upraised hands in chains, an American flag to wave overhead."[5]

Slave auctions were held regularly in the District of Columbia, Georgetown, and Alexandria. James Martin, who was born on a Virginia plantation in 1847, described one such auction to an interviewer with the Works Progress Administration in 1937, when Martin was ninety years old:

> The slaves are put in stalls like the pens they use for cattle—a man and his wife with a child on each arm. And there's a curtain, sometimes just a sheet over the front of the stall, so the bidders can't see the "stock" too soon. The overseer's standin' just outside with a big black snake whip and a pepperbox pistol in his belt. Across the square a little piece, there's a big platform with steps leadin' to it. Then, they pulls up the curtain, and the bidders is crowdin' around. Them in back can't see, so the overseer drives the slaves out to the platform, and he tells the ages of the slaves and what they can do. They have white gloves there, and one of the bidders takes a pair of gloves and rubs his fingers over a man's teeth, and he says to the overseer, "You call this buck twenty years old? Why, there's cut worms in his teeth. He's forty years old, if he's a day." So they knock this buck down for a thousand dollars. They calls the men "bucks" and the women "wenches."
>
> When the slaves is on the platform—what they calls the "block"—the overseer yells, "Tom or Jason, show the bidders how you walk." Then, the slave steps across the platform, and the biddin' starts.
>
> At these slave auctions, the overseer yells, "Say, you bucks and wenches, get in your hole. Come out here." Then, he makes 'em hop, he makes 'em trot, he makes 'em jump. "How much," he yells, "for this buck? A thousand? Eleven hundred? Twelve hundred dollars?" Then the bidders makes offers accordin' to size and build.[6]

Rose and her family owned slaves throughout most of her life, and a personal servant traveled with her on many of her most challenging adventures. She rarely referred to them in her writings, but they appear in numerous property records, on ship passenger lists, and in at least one legal document in which her husband permitted one of his slaves to buy his freedom with cash and five years of labor. Rose never hesitated to defend the ownership of one race by another.

In the early 1800s, slavery was an accepted part of American life, an integral element of the young nation's economy and so deeply woven into the fabric of society that many people never gave it a second thought. Northern whites frequently owned one or more black servants, but the plantation economy of the South rested firmly on the institution of human bondage. For both moral and economic reasons, however, slavery was declining in the North, where laws were passed to phase out the practice over a generation or two. New York finally outlawed slavery in 1827. A handful of slaves remained private property in New Jersey at the outbreak of the Civil War, but by that time they were referred to as "apprentices." The census of 1830 counted almost 13 million Americans, of whom about 2 million were slaves. By 1840, the total population was about 17 million, including 2.5 million slaves.[7] Even in the South, where slaves outnumbered whites in some states, most free people didn't own slaves, but they were willing to fight a war to preserve the rights of those who did.

As the country expanded westward, furious debates erupted over which new states would permit slavery. Yet the issue of abolition often gave way to economic imperatives. The regions of the country depended on each other; the textile mills in the North needed cotton from the South, where the economy was based on slave labor. As historian William Lee Miller wrote, slave owners were among the wealthiest men in the country and among the most powerful. Five of the first seven presidents owned slaves; the office of Speaker of the House was held by a slaveholder for twenty-eight of the nation's first thirty-five years. The president pro tempore of the Senate was nearly always a slaveholder, as were cabinet members and justices on the Supreme Court. Rose's family friend Chief Justice Roger Brooke Taney, appointed in 1835 by the slaveholding president Andrew Jackson to succeed the slaveholding John Marshall, served nearly to the end of the Civil War and owned slaves almost all his life.[8] His Court's 1857 ruling in the Dred Scott case that blacks, free or slave, could never gain U.S. citizenship would hasten dissolution of the Union.

In the antebellum South, slavery was deeply embedded in tradition and culture and as central to the largely agricultural economy as sun and rain. Eli Whitney's invention of the cotton gin in 1793 and the purchase of the Louisiana Territory in 1803 had increased the demand for cheap labor to grow and harvest cash crops such as cotton and tobacco. Defenders of slavery insisted they had no feasible alternatives.[9]

Brother Joseph Mobberly, one of the Jesuits who helped administer the Maryland plantations of the Society of Jesus, dismissed religious arguments against slavery in a lengthy treatise written about 1818 that accused the Presbyterians, Baptists, Quakers, and Methodists of reinterpreting the Scriptures as they chose. He cited numerous passages in the Bible to show Abraham and others owned slaves and were not admonished for it by God. "Would not God have forbidden slavery, had it been unlawful?" Mobberly reasoned.[10]

Well-to-do Southern white women like Rose used black servants to free them from domestic work and prided themselves on mothering not just their own children, but their many black "children," a euphemism for slaves of all ages.[11] With reports of occasional slave rebellions, many white women lost trust in their slaves and complained of them as uppity, insolent, and lazy. Wives trained themselves to look the other way or feign indifference when a slave's child was born light of color and with features favoring those of the plantation's owner. People commonly said it was black women, not white men, who had loose morals.[12]

Foreign visitors were most open in their disapproval of slavery. "It is impossible for any mind of common honesty not to be revolted by the contradictions in [America's] principle and practice," wrote English traveler Frances Trollope when she visited Washington in 1827. "You will see them with one hand hoisting the cap of liberty, and with the other flogging their slaves. You will see them one hour lecturing their mob on the indefeasible rights of man, and the next driving from their homes the children of the soil, whom they have bound themselves to protect by the most solemn treaties."[13]

Martha Elizabeth Wright Morris, a Cincinnati native who spent several winters in Washington visiting her grandfather in the 1850s when she was a teenager, wrote: "The devotion of house servants was a new phase of life to me. The inactivity of some of the fancy girls I could not understand, to allow a black woman to dress & undress them did not strike my fancy, and when I rebelled against their insistence, one said to me, 'Why Miss Martha, quality folks never takes off their own shoes and stockings. Never.'"[14]

When Rose and Ellen O'Neale arrived in Washington at the end of the 1820s, blacks were barred from the Capitol, except when handling menial tasks, like cleaning.[15] *The Washingtonian* newspaper advocated hanging Northerners who invaded the South to stir up slaves. Not to be deterred, Northerners petitioned Congress to outlaw slavery in the District.[16] "Tell your representatives that Slavery and all traffic in human flesh at the Seat of Government must be TOTALLY, IMMEDIATELY AND FOREVER ABOLISHED," one petition read.[17]

In large ways and small, the capital became a hornet's nest of conflicting values and allegiances as debate centered on whether or not slavery should exist in a nation based on equality and democratic rule. Because the District was under the direct control of Congress, there were no issues of state sovereignty, but the even split in the Senate between slave and free states made outlawing slavery difficult. Nonetheless, the growing power of Northern abolitionists and support for helping slaves escape made Washington a hotbed of antislavery agitation.

The symbolic importance of the Federal City in the struggle was evident to both sides. To pro-slavery politicians, it bespoke the South's pre-eminence in political matters, while abolitionists imagined that slavery's demise in Washington would make it morally untenable throughout the nation.[18] Geographically, too, the District was in the thick of it. Bordered on the north by Maryland and on the south by Virginia, both steadfast slave states, the Federal City was connected to the South by rivers and roads, which made it a convenient depot for slave dealers.[19] But the availability of jobs in the growing city also made it a haven for freed blacks, who by 1830 outnumbered slaves in the city of nineteen thousand people.[20] Free blacks formed a tightly knit and largely self-reliant community, built around their churches and schools.

Music was a vital cohesive force in the black community, both slave and free. The songs, sometimes joyous, sometimes mournful, were not evidence of happiness and contentment, as many white people claimed, but lyrical expressions of the deepest sorrow, haunting melodies born of aching hearts. "They told a tale of woe which was then altogether beyond my feeble comprehension," wrote abolitionist leader Frederick Douglass. "They were tones loud, long, and deep; they breathed the prayer and complaint of souls boiling over with the bitterest anguish. Every tone was a testimony against slavery, and a prayer to God for deliverance from chains."[21] Music provided spiritual release from a world that offered little respite from toil and a safe way of resisting and mocking those who held power over the powerless.[22]

The community of free blacks in the District was a diverse mix of those who had been born free and some who had been freed by their masters or permitted to purchase their own liberty. Slave owners who saw their tobacco fortunes decline sometimes gave up their human property to relieve themselves of the financial responsibilities of feeding and housing their slaves. Some slaves were "willed" free by owners who died. But slaves were valuable commodities, and it was more common for owners to leave their slaves to their heirs. Occasionally, an owner would decide slavery was morally wrong and free his slaves, but that was sure to outrage his fellow slaveholders. Sometimes slaves were permitted to purchase their freedom with money they earned from menial jobs as servants, cooks, carriage drivers, and washerwomen.

Washington's land and water routes connecting Northern and Southern states made it a gateway for runaways. By the early 1840s, an elaborate, highly organized "underground railroad" run by former slaves and abolitionists was operating in and around Washington to help individuals and even entire families flee their owners.[23] Escapees would be met by a guide at secret rendezvous points, which were constantly changed, harbored in sympathetic homes, and transported by carriage at night to Pennsylvania.[24] It was claimed that in a single month in 1843, the Washington operation helped 150 slaves escape, an estimated loss of slaveholders' "property" of $75,000.[25] The escape route continued to function through the Civil War, even though one of its first organizers, white abolitionist Charles T. Torrey, would die in a Maryland prison for his efforts.[26]

Periods of toleration followed others of harsh repression. Washington's first black code, adopted in 1808, was moderate by Southern standards. Slaves would be jailed for disturbing the peace, and there was a $5 fine for any black person found on the streets after 10:00 P.M. "They put me in the cellar and put me in double irons, hand and feet," wrote Michael Shiner, a freed slave who got drunk one Christmas Eve, set off "fier crackers," and got into a slugging match with the local justice of the peace: "He hauled of and struck me and I hauled of and struck him. But if I had of known at that time he were a justice of the peace I never would of offer to raise my hand to him."[27]

On January 1, 1831, a Boston journalist named William Lloyd Garrison launched The Liberator, a weekly newspaper dedicated to the immediate emancipation of all slaves. Unable to raise the money to publish his paper in Washington, Garrison put out The Liberator in Boston, promising it would make slaveholders tremble, that he would stir a spirit of patriotism, making "every statue leap from its pedestal," and issue a trumpet call that would "hasten the resurrection of the dead." The front page of the first issue carried an article about the campaign to abolish slavery in the District of Columbia. "I do not wish to think, or speak, or write, with moderation," Garrison wrote. "I am in earnest—I will not equivocate—I will not excuse—I will not retreat a single inch—AND I WILL BE HEARD."

EIGHT MONTHS AFTER *The Liberator* appeared on the streets in the North, a band of eight slaves, led by a slave preacher named Nat Turner, entered the home of the Travis family in Southampton County, Virginia, sixty-five miles south of Richmond, and killed all five family members in the house. In the next thirty-six hours, the rebel band swelled to forty angry slaves who went house to house, stabbing, clubbing, or shooting fifty-five whites before the local militia, including some blacks, caught up with the insurrectionists, captured some, and scattered the rest. Turner himself was found several weeks later, and after his "confession" was taken, he was hanged and his body skinned. The rebellion terrified whites, who rounded up and killed slaves suspected of conspiring with Turner as far away as North Carolina.

For weeks after the Turner rebellion, Virginia legislators were divided over whether or not to gradually abolish slavery, but greed prevailed. Slavery was too profitable to give up, and instead, stricter laws were adopted to punish blacks—slave or free—who caused trouble for the white community. In Richmond, whites organized patrols and had orders "to shoot with mustard seed any Negroes" on the street after the 10:00 P.M. curfew.[29]

Washington was not immune to growing resistance and fear. Four years after the Turner rebellion, a race riot broke out in the city when a slave allegedly tried to murder Mrs. William Thornton, widow of the architect of the Capitol, while she slept. Dr. Reuban Crandall, a young physician from the North, was arrested for possession of some botanical samples that were wrapped in abolitionist newspapers. He was falsely accused of inciting slaves. In the ensuing riot, a white mob destroyed a black school and some tenements and broke the windows of a black church in two days and three nights of unrest. When a free black named Beverly Snow, the proprietor of a popular tavern at 6th Street and Pennsylvania Avenue, insulted men in the mob by making disparaging comments about their wives and daughters, the mob destroyed his business.[30] As a result, the city council strengthened the black code and denied free blacks licenses to run restaurants and taverns.[31]

SLAVERY WAS EXPENSIVE to maintain. Families had to be fed, clothed, and housed. When the economy faltered, some slaveholders in the upper

South and around Washington chose to sell their slaves to prosperous farmers in the Deep South, where crops and climate were more conducive to slave labor. On September 27, 1836, the *National Intelligencer*, Washington's first daily newspaper, ran a front-page ad purchased by one of the largest slave dealers in Virginia:

CASH FOR 500 NEGROES

Including both sexes from 12 to 25 years of age. Persons having likely servants to dispose of, will find it to their interest to give us a call, as we will give higher prices, in cash, than any other purchaser who is now, or may hereafter, come into the market.

Franklin & Armfield, Alexandria[32]

The District of Columbia Circuit Court kept records of blacks arrested and fined or jailed, an overwhelming number for such minor offenses as stealing a pair of shoes, a coat, or "one silver spoon." Robert Ellis, an archivist in the National Archives and Records Administration in Washington, compiled a list of more than one thousand names of blacks brought before the court between 1828 and 1850, including several hundred who petitioned for their freedom. The following is a sample of the court records.

DECEMBER TERM 1828
CRIMINAL APPEARANCES

129 *U.S. v. Ann Talbutt*	stole three pairs of shoes worth $4.00
148 *U.S. v. Nancy Ashton*	stole one cloak worth $1.00
156 *U.S. v. Caroline Calvert*	cut Nancy Ashton with an axe
161 *U.S. v. William Chubb*	stole eight dozen herrings worth 80 cents
172 *U.S. v. Jim Davis*	stole $50 in banknotes and $3 in silver money
175 *U.S. v. John Barnes*	stole one cheese worth $1.00
177 *U.S. v. Thomas Johnson*	stole one blanket worth $1.25
187 *U.S. v. Rezin Barker*	stole one overcoat worth $15; 1 pr gloves worth 50 cents.[33]

MARCH TERM 1837
CRIMINAL APPEARANCES

36 *U.S. v. Negro James Kennedy*	assault on Maria Williams (negress); $5 fine
62 *U.S. v. Negro Martha alias Judy Nokes*	larceny (goods worth $6.47); $1 fine, 1 day jail
677 *U.S. v. Negro William Williams*	larceny (goods worth $66.50); 3 years penitentiary[34]

THE DAUGHTER OF a slaveholding family, Rose grew up with slavery all around her. It was part of her heritage and her everyday life in Washington, and she defended the practice to the end of her days. When she developed an interest in politics and learned to articulate her views, she built her beliefs on those of her hero, former vice president and longtime South Carolina senator John C. Calhoun. He was her friend and mentor and, in some ways, a surrogate for the father she had barely known.

CHAPTER 9

John C. Calhoun

CALHOUN WAS A stubborn Southern statesman. A tall, spare man with long hair pulled back from his forehead and flowing past his ears, he intimidated with his stern demeanor and mesmerized with his speech. Though he rarely smiled and usually dressed in black,[1] Calhoun's silvery voice charmed the ear, and his bearing radiated civility and decorum. Rose Greenhow called him "the best and wisest man of this century."[2]

Born to a slaveholding farmer, Calhoun read for the law and first went to Washington as a member of the House of Representatives in 1811. He was among the South's young war hawks urging war with England, which came in 1812. Through his marriage to a second cousin, Floride Bonneau Calhoun, he attained both wealth and social prominence. His plantation, Fort Hill, was one of the largest in South Carolina. President James Madison named Calhoun secretary of war in 1817, when he was just thirty-five. Calhoun sought the presidency himself in 1824, then withdrew to run for vice president without serious opposition, leaving John Quincy Adams to battle Andrew Jackson for the top spot. Adams lost both the popular and electoral votes to Jackson, but no candidate took a majority of the electoral college; this threw the contest into the House, which put Adams in the White House. Calhoun was reelected vice president in 1828 under Jackson but grew increasingly extremist in his view that states ought to be able to nullify federal laws they didn't like. He broke with Jackson when the president threatened to use force to block South Carolina's attempt to nullify the tariff of 1832. Calhoun was elected to the Senate in December 1832 to fill a vacancy and resigned the vice presidency to represent his home state in Washington.

During their early years in the capital, the Calhouns entertained with great style at their summer home, Oakly, later known as Dumbarton Oaks, one of the great mansions of Georgetown.[3] "In his dress he affected a Spartan simplicity, yet he used to have four horses harnessed to his carriage, and his entertainments at his residence on Georgetown Heights were very elegant," wrote the *Boston Journal*'s Ben: Perley Poore.[4]

Floride, however, found Washington a difficult place to raise her nine children and preferred living at Fort Hill in South Carolina. That left Calhoun alone during much of the time Congress was in session. The Southern senator tired of the social scene and preferred returning in the evening to his Capitol Hill boardinghouse, but like any number of politicians whose wives remained back home, he had a roving eye.

Isaac Bassett, who rose from page to assistant doorkeeper in the Senate,[5] described one incident he observed while delivering mail to Calhoun's boardinghouse: "After the adjournment of the Senate one evening, Mr. Calhoun told me always to bring his mail in his room and lay his mail down on his table. It was just getting dark. I heard a great rustling of clothes, looked around, and saw a very fine looking lady on the sofa with Mr. Calhoun. She seemed to be very excited and said, 'Let me go! He will expose me!' Calhoun replied, 'Oh, no, it is only the messenger with my mail. I don't mind him.' " Bassett said he left the room as quickly as possible and learned the next day that Calhoun was bedding the wife of a navy officer who boarded in the same house.

Bassett described Calhoun as courteous to his colleagues but sharp with aides. Once, after summoning Bassett from the other side of the Senate floor, Calhoun scolded him when the page did not move fast enough. "Sir, why don't you come to me when I call you?" Bassett quoted Calhoun saying. "I have you know that there are no two sides to this Chamber." Bassett learned also that he should never disturb Calhoun while he was working. "John C. Calhoun was very distant," Bassett wrote. "I kept out of his way as much as possible. . . . He was very short in his speech. Said as few words as possible, quick and to the point."

When Calhoun was excited, Bassett wrote, "he would get up from his seat and walk much of the time in the lobby in the rear of the presiding officer's chair. When he spoke, he maintained a stern attitude and stood in the aisle at the side of his desk. His gesture was short and nervous, chiefly with the right hand, his articulation was rapid, his keen eyes was fastened upon the senator to whom he was replying."[6]

From her earliest years in Washington, Rose was captivated by Calhoun. She probably met the senator through his daughter Anna Maria, who was about Rose's age and, like Rose and many young ladies of the period, visited the Senate gallery to listen to the debates, admire the oratory of their heroes—and socialize. But Calhoun became much more than the father of a friend. He and Rose corresponded. Rose sought his counsel and later helped her husband get a job with him; she supported his candidacy for president and nursed him on his deathbed. Calhoun articulated what Rose and many Southerners felt in their hearts: that liberty and equality, the core beliefs on which the nation was founded, applied only to white people. Calhoun argued unapologetically that slavery was morally sound and essential to the economy of the South, a fair deal for both races. He bitterly opposed anyone from outside the South trying to tell his region what to do about it. Calhoun, Rose said, was the person most responsible for shaping her political philosophy.[7]

Floride Calhoun had mixed feelings about slavery. When she was six years old, some of the slaves on her family's South Carolina plantation, Twelve Mile River, tried to poison her father and run away. Court records show that Will, the young slave who put the poison in his master's food, was sentenced to be hanged. Two other slaves, Sue and Sukey, were to have their ears cropped in public, be branded on their foreheads, and receive one hundred lashes. The other conspirator, "Old Hazard," was to be branded, have both ears cropped, and be dealt twenty-five lashes.[8]

As an adult, Floride Calhoun was afraid of her slaves. On some occasions, she bragged about the skill of her cook, but she preferred white servants and had a white nurse care for her children. When a slave called Young Sawney was captured after running away and wanted to return, Floride refused to have him back. "I think he ought to be sold, or he will do more mischief," she wrote to a son. "He is a bad boy . . . he might set fire to the gin house."[9]

Northerners claimed that slavery was at the heart of the national debate over tariffs and states' rights. Certainly there were Northerners who supported states' rights; but over time, it became known as a Southern doctrine.[10] The three giants of the Senate—Daniel Webster, Henry Clay, and John C. Calhoun—defined the debate for years and battled one another to shape the outcome. Calhoun insisted that tariffs were responsible for the decline of the South's economy, which was based largely on cotton and rice produced with slave labor. As vice president, he vehemently opposed a tariff bill President John Quincy Adams signed in May 1828 to raise duties on imported goods, a measure the South contended was aimed at protecting Northern manufacturers at the expense of Southern planters, who traded their crops for European imports made more expensive by the tariffs.[11] The power of the federal government to impose tariffs that all states had to collect was at the heart of the struggle over whether the young Republic was a single nation or a federation of sovereign states. Calhoun was presiding over the Senate in January 1830 when his friend and colleague from South Carolina, Senator Robert Y. Hayne, faced off with Daniel Webster of Massachusetts over that question and brought the issue of slavery into the open. Hayne, a public spokesman for Calhoun's covert authorship of the nullification principle, maintained the right of states to refuse to enforce specific federal laws within their territory. And he defended slavery as the obligation of white Southerners who inherited a helpless and inferior race owing largely to Northern traders.

"We found that we had to deal with a people whose physical, moral, and intellectual habits and character totally disqualified them from the enjoyment of the blessings of freedom," he told the Senate and a rapt audience in the gallery. "We could not send them back to the shores from whence their fathers had been taken; their numbers forbade the thought, even if we did not know that their condition here is infinitely preferable to what it possibly could be among the barren sands and savage tribes of Africa; and it was wholly irreconcilable with all our notions of humanity to tear asunder the tender ties which they had formed among us, to gratify the feelings of a false philanthropy." He accused Northerners of seducing slaves away from their masters and dumping them in Northern cities as "outcasts of the world."

"There does not exist on the face of the whole earth, a population so poor, so wretched, so vile, so loathsome, so utterly destitute of all the comforts, conveniences, and decencies of life as the unfortunate blacks of Philadelphia and New York and Boston," Hayne claimed. "Liberty has been to them the greatest of calamities, the heaviest of curses."[12]

On the coldest day of winter, with the wind whipping enormous clouds of dust from the streets, hundreds of spectators made their way to the Capitol to hear Webster's response. Records don't show whether Rose was among the three hundred brightly attired ladies in voluminous crinolines who jammed the Senate gallery when Webster rose to defend the supremacy of the Union. People poured into the Capitol beginning three hours before the Senate convened at noon, and by the time the senators entered the chamber, the galleries, floor, and even lobbies and stairways were overflowing. Ladies were permitted on the Senate floor, and some members gave up their seats for women in gay bonnets and brilliant dresses.[13]

Webster was not a large man, but with his swarthy complexion and shaggy eyebrows, he was majestic in appearance and commanded attention. For the occasion, he was dressed in his Whig uniform, copied from those of his Revolutionary heroes: a blue dress coat with bright cottons, a buff waistcoat, and a high white cravat.[14]

As Webster rose to speak, his deep, resonant voice echoed through the chamber, hypnotizing his audience. Starting slowly, he dismissed his Southern rival's charges, presumed to give him a history lesson about the founding of the country, and denied any interest in ending slavery in the South, insisting that was a state matter.

"The domestic slavery of the Southern States I leave where I find it," Webster said, "in the hands of their own governments. It is their affair, not mine." But winding up, he challenged South Carolina's claim to a right of nullification and defended the Constitution as the supreme law of the land: "It is, Sir, the people's Constitution, the people's government, made for the people, made by the people, and answerable to the people." Then, in a bellowing voice, he declared that no state law could stand in conflict with the Constitution.

Webster glared at Calhoun, who was presiding over the session, and his words filled the chamber; all eyes were riveted on him as he pounded his message home. The senator's arms moved up and down as he spoke, as if, wrote *Boston Journal* correspondent Poore, "he were beating out with sledgehammers his forcible ideas."[15]

His closing words rang through the gallery: "Liberty *and* Union, now and forever, one and inseparable."[16]

Southern ladies kept their hands clasped tightly in their laps, determined not to stand or applaud. One spectator feigned boredom by reading his newspaper upside down.[17] There was an occasional bustle, a rustling of silks and waving of feathers, but for the most part, the chamber was silent, transfixed. "It is a kind of gladiatorship in which characters are torn to pieces and arrows, yes, poisoned arrows, which tho' not seen are deeply felt, are hurled by the combatants against each other," wrote diarist Margaret Bayard Smith. "Every seat, every inch of ground, even the steps, were compactly filled. One lady sat in Col. Hayne's seat."[18]

Although triggered by an obscure bill governing western lands, the

Hayne-Webster debates carved in sharp relief the regional divide between North and South, exposing the growing suspicion and philosophical differences that frustrated Henry Clay and those who would compromise almost anything to save the Union. The "Battle of the Giants" defined the issues that would dog the country for three more decades, ultimately leading to war. Rose was still a teenager, but the debate helped shape her own thinking for a lifetime. She would listen to the counsel of her stalwart hero for years to come.

CHAPTER 10

Romance in the Wind

WHILE GOVERNMENT OFFICIALS debated issues dividing the country, their wives concentrated on concerns closer to the heart: marrying off sisters, daughters, and nieces. Virtually every woman had her eye on a new bachelor in town, Dr. Robert Greenhow, a Virginia gentleman and physician recently arrived from New York, where he had received his medical training. The married women wanted to play matchmaker. Single ones like Rose O'Neale could hear their hearts flutter.

Dr. Greenhow, the son of a Williamsburg and Richmond mercantile family, moved to Washington in 1831. The young physician was sophisticated, worldly, and wealthy, with none of the raw edges of the congressmen at Hill's Boarding House. Greenhow had lived in Europe and was fluent in several foreign languages, including French, Spanish, German, and Italian. He had been hired as translator and librarian at the State Department, which ranked him number three in its sixteen-person bureaucracy. Polished, highly educated, and studious, with a passion for history and science, he also was reserved, prone to illness, and somewhat melancholy. Unlike Rose, he was neither a social climber nor personally ambitious. Socially, Greenhow was a bit of a bore.

His grandfather John Greenhow left England and settled in Williamsburg, Virginia, where he opened a general store. It advertised "Useful & fashionable Goods . . . from London and Liverpool." John Greenhow was a clever merchant whose eight-ton three-masted schooner the *Robert* ferried merchandise between the James River and Philadelphia.

Advertising that his stocks were "for ready money only," Greenhow sold a wide assortment of household goods: "Calicos and Irish linens, Wool Cloaks and Fine Night Caps, Feathers and Livery Laces, Trimmings and Buttons; Mixed Tulips, Anemone, Fine large Hyacinths and Double Narcissus; Confectionaries and Candies, Whistles for Children, Pewter and Tin Wares and Seeds of every variety."[1]

The store, with its rich scents of fresh spices and cured leather, has been re-created in Colonial Williamsburg on Duke of Gloucester Street and still carries the name Jn̊ Greenhow. John's son Robert Greenhow Sr. was a community leader in Williamsburg who moved to Richmond, the booming new capital of Virginia, and opened a store there called the Sign of the Golden Padlock. An upstanding citizen, he was admitted to the Amicable Society, one of three associations whose members essentially ruled the charitable, literary, and social life of the insular city from the late eighteenth century.[2]

Robert's wife, Mary Ann Wills Greenhow, gave birth to a son, named Robert Jr. after his father, on June 16, 1800. The little boy grew up visiting his grandparents and relatives in Williamsburg and being cared for by his parents' household slaves, as were the children of most well-to-do Southern families. They frequently visited a fellow Virginian and family friend, Thomas Jefferson,[3] at Monticello, the former president's hilltop estate overlooking Charlottesville, about seventy miles west of the Greenhows' home in Richmond.

On December 26, 1811, when young Robert was eleven years old, his parents took him to the Richmond Theatre for a special benefit performance to help a baby boy named Edgar Allan Poe, who had been left a penniless orphan just before Christmas by the death of his mother, a favorite actress in the city. The cream of the city's social set filled the theater to see a play and a new pantomime, *The Bleeding Nun,* selected for the occasion. Eighty of the 598 tickets sold were children's seats. The play ended and the pantomime had just begun when the stage manager started to lower a chandelier that had been raised toward the rafters after the first act. The lines became tangled, the huge light started to swing, and the flame from the lamp ignited the elaborate painted scenery panels aloft. Flames shot into the air over the heads of the patrons and quickly reached the theater's pine rafters. People raced for the only exit door as flames engulfed the building. Most of those in the orchestra escaped, but people in the boxes and balcony were trapped.[4]

Robert Greenhow Sr. wrote afterward to a friend, John T. Mason, that his wife was sitting on the front seat of the third box from the stage, reclining in his arms, when the flames broke out. The last words he heard from her were "Save my child!" Greenhow grabbed young Robert, but the crowd lunged forward, and they were thrown to the floor. Greenhow was sure they were about to suffocate. "A blast of flame & smoke was inhaled by us both," he wrote.

Terrified, young Robert wrestled himself from his father's grasp. "Oh, Father! I am dying!" the boy cried.

"My Son, I will die with you," the father told him, then seized his child by the skirt of his coat.

Standing at the top of the staircase with the boy in his arms, Greenhow jumped over dead bodies and pieces of flaming wood as he made his way to the ground floor and rushed through the theater doors to put his child out of danger. Greenhow tried to return to search for his wife, but the fire was too hot for him to go back inside.

"My wife! My wife! & friend of my heart; of my best and warmest affections," Greenhow lamented to his friend. "My wife for near 26½ years! With whom I had enjoyed as much of connubial bliss as ever fell to the Lot I dare venture to pronounce for any one pair."[5]

Mrs. Greenhow was one of at least sixty-eight victims of the fire. Others included the new governor of the state, the president of the Bank of Virginia, the publisher of one of the city's newspapers, and the wife of the theater's owner. Dozens more were severely burned. The toll would have been even higher but for the heroism of a young slave, Gilbert Hunt, who raced to the scene, leaned a ladder against a wall, and caught about a dozen ladies as a doctor in the theater dropped them from an open window above. Hunt pulled the doctor to safety just as the burning wall collapsed.[6] The city was plunged into mourning; all public events were canceled for months.

Robert Greenhow Jr., a child of privilege and a happy family, lost his mother. He became a scholarly, bookish child, reserved and frequently sick. His father, who had barely survived with him, became mayor of the city less than two years later. Edgar Allan Poe, the orphaned beneficiary of the charity event, was destined to become one of the nation's best-known writers—and a master of the macabre.

A few years after the theater fire, young Greenhow, as an adolescent of the Richmond social set, took dance lessons from a French dancing master named Charles Fremon who taught most of the belles and beaux of the city in those days. Charles's illegitimate son, John C. Frémont, grew up to be a famous explorer and candidate for president of the United States. He and his wife, Jessie Benton Frémont, were lifelong rivals of the Greenhows and brought out the worst in Rose.[7]

At the age of sixteen, Robert Greenhow graduated from the College of William and Mary and went to New York City to study at the College of Physicians and Surgeons, one of the country's first medical schools, now part of Columbia University. He received an MD degree in 1821.[8]

But Greenhow, like his family's friend Thomas Jefferson, had broader horizons than the practice of one profession, such as medicine, which did not hold his interest long. He delved into science, literature, and law, traveled, studied the arts, and read history. A gentleman and a scholar, Greenhow sailed for Europe, where he spent seven years pursuing his interests in medicine, science, and political history. He studied at Edinburgh University as well as in hospitals in London and Paris, and he took a law degree from the Sorbonne.[9]

In the early 1820s, Greenhow moved back to New York and opened a medical practice on Canal Street. Dr. Thomas Cooper, a controversial scholar, physician, and lawyer who was president of South Carolina College, was a good friend. So was J. W. Jarvis, the American portrait painter, whom Greenhow introduced to friends in Richmond when the painter visited the city.[10]

Jefferson sought Greenhow's help in obtaining anatomical castings from Italy for Jefferson's School of Anatomy and Medicine at the fledgling University of Virginia at Charlottesville, which opened in March 1825 with 123 students. In a series of seven letters from March 8 to July 24, 1825, many with phrases and sentences crossed out and in handwriting that was increasingly difficult to decipher owing to his advancing years, Jefferson agreed to Greenhow's suggestion that he purchase from France several castings to be used as teaching aids: two human skeletons, one male, one female, for $42 each, and the "injected preparation of the veins school and arteries of the whole system of a boy 12-years old," which would cost $100.

Greenhow told the former president that he could obtain any number of anatomical preparations, including "the female genital organs and parts adjacent . . . the penis . . . and the testes with artery veins. . . ." He asked Jefferson to convey his "best respects" to the Jefferson family and especially the elderly statesman's grandson Thomas Jefferson Randolph, who was eight years older than Greenhow.[11]

In time, Greenhow found the practice of medicine "irksome" and leaned more toward scientific and historical research.[12] In 1830, as nationalist revolts broke out in Europe, he founded and edited a newspaper in New York he called *The Tricolor* to support the return of liberal government to France. When the Bourbon monarch Charles X was overthrown a few months later and Louis-Philippe d'Orléans ascended the throne as a constitutional monarch, the paper suspended publication.

In 1831, Edward Livingston, a Louisiana lawmaker whom Andrew Jackson had just named secretary of state, tapped Greenhow to come to Washington to join his department.[13] That September, Greenhow accepted a post that kept him in government throughout most of his life. Many of his fifteen full-time colleagues at the State Department were Marylanders and Virginians from socially prominent families with good political connections.[14] His title was librarian and translator, and his annual salary of $1,000[15] made him one of the three highest-paid officials in the department.[16] He was so dedicated to his new boss that he later gave his daughter Gertrude the middle name Livingston.

The country was in the midst of expansion across the continent, and the national debate focused more on domestic concerns than on foreign affairs. There was a tendency to discount the importance of diplomacy. Secretary of State Livingston[17] acknowledged that view, conceding that Americans thought of their diplomats as privileged characters "selected to enjoy the pleasures of foreign travel at the expense of the people; their places as sinecures; and their residence abroad as a continued scene of luxurious enjoyment."[18]

In 1832, Greenhow asked Livingston to appoint him secretary of a commission to liquidate claims against the French government, but the appointment did not appear to go through, and Greenhow remained in Washington.[19] With his cultured background and impeccable family connections, he was much in demand on the city's social circuit.

But Robert Greenhow was not just another Southern gentleman living in Washington to pursue politics and spend his leisure hunting or playing poker or drinking whiskey at Gadsby's Tavern until he was too drunk to stand. Instead, he relaxed by losing himself in books about architecture and anatomy and corresponding with friends—distinguished painters, sculptors, and scientists. Over dinner, he was more likely to tell a story about the poet Lord Byron, whom he met in Italy, than rehash the yeas and nays of the last Senate vote.

At heart, Greenhow was a historian, happiest alone and uninterrupted in his study, deciphering faded, handwritten accounts of territories and bodies of water in uncharted areas of the world. He pored over maps and traced competing claims to virgin lands, establishing himself as an expert in a field that grew vitally important as new territories were added to the Republic. The urbane Virginian took enormous pride in his precise translation of documents from their original language into English. His first work, "The History and Present Condition of Tripoli," appeared in 1835 in the *Southern Literary Messenger,* a magazine founded the previous year in Richmond and meant to appeal to Southern readers. Greenhow was greeted as a solid researcher and a clear, objective writer.

At thirty-five, the well-educated bachelor from a good family was a most eligible catch. Rose O'Neale, in her early twenties with two older sisters married into the cream of Washington society, was well positioned to find an attractive match. Robert Greenhow was younger and certainly more refined than her regular escort, Congressman Cave Johnson of Tennessee. While reserved, Greenhow had considerable cachet and could be presumed to offer Rose comfort and a secure place in Southern society. Though never the life of the party, he was a successful man, respected by the community. Rose was from a good Maryland family, even if it went broke after her father died. She was charming and beautiful, and she needed a husband.

The impetuous young lady could do more than simply follow in her husband's footsteps; she could promote his career and rise with him in Washington. Rose was bright, well-read, and a language student herself. Robert explained his work to her, and she helped him with politics, both partisan and in the office.

Like many of Virginia's established families that came from England, Greenhow had been raised an Episcopalian. Rose was Roman Catholic. When her family settled in the New World in the 1700s, Maryland was a haven for Catholics barred from many of the other colonies. But both believed in God. The rest was not that far apart.

On May 26, 1835, Rose O'Neale and Robert Greenhow were married at St. Patrick's Catholic Church in Washington at 10th and G streets, a few blocks from the Avenue. Roger Brooke Taney, an O'Neale family friend who would become chief justice of the United States the following year, was among the parishioners, as was Henry Clay, the distinguished senator from Kentucky. The Reverend William Matthews, the first American to be ordained a Catholic priest in the United States, officiated at the wedding.[20]

Rose was radiant. She had found an engaging partner, a man who inspired confidence and did not seem to mind living in the shadow of a gregarious, headstrong wife. He would also assure his new bride's entrée to the elite circle of Washington society, and her financial problems were now a thing of the past. The future of these two children of tragedy looked bright and promising. Or so it seemed.

Part Three

SADNESS AND
SETBACKS

Journey to Mexico

NINE MONTHS AFTER their marriage, on February 29, 1836, Rose gave birth to her first child, a daughter, whom the couple named Mary Florence and called by her middle name.[1] That spring, they bought a three-story house on North K Street between West 12th and West 13th streets, right across from the home of former president John Quincy Adams. The house, which cost $2,500,[2] was built on a long, narrow lot that backed up to an alley where slaves who served families on the block were quartered. The new family settled in comfortably.

While Rose supervised the household, Robert spent long hours at the State Department, located just east of the White House on a site occupied today by the Treasury Department. It was a pleasant ten-minute walk to the office, down K Street and through Lafayette Square, a lovely park with tall white magnolias that blossomed in early spring. Dolley Madison would soon return to her home here as a widow.

The State Department took up eleven rooms on the second floor and six in the attic. The exterior of the building was painted a leaden gray with white trim, and the library where Greenhow worked extended the length of the portico with five large windows overlooking the Avenue.[3] He could stand by his desk and watch Rose pass by with Florence in a carriage when they called on Mrs. Madison.

Andrew Jackson's vice president and handpicked successor, Martin Van Buren of New York, was sworn in as president in March 1837. Only the year before, Texas had declared independence from Mexico, and the American-born founders of the new Republic hoped to bring Texas into the Union. Van Buren favored the territorial expansion that annexation of Texas would provide, but Texas tolerated slavery, and he worried that adding another slaveholding territory would further strain the country's growing regional divide.

Van Buren had pledged to continue Jackson's policies, but the fiscal policies of Old Hickory had sent the economy into a tailspin, and the country was teetering on the edge of depression. People were in a panic. The new president, a non-slaveholding Northerner determined to hold the Union together, did not want to make matters worse by angering either abolitionists in the North or pro-slavery forces in the South.

Van Buren understood that in order to strengthen U.S. designs on Texas, a number of long-standing claims by American citizens against Mexico needed to be resolved.[4] Scores of cases were pending, many dealing with American ships that had been seized by the Mexican government and their cargoes sold to replenish the national treasury of Mexico.

In May 1837, Van Buren asked Robert Greenhow to travel to Mexico as an executive agent, exempt from congressional oversight and reporting directly to the president. It was a sensitive intelligence-gathering mission.

Relations between the two countries were growing increasingly tense, and the president needed a careful assessment of how Mexico would react if the U.S. claims were pressed. In his letter outlining the assignment, Secretary of State John Forsyth gave Greenhow a $700 advance for what was expected to be a three-month trip.[5]

Greenhow was a studious man, an intellectual, but he was not particularly ambitious. Rose was better at promoting his career than he was, never missing an opportunity to attend dinner parties at Forsyth's home, where she could engage the secretary in discussions about the latest foreign crisis and suggest—tactfully, of course—how Robert's skills might be used to the best advantage. Rose was already a pro at the art of social climbing, which in Washington is an acquired art form for anyone not wanting to be swallowed up by the bureaucracy.[6]

Greenhow knew the trip offered an opportunity to impress the new president with his diplomatic skills on an issue of considerable importance. For a Southern gentleman brought up in comfortable circumstances, however, the logistics of travel through the Deep South and across the Gulf of Mexico were daunting. Unpredictable weather made sea travel treacherous, and Greenhow suffered terribly from seasickness. The narrow, rutted dirt roads were often impassable, the lodging miserable, and it was frequently necessary to travel by overnight stagecoach, which made sleep impossible. Rose and Robert had been married for only two years, and this was probably the first time they would be separated for more than a few days. There were dangers as well: unfriendly Indians, pirates, Mexican bandits, and, most uncontrollably, disease.

Greenhow accepted the assignment and kept an eighty-page, largely impersonal diary in which he recorded every expense and his impressions of the people, buildings, and food he encountered along the way. In his clear, precise handwriting, the presidential agent detailed the cost of every hotel, meal, stage ride, tip, and tavern bill; for example:

MAY 28

Steamboat from Washington to Potomac Creek	$2.
Breakfast on steamboat	.50
Passage to Richmond	4.
Porter at Potomac Creek	.18¾
Porter in Richmond	.25

MAY 29

Stage to Petersburg	2.00

MAY 30

Tavern bill at Petersburg	1.50[7]

The diary, previously unpublished, showed that Greenhow enjoyed the challenge of his diplomatic mission, as well as the unusual opportunity to travel through parts of the United States he had never seen. In every city, he wrote a careful critique of the architecture of the buildings, the width of the streets, and the lushness of the vegetation. "The state house at Raleigh is upon the whole the best piece of architecture in plan, in material and in execution which I know in the U.S.," Greenhow wrote in North Carolina. "The porticos have not sufficient width for their height. They should each have six columns at left instead of four. Better yet have had eight and then they would have formed part of the center building instead as they do of the wings."

The news reaching Washington about Americans traveling in Mexico was chilling. On Monday, May 29, the day after Greenhow left Washington, the *National Intelligencer* reported, "We have received confirmation of the capture of the *Independence* after sustaining an action of 2 hours with two Mexican brigs. We learn, also, that the merchant schr. *Julius Caesar,* an American vessel, was captured and that all passengers and crew of the two schooners were condemned to death as pirates by the Mexican authorities."[8]

Rose, an avid newspaper reader and friend of the editor of the *Intelligencer,* must have been terrified.

Mexico seemed to be clamoring for war with the United States to head off a feared invasion and seizure of Mexican lands. Diplomacy wasn't working, and the two countries' navies fired at each other's ships at will.[9]

Greenhow was shocked by the poverty he saw in the Deep South but captivated by the scenery. On June 2, passing the courthouse in Camden, South Carolina, he noted a monument to the German-born Baron Johann de Kalb, a spy for the French who joined the American war for independence and who was mortally wounded in a disastrous defeat at the Battle of Camden. He was so beloved that the Marquis de Lafayette traveled to Camden to lay the cornerstone of the monument, one of the country's first war memorials.

"DeKalb's monument in front of the court house is a short obelisk upon a die, standing on steps of fine red granite with black specks," Greenhow wrote. It was the sort of historical detail that fascinated him. Greenhow could not imagine that the technological advances of his generation would make even a minor battle in the next war ten times as bloody as the Americans' defeat at Camden.

ON JUNE 16, Greenhow celebrated his thirty-seventh birthday in Pensacola, Florida, eating figs and writing "to my dear Rose."[10] It would be three long weeks, desperately seasick on the high seas, before he arrived in Mexico, exhausted and suffering from dysentery.

Greenhow presented his credentials to the Mexican foreign minister on July 20 and gave an oral recitation of the U.S. position on American territorial claims against Mexico. Greenhow spoke to the Mexican minister in French rather than Spanish "in order to be more certain of what I conveyed." Greenhow explained that the United States had acknowledged the independence of Texas. Before the meeting ended, Greenhow was taken to meet Mexico's president, Anastasio Bustamante. "The president," wrote Greenhow to Secretary of State Forsyth, "is a stout, dark-featured man without any Indian blood, I think, about 55 years old, with much amenity as well as dignity in his address."[11]

Greenhow's mission accomplished little in tangible terms, but he took the measure of the Mexican government and returned home invigorated by his travels, which took him from Washington to Mexico City and back in just over three months. Whether or not Robert was a spy is not apparent from available records, although it is clear he was dispatched on the president's personal authority with the intention of keeping his work from public view.

For Rose, who took enormous interest in her husband's work, studied the maps and plans he showed her, and helped him navigate the back channels of the federal bureaucracy to get ahead, it was an introduction to secret statecraft at the highest levels, a primer for all that lay ahead.

CHAPTER 12

Life on K Street

ON HIS RETURN from Mexico at the end of the summer of 1837, Robert Greenhow stopped in Richmond to pick up his half-sister, Mary, to bring her to Washington for an extended visit. They made the journey by steamship and stagecoach, because even though the two cities were but one hundred miles apart, there was no good highway linking them. Rural roads were little more than deep ruts that wrecked wooden carriages or sucked their wheels into the mud during fierce summer thunderstorms. "I arrived in Washington on Saturday and 'oh, for a quill plucked from a Seraph's wing' to write a description of my journey," Mary Greenhow wrote on Monday night, September 4. "The accidents were innumerable; the most unpleasant were the loss of our bandboxes containing sundry bonnets and dresses."[1]

Mary's diary provides a chatty and often intimate account of Rose's skill at building a network of powerful contacts, as well as a glimpse into the family's day-to-day routine. It portrays Rose as witty, willful, and eager to jump through the hoops necessary to boost her husband's career and rise to the top of Washington society.

A week after Mary's arrival, she turned eighteen.[2] Vain, witty, and supremely self-centered, the Richmond belle had much in common with her sister-in-law, who was four or five years older but considerably more sophisticated.

Rose had already developed a knack for sizing up who was important and who wasn't; and she understood that a man's title did not always make that distinction. Rose was learning to entertain not only those in power, but their deputies, assistants, and the *secretaries* of the secretaries, for they were often more accessible and willing to trade the tidbits of gossip that were a social climber's coin. Robert may have had several impressive degrees and traveled the world, but Rose would teach her husband that in Washington, *whom* he knew was more important than *what* he knew.

Though married only two years, the Greenhows were already mixing with the cream of the crowd, and they introduced Mary to their circle of fashionable friends.

Two or three times a week, they attended glittery diplomatic receptions and formal dinners thrown by members of the cabinet and other luminaries in the Washington galaxy.[3] They were invited to the Executive Mansion by President Van Buren, had tea with Dolley Madison, threw a party to honor Chief Justice Roger Brooke Taney, and watched with amazement as Sioux and Black Hawk Indians wearing war paint and feathers performed a war dance in Lafayette Square. Mary flirted with Martin Van Buren Jr., the president's younger son. Occasionally Robert called on the president after dinner while Rose and Mary stayed home, reading the latest novels aloud to each other by the fire. The women would become close as sisters—and addressed each other as such as long as they lived.

The two often climbed into a horse-drawn carriage for a bumpy ride to Georgetown, where they shopped in lovely boutiques for the latest Paris fashions or visited Rose's sister Susannah, who had married into the respected Peter family. Sometimes Rose and Mary strolled arm in arm down the Avenue and stopped to get ice cream at one of the small sweetshops. When the family needed fresh meat, fruits, and vegetables, the women had one of the slaves[4] accompany them to the sprawling Center Market a few blocks from Capitol Hill.

Mary Greenhow recorded the details of a world that revolved around fashion, French lessons, parties, and a full schedule of formal social calls to family and friends. Her diary shows that Rose was learning to entertain with flair, making up her guest lists to ensure people were put at ease when they arrived and could engage one another in pleasant conversation. Mary also wrote about Rose playing with Florence, then a toddler just learning to talk, and sewing clothes for her daughter.

Mary sometimes tired of all the activity and got annoyed with Rose for insisting that they call on people who struck her as boring as they were important. She adopted the overstatement common to the romantic stories she was reading, such as when she told her diary she was so overcome by homesickness for Richmond and her brother, James Washington Green-how, that she went to bed in "a vale of tears."[5]

Rose and Mary were voracious readers, with a particular weakness for the latest novels. Every week they would pick up two or three books from the Waverly Circulating Library, which advertised "**NEW BOOKS** for sale by vendor F. Taylor" on page one of the *National Intelligencer.* "I am really ashamed to say I spent the day, in no other manner than lying in bed reading *Venetia,*" Mary wrote one September evening. "I like it very much, and it is impossible not to be interested in it, when you know that Lord Byron's character is portrayed in the hero of the tale, or rather the he-roes, for his youth is described in one person and his manhood in another. I do not like it in that it produces confusion and keeps the mind on a stretch, but on the whole, it is a thousand times better than *Henrietta Tem-ple* [another love story by Benjamin Disraeli published that year about Disraeli's affair with Henrietta Sykes]." *Venetia* was a popular romantic novel in which the main characters, Venetia and George, Lord Cadurcis, marry and live happily ever after: "Perhaps the reader will not be surprised that, within a few months of this morning walk the hands of George, Lord Cadurcis, and Venetia Herbert were joined in the Chapel at Cherbury by the good Masham. Peace be with them."[6] Mary said the book "had an ef-fect on me that few novels have, namely to make me cry."[7]

Mary was looking forward to the winter social season and had her heart set on meeting handsome young bachelors. As with most young women of her taste and background, marriage was foremost in her mind, and she measured every young man she met by his prospects as a husband. Social engagements with older members of Washington society strained what lit-tle patience she had, often leading to arguments with Rose, who insisted that the young Virginian dress to receive guests whether or not she felt like it. Both women were used to getting their own way, and while Rose usu-ally won, Mary was not shy about expressing her feelings. "It is very stu-pid to sit up with a parcel of old people who you do not know, and for whom you do not care a copper," she wrote in her diary the night of Sep-tember 11, after Rose took Mary to meet Secretary of War and Mrs. Joel R. Poinsett of South Carolina. "Mrs. Poinsett is a matronly woman, appar-ently about fifty-five-years old. . . . I spent the evening more pleasantly than I expected, but still was delighted to get home."[8]

The next morning, right after breakfast, Mary and Dolley Madison Cutts, nieces of former first lady Dolley Madison, paid a visit, and Mary

Greenhow was favorably impressed. "They are very agreeable, very witty, very ugly and seem inclined to be very sociable," she wrote in her diary.[9]

"Miss Mary," as she jokingly referred to herself, prided herself on dressing stylishly, with her hair curled and set off with fresh flowers, but she despised the tightly laced corset that drew her figure into an hourglass. It was uncomfortable in the extreme, but very much in vogue. "Mr. Palmer spent the evening here and I should have enjoyed myself if I had not been tortured by a pair of corsets which I should imagine have as many bones as I have," she wrote. "I will never sit down in them again, as they are not unpleasant when walking."[10]

At first, Mary seemed to enjoy the rhythm and routine of the Greenhows' life. Once or twice a month, Rose's mother, Eliza O'Neale, came to visit, and the ladies would hail a carriage to call on the Hills, who still operated their boardinghouse on Capitol Hill. Rose's younger sisters, Mary Ann, who was twenty-two, and Eliza, a year younger, visited occasionally, and the women spent many afternoons shopping in Georgetown for a trousseau for Mary Ann, who had announced her engagement to a Philadelphia physician.[11] Occasionally in the evening, when Robert was out on business, Rose and Mary would amuse themselves by sitting in the parlor and smoking cigars.[12]

That autumn Dolley Madison, recently a widow, moved from Montpelier to her home in Lafayette Square, a few blocks from the Greenhows'. Owing to the excessive spending habits of an irresponsible son, the former first lady had fallen into difficult financial straits and struggled to keep up the lifestyle she had enjoyed when her husband was president. Sympathetic friends and even her husband's former slave Paul Jennings took gifts of food and money to the national heroine. Rose and Mary often stopped by for tea. The aging doyenne, always gracious, welcomed the company of younger, vibrant women. "I saw Mrs. Madison who had just arrived, and in her long black dress and white turban, looked like a tragedy queen," Mary wrote on Sunday night, October 22.[13]

The Greenhows' busy social life eventually lost its allure for Mary, who was more interested in a gay time with people her own age than tagging along after Rose to meet people of prominence, the wives of high-ranking officials who could advance her husband's career. When Rose insisted that Mary accompany her on a visit to Sarah Gales Seaton, whose husband and brother edited the *National Intelligencer,* Mary groaned. When no one was home, she cheered.[14]

The *Intelligencer* was an influential newspaper in Washington whose editors, William W. Seaton and Joseph Gales Jr., did not share the politics of the Greenhows. The two brothers-in-law wielded power, however, and Rose continued to call on the Seatons. Mary resigned herself to do as Rose asked, but not without protest: "It is a great bore to me to pay morning calls to old married people, but when you are in Turkey, you must do as the Turks," she wrote one night before nodding off to sleep. "Went on the Avenue this evening, chose a ribbon for a bonnet, and at last came to the conclusion that every article of dress is prettier in Richmond than in Washington."[15]

On Saturday evening, September 23, Rose took Mary for their regular after-dinner promenade on the Avenue. There had been no rain for several days, and as they passed a clay-covered street, the wind whipped at their skirts, covering them with a thin veil of orange dust. When the cloud settled and the air cleared, they were startled by what they saw ahead. "There are 27 Indians chiefs in town who are perfectly wild, never having left their forests before," Mary wrote. "Their faces are painted and tattooed, and their heads draped with feathers of every colour of the rainbow. They are wrapped up in blankets, and carry their tomahawks. They speak to everyone they meet and attempt[ed] to kiss a young lady in the street. We met them, and as soon as they saw us they quickened their pace and said something which of course we could not understand."[16]

The Sioux had come to Washington to sign a treaty in which the Indians agreed to sell their land east of the Mississippi River in what is now Wisconsin. As secretary of war, Joel R. Poinsett was the government's chief negotiator on the treaty.[17] Poinsett consulted frequently with his friend Greenhow, who studied maps and land claims in the region.

Several days later, Rose and Mary were standing in the kitchen, peeling peaches. They planned to visit friends in the afternoon, and Mary had her hair wrapped in papers to make it curl. Robert Greenhow had ordered a carriage to arrive for them at 2:00 P.M. Suddenly, he burst into the kitchen and announced excitedly that the government's treaty with the Indians was about to be signed; if the women wished to see the ceremony, they must drop everything and leave immediately. "I pulled the cap of my bonnet over the papers (not having time to take them out) and was dressed in two minutes," Mary wrote that night.

When the Greenhows arrived at Dr. Laurie's Presbyterian Church on F Street, between 14th and 15th, it was so crowded that people were already being turned away. A friend found the women a place where, standing on a pew, they had an excellent view. "There were about thirty chieftans in their high day dresses, with their faces painted in the most horrible manner," Mary wrote. "They smoked the calumet [a long-stemmed, ceremonial pipe], and they were addressed by Mr. Poinsett in English, and what he said was interpreted to them by their guide."

Mary was fascinated by the proceedings and sympathetic to the plight of the Indians. "It made my blood run cold to hear the deep grunt by which they signified their assent to his proposition," she wrote. "The object was to buy their lands, and send them to the other side of the Mississippi, and I felt sorry for the poor wretches, who were sitting quietly to be cheated out of their lands by the great father, for they will not receive one-tenth part of the value of their hunting grounds. One of the chiefs made a reply in Cherokee, and I never heard such jargon in my life; he had no other covering but a very short hunting shirt of calico, some leggings which reached to his knees; the intermediate space being perfectly bare."[18]

A few days later, on the evening of October 4, Mary and Dolley Madison Cutts accompanied Rose and Mary to watch the Indians stage a well-publicized dance in Lafayette Square. The block was so crowded that many people were not able to see them at all. Two of the chiefs, Black Hawk and Keokuk, drew the most attention.[19] "There are two tribes," Mary wrote, "the Sioux and Black Hawk's, and this band, the Sioux, danced the war dance and accompanied it with the most horrid yells or rather the war whoop; the dance consists of nothing more than hopping, and jumping around in a circle; they are almost in a state of nature. Black Hawk and his followers were mainly spectators and are mortal enemies of the Sioux, and I feared the scene would have a tragic termination, but they left in different directions and did not come in contact."

As she watched them leave, Mary climbed up on a fence rail to get a better view. "Mr. Cutts [Dolley Madison's nephew] was with me and seems to be amused at me jumping over the fence without falling," she wrote. But when she saw Martin Van Buren Jr., the president's pudgy son, approaching the group, she jumped down, "fearing his weight would prostrate us to the ground."[20] Martin was a flirt. He and his older brother, Abraham, served as private secretaries to their father, but Martin, who was the alternate, seemed to have plenty of time for seeking out the ladies.

On October 9, the Greenhows held a party in Mary's honor, and the young belle spent hours debating what to wear for the occasion. She finally settled on a loose muslin dress with a pink sash, her sleeves tied with pink ribbon and her hair curled "and dressed with rose buds." She was thrilled when Martin Jr. presented her with a beautiful rose. "He is quite handsome and has excellent manners," Mary wrote, apparently so impressed with the attentions of the president's son that she quite forgot how fat she found him only a few nights before. "He is thirty and does not look to be more than twenty-one."[21]

Mary liked being the center of attention but did not warm to the responsibility of receiving guests and making them feel welcome, as Rose did with apparent ease. "I was worried at being compelled to help play lady hostess and [having to make sure there were] agreeable persons to talk to stupid ones who were alone," she wrote. "This party went so well that Robert means to have several in the course of the winter. The next will be in December when Wash [Mary's brother] comes."[22]

One evening, the Greenhows accepted an invitation to dine at the home of Secretary of State John Forsyth of Georgia, who had been responsible for Robert Greenhow's trip to Mexico. "The party was very small and consisted of the elite of the elite," Mary wrote. "I wore my new chally with short sleeves, and my hair curled with roses on each side." She flirted with "the little Major [Martin] Van Buren," but he by now had lost some of his appeal. Young Martin, Mary noted, "is small and has a good natured countenance, but nothing very striking in his appearance."[23] Mary was surprised that unlike most of her family and friends who owned slaves, the president's son, a New Yorker, had "a white servant." She found Mr. [Arthur] Fox, the English minister, "the ugliest man I ever saw. He is completely lost in his shirt collar, which comes to his eyes and looks as if he were just dug up from the grave."[24] Mary thought her hostess less stuck-up than some of the other society matrons. "Mrs. Forsyth is a charming old woman," Mary wrote. "The whole family are free from anything like pride or haughtiness; their elevated situation would make some people give themselves airs."[25]

On the afternoon of Friday, October 20, the Greenhows called on General Alexander Macomb and his family. Only Mrs. Macomb was at home. "Saw the old lady, but no sign of her handsome son," Mary wrote sadly. "Miss Rose had the impudence to ask me if I would leave a card for him, but I do not believe Mrs. Macomb heard her."[26]

Like many young women, Rose and Mary took French lessons every week, probably at Mrs. Smith's French School, which had a roster of fashionable female students. Robert Greenhow, an accomplished linguist, undoubtedly encouraged the women in their studies, and Rose became fluent enough to converse in French at diplomatic functions and read the latest French novels. The ability to speak French was considered a sign of education and sophistication. Rose and Mary liked to drop little French phrases into their letters and conversation, *robe de chambre* for "bathrobe"; *déshabillé* for "disheveled"; *passer le temps* for "pass the time"; *pour m'amuser* instead of "to amuse myself."[27]

While she was intent on finding a husband, Mary was uncomfortable with any hint of the intimate aspects of marriage and confessed to collapsing into a fit of giggles whenever a friend announced that she was about to wed. The thought of actually *being* married was rather horrifying. After attending a wedding, Mary wrote in astonishment: "I never saw such brides as they have here. They don't mind being married and are as unembarrassed as if it were an everyday affair."[28] She also joked about the physical changes she saw in friends who seemed to age the moment they took their vows, replacing feminine flirtations and frilly crinolines with sedate manners and dark silks as they settled into the responsibilities of raising families and overseeing a household. One morning a woman called on Mary, and the young maiden did not immediately recognize her old friend. "Until sister called her name, I did not know Elizabeth Vankleek to be the stiff, prim-looking Presbyterian before me," Mary wrote. "I never saw a girl so much altered by Hymen in my life; from a pretty, cheerful girl, she is changed into an ugly, grave-looking woman."[29]

The Greenhows entertained distinguished visitors from all over the country and the world, including many diplomats and scientists whom Robert met on his travels. Their dinner parties were formal occasions, with fine china, good linen, and several crystal glasses at each place setting for the various wines and champagne.[30] Clarence, the Greenhows' male slave, served as butler. One evening, the guest of honor was Hartley Rennick, a professor of natural philosophy from Smith-Olive University in New York. After dinner, Robert Greenhow took Rennick to call on President Van Buren.[31] Another evening, General Macomb called on the Greenhows, as did young Martin Van Buren, who spent the evening laughing and joking with Mary. Rose took her duties as chaperone for her young sister-in-law seriously, but she sometimes slipped quietly out of the parlor for a few moments to leave Mary alone with whichever beau had taken a fancy to the pretty Virginian. "I will be as wild tonight as I can," Mary wrote, "that is to say if my confidence does not fail me."[32]

In whatever free time she could find, Rose read and discussed the latest books. One evening, she read aloud to Robert from *The History of Arabia, Ancient and Modern* by Andrew Crichton. Rose and Mary argued about the merits of British writer Harriet Martineau's account of her travels in

America, *Retrospect of Western Travel*, in which the author described her
visit to Washington as the most disappointing part of her trip. Rose, who
took pride in living in the nation's capital, didn't like Martineau describing
it as boring. "Quarrelled with sister about Miss Martineau's book," Mary
wrote.[33] During the course of a week, Rose and Mary read Baron Edward
Bulwer-Lytton's just-published novel, *Ernest Maltravers*, about British
high society. Daniel Defoe's *Robinson Crusoe* was another favorite that
they read aloud with Robert. Mary spent many evenings lost in William
Godwin's powerful novel *The Adventures of Caleb Williams*, an exposé of
political social life in Britain in the 1790s. They were mesmerized by the
romance *Memoirs of a Peeress* by Lady Charlotte Susan Maria Bury.

On Sundays, Rose made an effort to attend Mass at St. Patrick's
Catholic Church, but if the weather was bad, she often didn't make it.
Robert Greenhow attended St. John's at 16th and H streets, a small but elegant church a few blocks from their home and across Lafayette Square
from the White House. Established in 1815, St. John's is known as the
"Church of the Presidents." Mary attended with her brother, but when he
was away on business, she did not like to go alone and wouldn't consider
a Catholic service. "I wish sister had a pew at St. John's," she wrote. "I
dread Sunday to come, as I cannot go to church and have no way of passing the time."[34]

Every few weeks, the Greenhows took a carriage to Georgetown to visit
Chief Justice and Mrs. Taney, the O'Neales' old family friends from
Maryland. Rose's mother, Eliza O'Neale, sometimes joined them. The
previous year, President Jackson had named Taney chief justice of the
United States, and Rose was planning a party for him and his wife. She
would have given considerable thought to the invitations, because
Supreme Court justices were prized guests. And like all good Washington
hostesses, she knew that the best way to put a good party together was to
"honor" someone who would draw other interesting people. Life in Washington was all about cultivating the right friendships, and Rose worked
hard at it.

Taney owned many slaves, and slavery was becoming increasingly controversial. Robert Greenhow owned two: Clarence, who served as driver as
well as butler, and a woman, who probably did most of the cleaning and
cooking and helped care for baby Florence. Several families on the Greenhows' block owned slaves who were married to free blacks, some living in
the same household.[35] There was growing anxiety that free Negroes were
encouraging slaves to seek their freedom, and more and more slaves were

fleeing their owners for safe havens in Washington or up north. Every day, the *National Intelligencer* ran half a dozen ads similar to one published on September 28, 1836:

$300 REWARD: Ranaway from the Subscriber, residing in Prince George's County, Md., about 15th of August 1834, a negro man named Sam or Sampson, thick lips, shows his teeth a little, wore rings in his ears when he left which he did for no provocation. I have been told he was persuaded away by his father who lives in Georgetown, a free colored man who calls himself William Williams. . . . I have no doubt the said Sam or Sampson is either secreted by his father in Georgetown or the City or employed on some part of the canal or has obtained a forged pass through his father. I will give the same reward if apprehended and brought home to the Subscriber. Thomas Berry.[36]

As a descendant of generations of slaveholders, Rose opposed the growing abolitionist movement, and she was not reticent about expressing her opinion. Whether out of bitterness stemming from her father's death or simply from the tradition she inherited, Rose believed blacks were inherently inferior to whites. "The Negro population but illustrate the race in every other place where the wholesome restraints and dominance of the superior race does not exist," she wrote in a diary she kept during a trip to Europe years later, speaking of blacks she encountered on the island of Bermuda. "They have no regular system of labor—and have no idea of provision for the future. Sufficient for the day seems to be their motto. . . . The Negros seem to have no idea of moral or religious restraint. And like the beast of the fields unconscious that they offend against the laws of God or Man."[37]

Rose and Mary Greenhow also shared a strong dislike for Northerners, whose brusque manner and outspoken views on abolition were offensive to Southern ladies. Decades before the country split between North and South, Mary wrote dismissively of a gentleman she met on the Avenue one evening: "He is quite a good looking little man, but bears the Yankee stamp on him beyond mistake. I made my escape as soon as possible. . . ."[38]

On Christmas Eve, Rose went to Kinchley's general store to purchase sugarplums for Florence's stocking. Later in the evening, one of the windiest and coldest of the winter, Rose and Mary fell into a "frolicsome humour." They dressed in white, wrapped themselves in sheets, and ran to a neighbor's house, interrupting a party disguised as snow angels. "We threw open the door and knelt down, much to their astonishment," Mary wrote. With much hilarity, all the guests made their way to the Greenhows' home. At one point, Rose ducked out of the parlor, and Mary found herself alone with "a thickset, big-headed, long-lipped ugly being . . . talking of poetry and romance and the like." Before anyone else came in, she "arranged [her] tresses which are very much disheveled."[39]

On January 2, 1838, Robert Greenhow had lunch with Major General Winfield Scott, who was charged with driving the Cherokee Indians out of the East to the Indian Territory, later named Oklahoma. The 1,200-mile journey, to become known as the Trail of Tears, had barely begun the spring before. Within two years, some sixteen thousand Cherokees who survived the journey were resettled on unfamiliar ground in the Indian Territory. The Cherokee tribe was devastated, with at least a quarter of its people dying along the way. Greenhow had been diverted on his trip to Mexico the previous year when some of the Indians being forced off their ancestral lands had risen up and attacked some whites in Georgia. He had felt endangered enough to send home a packet of his expense vouchers "in case anything happened to me."[40]

After lunch with Scott, Greenhow went home to meet Rose and Mary, who had dressed to go to the White House. Mary had on a new black crepe dress that she thought "beautiful & very becoming." Just as they were leaving, a carriage pulled up to the house and two gentlemen stepped out. Instead of explaining that the Greenhows had a social invitation from the White House, Clarence escorted the visitors into the parlor, where they promptly sat down and made themselves comfortable. "Although they knew we were impatient to be gone, [they] paid a very long visit," Mary wrote with annoyance. "I wished them at the bottom of the Potomac."[41]

By the time the Greenhows arrived at the White House, most of their friends had left. "The rooms, however, were filled with well dressed persons promenading up and down to the sound of a full band stationed in the hall," Mary wrote. "The president stood at the door of the reception room, and I had the pleasure of shaking hands with him and wishing him a Happy New Year." From the White House, the Greenhows walked across Lafayette Square to the home of Dolley Madison, whose New Year's party had become a popular tradition. "She also had a levee and her rooms were as crowded as the president's."[42]

January was windy, rainy, and raw, and Mary spent many days in bed "with a pain in my breast and constant sick stomach." Robert insisted she

LIFE ON K STREET · 119

would die of consumption if she didn't wrap her chest in flannel. "I preferred incurring the risk of seeing the devil,"[43] Mary wrote. At the end of the month, Rose's sister Eliza came to stay. They called her "Liz." "She is a sweet girl and will make me pass the time more pleasantly," Mary wrote.[44] Liz was only a year or two older than Mary, and because the Greenhows' residence was small, the two young women shared a bed. Mary enjoyed Liz's company so much that she accompanied her to St. Patrick's Church, where they "saw all the foreigners,"[45] probably Irish laborers who were flocking to Washington to work on the construction of the C&O Canal.

In February, "when the wind was blowing hurricanes and the night was intensely cold,"[46] Robert Greenhow took ill. He was often confined to bed "with an attack of pain in his face"[47] that suggested he may have suffered from shingles, facial neuralgia, or migraine headaches. Rose and Mary tried to entertain him with a card game called whist, but Robert wasn't well enough to play. Then Rose fell sick as well. She complained of eye strain—perhaps migraines—that sometimes sent her to bed for days at a time.

The winter continued to be unusually cold and wet. Frequent snowstorms stopped most carriage traffic, forcing people who had to go out to travel on foot or horseback. "Brother Robert declares he will not go out again this winter," Mary wrote. She entertained Robert and Rose by reading aloud from another historical romance by Bulwer-Lytton called *Leila*. Rose listened intently to the description of beautiful Leila, whose "form was of the lightest shape consistent with womanly beauty; and there was something in it of that elastic and fawn-like grace which a sculptor seeks to embody in his dreams of being more aërial than those of earth."[48] Rose, apparently quite touched by the description of the book's heroine, would name a daughter Leila.

After the worst of the winter had passed, Rose's younger sister Mary Ann married Dr. John R. Rowand,[49] a Philadelphia physician. The ceremony took place on Tuesday evening, March 27, at St. Patrick's Church. The Reverend J. P. Donellan officiated. Rowand, wrote Mary Greenhow, was "a nice little man no bigger than my thumb."[50] At twenty-one, Mary Ann was a lovely bride, and many family members and friends attended the wedding. Susannah O'Neale Peter, Rose's eldest sister, arrived with several members of her family. Mary Greenhow was delighted to be a bridesmaid. The Greenhow family arrived at the church in four horse-drawn carriages. The bride and her attendants walked up one aisle, while the groom and groomsmen went up another. The couple met at the altar. "The church was very badly lighted, but the ceremony was imposing," Mary wrote. "The responses were very distinctly made."⁵¹

The March winds were fierce that year and the church brutally cold. The next day, Mary came down with influenza. She was tired of the winter and tired of Washington and looking forward to returning to the familiar hills of Richmond and the slower, more familiar rhythm of home. It had been a longer visit than she had anticipated. "This time next week I shall be on board the boat on my return to <u>home sweet home.</u>" Mary wrote. And like a heroine in one of her favorite novels, she finished her diary with flair: "Here endeth my adventures."⁵²

CHAPTER 13

Reversal of Fortune

THE GREENHOWS LIVED comfortably on Robert's State Department salary, perhaps supplemented by some family money, and the family was growing. Their second daughter, Gertrude, was born in 1838,[1] and others would soon follow. On the surface all seemed well, but the Greenhows' carefully planned life was about to be turned upside down.

Robert Greenhow's interest in Mexico and the West kept him professionally engaged in the nation's expansion. But a severe depression, blamed on the Jackson administration's economic policies, and wild land speculation in the West were leading to a major banking crisis and widespread financial instability that stretched the Greenhows' personal finances and left them in debt.

In October 1840, Robert sought the help of his father—and his wife—to obtain a short-term loan, probably to make overdue mortgage payments on his K Street house. A deed of trust shows that Robert Greenhow Sr. and his son, Robert Greenhow Jr., signed a note for $1,400—more than half the value of the house—on April 19, 1840, payable to the Bank of Metropolis in sixty days. In a departure from its usual practice, the bank had Rose cosign the note, stipulating that she did so "willingly and freely and without being induced thereto by fear or threats of or ill usage by her husband or fear of his displeasure."[2]

The day after the note was due, Robert's eighty-year-old father was stricken at his son's home in Washington and died.[3] The old man's body was returned to Richmond for burial in the cemetery on Poor House Hill.[4] Robert inherited the family plate silver and two properties valued at $18,130,[5] a substantial amount of capital at that time.

Rose and Robert paid off their real estate loan and sold their house in September 1843 for $2,700[6]—$200 more than they had paid for it six years earlier.[7] They moved to F Street between 13th and 14th streets, a neighborhood of two-story single-family houses, conveniently located just a block from the State Department and right off the Avenue, where Rose could stroll with her daughters.[8]

Rose gave birth to a third daughter, christened Alice Rose, on October 8, 1842,[9] and two years later produced a son, named Robert in honor of his father and grandfather. Yet another daughter followed, and Rose named her Leila, after the beautiful, dark-haired heroine in Bulwar-Lytton's popular romantic novel that she and Mary had read together many years before.

In less than a year, however, the Greenhows suffered two devastating blows. Alice Rose died at four in October 1846, and young Robert died in June 1847 at two and a half. The children's deaths were noted in the *National Intelligencer,* but no cause was reported.[10] Childhood diseases, of course, ravaged families before vaccines were developed to combat smallpox, diphtheria, and similarly deadly epidemics.

But Rose was resilient. She became pregnant again and in March 1848 would give birth to a son named Morgan Lewis. He was a strong and merry baby.[11]

Yet Robert Greenhow seems to have become more detached, concentrating almost entirely on his own intellectual world. He focused on his academic pursuits, spending countless hours hunched over old charts and maps, tracing boundaries, and studying geography and history. He also translated into English the notes and memoirs of early European explorers.

Rose had a more passionate and outspoken nature and was more interested in political issues. Like Calhoun, she defended the South and its cherished institutions and sought ways to strengthen them. As she put it herself in her memoir years later: "I am a Southern woman, born with revolutionary blood in my veins."[12]

Tension over the slavery issue had been mounting for years. Calhoun threw down the gauntlet himself in a speech to the Senate on February 6, 1837. It was a bitterly cold day, with a raging wind that rattled the windows of the Capitol, when he took the floor in the Old Senate Chamber and demanded that his colleagues from the North stop trying to impose antislavery measures on the rest of the country. With his black cloak and flowing hair, Calhoun commanded rapt attention as he insisted the existing relationship between the races in the South was "indispensable to the peace and happiness of both." The institution of slavery was not an evil, Calhoun said, "but a good—a positive good."[13]

Rose had heard those sentiments expressed many times, often in the same blunt phrases. Calhoun stayed in the Greenhows' home, sometimes for days at a time when Congress was in session,[14] and he spent many evenings in their parlor, sipping old port and discussing the rich possibilities of America's westward expansion and what it meant for slavery.

Calhoun argued that for slavery to survive in the South, its defenders needed to form an alliance with the West to avoid being overwhelmed by a united North and the fast-growing western states. Expansion was becoming a tug-of-war between North and South, with each side demanding that states entering the Union declare themselves for or against slavery.[15]

In Washington, the illegal escapades of abolitionists and runaway slaves were matched by the brazen acts of slave traders and bounty hunters. Free blacks outnumbered slaves in the capital, but free blacks lived in constant fear. As they arrived in the city to search for work, they were frequently kidnapped by slave dealers who would steal and burn the papers proving their status as free people.

Solomon Northup, a free black man from Saratoga Springs, New York, recounted his own nightmare that began when he came to Washington in 1841 to attend the funeral of President William Henry Harrison. He was earning $1 a day as a carriage driver. Northup was dining at Gadsby's Hotel with two white men when he suddenly passed out. He probably had been drugged with laudanum, a powerful opiate used as a painkiller.[16] After a period of unconsciousness—hours or days, he didn't know— Northup awoke, imprisoned. "When consciousness returned I found myself alone, in utter darkness, and in chains," he wrote. "The pain in my head had subsided in a measure, but I was very faint and weak. I was sitting upon a low bench, made of rough boards, and without coat or hat. I was hand cuffed. Around my ankles also were a pair of heavy fetters. One end of a chain was fastened to a large ring in the floor, the other to the fetters on my ankles."[17]

Northup had been abducted, shackled, and thrown into Thomas Williams's slave pen within sight of the Capitol. As he later recounted in his memoir, *Twelve Years a Slave,* he was caught by James H. Burch, a well-known slave dealer.

Northup insisted he was a freeman, but Burch responded by whipping him with a paddle until it broke, then with a cat-o'-nine-tails, giving him a hundred lashes. Burch swore he would kill Northup if he ever said aloud to anyone that he was a freeman. Northup was kept in the pen for about ten days before being sent by steamboat with forty-eight other slaves to New Orleans. Another slave dealer met the ship and slapped the prisoners in holding pens to await sale in the Deep South.[18] Northup was rescued in 1853 when a Canadian laborer mailed a note for him to his hometown and a prominent resident came to Northup's aid.

Rose and Robert Greenhow certainly understood slave conditions in Washington, but the unsavory details were rarely discussed, except when servants tried to escape or threats of uprising panicked white neighbors. Rose ridiculed foreigners who questioned Southerners' treatment of their slaves[19] and defended the practice, as Calhoun did.

By 1841, the South Carolinian was thinking again of running for president. He had fashioned the doctrine of states' rights as a means of preserving the South's culture and economy in the face of growing Northern power. Political committees were set up in the South to prepare for his campaign. Robert Greenhow's half-brother, James Washington Greenhow, was editor of the *Petersburg Republican,* a pro-Calhoun newspaper, and Robert probably supplied editorial advice.

Rose not only agreed with Calhoun on the issues but knew that having a close friend in the White House might well enhance her husband's career, and she was eager to help. In 1843, a confident Calhoun quit the Senate and returned to his Fort Hill home to plot his campaign; but to the dismay of his supporters, he preferred writing lofty essays in his hideaway office on the plantation to getting out on the hustings and taking his ideas to the people. His devotion to principle and intellectual approach to problems may have appealed to the Greenhows, but not to the general public, and his candidacy stalled.[20]

Robert turned his attention to the mineral-rich lands and deep ports of the Pacific Northwest. Britain was pressing its territorial claims in Oregon to the point that officials feared another war between the British Empire and its former colonies. Robert documented the Spanish, Russian, British, French, and American explorations and settlements in the region and argued in "Memoir on the Northwest Coast" that Oregon should belong to the United States. In the ultimate expression of Manifest Destiny, expansionists sought unchallenged control of the Oregon Territory to stretch

U.S. borders from sea to shining sea in an unbroken land across the continent.

At the instigation of James Buchanan of Pennsylvania, chairman of the Senate Foreign Relations Committee and a friend of the Greenhows, the committee ordered the government to print 2,500 copies[21] of Greenhow's treatise. He quickly expanded the memoir into a 482-page book, *The History of Oregon and California,* which was published in both Boston and London in 1844. The respected work was used extensively in congressional debate and diplomatic negotiations.[22]

But Greenhow's intellectual treatise was overshadowed by the derring-do of John Charles Frémont, a brash and handsome explorer of the American West. The Greenhows and Frémonts would soon become bitter rivals, clashing politically and in social circles for years. While the men hammered away at their policy differences, Rose and Jessie Benton Frémont were downright bitchy to each other.

Jessie Benton, the beautiful and rebellious daughter of Senator Thomas Hart Benton of Missouri, scandalized her famous family at seventeen when she eloped with Frémont, the illegitimate son of a French dance instructor who schooled young ladies in Richmond and Atlanta. Like Rose, Jessie was bright, ambitious, and politically astute, helping advance her husband's career at every opportunity. But the ladies were on opposite sides of the slavery issue and despised each other.

Frémont, who was cashiered from the army for insubordination during the Mexican War, led three long and difficult surveying expeditions to map the rugged West between the Rocky Mountains and the Pacific, guided on horseback by the famed scout Kit Carson. Unlike Greenhow, who charted some of the same regions by studying and translating the work of early explorers, Frémont spent months traversing the frontier, sleeping under the stars, braving harsh winters and parched deserts to find routes to the coast and identifying the most promising lands for an expanding United States. In an expedition sponsored by his father-in-law, he mapped the Oregon Trail, which opened the western territories to settlement. He called himself the Pathfinder.

After each journey, Frémont returned east to tell of his adventures and raise funds for another trip. He entertained dignitaries and government officials in their parlors, mesmerizing them with tales of his travels, all recorded in notes that he dictated to his wife, who helped him write richly detailed accounts of his travels for submission to the Congress. The narratives, which combined the human drama of the expeditions with descriptions of the magnificent wilderness and precise maps of the region, made riveting reading, and newspapers around the country printed long excerpts. Under strict instructions from Benton, Frémont produced glowing tales of excitement and opportunity that inspired the great westward migration of settlers who joined trains of covered wagons to cross the mountains in search of land, riches, and adventure.

James Buchanan played both sides of the rivalry. After being appointed secretary of state, he frequently consulted Benton, his former Senate colleague, who sometimes brought Frémont to their meetings. This could not have pleased Robert Greenhow, who considered himself an expert both on the U.S. dispute with Mexico and on the struggle with Britain over the rightful boundaries of the western territories. In public and in private, Robert Greenhow and John Frémont were pitted against each other, and their wives, each jealous of the other, took any opportunity to sully each other's reputations, to the point that Jessie Frémont accused Rose of being a spy—long before there was a Confederacy.

Jessie Frémont claimed that during the Mexican War, when the United States and Britain were engaged in a dangerous boundary dispute in the U.S. Northwest that could have brought fighting on two fronts at once, Rose passed secret documents to the British that she got from her husband. According to Jessie's account,[23] Secretary of State Buchanan knew of Rose's treachery, but thinking it best "to cut off opportunities but not betray knowledge of being watched," he quietly circumvented Robert Greenhow as his translator, bringing sensitive Spanish-language documents to the Frémont house instead, where Jessie and her sister would translate them.[24]

Rose was never publicly accused or charged with aiding a foreign power, yet the suggestion that she and her husband were engaged in espionage a decade before the Civil War is tantalizing. If Rose had been spying for the British during the Mexican War, as Jessie Frémont charged, she would have been working against U.S. interests—and Robert's position—regarding westward expansion.[25] That means if Jessie were right, Rose would have been betraying her own government, her husband, her mentor, and her beloved South. No evidence ever surfaced to support Mrs. Frémont's claim, and if Buchanan knew about and circumvented Rose's spying, it does not appear to have affected their friendship, which continued for many years, through and beyond Buchanan's presidency.

For her part, Rose devoted nearly an entire chapter of her memoir to an attack on Frémont, accusing him of being incompetent, a swindler, land thief, and a poseur. Alluding to his being the product of a philandering father and adulterous mother, she added he "is entitled to the bar sinister on his shield."[26]

In the midst of their personal troubles and social disputes, the Greenhows nearly lost the sponsor they had counted on when Calhoun's presidential campaign stalled. In 1844, he withdrew his name from consideration by the Democratic National Convention. Having resigned from the Senate, the South Carolinian planned to return to the comforts of Fort Hill and the embrace of family and friends. But suddenly disaster struck, a tragedy that stunned the capital and the nation, and the president asked Calhoun to stay. The Greenhows' friend and mentor would soon return to power.

CHAPTER 14

Explosion of the Peacemaker

THE STEAM FRIGATE USS *Princeton*, a marvel of modern engineering, was cruising down the Potomac River on Wednesday, February 28, 1844, with President John Tyler and a host of dignitaries aboard, including seventy-six-year-old Dolley Madison and twenty-three-year-old Julia Gardiner, future wife of the widowed president. It was a huge social event celebrating the navy's technological achievements—the first screw propeller mounted on a warship and the two largest guns in the U.S. Navy. The ship's commander, Captain Robert F. Stockton of Princeton, New Jersey, whose grandfather signed the Declaration of Independence, had assembled nearly four hundred guests for the cruise and a demonstration firing of the huge "Peacemaker" cannon. It was given the name under the assumption that no foreign leader would dare to declare war on a country with such a deadly weapon.[1] While a long line of black carriages waited at the wharf, the ladies were piped aboard and received by Stockton, attired in full dress uniform. This was Rose Greenhow's crowd. The guest list has not survived, but there is no question she and Robert would have been invited.

It was a clear, beautiful day, and the water sparkled. After the ship weighed anchor and fired a national salute of twenty-six guns, one for every state in the Union, the sailors pulled off their hats and gave three cheers, and the brightly clad Marine Band—"the President's Own"—played "The Star-Spangled Banner." As the ship's sails were unfurled by sailors hanging high in the rigging, the *Princeton* moved majestically down the Potomac.[2] What a glorious day! What a glorious event! The lucky guests were participating in a momentous occasion.

Below Fort Washington, where the river widens, the Peacemaker was loaded with forty pounds of powder and a twelve-inch iron ball. When the cannon was fired, guests startled at the thunder as the 228-pound projectile "arched into the air, hit the water two miles away and skipped along the surface for another mile until it disappeared from sight," as one historian described it. With a maximum charge of fifty pounds of powder, the cannon could fire a ball five miles.[3] The gun was discharged a second time, again to an enthusiastic crowd,[4] and as the ship passed Mount Vernon, the home of President Washington, the band played "Hail to the Chief."

About 3:00 P.M., most of the two hundred ladies aboard retired belowdecks to begin an elegant lunch of roast birds, ham, and fine wines bought for the occasion from a caterer in Philadelphia. As they finished, Secretary of State Abel Upshur stood to give the customary toast to the president of the United States. Accidentally picking up an empty bottle of champagne, he remarked pleasantly that the "dead bodies" must be cleared away before he could begin. "There are plenty of living bodies to replace the dead ones," Captain Stockton joked, and passed the secretary of state a full bottle of bubbly.[5] Then President Tyler stood to give a return toast: "To the three great guns: the *Princeton*, her commander, and the Peacemaker."[6] The ladies clapped appreciatively.

As several cabinet officers left the table to make room for other guests, an officer whispered to Stockton that someone wished the great gun to be fired again. "No more guns tonight," Stockton replied. But when he heard that the request had come from the secretary of the navy, Stockton interpreted it as an order and went immediately to the deck.[7] There was an announcement that the gunnery was about to fire Peacemaker for a third and final time to honor George Washington. "Though secretary of war, I do not like this firing and believe I shall move out of the way," joked William Wilkins, who had held his post for less than two weeks.[8] The president started up the ladder to observe the shot but paused to listen to his son-in-law William Waller sing a patriotic ditty about 1776. Just as the young man came to the word *Washington* in the lyrics, the great gun exploded, hurling fiery iron in all directions.

The blast killed Secretary of State Upshur, Secretary of the Navy Thomas Gilmer, Virgil Maxcy, the American chargé d'affaires to Belgium; Colonel David Gardiner of New York, father of Julia Gardiner, the president's fiancée; Beverly Kennon, the navy's chief of construction; and the president's personal valet, a slave named Armistead.[9]

Lieutenant R. E. Thompson wrote in the ship's log that the gun broke off at the trunnion band and the breech and split in two.[10] As the ship trembled, a dense cloud of white smoke smothered the deck, making it almost impossible to see or breathe.

According to the editor of the *Boston Times,* an eyewitness, when the smoke cleared, dead bodies and detached arms and legs littered the deck. Unconscious guests with open head wounds seeping dark, venous blood lay near the destroyed gun. Some of the wounded were struck deaf by the explosion, their eardrums ruptured. Upshur's arms and legs were broken and his bowels torn out. Colonel Gardiner had both arms and both legs blown off. Gilmer was killed by a metal fragment in the head. Virgil Maxcy's severed arm struck a lady in the head, covering her face with blood and knocking off her bonnet.[11] Another man had his arm and leg blown away. The president's slave, hit by a piece of the exploding gun, survived for only ten minutes. The daughter of New Hampshire senator Levi Woodbury was standing so close to one of those killed that her dress was spattered with blood. Senator Thomas Hart Benton of Missouri was blown flat on his back and suffered a concussion, and a woman who was holding on to his arm was thrown into the rigging but unhurt. Benton was carried off and placed on a mattress. Captain Stockton, who was standing at the base of the gun, received severe powder burns on his face, and all the hair on his head was burned off. "My God! Would that I were dead too," he shouted. Stockton was carried to his cabin in a state of delirium and burst into tears.[12] When President Tyler saw the bodies of Upshur and Gilmer, he wept as well.

None of the women on board were injured, but they were not allowed to see the dead bodies of their husbands, brothers, and fathers. Julia Gardiner fainted. Mrs. Gilmer became hysterical.[13] They were led off the ship as quickly as possible and taken to their homes. Miss Gardiner was escorted to the White House. When Dolley Madison entered her drawing room, she found it "filled with anxious friends waiting to be assured of her safety," wrote Lucia B. Cutts in a memoir edited by Dolley Madison's grandniece. "She came in quietly, bowing gracefully and smiling but unable to say a word . . . nor could she ever afterwards trust herself to speak of that terrible afternoon, and she never heard it mentioned without turning pale and shuddering."[14]

News of the explosion was first announced at Gadsby's Hotel by John

Sable,[15] a black waiter, and word spread quickly through the city. Calhoun learned of it from his son Patrick, who was on board when the accident occurred.

The explosion on the USS *Princeton* was the greatest peacetime disaster the country had ever known. The Senate and House of Representatives immediately adjourned to reconvene for the funerals. The ship returned to the Washington Navy Yard, where crowds poured onto the wharf the next day to wait, hour after hour, until each coffin, borne by seamen and escorted by naval officers, left the ship to be loaded into one of six hearses, drawn up side by side on the wharf. Five of the coffins were mahogany. The sixth, bearing the president's slave, was made of cherry.[16] More than sixty carriages followed the cortege to the White House, where Tyler ordered that the bodies lie in state until the funeral Saturday morning.

Drawn to the tragic scene, spectators filed past the flag-draped caskets lined up in the East Room, which had been converted from a scene of brilliant festivity into "a sepulchral chamber, cold and silent as the grave."[17] Four of the five caskets were open for public viewing. The fifth was closed, probably empty, because the body of Virgil Maxcy, the U.S. chargé to Belgium, had already been moved to his family estate on the West River in Maryland for burial.[18] No mention was made in the public ceremonies of the sixth victim, Armistead. The *National Intelligencer,* reporting the fatality a day after the others, said: "No death has occurred, in consequence of the terrible accident, besides those mentioned yesterday, except that of a servant of the President (a colored man) who was near the gun at the time of its exploding."[19] He was buried by his family the next day.[20]

The mayor of Washington ordered all stores and businesses to close on the day of the funeral, a Saturday. At 10:30 A.M., members of Congress boarded carriages and rode to the White House, where the procession formed behind a military escort in reverse order, with Major General Winfield Scott, commanding officer of the army, in the rear. The Executive Mansion was draped in black crepe, and each of the hearses for the five white victims was drawn by a pair of jet-black horses.[21] They were followed by the president's carriage, surviving members of his cabinet, former presidents, officers and members of the Senate and House, the chief justice and associate justices of the Supreme Court, the diplomatic corps, governors, and state and local officials, all in order designated by protocol and all wearing armbands of black crepe.

At precisely 11:00, under a cold, gray sky, an artillery detachment stationed near St. John's Church across the square from the White House fired the first salute that rattled windows across the city. Every sixty seconds, the crack of rifles and the boom of cannons echoed through town as the mile-long procession passed military units posted outside City Hall at Judiciary Square, the Capitol, and the Navy Yard. Bells tolled from church steeples throughout the city at measured intervals. Thousands of spectators lined the route, craning their necks for a view of the grim parade. At the gates of the Congressional Burying Ground, now the Congressional Cemetery, the military halted, the coffins were lifted from their hearses, and the pallbearers led a civic procession into the graveyard.

On the way back to the White House, as President Tyler's carriage passed the Capitol, something startled Tyler's horses, and the presidential coach, shrouded in mourning, raced up Pennsylvania Avenue, "still crowded with hacks and vehicles of every description, and persons on horseback and on foot returning from the funeral."[22] As it passed the heart of the market district at 7th Street, the horses were galloping at top speed, and people and carriages hurled themselves out of the way of the runaway president. Tyler's son John Tyler Jr. tried desperately to help the driver get the team under control, but they couldn't. When the carriage reached Galabrun's European Hotel at the corner of Pennsylvania Avenue and 14th Street, where the Willard Hotel stands today, an unidentified black man stepped out and stopped the team, saving the president from harm for the second time in four days. Tyler, who had become the first "president by accident" upon the death of William Henry Harrison after barely a month in office, was forever tagged "His Accidency."

In a special message to Congress, the president announced that the *Princeton* disaster was not caused by carelessness or inattention of the captain or crew. A naval court of inquiry quickly absolved Stockton of blame.[23] In true Washington tradition, no one was held responsible, and nobody lost his job.

With the death of Upshur as secretary of state, there was no one left in the cabinet to uphold the South's interest in obtaining the annexation of Texas. Virginia congressman Henry A. Wise, who had been in Gadsby's Hotel when the disaster was announced, realized the political significance of the event and, uninvited, made an early morning visit to the White House to persuade Tyler to name fellow Southerner and states' righter John C. Calhoun to the post.[24] Although initially reluctant, Tyler agreed, and the Senate hastily confirmed the appointment of the man who had presided over the chamber as vice president and later become one of its staunchest orators.[25] Robert Greenhow, whose expertise in Mexican affairs and the Oregon Territory was well known by that time, now had a family friend as his new boss, a cousin and fellow Virginia gentleman in the White House, and his two favorite issues at the top of the administration's short agenda. Tyler named John Y. Mason of Virginia, another Greenhow friend, as secretary of the navy.

The country was caught up in westward expansion, but Americans were divided over the annexation of Texas. The republic sanctioned slavery, and Southerners like Calhoun wanted the pro-slavery votes that a state of Texas would send to Congress. The issue split the Democratic Party into a moderate faction led by James Knox Polk and James Buchanan of Pennsylvania and a growing antislavery wing represented by Missouri senator Thomas Hart Benton and Martin Van Buren.

Thousands of Americans were moving to Texas, attracted by offers of free land, and the republic was eager to join the Union. But Congress was reluctant to upset the balance of free and slave states and did not want to risk war with Mexico, which still claimed Texas as its own.[26]

The U.S. Senate voted down an annexation resolution in 1844 in a slap at Calhoun's diplomatic skills, but when James K. Polk was elected president in November, he pressed for quick annexation to head off an attempt by England and France to guarantee its independence. Congress formally invited Texas to join the Union in December 1844, and the deal was completed a year later.

In the end, Calhoun had helped bring Texas into the Union, adding another slave state to the increasingly divided Congress. But Polk, who was anxious to deemphasize the slavery issue, dropped Calhoun from the cabinet and named Senator James Buchanan of Pennsylvania to head the State Department.[27] He made a fellow Tennessean, Rose's old suitor Cave Johnson, postmaster general. Buchanan moved into an elegantly furnished house on F Street North, right across the street from Rose and Robert Greenhow.[28] He was a welcome neighbor.

CHAPTER 15

Pursuit of the *Pearl*

ROSE KNEW HOW to cultivate Buchanan. They had a teasing friendship, and Rose charmed the lifelong bachelor with her outspoken political views as well as her social graces. Her husband, however, got caught in a classic bureaucratic backstabbing that could have cost him his relationship with his boss and probably contributed to a serious decline in his health.

Robert had stayed at State through yet another presidential transition and was concentrating on Mexico and Oregon, the two critical foreign policy issues for President Polk. The United States was prepared, even eager, for war with Mexico and was standing tough on Oregon. Polk had been elected on the campaign slogan "54-40 or fight!" which meant the United States was prepared to battle Britain for the entire Oregon country up to the recognized southern boundary of Russian America. With Mexico ready to go to war over U.S. annexation of Texas, however, Polk was reluctant to fight on two fronts and agreed to split the northwest region with Britain at the forty-ninth parallel. Robert Greenhow's history and maps of the region were cited by lawmakers on both sides of the Senate debate over the boundary treaty with Britain. Thomas Hart Benton, the master of Manifest Destiny, carped about a few of Greenhow's points, implicitly backing his son-in-law John C. Frémont, the other presumed expert on the region.

Since Robert Greenhow's journey to Mexico eight years earlier, Texas had organized itself into a republic modeled on the United States, and

Mexico reluctantly acknowledged its independence in a vain attempt to keep the vast territory from becoming part of its threatening neighbor to the north. Both President Tyler, before his defeat for renomination, and President Polk were strong supporters of Texas annexation, and the Lone Star republic was admitted to the Union before the end of Polk's first year in office.

Conflicting claims about the southern boundary of the new state of Texas and U.S. designs on New Mexico and California, both then part of Mexico, exacerbated tensions between the two countries. In a display of provocation, President Polk dispatched an "Army of Observation" to the Rio Grande in a region Mexico considered its territory, and the Mexicans interpreted that as an invasion. War broke out in April 1846.

Robert's knowledge of Spanish and experience with the people and issues put him in the thick of diplomatic maneuvers to settle the dispute, but a few months into the war, he found himself a victim of Washington's favorite blood sport: bureaucratic backbiting. In December 1846, he received a polite reprimand from Secretary Buchanan for a supposedly careless translation of a letter from the Mexican foreign minister. Greenhow suspected he was being undermined by a colleague, and he was right.

Nicolas Trist, the chief clerk at the State Department, who later played a key role in negotiating the treaty to end the war with Mexico, had altered Greenhow's translation of the letter, producing what Greenhow considered embarrassing errors. Trist plunged the knife deeper when he sent the letter to Congress and leaked it to the local newspaper for publication. A vain and arrogant man, Trist may have thought he was improving the translation, but it was a professional blow to Greenhow. In the course of a week, Robert wrote two scathing letters to Buchanan accusing his colleague of undermining him. He offered to resign if Buchanan sided with Trist.[1]

The secretary was an indecisive cabinet officer who avoided controversy, and he did not respond, leaving Greenhow in an even more precarious position. Robert Greenhow was not the type who handled such stressful office politics well. Trist went off on a secret mission to Mexico to negotiate an end to the war, and Robert grew increasingly distressed, his physical and mental health following a downward spiral.

The United States handily bested the Mexican army, and Congress took up the question of what to do about Mexican territories such as New Mexico and California that expansionists had coveted since before the war. On January 4, 1848, Calhoun broke with the Democratic Party and offered a resolution denouncing annexation as a threat to American institutions. "Ours is the government of the white man," declared the venerable senator, his health failing at sixty-six and his bushy hair streaked with gray. Mexico, with its large population of Indians and mixed bloods, had made "the fatal error of placing the colored race on an equality with the white," Calhoun told the Senate, insisting that "in the whole history of Man," there was no record of any "civilized colored race" maintaining free institutions. "Are we to overlook this great fact?" he asked. "Are we to associate with ourselves as equals, companions and fellow citizens the Indians and mixed races of Mexico? I would consider such associations as degrading to ourselves and fatal to our institutions."[2]

Greenhow's State Department nemesis Trist, in a brash gamble, disobeyed his orders from President Polk to return to the United States and negotiated a settlement with Mexico at Guadalupe Hidalgo. Despite Polk's peevish displeasure with Trist—the president refused to pay his negotiator's expense account—the treaty contained the conditions Polk wanted for acquisition of New Mexico and California, and it was sent to the Senate for ratification.[3]

Greenhow, now sidelined by his poor health—probably migraines and depression—took a parting shot at Trist in a letter to Buchanan, warning the secretary of state about potential border problems with the treaty; but it was too late to affect the Senate vote. The treaty passed 38–14, three votes more than the required two-thirds' majority. Greenhow also thanked Buchanan for allowing him to take a medical leave: "The extreme sensibility of my eyes to the light has been much relieved, though I am, I fear, incapacitated for continued exertion of the eyes to an extent which fills my mind with anxieties the most painful and gloomy."[4] He turned his attention to less stressful matters, preparing a sixteen-page handwritten memo to the Virginia Historical Society concerning European exploration of the Chesapeake Bay. In it, he suggested that the bay was not discovered by the English in 1607, as was commonly claimed, but first visited by Spaniards in 1573.[5]

The country was barely over the war with Mexico when Washington was again racked by trauma sparked by the slavery question. On April 16, 1848, a month after the ratification of the U.S. treaty with Mexico, a small schooner named the *Pearl,* sailing from Whitehill, New Jersey, made its way up the Potomac and tied up at Steamboat Wharf on 7th Street. The instigator, Daniel Drayton of Baltimore, financed by a wealthy New York abolitionist he refused to identify, had quietly put out word that he would carry off as many slaves as the vessel would hold. It was a Sunday, the day when many blacks gathered in church, the center of their religious and social lives. This was where they caught up on the latest gossip and news.

That night, by prearranged signal, seventy-seven slaves slipped through the darkness in a light rain, crossed the Mall where construction was about to begin on a huge obelisk to be called the Washington Monument, and boarded the *Pearl* downriver, where she had been moved to a secluded wharf to keep from attracting attention. Drayton told the sole crewman aboard that as black people crossed the open field nearby and glided silently on board, he should lift the hatch, let them enter the hold, and shut the hatch cover quickly behind them. "Their destination was freedom in the North," writes Washington historian Mary Kay Ricks, who has documented the escape. At 2:00 A.M., the vessel weighed anchor, carrying a "cargo" of thirty-eight men, twenty-six women, and thirteen male children, all huddled together in the hold. Edward Sayres, owner and captain of the *Pearl*, Drayton, and Chester English, a young sailor and cook, were the only white men aboard. Drifting down the Potomac in a predawn mist, the small schooner headed toward the Chesapeake Bay one hundred miles to the southeast, passing slave pens and the comfortable homes of their owners on both sides of the river. The plan was to round Point Lookout at the mouth of the river and head north up the bay through the slave state of Maryland, pass through the Delaware Canal at the head of the bay, and make for New Jersey. It was a daring plan for a small sailing vessel in the age of steam.

The *Pearl* cast off in a dead calm, and she lay becalmed most of the night, her passengers too far from shore to swim back and sneak off to their homes. When the wind picked up after daybreak, about the time slave owners on both sides of the river were waking up to find no one to serve them breakfast, the *Pearl* was barely past Alexandria, still within sight of the capital. With a northwest wind behind her, the schooner sped down the river, making good time, well ahead of a posse that learned of the mass escape and gave chase in a privately owned steamboat named the *Salem*. The favorable breeze freshened into a northwesterly squall, and Captain Sayres sought shelter in Cornfield Harbor, just above Point Lookout. According to Ricks's reporting, Drayton demanded that Sayres sail south down the bay and out into the Atlantic off Hampton Roads, Virginia, but the captain refused, insisting his small, crowded vessel would founder in the open sea.

The *Pearl* dropped anchor to wait out the storm. The thirty-five armed men aboard the *Salem* were about to give up their search when they spotted the *Pearl* hiding near the marshes and quickly captured their prey.

The schooner was towed back to Washington, where, as Ricks explains, Drayton, Sayres, and the male slaves were manacled, and all the fugitives were marched north from Steamboat Wharf to the D.C. jail at Judiciary Square, known as the "Blue Jug." Jeering crowds taunted the captives, and when the prisoners passed Gannon's slave market, the owner lunged at Drayton with a knife. A mob estimated between one thousand and three thousand gathered outside the abolitionist newspaper the *National Era,* demanding the publication be shut down and threatening to lynch the editor, who was rumored to have participated in the largest slave escape plot in history. The three-day standoff that followed became known as the Washington Riot of 1848.[6]

One of the organizers of the foiled escape was Paul Jennings, the longtime body servant of President Madison. In 1846, ten years after her husband died, Dolley Madison sold Jennings for $200, and Senator Daniel Webster, who had known the slave when he was the president's butler, bought Jennings for $120 and granted him freedom—on condition that Jennings work off the purchase price at the rate of $8 a month.

Before leaving Webster's house on the night of April 15 to aid in the conspiracy, Jennings wrote Webster a letter expressing his admiration for the senator, as well as his gratitude, but explaining his obligation to act: "From the daily contact with your great personality which it has been mine to enjoy, has been imbibed a respect for moral obligations and the claims of duty. Both of these draw me towards the path I have chosen." The note was signed simply: "Jennings."

Jennings left the note for Webster, who was not at home, and told the cook that he would be away for a few days. Then he set off to meet the schooner. But Jennings, who was already a freeman, did not join the other passengers. Some say it was his loyalty to Webster; others insist that as a freeman, he would have been taking a needless risk of being captured and punished. Perhaps the letter was only a precaution, in case Jennings was apprehended at the scene. However, when he returned home, Jennings retrieved the letter he had written.[7]

Those aboard the captured vessel were not so fortunate. Some were returned to their owners; others were sold "down the river" to New Orleans, one of the busiest slave markets in the South. Through the intervention of abolitionists such as the Reverend Henry Ward Beecher, two beautiful teenage sisters who were to be sold as sex slaves were purchased with parishioners' donations and brought north to freedom. The sisters, Mary and Emily Edmondson, later met Beecher's sister Harriet Beecher Stowe, who used their story to document the horrors of slavery she had described in her novel *Uncle Tom's Cabin.* Drayton and Sayres, after narrowly escaping a lynch mob in the first days after their capture, spent more than four years in jail in Washington before being pardoned by President Millard Fillmore.[8]

The *Pearl* incident inflamed passions on both sides of the slavery issue in Washington and beyond. President Polk asked his cabinet to try to calm the mob and wrote in his diary that "the outrage committed by stealing or seducing the slaves from their owners and the attempt of abolitionists to defend white men who had permitted it was the real cause of all the trouble." In the Senate, Henry S. Foote of Mississippi invited abolitionist John P. Hale of New Hampshire to visit his state, where, Foote promised, Hale "would grace one of the tallest trees of the forest, with a rope around his neck."[9]

That fall, Robert Greenhow agreed to let a slave, Robert Evans, buy his freedom. The price was $300 with interest, payable at the rate of $70 a year for five years. The deed, dated September 20, 1848, said Greenhow acted "for and in consideration of the faithful services rendered to me by my Servant Robert Evans, a man of colour aged about thirty years bought by me from my Sister in 1840." Greenhow agreed to allow Evans "to dispose of his time and labour as he may please, within the District of Columbia," for the five-year period for payment of the slave's debt, after which Evans would have "his full and entire freedom."[10]

It is not clear whether Greenhow was responding to the changing climate in Washington or whether his finances were so strapped that he was unable to afford to keep the slave. But the audacious escape attempt by the passengers of the *Pearl* prompted many people to free slaves, and Greenhow may have been one of them.

It had been a difficult summer in the capital, but the city continued to grow and prosper. On July 4, 1848, President Polk presided over the laying of the cornerstone of the Washington Monument and signed the treaty formally ending the war with Mexico. The newly incorporated Washington Gas Light Company placed a lantern, six feet in diameter, atop the Capitol, so bright that it was visible from Alexandria across the Potomac River. The company laid pipes made from hollowed-out logs, erected iron lampposts, installed lanterns, and brought gaslight to the White House and

Pennsylvania Avenue, making it the only illuminated street in the city for several years.[11]

Rose and Robert could now take a walk after dinner and admire the quiet beauty of the new lights flickering along the Avenue. Summer evenings in Washington can be long and leisurely, and it was becoming a beautiful city. That offered some comfort, but it wasn't enough to satisfy Rose's restless spirit.

CHAPTER 16

End of an Era

THE 1840S OPENED with Rose and Robert in good health and optimistic spirits, but in less than a decade events had rendered them physically and emotionally drained, financially stretched, and uncertain about their future. Robert's career was in eclipse. He and Rose were thinking about going somewhere that would offer new challenges and a chance to pull their lives back together. Washington, with memories on every corner, was growing more polarized by the day.

In January 1849, a young congressman from Illinois named Abraham Lincoln introduced legislation to outlaw trading in slaves in the District of Columbia, at that time the largest slave market in North America. Opponents argued the measure would lead to the abolition of slavery throughout the nation. Although Lincoln left the House and returned to practice law in his home state, the action he proposed was adopted the following year as part of the Compromise of 1850, another attempt to hold the Union together by maintaining the balance of free and slave states.

Rose confided to Calhoun, whom she called "my kindest and best friend," that she didn't think her husband could return to work at the State Department. She asked him for a letter of introduction to the new president, Zachary Taylor, hero of the Mexican War, saying Robert desperately needed a change in location, perhaps a warmer climate. "Mr. Greenhow's situation is one which . . . is alarming in the extreme," Rose wrote. "The irritability of the nervous system is greater than at any previous time, together with intense pain in the head and eyes—I am haunted by the fear of paralysis or blindness, and my first feeling in the morning is to ascertain if he is worse than on the previous day."

Rose told Calhoun she knew her husband would like a diplomatic appointment to Mexico but didn't think that was a possibility. In a stroke of audacity or desperation, she suggested that he be assigned instead to—of all places—Italy: *Rose's* choice, not Robert's. "Turin or some place in southern Europe is where we desire to go," she wrote. "Mexico is where my husband would desire to go, as he feels that he would be of great use there; but that we conclude to be out of the question."[1] Whether she ruled out Mexico because of her husband's bureaucratic tiff with Trist or her concern that Mexico was an unhealthy environment for Robert, Rose wanted to revive their marriage and health in a romantic place like Italy, where Robert had traveled as a young man.

Three weeks later, they lost their son. At thirteen months, Morgan Lewis Greenhow was racked with severe convulsions, followed by a fever that his physician-father and the family doctor were powerless to control. On Sunday evening, April 29, 1849, the baby died[2] after a struggle that left his mother utterly exhausted. Morgan Lewis was the third child the Greenhows lost in three years.

Robert, already in the depths of depression, mourned openly. On the day after his son's death, he wrote a plaintive letter to John Calhoun echoing the grief his own father had expressed when young Robert's mother died in the Richmond Theatre fire thirty-seven years earlier. "Dear Sir," Greenhow wrote, ". . . my little boy, my only little boy, whom you may remember as a strong and merry baby, was seized with convulsions. . . . His brain was probably injured, during the convulsion, as he never after exhibited any farther sign of consciousness, other than a preference for his mother. All that could be done by the courage and watchfulness of his mother, and the skill of his physician, was vain, as the symptoms constantly became worse, until the close. . . . Mrs. Greenhow is much reduced in flesh and strength, by her unwearied attentions; never have I seen more courage, and perseverance displayed, than by her. She is only able at present, to express to you, through me, our recollection of your kindness, so promptly received."[3]

The indomitable Rose eventually regained her strength, and a few weeks later she herself wrote Calhoun to inquire about his failing health—and offer to help him get some good press in a new newspaper, *The Union,* which had just begun publishing in Washington. The editor was Thomas

Ritchie, the powerful Democratic voice of the *Richmond Enquirer*, and Rose offered to use her connections to serve as a confidential intermediary between Calhoun and *The Union* "should you desire it, indirectly or otherwise."[4] She didn't mention that she was already pregnant again.[5]

Rose confided to Calhoun that with the change in administrations that saw Buchanan depart as secretary of state and a Whig lawmaker, John M. Clayton, take that post under Taylor, her husband's job was in jeopardy. Publicly, Clayton praised Greenhow's qualifications, according to Rose, but he appeared to be preparing a run for the presidency himself, and "all his patronage will be used to that end."

"For my part," she wrote, "I long to escape from this infected political atmosphere—else to plunge more deeply into it. Nothing would please me better than that my husband should be connected with a newspaper at this time."[6] Rose seemed to feel that *any* change, whether a new government assignment or a return to editorial work, would help Robert recover.

On July 12, Dolley Madison died. The former first lady and doyenne of Washington society for almost half a century had taken special interest in Rose and her sister Ellen from the time they arrived in Washington. With Ellen's marriage and Robert's Virginia connections, the Greenhows were part of the family. And Dolley Madison had been a model for Rose.

In August, Robert reported to Calhoun that he was "unable to read, think or sometimes, even to stand." In hopes of finding rest and relief, he took a vacation to Warrenton Springs, Virginia, where the state legislature was meeting. As sick as he was, he summoned the strength to pass along some potentially crucial intelligence. Greenhow reported "in entire confidence" that a Latin revolutionary (General Narciso López) planned to invade Cuba, oust its Spanish rulers, and deliver the island to the United States for annexation. He offered to pass along any advice Calhoun might have for the leaders of the daring plot that could, conceivably, bring Cuba into the Union as another slave state to offset the impending statehood of California, destined to be a free state.[7] Rose went even further and met López for breakfast before he left on his expedition.

Without naming the general, she wrote Calhoun, "The main spring or mover in the matter has just left me, having taken a parting breakfast, before starting on the perilous undertaking." She reported that one steamer with 1,000 men aboard would sail from New York or some point north, and another steamer with 1,200 to 1,500 men would sail from New Orleans, "well armed and equipped composed of picked men, and officers, ready for the perils, the profits and honours of the venture." Rose had traveled to Pennsylvania to visit Buchanan at his estate and assured Calhoun the former secretary of state was confident of the mission's success.[8]

Rose got her meeting with President Taylor, whose nickname, "Old Rough-and-Ready" (from the Seminole wars), had followed him to the White House; but Robert reported to Calhoun that his wife returned "unfavorably impressed as to the capacity and character of the head of our government, whom she found far more rough than ready."[9]

In her own letter to Calhoun on August 29, Rose told her iconoclastic friend that Buchanan believed the future of the country rested on Southern unity. "He says the fate of this Union depends upon the firm and unwavering front which the South may present next winter," Rose wrote. Buchanan, a Southerner by preference if not geography, wanted the South to insist that there be no ban on slavery in territory acquired from Mexico, that Congress pass laws to enable Southern slaveholders to reclaim their property, and that there be no more pressure to abolish slavery in the District of Columbia. Buchanan wanted to defuse the explosive issue by abolishing the use of slave pens and dropping the question of slavery in the new territories "as the laws of nature, which is paramount, will settle how far that institution can exist." Rose's letter showed an increasingly sophisticated understanding of the nuances of Southern politics, as well as her fascination with revolutionary intrigues and interest in sharing the intelligence she gained with trusted friends. Rose was unaware, however, that President Taylor had ordered the navy to block the Cuba enterprise as a violation of U.S. neutrality. He had sent three warships the day before to surround the would-be invasion force on Round Island in Mississippi and disperse the band of several hundred soldiers of fortune. With support from American Southerners, López tried twice more to invade Cuba. In August 1851, he landed a small force on the island, was captured by the Spanish, and was taken to Havana, where he was executed by the garrote for high treason.

In her letter to Calhoun about the plot, Rose mentioned she was still worried about Robert's declining health: "He is at this moment laboring under great depression of the nervous system—so soon as he is able travel he will go to the north for awhile as I think that he will not otherwise recover his strength. . . . I cannot say what my husband's prospects are—yet I do not despair as yet—though I think nothing will be done before the next Congress."[10]

Disaster struck the Greenhows yet again on October 10, 1849. The daughter Rose had been carrying when she lost Morgan Lewis died in infancy. Her mother had named the baby Rose, the second daughter to carry her mother's name. The notice in the *National Intelligencer* did not list a cause of death.[11] The couple had lost two sons and two daughters in an excruciating three years, but tragedy still stalked them. On February 18, 1850, Rose lost her mother, Eliza O'Neale. The widow of John O'Neale, who had pulled her own life together and raised five daughters to adulthood, was fifty-five years old.[12]

THE INTENSIFYING DEBATE over slavery and its future in an expanding nation threatened to tear the tenuous bonds that had held the country together since the Missouri Compromise preserved the balance of free and slave states thirty years before. The Senate's sixty members were split evenly between the fifteen free states in the North and fifteen slave states in the South. The addition of California as a free state would tip the balance and deepen the crisis atmosphere in the beleaguered South.

It remained for the Senate's grand old men, the Great Triumvirate, to battle for the future of the Union.

Henry Clay of Kentucky had returned to the Senate in March after a fourth and final failed campaign for the presidency and was welcomed back by his longtime rivals Daniel Webster and John C. Calhoun. Clay had shaped the Missouri Compromise, which split Maine from Massachusetts and admitted it as a free state to offset the admission of Missouri as a slave state in 1820. Thirty years later, despite worsening tuberculosis, "the Great Pacificator" braved a winter storm to pay an unexpected visit to Webster's home. He sought the Massachusetts senator's support for another plan to buy time with a series of new provisions to preserve slavery where it already existed and ban it in California and the new territories of the Southwest. Clay, who owned slaves but professed to hate slavery, appealed to his Northern colleague to go along, even if the compromise would be unpopular in the North. He also proposed to abolish the slave trade in the District of Columbia and strengthen existing fugitive slave laws. Webster listened carefully and agreed to think about it.[13]

Eight days later, Clay took the Senate floor to make his proposal. Around him stood the most powerful abolitionists: Webster, Thomas Hart Benton, William Seward of New York, and Stephen Douglas of Illinois. Calhoun, too sick with pneumonia and tuberculosis to go to the Capitol, followed the debate in the newspapers from his room in Hill's Boarding House, where Rose had lived as a teenager and tended him now.[14] On

March 4, Calhoun's strength returned enough for him to make an appearance on the Senate floor. "Mr. Calhoun entered the Senate chamber supported by two senators," wrote assistant doorkeeper Isaac Bassett in his memoir. Calhoun was very feeble, but after a short rest, he rose to address the Senate. "But as he was too weak to perform the task," Bassett wrote, he asked the Senate to allow his friend Senator James Murray Mason of Virginia to read his remarks.[15] Calhoun sat upright in his chair, bundled in a cloak, as Mason delivered Calhoun's last speech: The North had all the advantages of wealth and power, and the South had been hurt by unfair economic policies. If the Union was to be saved, the South would require justice. The West must be opened to slavery. And if California was admitted to the Union as a free state, the South would have no choice but to leave the Union.[16]

It was pure Calhoun, conceding nothing. On March 7, Webster rose to support Clay's compromise in a bold gamble that would carry the day—but cost him dearly in his native New England. "I wish to speak today, not as a Massachusetts man, nor as a Northern man, but as an American, and a member of the Senate of the United States," Webster declared. "I speak for the preservation of the Union. Hear me for my cause."

For three and a half hours, he argued that it was pointless to try to abolish slavery where it already was entrenched, but that the institution would not expand westward in any case. He closed by appealing to the noble cause of union: "Instead of speaking of the possibility or utility of secession, instead of dwelling in those caverns of darkness, instead of groping with those ideas so full of all that is horrid and horrible, let us come out into the light of day; let us enjoy the fresh air of Liberty and Union; let us cherish those hopes which belong to us; let us devote ourselves to those great objects that are fit for our consideration and our action; let us raise our conceptions to the magnitude and the importance of the duties that devolve upon us; let our comprehension be as broad as the country for which we act, our aspirations as high as its certain destiny; let us not be pigmies in a case that calls for men. Never did there devolve on any generation of men higher trusts than now devolve upon us, for the preservation of the Constitution and the harmony and peace of all who are destined to live under it."

The Compromise of 1850 gained ten more years of peace—but without Calhoun. The South Carolina patriot returned to the Senate floor once more six days later, when he rose to object to charges that he was fostering division, insisting that his intention was to save the Union.

Two weeks later, Calhoun requested that Senate debate on Clay's resolutions be postponed until the following Tuesday, when he thought he would feel well enough to speak. But his health did not improve. On Sunday, March 31, at 7:10 A.M., Calhoun died in his room at Hill's Boarding House.[17] Rose Greenhow sat at his bedside and nursed him during his last illness, treasuring his words.[18]

"In the room in which I now sat waiting . . . ," she wrote later, "I had listened to the words of prophetic wisdom from the mouth of the dying patriot. He had said that our present form of Government would prove a failure, that the tendency had always been, towards the centralization of power in the hands of the general Government; that the conservative element was that of States' rights. . . ."[19]

Rose attended the memorial service for her old friend in the Senate chamber and walked in the procession with his Senate colleagues: "Mr. Webster walked by my side as we turned from the tomb, and, with tears trickling down his face, made use of these words: 'One of earth's princes hath departed—the purest, best, and greatest man I ever knew! He was a Roman senator when Rome was.' . . . Mr. Clay, in his eulogy upon him in the Senate at the same time, said, 'He was my senior in everything but years.' "[20] Both men would survive but two more years.

It was the end of an era. Rose had lost her mother and four children, and her husband was in poor health. Now the man whom she had loved like the father she had hardly known was gone as well. They had reached a turning point.

Robert Greenhow was fifty years old, Rose nearing forty. She was still an attractive woman, her hair immaculate and her face only lightly lined, but she had been devastated by loss. Once again, she was draped in black, a woman in perpetual mourning. There was talk among Southern extremists of forming their own country with boundaries that extended to the Pacific and included parts of Mexico and Cuba. The Greenhows might even cash in on the gold rush fever in California that followed discovery of gold at Sutter's Mill in 1848 and made Frémont a millionaire. It was time to stop dwelling on the past and concentrate on their future, time to move on.

Part Four

DARING
DANGER

CHAPTER 17

Leaving Washington

TWO WEEKS AFTER Calhoun's funeral, debate in the Senate struck a flashpoint. As Senator Henry Foote of Mississippi was praising Calhoun and denouncing his colleague Thomas Hart Benton, Benton rose from his seat and lunged for Foote, who retreated backward toward the vice president's chair. Foote drew a loaded revolver and pointed it at the Missouri abolitionist. Benton, who with his brother had wounded and nearly killed Andrew Jackson in a gunfight many years before, cried out, "I have no pistols!" Senators rushed about, calling for order and the sergeant-at-arms. Several senators jumped up on their chairs. Vice President Millard Fillmore, the presiding officer, demanded that everyone, senators and spectators alike, be seated. "Stand out of the way, and let the assassin fire!" Benton shouted. Senator Henry Dodge of Wisconsin grabbed Benton and tried to force him back into his seat, but the burly Missourian broke away and lunged again toward Foote. Another senator, Daniel S. Dickinson of New York, snatched Foote's pistol from his hand and hastily locked it in his desk. Foote returned to his chair, and the flare-up subsided.[1] But the regional divide deepened.

The capital was so split that families, friends, and colleagues were feuding openly. Hostesses scrutinized their guest lists to assure that people of opposing views were not invited to the same parties.[2] Rose was not intimidated by anyone, but she had run out of fight. Robert was ill, and his career was at a standstill.

One week after the Foote-Benton showdown in the Senate, Robert Greenhow tendered his resignation as translator and librarian at the State Department, giving up his annual salary, which after twenty years of service had climbed to $1,800.[3] They were leaving town.

Greenhow wasn't the only fed-up bureaucrat with gold on his mind. "The California fever has reached the public offices of this city, and a stampede is threatening among the twelve hundred clerks," wrote one Washington correspondent. "Three or four intelligent clerks . . . resigned during the last week and are going to seek a better lot in the land of promise. The well-known and intelligent translator of the State Department, Mr. Greenhow, is about to go to California."[4]

Unlike most of those racing west, Greenhow had arranged a diplomatic mission that would take him—and Rose—to Mexico, which he had been hoping to revisit for a long time. So much for Rose's dream of going to Italy.

President Taylor named Greenhow a special diplomatic agent with instructions to settle land claims of American citizens that had been assumed by the United States on the signing of the Treaty of Guadalupe Hidalgo.[5] The war had lasted less than two years, and the United States had ended up with half of Mexico, taking land that would become America's Wild West: California, New Mexico, Arizona, Nevada, Utah, and more. Secretary of State John M. Clayton sent Greenhow a list of unsettled claims and asked him to find proof for the legitimate claims and tag the many he thought were fraudulent. He gave Robert five months.[6]

Rose arranged for her sister Ellen Cutts to care for the couple's three surviving daughters, then between seven and fourteen, and she set off on the perilous journey with her still ailing husband.[7]

The Greenhows took a California-bound steamer and got off in Mobile Bay, Alabama, in mid-May 1850, after what Robert reported to the secretary was a "most fatiguing" seven days.[8] Rose ever after was subject to awful bouts of seasickness, but she never let it stop her from traveling. They waited there for the British steamer Severn, which took them via Havana to Vera Cruz on the Mexican coast. The voyage across the Gulf of Mexico took about four days.[9]

The Severn, known as an "ocean stagecoach," was heavy and cumbersome,[10] which made her ungainly and uncomfortable under way. But in good weather, passengers enjoyed watching a wide variety of birds, pods of whales, playful dolphins, and pastels of flying fish that, when caught by the sunlight, seemed to hang in the air like an iridescent rainbow.[11] When the moon was nearly full, as it was the night the Greenhows left port,[12] it seemed to rise from the horizon "like a mass of fire, unlike anything seen in the northern hemisphere," according to a local guidebook. And when there were occasional *nortes*—fierce blasts of wind from the north—the air filled with sand, the sky darkened, and waves pounded with such force on the beach "that the whole line of coast was one sheet of foam."[13]

The vessel had cabins that opened onto one of two saloons. The ladies had one saloon for their exclusive use between 9:00 A.M. and 9:00 P.M. Men congregated in the other,[14] often gambling, which began as soon as the breakfast dishes were cleared away.[15] Dinner was served at 4:00 P.M., tea at 7:00 P.M. "Rats were always troublesome," wrote one passenger. "They ate the mail bags (which were made of hide) and gnawed the corks out of many champagne bottles."[16]

The *Severn* entered Vera Cruz through a narrow channel lined with sunken coral reefs and dropped anchor under the western wall of the castle of San Juan de Ulna, a fortress that guarded the entrance to the port. The weather was soft and balmy, the city surrounded by mountains of sand formed by the blustery *nortes*.[17] Trees were heavy with tropical fruit— papayas, guavas, bananas, oranges, and lemons. There were palms and cacao trees bearing cocoa pods, whose beans were roasted to make chocolate. The main street was long and wide, with large houses and flowers of every color and fragrance. "There is not a carriage in the street," wrote visiting author Frances Erskine Inglis Calderón de la Barca, "nothing but the men with wide trousers slit up the side of the leg, immense hats and blankets or serapes, merely a closed blanket, more or less fine, with a hole for the head to go through; and the women with rebozos, long colored cotton scarves, or pieces of ragged stuff, thrown over the head and crossing the left shoulder." Indian women with plaited hair wore large straw hats and petticoats of two colors, with their babies slung over their backs.[18] Rose had never seen such exotic sights. The colors were breathtaking, the poverty appalling.

A nine-passenger coach took the Greenhows from Vera Cruz to Mexico City, a four-day, 250-mile trip from the warm, humid coast through barren desert sands and lush jungle into the mountains of the interior. Passengers sat three abreast, with the person in the backless middle seat leaning on or clinging to a leather strap for safety and support.[19]

In Mexico City, the Greenhows settled into a residence in the Calle de

Palmas y Plateros. As American diplomats, they were quickly swept into the social life of the city and became frequent guests at the French embassy, where their fluency with the language made them welcome.

Shortly after they arrived, the Greenhows were introduced to José Yves Limantour, a charming and courageous French entrepreneur and land speculator who had been active in the arms trade along the California coast for several years. "Cool, self-possessed, and as brave as a man could be, he had confronted death in almost every form by land and sea,"[20] wrote one of his contemporaries. Limantour was not well educated, but he had traveled widely and had good business sense. With Mexico in a perpetual state of revolution, his weapons trade was thriving.[21]

Limantour told Robert Greenhow he held title to hundreds of thousands of acres of land in and around Yerba Buena, the little Mexican settlement that was fast becoming the city of San Francisco.[22] He sought Robert's advice on how to prove his claims to the California Land Commission, the U.S. panel being set up to rule on the legitimacy of thousands of Mexican land grants in what had suddenly become hugely valuable U.S. territory.[23] If Limantour's documents were defensible, the Greenhows might have struck their own source of gold in California.

The French speculator and the American diplomat met several times to discuss the prospects, switching between French and Spanish in their conversations. At least once, Limantour brought a bundle of papers to the Greenhow residence, and Robert pored over them for hours, with Rose leaning over his shoulder.[24] The documents, written in Spanish and English, included maps of Goat Island in the middle of San Francisco Bay and the island of Cedros in lower California, lands Greenhow recognized because he had written about them in his history of Oregon and California. There was much more, including a large section of what would soon be the waterfront district of San Francisco. After the Frenchman left that evening, Robert spread out a map of California and explained carefully to Rose the geography of the bay area—and Limantour's claim to the heart of the most exciting, fastest-growing boomtown in the world.[25] This could make them all rich.

Greenhow's diplomatic mission, meanwhile, was going nowhere, and he and Rose decided to head straight for California.[26] He sent a dispatch to the new secretary of state, Daniel Webster, on October 23 saying the Mexican government had failed to provide the documents necessary to settle U.S. claims. His efforts to persuade the foreign minister to live up to Mexico's treaty obligations had been "a mere waste of word," Robert reported.

He said he was leaving for Acapulco on the Pacific coast to catch a steamer for San Francisco, "where I intend to establish myself."[27]

The terms of Robert's deal with Limantour were never revealed, but the Greenhows traveled overland to Acapulco,[28] where they booked passage on the new three-masted sidewheel steamship *California*, a packet that carried mail and passengers between Panama City and San Francisco.[29]

By the time the Greenhows boarded the vessel, the *California* was already crowded with gold seekers who had embarked at Panama City. The ship, built to carry 180 passengers, had 214 aboard, including 5 families with slaves. There were cabins for only 50 or 60, which left the rest, mostly laborers and miners, relegated to steerage.[30]

The Greenhows found some familiar faces among their fellow passengers, including their old rivals John and Jessie Benton Frémont, who were traveling with a child and servant.[31] California had just been admitted to the Union as a free state, and Frémont had been sworn in as one of its first two senators. Jessie, almost four months pregnant with their second child, was suffering from a fever and not happy to see Rose heading for her new home state. "I barely spoke to her," she sniffed in a letter to her closest friend, Lizzie Blair Lee, the daughter of an influential Washington newspaper editor.[32]

The Greenhows found a friendlier traveling companion in Richard D. Cutts, Dolley Madison's brother-in-law, who likely could give them news of the Greenhow girls, then living with his niece and nephew.

The ship's log shows that the voyage from Panama to San Francisco took 19½ days, with stops at Acapulco and Mazatlán in Mexico and San Diego, Santa Barbara, and Monterey in California.[33] That was a long time to avoid bumping into an unfriendly face on deck or in the dining room. Yet even in tight quarters, the atmosphere was usually enjoyable. Levi Stowell, a passenger on his first voyage to San Francisco, wrote in his journal that people had "plenty of fun on deck, all kinds of games going on, singing, stories, etc."

The Greenhows had spent almost six months in Mexico. Robert regained his health, cut his ties with the federal bureaucracy—at least temporarily—and he and Rose had high hopes for a new start in the American West.

CHAPTER 18

San Francisco

City of Dreams

THE *CALIFORNIA* STEAMED into San Francisco Bay on November 21, 1850. From the deck, Rose and Robert could see a harbor bristling with the masts of a thousand vessels of every size and design, many lying low in the water, their cargoes still on board after their crews abandoned ship in the pell-mell rush to the goldfields. The city, built on and around the hills rising from the bay, was beginning to take shape, with streets and well-designed commercial buildings supplanting the ramshackle huts and cabins that had previously been thrown up on any available hillside. For the Greenhows, a new chapter in life was opening. Little did they know how short and sad it would be.

Eleven well-equipped wharves jutted into the bay[1] to serve even the largest ships. The wharves were small cities unto themselves, with shops, restaurants, and bars lining the waterfront. They were busy night and day, teeming with sailors, merchants, and dockworkers, wagons, horses, and ships' cargoes of every description. Lining the shore were tents, shanties, and shacks where transient miners camped. Only a few blocks away, workmen were building comfortable homes and offices for the bankers, businessmen, and lawyers who hastened to serve the new mining business and establish themselves.

The lack of roads across the rough terrain was a major problem, and city fathers were working with contractors to build plank roads along the steep hillsides, over deep gulches, and across soft ground. Rock, gravel, and brick were in short supply, but timber was plentiful, and redwood made particularly sturdy frames and roadbeds because it was hard and didn't rot. But the plank roads were uneven and difficult to negotiate on foot. Accidents were frequent.

A great fire had swept San Francisco the previous year, and when the Greenhows arrived, reconstruction was still under way. The city, which before the discovery of gold two years earlier had been the tranquil Mexican village of Yerba Buena, was growing so fast that even fire couldn't stop it.

California had become the nation's thirty-first state on September 9, and fortune seekers of every description were pouring into San Francisco, the closest major port to the goldfields north and east. More than thirty-six thousand people a year came from Mexico, New England, the American South, Europe, and even Canton, in China. Thousands raced to the goldfields, of course, but many more, including a few women, remained in San Francisco as traders and merchants, bent on profiting from those who beat the odds and struck gold—or didn't. The city boasted dozens of restaurants, hotels, refreshment stands and vendors, boardinghouses, and saloons, many featuring a bevy of "soiled doves," as women of questionable character were called.[2] Built on the uncertain prospects of men panning for gold, the economy gyrated between boom and bust, but growth was everywhere. So was disease. The air was filthy with construction sand, and dust hung in the dense fog that often engulfed the harbor. People dumped buckets of slop out of their windows into the streets, and cholera broke out, killing a dozen people a day.[3]

Sometime after the Greenhows' arrival, Robert set up an office at 135 Montgomery Street, which ran along the shore before the bay was filled in to create more land in the waterfront district.[4] Montgomery Street was popular with local businessmen, bankers, lawyers, assayers, gold buyers, and shippers. The Pacific Bath Company opened at 8:00 A.M. and closed at 10:00 P.M. An auction house called F. B. Folger & Company sold off the properties of other merchants who went broke. Collins & Wheeland, a restaurant across the street from the Mining Exchange, served up fifty-five barrels of whiskey a week. Warehouses were built on the land closest to the water, but the ground was never firm. Quicksand swallowed several animals and a few men, probably drunks, who fell into it unseen every year.[5]

Despite the chaotic atmosphere, the Greenhows and other Southerners established their own small social circle, built lavish homes, and entertained one another in the manner they knew and brought west with them. Although outnumbered three to one by Northerners, the Southerners, led by Senator William Gwin, formerly of Tennessee, observed family tradition, employing black servants to look after their grand mansions and hosting elegant balls and receptions for the city's elite. Gwin introduced the Greenhows to San Francisco society, inviting them to a party at his home, where guests sipped champagne from crystal glasses imported from France.[6]

The other U.S. senator in those first days of statehood was John C. Frémont, whose wife still would have nothing to do with Rose, even in a new city where the two ladies had more in common with each other than they did with the relatively few other women in town. "I never spoke to her after we left the ship or visited her which piqued her very much," Jessie Frémont wrote.[7] Rose ignored Jessie in her memoir but expressed her low regard for the state's second senator with an editorial stiletto: "He seemed really to long for the primitive life he had marked out, and confessed himself utterly unsuited for the part he had been appointed to play upon the world's great stage—in which opinion I heartily concurred."[8] The Pathfinder lost his bid for a full Senate term three months after they all arrived, but the Frémonts stayed on in San Francisco while planning to build an adobe house on a forty-four-thousand-acre ranch they called Las Mariposas—the Butterflies—in the gold-rich Sierra foothills near Yosemite Valley.

On Saturday evening, May 4, 1851, the anniversary of the big fire, an even more devastating inferno swept the city. It started in Mr. Oliver's paint store on Clay Street, and within minutes flames engulfed one block after another. The fire swept down Battery Street north of Clark's Point,[9] and sparks ignited ships in the harbor, burning many to the waterline. "Its progress was so rapid that people occupying houses only a block away were unable to remove their goods," wrote witnesses T. A. Barry and B. A. Patten. "The roofs of buildings, seemingly too remote for danger, caught fire like powder, the flames creeping from street to street like a laid train, finding fresh combustible in the dry board walls, paper and cloth interiors; and the wind—sleeping at the fire's commencement—now roaring like a pyromaniac . . . adding new dire to the dire confusion."[10] The flames scorched the paint off the walls at John and Jessie Frémont's home on Stockton Street. "On and on through the long night it raged and roared," wrote Jessie Frémont, who was in bed recovering from childbirth when the sirens sounded.[11]

Records don't show where in San Francisco the Greenhows were living when the fire broke out, but like the Frémonts, many watched helplessly as houses, businesses, and belongings went up in flames. More fires erupted in the months to come, sometimes set deliberately by looters and thieves. To Robert Greenhow, who had lost his mother in the Richmond Theatre fire and nearly died himself, it was a nightmare returned.

Rose stuck it out in San Francisco four months longer, but she had been away from the children for more than a year, and in September 1851, she left her husband to fend for himself while she began the long journey back home to the East Coast.

She did not travel alone. Passenger lists show she was accompanied by a servant and sailed on the same ship with her friends the Gwins, her social benefactors in San Francisco. After taking a ship to Panama, they crossed the sixty-mile Isthmus of Panama via an overland route that was fraught with danger but faster than the much longer and even more hazardous sea route around Cape Horn. A British writer, Frank Marryat, made the trip a few months before Rose and described the "tortuous path, which had been burrowed through the forest."

From the old ruined houses of Panama, a run-down Spanish city enjoying a sudden burst of popularity from the traffic to and from California, home-bound travelers hired mule trains to take them in groups up into the mountains. The traffic along the stretch of land between Pacific and Atlantic was two-way, with wild-eyed fortune hunters heading west and at least as many "emigrants from the land of promise" making their way home. "Some were returning rich in gold dust and scales, but the greater part was far poorer than when first they started to realize their golden dreams," Marryat wrote. "Stamped with vice and intemperance, without baggage or money, they were fit for robbery and murder to any extent." For a lady accustomed to dining at the president's table, Rose was keeping rough company.

At nightfall, the travelers reached the Washington Hotel, which advertised forty beds and food for the weary, but there they found a log hut perched on a hill with an interior "sufficient to destroy all appetite. Round it, and stretching for yards, there were mules, drivers and passengers, clustered and clamorous as bees without a hive." Even with the inflated prices charged by its Yankee owner, the Washington ran out of food long before all the hungry had been fed, and the "forty beds" advertised along the road consisted of frames of wood five feet long, stacked three high, with soiled canvas stretched over the frames. Altogether they occupied about the same space as two four-poster beds—and there was no vacancy.

From the hotel, the mule train wended down a narrow rocky path through thick forest, where palm trees and creepers blocked the light. Marryat described "splashing through gurgling muddy streams that concealed loose and treacherous stones, stumbling over fallen trees that lay across our road, burying ourselves to the mules' girths in filthy swamps, where on either side dead and putrid mules were lying amidst lightning, thunder and incessant darkness."[12]

At Gorgona, the east-bound travelers gave up their mules and bargained with the local Indians for dugout canoes that would take them down the notorious Chagres River to the sea. Naked boatmen poled the boats through strong currents and around downed trees and obstacles that jutted into the river, watching for alligators that slithered into the water from the muddy banks. The jungle was lush with tropical vegetation—palm, cocoa, orange, lemon, and banana trees—and passengers shivered at the shrill cries of monkeys and baboons hanging from the branches. Insects swarmed in the sultry air, carrying malaria, yellow fever, and the local menace, Chagres fever, to unwitting travelers who did not yet know how they contracted such horrible diseases.[13] The next time Rose came this way, there would be a train.

When the party finally emerged at Chagres on the Mosquito Gulf in early October,[14] Rose and the Gwins boarded the United States mail steamer *Illinois,* another packet built for the California run after the discovery of gold created demand for regular service between east and west.[15] They arrived in New York on October 18[16] and soon headed south, where Senator and Mrs. Gwin would now be her neighbors in the Federal City.

Rose was suffering from a tropical disease she had picked up on the long journey, but once home, she recuperated and quickly got back to work. She and the children settled into a small house on H Street, between 15th and 16th, a few blocks from the White House. Her correspondence shows that while she was happy to be back in a city that lived and breathed politics, she was already planning another trip.

Rose wrote Virginian John Y. Mason, who had been secretary of the navy and attorney general under President Polk, to arrange a business meeting at Mason's home in Richmond. "I arrived here about three weeks ago from San Francisco, after a passage of 35 days," she told him. "I was very ill for the first ten days with Chagres fever. I was fortunate however in having only a slight attack and am now almost restored to health." She probably suffered from malaria contracted during the trip across Panama or perhaps a somewhat less virulent fever caused by the bite of a Panamanian sand fly. "I left Mr. Greenhow quite well and am charged with many

SÁN ʃ⋅ⁿ⋅ʃCISCO • 161

<u>commissions</u> to you," Rose wrote, adding that she would like to visit the Masons in Richmond "for my commissions far exceed the capacities of a letter."[17]

One reason Rose wanted to see John Mason was to seek his support for James Buchanan, the Greenhows' longtime patron, who was running against Senator Stephen A. Douglas for the 1852 Democratic presidential nomination. Mason was active in Virginia politics, and Buchanan, a Northerner whose sympathies lay with the South, needed Virginia to solidify his Southern base. Buchanan was a serious contender, and Mason did offer to help, but at the convention in June, Franklin Pierce of New Hampshire emerged as a compromise candidate and went on to win the election by a narrow margin. Buchanan returned to Wheatland, his country home in Lancaster County, Pennsylvania.[18]

Robert Greenhow had not found steady work yet in California, so family finances were tight. After visiting her sister-in-law, Mary Greenhow, in Winchester, Virginia, Rose sought help from a family friend, Peter G. Washington, assistant secretary of the Treasury. In a letter written with black ink on fine white paper and fixed with red sealing wax, she acknowledged receipt of an order for $1,000 and asked for a draft to allow her to cash it immediately: "You will increase the obligation I am already under to you sir by attending to this."[19]

Rose was unabashed about soliciting favors from influential friends, and she appears to have sought a position for Robert—it's not clear from whom. On August 28, 1852, Buchanan wrote to congratulate her on having "successfully accomplished your mission in behalf of Mr. Greenhow," that Buchanan supposed she was "now reposing on your laurels at Warrenton Springs and receiving the homage of all persons of good taste there assembled." Buchanan invited Rose to visit him in Lancaster County, insisting that his election defeat did not weigh on him and that he was in good spirits: "Never have I been so contented and even happy as since I have lived at Wheatland. I find that a life . . . in which I can just employ myself as I please is exceedingly agreeable. I no longer indulge any ambitious aspirations. My defeat cost me not a single pang. Indeed, I felt this more on account of my friends than on my own account."[20] Even then, the well-worn line of a defeated candidate was painfully transparent. Buchanan's political ambition would soon get the best of him again.

As the Pennsylvanian surmised, Rose was spending part of the summer in Warrenton Springs, a famous mountain resort and mineral spring that attracted prominent visitors escaping the insufferable heat of Washington,

Richmond, and Southern plantations. Robert Greenhow had not seen Rose and the children in more than a year, and records suggest he joined them for a family vacation. The Rasmussen San Francisco passenger list shows "R. Greenhow," most likely Greenhow, arriving in San Francisco via Panama aboard the *Golden Gate* on August 18,[21] probably returning from the East to accept the appointment Rose had helped arrange for him as associate law clerk of the California Land Commission. Rose remained in Washington with her daughters Florence, then sixteen; Gertrude, fourteen; and Leila, not yet ten. Rose was thirty-nine years old—and pregnant again.

The California Land Commission was established by Congress in 1851 to deal with hundreds of property claims that Mexican rancheros, prospectors, and settlers attempted to establish under the laws of the new state, following its transfer from Mexican sovereignty. The sparsely settled but suddenly valuable land was being seized by squatters and opportunists of every stripe following the discovery of gold, and the commission was charged with sorting out conflicting claims, some of which dated back to Spanish rule and were based on uncertain documentation and vague boundary descriptions. Greenhow, a founding member of the Historical Society of the State of California,[22] had hoped to be one of the three commissioners appointed by the president, and his Spanish-language skills and knowledge of California and its history undoubtedly qualified him. But the commissioners, none of whom spoke Spanish or had any background in Mexican culture, already had been named. As a result, the physician-turned-diplomat-turned-lawyer accepted the post of associate law agent at a salary of $1,500, less than he had made in Washington.[23] Greenhow went to work in the commission's offices on the third floor of the Parrott's Iron Building at 148 California Street. It was good to be working, but he was disappointed to find the job distasteful. Greenhow spent most of his time taking testimony from poor, uneducated Mexicans who had no understanding of how to prove they owned their land.[24]

Many of the land claims and counterclaims were poorly documented or downright fraudulent, but one stood out for its sheer audacity. In February 1853, barely a month before the commission's deadline for filing new claims and nearly three years *after* he had first carried his bundle of documents to Rose and Robert Greenhow's door in Mexico City, José Yves Limantour formally declared that some sixteen thousand acres of land within San Francisco—roughly half of the occupied portion of the city—belonged to him.[25] On March 2, the last day for filing, Limantour presented an additional six claims to the commission covering even larger stretches of land across most of the state.[26]

If approved, Limantour would become a very rich man. And if Greenhow was still advising him, there was every reason to believe he would become rich as well.

Rose, sensing an opportunity, wrote Buchanan asking him to prevail upon President Pierce, who had defeated Buchanan, to elevate Robert from a staff position to a voting commissioner on the land commission. It could have given him a key role in judging the Limantour case. It is not clear whether or not Greenhow, who had once advised Limantour, still had an understanding with him, but documents reveal he was involved in the case as a lawyer for the commission.[27] Even more intriguing, Rose herself later became embroiled in the case.

Her request put Buchanan in an uncomfortable position. He admired the Greenhows and was happy to help a friend, but he didn't want to offend President Pierce, who had been in office only two weeks. Buchanan was in line to become ambassador to the Court of St. James's in London and did not want to jeopardize his chances.

On March 21, 1853, Buchanan composed a careful reply to Rose, saying he had refused to recommend a niece's husband for an appointment as a naval officer, nor had he sent up a friend's son for a job with an Indian agency, but he would do his best to help Greenhow. However, he told Rose, he would have to act discreetly and not write to Pierce because the three commissioners had just been appointed and he couldn't ask that one be removed to make a place for Robert. "I doubt very much whether he will do it," Buchanan wrote, "but when the deed has been actually done then I will adopt my own mode of processing, without informing you of it, at least for the present."[28]

If Buchanan intervened with President Pierce on Greenhow's behalf, he did not meet with success, for Greenhow's position with the land commission remained unchanged. But the Virginia gentleman, who had grown up in comfortable circumstances, appeared to live well in San Francisco. He moved into newly built living quarters at 8 and 9 Montgomery Block, on the corner of Montgomery and Washington streets, a lavish building where many of the most prominent men in the city rented rooms.[29] The design was more garish than anything in Washington, with its doorway of cut stone and Roman Doric columns modeled after the Diocletian baths.[30]

Greenhow furnished his quarters in equally grand fashion, outfitting his rooms for entertaining eighteen guests for dinner with the requisite punch bowls and punch glasses, soup plates, finger bowls, champagne glasses, and forty-eight dinner plates. Two candelabra and six decanters were on hand, as was a child's chair,[31] suggesting that he expected Rose to join him with the children after the new baby was born.

ON APRIL 2, 1853, Rose gave birth in Washington to another daughter. She named the baby Rose, the third girl the mother named after herself.[32] Little Rose would never know her father.

On February 17, 1854, when she was ten months old, Robert Greenhow was walking along Pacific Street near Mason, a few blocks from his San Francisco quarters, when he slipped off a section of planked road and fell six feet to the ground, disabling his left leg and suffering what the local newspaper described as "intense pain in his hip."[33] The injury was more extensive than that, or more likely an infection set in, for on Monday, March 27, six weeks after his accident, Greenhow died. News of his demise was published three hours later in the *Daily Alta California*'s evening edition: "Sudden death—Hon. Robert Greenhow, late Associate law agent of the United States before the U.S. Land Commission, died suddenly about 11 o'clock this morning."

The next day, the newspaper ran a longer story, reporting that "his nervous system appears to have been fatally injured by the accident. He remained in complete possession of his senses until Sunday morning." The story described Greenhow as a "man of great industry and varied attainments . . . universally respected among his acquaintances, of singular purity, brightness and singleness of character and purpose." His funeral, held the next afternoon at 3:00 P.M. in his rooms on Montgomery Block, was attended by his associates on the land commission, the judge, officers of the district court, and several members of the California bar. As was the custom, the land commission adjourned for a week in a gesture of respect, and the commissioners wore black badges of mourning for thirty days.[34]

News of Greenhow's death did not appear in the East until April 27, 1854, after the *Illinois* steamed into New York carrying the latest dispatches from California.

The Baltimore *Sun,* in a front-page report that day in "Further News from California," noted, "From the California papers to the 1st of April: Robert Greenhow, late associate law agent of the United States for the California Land Commission, died in San Francisco on the 27th March."[35]

Washington's *Daily Globe* and the *Washington Sentinel* ran slightly longer pieces the following day.[36]

Rose may have learned of her husband's death from the newspapers, or a letter sent by mail packet could have reached her first. It would be seven years until Western Union would string a telegraph line across the continent.[37] Rose's official notice, written on pale blue stationery and signed by George Fisher, head of the California Land Commission, was dated March 31, 1854:

> Madam,
>   The painful duty, under the instructions of the Board, devolves upon me, to communicate to you, that Robert Greenhow Esq, your late consort and the Associate Law Agent of the M.S. to this Commission, is no more. He departed this life on the 27th inst. At 11 o'clk A.M.[38]

Is no more. That message—stark, without details, without explanation, and with barely a hint of sympathy—informed Rose Greenhow she was a widow.

CHAPTER 19

Widow

ROBERT'S DEATH LEFT Rose achingly, overwhelmingly, alone. She had to comfort her grieving daughters and settle Robert's estate, bringing back painful memories. There were long winter evenings when the widow, once more in mourning silk, repaired to her writing desk to share a glimpse of her world with her old friend James Buchanan. As weeks turned to months and the pain eased some, Rose gradually began to embrace life again. But she carried herself with a dignity and sadness that caused many a man to reach out to her, if only to extend a protective arm.

While Rose was grieving, the country took an ominous step that abrogated the Missouri Compromise and reopened bitter wounds by proposing to let white settlers decide for themselves whether or not to allow slavery in the Kansas and Nebraska territories. Senator Stephen A. Douglas of Illinois sponsored the Kansas-Nebraska Act, expecting that Kansas, the southernmost of the two territories, would vote to join the Union as a slave state. Under the Missouri Compromise that had held for more than thirty years, the lands of the Louisiana Purchase above 36 degrees 30 minutes north, which would include both Kansas and Nebraska, were to remain free, but Douglas thought he could win Southern support by leaving open the possibility for one more slave state in the growing nation. He got his bill passed, but he badly miscalculated the outcome. Pro- and antislavery settlers poured into Kansas, a strategic junction of north, south, and west, and the frontier erupted in violent clashes that signaled the anger and intransigence of the long, smoldering race issue. As the rest of the nation watched with growing horror, "Bleeding Kansas" presented a precursor to the bitter civil war drawing ever closer.[1]

Once again, Rose became a fixture in the Senate gallery and wrote Buchanan, who was by then United States ambassador to Great Britain, to keep him abreast of political developments.

Having lost none of her savvy, Rose also filed a damage suit against the city of San Francisco, and five months later, on August 28, 1854, the city's Board of Aldermen awarded her $10,000 as compensation for Robert Greenhow's life.[2] That same year, probably thanks to the lobbying of influential friends, the Thirty-third Congress awarded her $42,000 to make up for Robert's "salaries and incidental expenses" as a staff member of the federally financed California Land Commission.[3]

The payments provided Rose with a substantial nest egg that would keep her comfortable for some time to come. She moved out of the H Street house in the autumn of 1855 and, with her baby daughter, into Brown's Indian Queen Hotel[4] on the north side of the Avenue between 6th and 7th streets. The fashionable hotel, once the principal lodging for Indian chiefs who came to Washington to negotiate treaties, was a gathering place for Southern congressmen who favored its proximity to the Capitol.[5] They often gathered at the bar, famous for its tall, smooth mint juleps made with old bourbon and bitters.[6] On rainy days, plantation owners warmed themselves by the fire while their slaves waited outside on the wet sidewalk.[7]

The older Greenhow daughters, Florence and Gertrude, had grown into beautiful young women. Florence, almost twenty years old, married S. Tredwell Moore, a West Point graduate from Ohio who had been an Indian fighter in California before becoming a prosperous miner in far west Minnesota, where the couple went to live. Gertrude, with long auburn hair and light blue eyes, was seventeen. She and Leila, then about ten, were enrolled at the Patapsco Female Institute, a Maryland boarding school about forty miles from their home. Little Rose was a toddler and her mother's only constant companion.

Barely forty, with only a hint of crepe at the neck and a few creases around her eyes, Rose Greenhow was still a handsome woman. She had spent almost twenty years raising children and promoting her husband's career. Now she embarked on a new course, disclosed in a few surviving letters of her correspondence with Buchanan. The Pennsylvanian, a reserved man who never married, kept a certain distance, even with friends.[8] But through flattery and gentle humor, Rose was able to pierce his armor. After two years in London, Buchanan tired of engagement in U.S.-British quarreling, most recently over Britain's maintenance of colonies in Central America, and wanted to run for president. He was ready to come home.[9]

In their correspondence, Rose and Buchanan also shared personal news. They loved to gossip and often opened their letters with the latest rumors. Buchanan told Rose in a four-page missive on November 23, 1855, that he had heard she had remarried, "and I scarcely knew by what name or where to address you." Rose, who had a serious suitor but was not contemplating marriage,[10] must have wondered who was passing on such stories—or if Buchanan was just fishing for news. He complimented her on her descriptions of her travels through California and allowed that he repeated her observations at dinner parties whenever he was asked about the American West. He also congratulated Rose on Florence marrying "so advantageously" and added: "She, as well as Gertrude, were great favorites of mine. Gertrude will, I think, resemble you much more than Florence though I doubt whether she will be handsomer than her mother."[11] They were comforting words for a lonely middle-aged widow.

By early winter in Washington, the days turned cold, and snow began to fall. On December 23, the Avenue was covered in deep white drifts.[12] Rose could hear carolers singing outside the entrance to Brown's Hotel, which was gaily decorated with ribbons and greens for the season. The festive atmosphere brought back memories of happier Christmases with Robert when the voices of the Greenhow children filled the house. Rose repaired to her room in a sad and reflective mood to answer Buchanan's letter: "Believe me, my friend, my heart clings with a jealous tenacity to its old memories and its old friendships, and I would treasure them as the evergreens of life when its dreary winter sets in." She assured Buchanan that she had no plans to remarry but confessed that "a gentleman of fortune and respectable position" had asked for her hand, "but there were many grave objections to such a step, wealth being the last important requisite."

Rose gave the diplomat no clue to the identity of the "gentleman of fortune," insisting only: "At this time I have not the most remote idea of any such entanglement."[13]

The man in question may have been Erasmus Darwin Keyes, a dashing widower and army officer who later confessed to finding Rose persuasive and charming.[14] Had Rose married him, however, she would have found herself the wife of a high-ranking Union officer at the outbreak of war in 1861, and history might have taken a different course at the First Battle of Bull Run.

In her letter to Buchanan, Rose teasingly turned the question of marriage back to him: "It has been confidentially said that you were coming home to marry Mrs. Polk," Rose wrote, referring to the widow of President James Polk, who had died six years earlier.

The primary purpose of Rose's letter was to persuade Buchanan to run for president. The Kansas-Nebraska Act had split the Democrats and given birth to the Republican Party, a political agglomeration composed of northern Whigs, Know-Nothings, and Democrats disillusioned with party leaders who tolerated the extension of slavery. President Franklin Pierce, a New Englander, had sided with the South and signed the legislation, enraging his fellow Northerners and effectively killing his chances for reelection. Buchanan was fortunate to be out of the country during much of the debate and in a position to return as a voice of security and moderation.[15]

Rose thought Pierce a timid leader and told Buchanan that the president's cabinet members "move him about, as a pawn on a chess board." Pierce had said he would not run for reelection, although he later changed his mind. For the sake of the Democratic Party, Rose wrote, Buchanan should seize the opportunity to run: "You are spoken of a great deal as the candidate, being as they say a safe man to rally upon. The South would rally upon you. I think so far it has been wise for you to be out of the way. But the time is approaching for you to be on the ground."

Rose appealed to her friend's vanity, saying she knew he would insist that he held no presidential aspirations and preferred private life, but it would be selfish of him not to think of the needs of the country. "The great statesman, the leader of a powerful party has no right to consult his inclinations and rest in inglorious ease when his services are necessary for the success of a great cause," Rose wrote, underlining her words for emphasis. "I do hope that if you allow your name to be used, that you will enter into the center with heart and soul."[16]

Rose had a personal stake in the campaign, too. With Robert Greenhow dead and the Democratic Party floundering, Rose was in danger of being eclipsed by her old rival Jessie Benton Frémont, whose husband was being urged to run for president as a Republican. Like his father-in-law, Senator Thomas Hart Benton, John Frémont had always considered himself a Dem-

ocrat, but he and Jessie understood that the Democratic presidential nominee would have to support the extension of slavery into Kansas. Rather
than compromise their long-held conviction that slavery was immoral, the
Frémonts chose to ally themselves with the fledgling Republicans.[17] If
they were to win, Rose would most certainly be on the outs.

Rose Greenhow had never hesitated to manage her husband's career
and frequently intervened with Buchanan on Robert's behalf. Now she
was trying to manage Buchanan's future as well.

She was also spending a lot of time alone. During the unusually cold
winter of 1856, Rose complained to Buchanan that she didn't like being
"brought in contact with the masses" in the crowded parlors of her hotel
and often retreated to the privacy of her own room, a "haven of rest." With
trepidation, she watched the Frémont campaign gaining momentum and
was delighted when Buchanan announced he was returning from England.
"I am so rejoiced that you are coming home that I would make of the
whole nation a fatted calf to welcome you," she wrote him on February 11.

Rose told Buchanan that Pierce had changed his mind and was running
for reelection, but that even Buchanan's detractors gave him an edge: "Mr.
Pierce is toiling hard to get the nomination," she wrote. "Isn't it strange
that cunning men are so often foiled with their own weapons? I am an
amused looker on. Your friends are all in good spirits and many who do
not wish it think that you will get the nomination. . . . The President looks
worn and anxious."

Rose closed her letter on a solicitous note: "Do I not seem somewhat
presumptuous to write you a long stupid letter whilst you are enjoying the
City of Cities—Paris. I hope you will see all its wonders, so as to give me
a vivid picture of your first impressions and do not let new scenes and new
friends efface the impression of old and tired ones."[18] Rose sent her letter
to Buchanan through Secretary of War Jefferson Davis, a friend she could
trust to give it special handling.

That spring, she returned to California to wrap up Robert's affairs. She
also had a continuing interest in the Limantour land claims, which by that
time were being challenged in court. She took Little Rose and a servant
with her on the long journey and sent Leila, not yet a teenager, to visit Florence in Minnesota.[19]

When Rose arrived in San Francisco, she found the city had lost its
magic. She was appalled by the increase in crime and told Buchanan in a
letter in early June that she was "very very homesick and shall embrace the

first opportunity that I prudently can to turn my back upon the land of the setting sun and its golden gates forever."

Everywhere she went the talk was of lawlessness and growing threats to the Union. In the evening, when Rose walked the city streets, she often encountered "citizen soldiers" bearing bayonets that glistened in the moonlight, and she didn't like the vigilante spirit. "The country at this moment is in a State of Revolution," she wrote to Buchanan. "People have in all ages held it as their sacred right to resort to revolution when the evils of government could not be amended in any other way."

Rose closed her letter by assuring Buchanan that her influential California friends considered him "a safe man for president." Then she added coyly: "You know how ardently I have always wished to hail you as our Chief."[20]

The Republicans, meanwhile, were about to hold their convention in Philadelphia, where they would choose John C. Frémont as their presidential nominee. Jessie Frémont was elated at the prospect of living in the White House, despite a bitter rift with her father, who refused to abandon his party and would campaign for Buchanan against his own son-in-law.

The Greenhow party, mother, daughter, and slave, left San Francisco on September 5 aboard the Pacific Mail Company packet *Golden Age* and arrived in Panama thirteen days later in the midst of the rainy season. The completion of the Panama Rail Road the year before made the trip across the isthmus a four-hour train ride instead of an arduous trek through mountains and jungle. It was the first transcontinental railroad, and Rose recognized the political potential of such a convenience in the United States.

In the new port of Aspinwall on the Caribbean, they boarded the *Illinois,* the same ship that had brought her home from California five years before and had carried the unhappy news of her husband's death. With no refrigeration to preserve meat, an assortment of live chickens, turkeys, geese, ducks, lambs, pigs, and cattle was carried aboard for consumption at sea, but Rose ate as little as possible to control her chronic seasickness.[21] A front-page article in the *New York Herald* reported the ship's arrival in New York on September 27, only 21½ days after the Greenhows left San Francisco.[22]

That same afternoon, Rose sat down in her room at Manhattan's fashionable Metropolitan Hotel to write to Buchanan, advising him how to campaign against Frémont in California. She predicted a "hard contest" against the celebrated explorer. The Democratic Party in California was deeply divided, and the "Black Republicans," as Rose and other Democrats labeled them, presented a strong challenge. She advised Buchanan to come out late in the campaign in support of a Pacific railroad, a move that would be extremely popular in the West and serve to emphasize the Pathfinder's repeated failures in his search for a railway route to the coast. "Our friends think that if you would express yourself upon that point in a letter which will reach there a few days before the election, it could be circulated throughout the country and give you the state by a large majority,"[23] Rose wrote.

Buchanan took her advice. On Tuesday, November 4, 1856, with former president Millard Fillmore running as a candidate of the American Know-Nothing Party, Buchanan captured every slave state but Maryland and five states in the North, including his native Pennsylvania. He won only 45 percent of the popular vote, but a comfortable 59 percent of the electoral college.[24] California, with four electoral votes, went to Buchanan, as Rose had predicted. "Words are feeble to express the fullness of my gratification at this just tribute to you, my old friend," she gushed in a letter to the president-elect, written from Brown's Hotel a few days after the election. "It is the fulfillment of my heart's dearest wish."[25]

The waning days of autumn 1856 were punctuated by long afternoon shadows, and leaves carpeted the ground in rich, soothing colors. Rose Greenhow had been a widow for two sad, difficult years, but now she had reason to rejoice. James Buchanan, one of her closest friends, had been elected the fifteenth president of the United States. And she was about to become one of the most powerful women in Washington.

CHAPTER 20

A Lady of Influence

SOON AFTER BUCHANAN'S election, Rose traveled overland across the Appalachians to visit her new in-laws in Columbus, Ohio, where Tredwell Moore's family lived. The conversation at supper turned to politics, and several guests were speculating about Buchanan's choices for his cabinet. Rose was amused that each person started by saying, "I heard from a confidential friend of his . . ."

The lady from Washington sat demurely listening to each guess, then— knowing her friend was keeping his cabinet selections to himself—finally spoke up: "Oh I know Mr. B. very well and I should not believe if his left hand were to tell me what he intended to do with his right."[1]

She delighted in relating the story to the president-elect and asked him if, in his season of triumph, he ever felt a sense of humility steal over him. "I always have, even in the small successes of life," she wrote curiously, "or is man's nature so different that success only makes him more Lordly and self-sufficient to meet the high behest of destiny."[2]

Rose seemed to be seeking a deeper, more thoughtful relationship with her old friend, or perhaps she was trying to warn him against the temptation to get carried away with his new high position. Arrogance, after all, has long been an affliction of those who occupy the White House. She knew Buchanan was a lonely man, a bachelor who had taken on his nieces and nephews as wards.[3] Except for his fascination with her gossip and Rose's relationship with other men, Buchanan did not appear interested in her romantically. Some modern historians insist he was asexual,[4] but he found Rose good company.

Following his election victory in November, Buchanan withdrew to his country estate at Wheatland to prepare for the change in administrations, which in those days took place in March. At the end of January, he visited Washington to confer with President Pierce and Senator Douglas, two rivals within his own party who bore much of the blame for the struggle over slavery taking place in Kansas.[5]

They dined at the National Hotel, where the president-elect and sixty or seventy other guests became violently ill with diarrhea and severe intestinal distress. The hotel closed in the wake of the "National Hotel disease," and rumors flew about the cause of the outbreak. Some suggested rats had fallen into the hotel water supply, others that poisonous sewer gas had seeped into the kitchen sink. A Philadelphia druggist told federal authorities he had discovered that thirty pounds of arsenic were sent to Washington from his office under suspicious circumstances while he was away. That led, of course, to allegations of a plot by abolitionists to assassinate the pro-South Buchanan.[6]

Rose, who loved intrigue, subscribed to the conspiracy theory. "This diabolical scheme was very near accomplishment, so far as regarded the life of President Buchanan, who was for a long time in a very critical condition, and it was only by the use of powerful stimulants that his constitution rallied from the effects of the poison," she wrote later in her memoir about the war years, disclosing also that she knew his supposed antidote. "He told me that often during the day at this time he was obliged to drink several tumblers of unadulterated brandy, to keep himself from entire physical exhaustion."[7]

Rose expressed dismay that after the inauguration Buchanan did not direct his attorney general, Judge Jeremiah S. Black of Pennsylvania, to investigate the incident. She claimed the president feared "the startling facts it would lay open to the world and that he shrank from the terrible exposure." Rose called it "a great weakness" on the part of her friend.[8] Modern historians attribute the outbreak to a contaminated water supply caused by broken pipes.[9]

Buchanan felt ill for weeks, but he recovered in time for his inauguration on March 4, 1857. The day dawned clear but windy,[10] and he was sworn into office by Rose's old family friend Roger Brooke Taney, chief justice of the United States.

Taney, by then almost eighty years old, "was an extremely plain-

Dolley Madison, wife of James Madison, the fourth president of the United States, was the most prominent social arbiter in Washington society for almost half a century. She was in many respects a role model for Rose Greenhow, who often had tea with Mrs. Madison at her home in Lafayette Square. *William S. Elwell, National Portrait Gallery, Smithsonian Institution/Art Resource, NY*

John C. Calhoun, a stubborn statesman from South Carolina and a key defender of slavery, was a friend and mentor to Rose Greenhow. In her memoir, she called him "the best and wisest man of this century." *G.P.A. Healy, National Portrait Gallery, Smithsonian Institution/Art Resource, NY*

Portrait of President Lincoln in 1864 by Anthony Berger. Lincoln had Rose Greenhow imprisoned on August 23, 1861, on charges of spying for the Confederate government. *Library of Congress*

31st July

All is activity. McClelland is busy night and day. but the panic is great and the attack is hourly expected. They believe that the attack will be made simultaneous from Edwards Ferry and Baltimore. Every effort is being made to find out who gave the alarm. A troop of Cavalry will start from here this morning to Harpers Ferry. dont give time for re-organizing.

Message from Rose Greenhow to General Beauregard written on July 31, 1861, ten days after the First Battle of Bull Run, the first major battle of the Civil War. *National Archives*

On July 10, 1861, Bettie Duvall carried this small silk purse with a coded message inside from Rose Greenhow to General Beauregard, telling him that Union forces were preparing to attack his headquarters in Manassas, Virginia. Miss Duvall hid the purse in her long silky hair, which she wound around her head. *National Archives*

"Scene in Uncle Sam's Senate. 17th April 1850." This lithograph by artist Edward W. Clay is a tongue-in-cheek portrayal of the scene on the Senate floor when Senator Henry S. Foote of Mississippi pulled a loaded revolver on Senator Thomas Hart Benton of Missouri. Benton (*center*) screamed, "Get out of the way, and let the assassin fire! Let the scoundrel use his weapon!" Foote (*left*) is being restrained from behind by Senator Andrew Pickens Butler of South Carolina. Also present in the scene are Daniel Webster and Henry Clay, as well as Vice President Millard Fillmore. In the background, gallery visitors flee in panic. *Library of Congress*

Explosion of the Peacemaker cannon on the USS *Princeton* on February 28, 1844, while it was cruising the Potomac River in Washington, D.C. Six people were killed, including the secretary of state, the secretary of the navy, and President Tyler's personal slave. *N. Currier lithograph, Library of Congress*

John C. Frémont, the explorer-politician who helped popularize settlement of the West by wagon train, was a longtime rival of Rose and Robert Greenhow. *Samuel Root, National Portrait Gallery, Smithsonian Institution/Art Resource, NY*

Jessie Benton Frémont, wife of John Frémont, made no secret of her disdain for Rose Greenhow. *National Portrait Gallery, Smithsonian Institution/Art Resource, NY*

James Buchanan, a stiff Pennsylvania legislator and lifelong bachelor, served as secretary of state and minister to Great Britain before being elected the country's fifteenth president. Buchanan corresponded with Rose Greenhow for years, and during his administration Rose was considered a grande dame of Washington society. *G.P.A. Healy, National Portrait Gallery, Smithsonian Institution/Art Resource, NY*

Presidential reception. President Buchanan and his niece Harriet Lane receive guests in the East Room of the White House. *Harper's Weekly*, March 13, 1858. *National Portrait Gallery, Smithsonian Institution/Art Resource, NY*

Balloon view of Washington and the U.S. Capitol before the dome was completed. *Harper's Weekly*, July 27, 1861. *Library of Congress*

INTERIOR OF LOWER BATTERY AT THE CHAIN BRIDGE.—[Photographed by Whitehurst.]

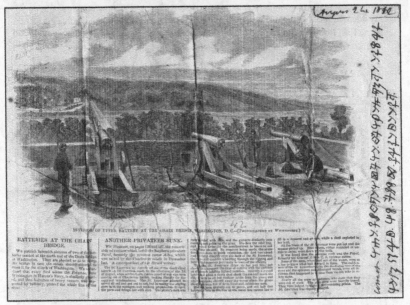

INTERIOR OF UPPER BATTERY AT THE CHAIN BRIDGE, WASHINGTON, D. C.—[Photographed by Whitehurst.]

Newspaper clippings showing the Chain Bridge over the Potomac River connecting Washington and Virginia. Bettie Duvall crossed Chain Bridge on July 10, 1861, carrying a coded message from Rose Greenhow to General Beauregard. These clippings, with Rose's coded message and cipher written on the side, were among the items seized from her house when she was arrested and charged with spying for the South. *National Archives*

The cipher found on Rose Greenhow's body after she drowned on October 1, 1864, provides a key to the messages she sent Confederate commanders. It is not known whether or not this is the same cipher Colonel Thomas Jordan gave her at the outset of the Civil War. *Courtesy of the North Carolina Office of Archives and History, Raleigh, North Carolina*

The First Battle of Bull Run. Rose Greenhow's coded message to General Beauregard that Union troops planned to attack him in a week gave him time to call for more troops and ultimately win the first battle of the Civil War. *Library of Congress*

General Pierre Gustave Toutant Beauregard, pictured here in his Confederate uniform, was commander of Confederate forces at Manassas. *G.P.A. Healy, courtesy of the Newberry Library, Chicago*

Coded letter, probably written by Rose Greenhow. It was among the correspondence seized at her house when she was arrested on August 23, 1861. *National Archives*

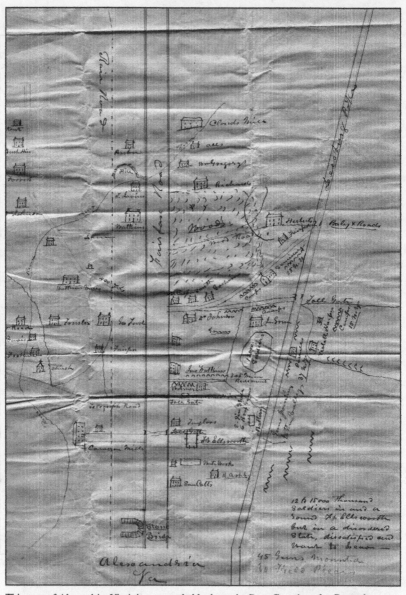

This map of Alexandria, Virginia, was probably drawn by Rose Greenhow for General Beauregard. *National Archives*

HOUSE OF DETENTION FOR FEMALE REBELS CORNER OF K AND SIXTEENTH STREETS WASHINGTON

Rose Greenhow's house at 398 16th Street, within sight of the White House. She was arrested on August 23, 1861, and kept here under guard for almost five months with her eight-year-old daughter, Little Rose. The Federals turned the residence into a female prison, which the press dubbed "Fort Greenhow." Published in *Frank Leslie's Illustrated Newspaper*, September 14, 1861. *Library of Congress*

The Old Capitol Prison at the corner of 1st and A streets on Capitol Hill was once Hill's Boarding House, where Rose Greenhow lived before she was married, and where she nursed John Calhoun on his deathbed in 1850. It was turned into a prison at the start of the Civil War. It is now the site of the U.S. Supreme Court. *Library of Congress*

Rose Greenhow and her eight-year-old daughter, Little Rose, posed for Civil War photographer Mathew Brady in the yard of the Old Capitol Prison. *Library of Congress*

Receipt from "E. J. Allen," the alias of detective Allan Pinkerton, confirming the receipt of "correspondence of a treasonable character" from Rose Greenhow. *National Archives*

Confederate president Jefferson Davis welcomed Rose to Richmond after she was exiled from Washington as a spy for the South, gave her a cash reward, and sent her on an unprecedented presidential mission to Europe to try to win recognition for the South. *National Portrait Gallery, Smithsonian Institution/ Art Resource, NY*

Confederate battle flags.

Rose Greenhow in England in 1863. *Georgetown University Library, Special Collections Division*

looking man, with frail body, which once rose tall and erect, but was now so bent that one thought of him as small, and with a head that made me think of a withered nut," wrote Virginia Clay-Clopton, wife of the Alabama senator Clement Claiborne Clay. "Swarthy of skin, but grey-haired, Judge Taney was a veritable skeleton, 'all mind and no body,' yet his opinion settled questions that agitated the nation."[11]

The chief justice was about to issue the High Court's decision in the much anticipated case of Dred Scott, a Missouri slave who claimed his freedom because he had lived twelve years in the free state of Illinois and free territory of Wisconsin before returning to Missouri with his master. Buchanan had taken the unusual step of asking friends on the Court which way the ruling would go because he wanted to include mention of the case in his inaugural address. Aware the Court was about to deny Scott's claim to freedom, Buchanan pledged in his speech to "cheerfully submit" to the High Court's decision, "whatever this may be."[12]

That night, thousands of people attended Buchanan's inaugural ball at Judiciary Square, decorated for the occasion in red, white, and blue bunting. Tickets cost $5 a head,[13] and Rose would not have missed the extravaganza. It was her evening to shine. "Such a jam, such heat I neither saw nor felt before," wrote one woman. "The members of Congress got so over-excited with wine that they had to be locked up in the upper rooms lest they should reappear in the ballroom."[14]

The revelry was short-lived. Two days later, nine aging Supreme Court justices, led by the frail but firm-minded Taney, filed into their courtroom in the basement of the U.S. Capitol to solemnly hand down their opinion against Dred Scott. Speaking in a weak, nearly inaudible monotone, Taney read the Court's ruling that as a black man—not just a slave, but any black man—Dred Scott was not a citizen of the United States and therefore had no right to sue in its courts. The case might have ended there, but the majority went further to find the Missouri Compromise of 1820 unconstitutional because by outlawing slavery in Wisconsin and other territories north of 36 degrees 30 minutes north, it was violating the Fifth Amendment property rights of slave-owning Americans. Dred Scott remained a slave, and the government was barred from telling people in the territories whether or not they could own slaves.[15] People of African ancestry, Taney wrote for the majority, "were not intended to be included, under the word 'citizens' in the Constitution, and can therefore claim none of the rights and privileges which that instrument provides for and secures to citizens of the United States."[16]

The landmark decision, intended to block the abolitionist movement, had the opposite effect, causing an outcry in the North and strengthening the Republican Party. It devastated blacks, who were left with no hope of ever attaining free and equal citizenship, and it wrecked the delicate balance of negotiated North-South parity that had kept uneasy peace among the states for more than thirty-five years. The South at first rejoiced, but the outpouring of rage in the North stirred passions that raced like wildfire across the country. James Buchanan, who had been president for two days, spent the rest of his term trying to keep the country in one piece.

The struggle divided Rose's family, as it did many others. A few days after Buchanan's victory, Rose's beautiful niece and namesake, Rose Adele Cutts, married Senator Stephen Douglas, whose doctrine of "popular sovereignty" had ignited the conflict in "Bleeding Kansas."

The "Little Giant," forty-three and a widower, stood only five feet four inches tall. Adie, as she was known, was twenty, a gifted linguist, and the tallest belle in Washington. They were popular guests at capital soireés, where she towered over her husband. Rose had every reason to be thrilled for her niece—Douglas's Kansas-Nebraska stance was popular in the South, and he was a wealthy man, accepted by the cream of Washington society—but Rose and Adie were destined to be caught on opposite sides of the coming conflict.

Adie was the daughter of Rose's sister Ellen and the grandniece of Dolley Madison. She had been raised in the comfort and elegance of Washington and Virginia society, but her marriage to Douglas elevated her to the national stage. Adie was a charming hostess who received guests wearing dresses of crêpe looped with pearls and her hair ornamented with green leaves and lilies. "Miss Cutts entered into the enjoyment of the wealth and position which her marriage with Stephen Douglas gave her, with the regal manner of a princess," wrote Virginia Clay-Clopton. "Her toilettes were of the richest and at all times were models of taste and picturesqueness. The effect she produced upon strangers was invariably one of instant admiration."[17]

Douglas, the father of two boys by his first wife, had been a major contender for the 1856 Democratic presidential nomination, but the divisiveness of his popular sovereignty doctrine in Kansas and Nebraska had derailed his hopes. After the convention, he worked tirelessly for Buchanan and expected a presidential appointment, but Buchanan distrusted him and had no intention of plucking him out of the Senate for a position in the new administration.

Buchanan understood the power of a White House invitation and invited people of varying political stripes to his table. The straitlaced chief executive did not permit dancing or gambling, but when Congress was in session, he gave state dinners and lively receptions and took pride in serving good food and liquor. With no wife for companionship, Buchanan considered his cabinet officers as family, and they and their wives became the center of his social life.[18] The president's beautiful niece Harriet Lane was her uncle's official hostess. Well educated and exposed to British high society when she lived with her uncle in London while Buchanan was minister to Great Britain, Harriet was by now a sophisticated woman of twenty-seven with poise, a tactful manner, and wide-ranging interests.

Rose was part of the small circle of Southerners who dominated Washington society during the Buchanan years. She was a frequent guest at the White House and entertained in her own parlor as well. Just when she was getting to enjoy her role as grande dame, however, Rose received a summons to return to San Francisco to testify in the Limantour land claims case. She had made the long journey to California only ten months before but quickly packed up to make the arduous trip again.

Correspondence shows that *before* Rose left, she tipped off Limantour about the government's case and later lobbied energetically in his behalf in Washington when his claim was on appeal—and asked for payment to finance the effort.

The land commission had ruled for Limantour in his most lucrative claim, but the decision was appealed to federal district court, and the government was about to indict Limantour on criminal charges, claiming he had pulled off a mammoth swindle. The Frenchman was safely back in Mexico, where Rose wrote him to say she could get help for him from some of her important friends in Washington. Rose, who got her information from U.S. attorney general Jeremiah S. Black, told Limantour that prosecutors were focusing on subtle differences between the engraved eagle on the Mexican state seal and a similar engraving used for the seal that appeared on Limantour's land grants. The discrepancy indicated to investigators that Limantour's documents, although they looked real enough to the land commission, were actually fake.[19]

"The enemy," Rose told Limantour conspiratorially, "are using it as their cheval de bataille." She implored him to explain the discrepancy in order for her to disabuse Black. Rose sent her letter through the Mexican ambassador and instructed him to send any private correspondence to Washington officials through her. "Believe me that I continue to take great interest in your success and that I am always warmly, your friend, Rose O'N. Greenhow."²⁰

When she testified as a witness for Limantour in the civil case in San Francisco two months later, spectators jammed the courtroom to get a glimpse of the society dame defending the Frenchman in the multimillion-dollar case. The trial record, which shows Rose as feisty, determined, and not intimidated by figures of authority, is the first official transcript of how she expressed herself, the first time her words—and her attitude—were captured verbatim.

When she was told to state her name, age, and place of residence, Rose stood before the judge, held her head high, and declared, "My name is Rose O'Neale Greenhow, and I reside in Washington City, District of Columbia. I am of lawful age."²¹ No one challenged the lady's refusal to disclose her date of birth, a secret she would take to her grave.

Rose testified that she met Limantour in Mexico "when he was brought to us at our residence." Then she added quickly, "When I speak of 'us,' I mean my husband and myself. Mr. Limantour's visits were to Mr. Greenhow, not to me." Rose said that after Limantour left that day, Robert showed her a map of the San Francisco Bay area and explained why the land was so valuable.

She told the court that her husband agreed to go to California to get the claims process under way and that Limantour would follow at the end of the year in time to file the necessary claims before a government-imposed deadline of March 1853.

Under cross-examination by the government, Rose bristled with indignation when asked if she had been paid by Limantour to testify in his defense: "I do not know anyone living who would dare to make me such a proposition," she replied—hardly a denial.

What, then, was her inducement in traveling all the way across country to California?

"I felt morally bound," Rose testified. "I consulted others. . . . I felt it my duty to come. In conversation with Mr. Black, the Attorney General, he told me I was obliged to obey a subpoena."

Had she ever been in Mexico before May 1850? "I never was," Rose replied.

The lawyer dug for details. What language did Robert and Limantour use to discuss the claims? "Sometimes French, sometimes Spanish," Rose replied. "When I did not understand, it was translated by my husband or Mr. De Joquet," secretary of the French Legation.

Were not Messrs. Limantour, Greenhow [and the secretary] all familiar with both the French and Spanish languages?

"Perfectly, as if it was their native tongues," Rose said.

Then why, the government's attorney asked, were any translations made?

"Simply to gratify me, when I did not understand any portion of it," Rose replied.

The attorney pressed Rose as to whether or not she had examined any of the papers herself and if she could identify them. "With a woman's natural curiosity, I leaned over my husband's shoulder while examining those papers, and read them with him in Spanish and in English," Rose said. "It would be an absurdity to suppose that a person unaccustomed to examine papers, could identify them, as it would require more knowledge than I could boast of."

Rose told the court that by the time Limantour got to California at the end of 1852, Robert Greenhow had already taken a job with the California Land Commission: "He was one of the few persons who was scrupulous here about being employed on both sides at the same time."[22] Perhaps.

Rose was excused after less than an hour on the stand, but the case dragged on for another year. After visiting her daughter Florence, whose husband was back in the army serving as quartermaster at the Presidio military base in San Francisco, Rose made the three-week journey home to Washington.

The government agreed to suspend the criminal case against Limantour until the court determined the validity of his claims,[23] and Rose sought an ongoing relationship with the Frenchman to help him with the powers in the capital. On December 4, 1857, Rose told Limantour in a letter sent through Mexican diplomatic channels that she knew he was "destined for some great purpose."

Addressing him familiarly as "Mon ami," she wrote: "An abstract sense of justice induced me against the strongest influence to go out to Cal. to testify in your case. Now that I know you, I am doubly interested in your success and my best services are yours."

Rose told Limantour that he would certainly have opposition, "but thank God our Supreme Court is considered irreproachably honest, and I have no fear that when your case reaches that tribunal, it will have a fair hearing." She reminded Limantour of her friendship with the attorney general, saying: "I try to keep his mind from prejudice, although I must tell you that the strongest and grossest misinterpretations have been made."

Then she made her pitch. "If my means were less circumscribed, I could do a great deal more than I am now able to do," she told him. "I have strong friends in this Congress, but this is a gay place and it is necessary to give our <u>friends</u> who <u>work</u> for us an occasional dinner and suppers, too, to stimulate their zeal; these are all honorable men who could not be bribed, but they discern much more clearly the justice of a case, when they have dined and supped well in pleasant company."

Others, she hinted, were not so honest: "There are men here however, who wield great power, <u>but they require material consideration.</u> One especially should be secured at once. He is a friend of mine and if fully authorized, I could approach him without any hesitation. But do not lose time. I have already spoken to the senator in virtue of the <u>discretion</u> you allowed me, but that is not enough."[24]

Rose was probably referring to her neighbor Senator William Gwin, who had helped set up the land commission and was a ranking member of the Senate Committee on Territories. As a pro-slavery Southerner who had known the Greenhows in California, Gwin was a friend who saw eye to eye with Rose on most issues. Chances were good that he would help.

Whatever the ethics of Rose's proposal—and they have changed little in Washington over the years—it was too late to help Limantour. On November 19, 1858, the United States District Court dismissed his claims as fraudulent, reopening the door to criminal prosecution, which the government seemed intent on pursuing. "The proofs of fraud," Judge Ogden Hoffman wrote in a scathing fifty-six-page opinion, "are as conclusive and irresistible as the attempted fraud itself has been flagrant and audacious."[25]

By the time the decision was handed down, Limantour had left the country and never returned. The government reactivated its criminal case against him in 1859, but without a defendant in the dock, nothing came of it.

Rose, however, seemed unfazed by the stunning setback of Judge Hoffman's unequivocal verdict. Two months later, on January 25, 1859, she wrote Limantour to report that she had taken his case to the Speaker of the House, the attorney general, and President Buchanan himself, assuring the president that Limantour was planning to appeal to the Supreme Court.

Sending her letter through another diplomatic friend, British minister Lord Napier, Rose assured Limantour that Buchanan was prepared to help as soon as he received an explanation of the problems and the evidence. "That there is a difference in the <u>seals</u> is a <u>fact</u> which <u>cannot</u> be <u>disputed</u>, but you must find a <u>satisfactory explanation of that</u>," Rose advised, again underlining her words for emphasis. "The Supreme Court will not be influenced by anything outside of the record, which is all in your favor. For God's sake, let no want of energy on your part mar your cause."

There was, however, no appeal. Limantour spent the rest of his days in Mexico, amassing a considerable fortune before he died in 1885.[26] Rose, for her part, did not suffer. She had established herself as a power broker, a woman whose legacy would be inextricably linked to the powerful men in her life.

Rose tried to keep her advice confidential.

"Much that I have told is secret," she said in closing her last letter to Limantour, "so burn this."[27]

CHAPTER 21

Downfall

ROSE'S REIGN AT *the pinnacle of Washington society was short-lived. The election of Abraham Lincoln in 1860 ended almost three decades of Democratic rule. After a bitter struggle over slavery, North and South were facing off, and Southern states began to secede from the Union. Jefferson Davis resigned from the Senate and was elected president of the Confederate States of America. War seemed inevitable.*

Throughout the winter, Rose continued to entertain Union and Confederate supporters at her table—and in her boudoir. If the passionate love letters signed with the initial "H" are to be believed, Senator Henry D. Wilson of Massachusetts, chairman of the Committee on Military Affairs, succumbed to her wiles.[1]

Two weeks after Lincoln's inauguration, Rose's beautiful daughter Gertrude died of typhoid fever, plunging the widow again into mourning. Gertrude, the second of eight children, was the fifth to die in Rose's lifetime.

In April, the South attacked Fort Sumter, and Lincoln called for seventy-five thousand volunteers to put down the rebellion of the Southern states. Sometime that spring, Captain Thomas Jordan tapped Rose to organize a Confederate spy ring.

In July, Rose sent General Beauregard two messages—one on July 9 and the other on July 16—informing him that the Union army was about to march south to attack his headquarters at Manassas.[2] *The messages arrived in time for Confederate general Joseph E. Johnston, protecting the Shenandoah Valley sixty miles northwest, to load his army onto trains and reinforce Beauregard at Manassas Junction. Two armies, not one, defended the Confederacy at Bull Run on Sunday, July 21, 1861, and routed the Union juggernaut in the first major battle of the Civil War. Lincoln's expectation that the insurrection would be put down in short order was dashed with the Yankees' devastating defeat.*

Rose continued to send messages south, but she probably knew she was under suspicion because she had come up with a risky escape plan. She spent hours at her sewing machine, stitching secrets about Union troop movements into the lining and cuffs of her gown. She sewed a pearl-and-ivory tablet on a silver chain and other contraband for Confederate soldiers into the voluminous quilted underskirt. Her acquaintance Mrs. Morris, who insists she heard it directly from President Lincoln, wrote in her memoir that Rose intended to hide maps of Federal forts in twists of her waist-long hair.[3]

But it was already too late.

Someone who undoubtedly knew Rose's Southern sympathies and suspected that she was seducing Federal officials in return for military intelligence reported unusual activity around Rose's house to Thomas A. Scott, the recently appointed assistant secretary of war.[4] Scott called in Allan Pinkerton, the noted railroad detective from Chicago who was directing counterintelligence operations in Washington for General McClellan under the nom de guerre "Major E. J. Allen." According to official records, Pinkerton was assigned to the Greenhow case shortly after he arrived in the city. Rose's neighbors soon noticed broad-shouldered men with revolvers stuffed in their belts lurking on the sidewalk outside her house. Yet her network of conspirators, "scouts," as she called them, continued to fan out across the city and report whatever they could learn about the Union army's preparations and expectations. Pinkerton's operatives observed the "fascinating widow," as they called her, receive a number of prominent men, including senators and congressmen, and took special interest in a couple of people who visited numerous times over several days. If Senator Wilson was among them, Pinkerton was careful not to say so.[5]

On August 21, Rose reported to Beauregard on the alert status in the capital and named Wilson as one of her sources: "No more troops have arrived. Great activity and anxiety here, and the whole strength concentrating around Washington, and the cry 'the Capitol in danger' renewed. . . . I do not give much heed to the rumors of Banks command arriving here, although he has advanced this way. Wilson told me last night, that they had [unintelligible] pieces, and over [unintelligible] and fifty guns of heavy calibre,—confirmed by my scouts."

Rose also told Beauregard that Wilson would join McClellan's staff, where he would provide "unflinching will and determination," but that as a result, she would have "greater access to the secrets of the Cabinet and War Office." Rose closed her message by asking for guidance on what kind of information to send, "as I know nothing from you of your wishes, and I may be wasting means in sending you what is of no use. . . . Give me instructions."[6]

Rose's August 21 message, later reassembled by archivists from scraps that had been torn to bits and thrown into a stove, apparently was the last she wrote before the Federals pounced.

Just before 11:00 A.M. on Friday, August 23, Rose was walking down 16th Street toward her house and stopped to inquire about the health of a neighbor's children. After several minutes of conversation, the neighbor leaned close to her friend and whispered that a guard had been stationed outside her house all day and night and that she had been followed on her walk. Rose looked across the street and saw two men, one in an army uniform and the other in civilian clothes, watching her. Looking down the street, she recognized a member of her circle of informers headed her way. "Those men will probably arrest me," she said quietly to her friend as her scout passed within earshot. "Walk to Corcoran's corner and see. If I raise a handkerchief to my face, give out the information." The person continued walking down the street toward the White House and began whistling a little tune. Rose took a handwritten note from her pocket, popped it in her mouth, and swallowed it.[7] Then she turned toward her house, held her head high, and crossed the street. As she reached her front door, the two men who had been watching the house raced up the porch stairs and asked awkwardly, "Is this Mrs. Greenhow?"

"Yes," she replied. "Who are you, and what do you want?"

"I have come to arrest you," replied Pinkerton, who was wearing his officer's uniform as "Major Allen."

"By what authority?"

"By sufficient authority," Pinkerton said.

"Let me see your warrant," Rose demanded, wiping a cheek with her handkerchief.

"Verbal authority from the War Department and the State Department," Pinkerton said. Then he and another detective stationed themselves on either side of her and escorted her into the house.

Rose glanced toward the street corner and saw that her signal had been understood. Turning to Pinkerton, she said coldly, "I have no power to resist you, but had I been inside of my house, I would have killed one of you before I submitted to this illegal process."[8]

Rose looked around the room as a dozen men swarmed into her parlor. "What are you going to do?" she asked Pinkerton.

"To search," he replied.

"Then I will facilitate your efforts," Rose snapped, and walked over to the mantel, where she took a torn piece of paper from a vase. According to Rose's detailed account of her imprisonment, written the following year, the note was dated "Manassas, July 23," and contained these words: "Lt. Col. Jordan's compliments to Mrs. R. Greenhow. Well, but hardworked . . ." The rest of the page had been torn away before it reached her. Rose said she suspected the message was an attempt to set her up because she had received it ten days earlier from the city post office, not a likely route for the Confederate military to use. To protect herself, she said, she had shown it to Captain Richard Cutts, one of the many well-connected Union officers in Rose's extended family, a Major Bache, and Senator Wilson, among others. She threw the letter at Pinkerton, saying, "You would like to finish this job, I suppose?" The secret service man took the letter—but discarded the city envelope in which it had arrived.[9]

The detectives had hoped to keep the arrest a secret, but Rose had flashed her signal to the collaborator on the corner, and eight-year-old Little Rose, terrified by the detectives, ran out the back door into the yard and blew their cover more loudly. After climbing a tree, she hung over the garden wall and called out to neighbors, "Mother has been arrested, Mother has been arrested."[10]

The detectives launched a frantic search of the house. They turned over beds, dresser drawers, wardrobes. They went through a hamper, leaving soiled clothes strewn across the floor. They ransacked Rose's library, taking every scrap of paper they could find. They found a small brown leather diary, inscribed in her handwriting, "R Greenhow, Washington, May 5." It contained several pages of notes about military preparations. They also found a printed, seven-page copy of orders from the War Department giving the organizational plan to increase the size of the regular army, as directed by President Lincoln. They even took the scribbled lessons of her children that she had saved carefully as childhood mementos. The papers were put in parcels marked "Highly Important," "Legal," and "Political."

The detectives weren't as thorough as they might have been. Rose described finding a number of items after the ransacking and arranged new hiding places for them. Inside the stove in the kitchen was a pile of letters, ripped into small pieces and partially burned. The singed scraps, which were seized at Rose's house after the arrest, are preserved today in Rose Greenhow's file at the National Archives.[11]

In her memoir, Rose wrote that as the detectives searched her house, they isolated her in the parlor. "Although agonizing anxieties filled my soul, I was apparently careless and sarcastic, and, I know, tantalizing in the extreme," she wrote. "My servants were subject to the same surveillance and were not allowed to approach me."[12] At 3:00 P.M., Lily Mackall and her sister stopped to check on their friend. As they entered the front door, a detective jumped out and seized them. Terrified, Lily put her head on Rose's shoulder and wept. "I did not know what they had done with you," she whispered.

"Oh, be courageous, we must whip these fiends," Rose replied.[13] A detective, whom Rose identified as Captain Dennis, stepped forward. In a loud, authoritative voice, he demanded the names of all visitors and ordered that they be detained.

It was an oppressively hot day, and a terrific late summer thunderstorm, for which Washington is notorious, turned the air even more muggy.[14] On the pretext of wanting to change her clothes, Rose asked to go to her bedroom. As soon as she was out of sight of the guard, she pulled several pieces of paper from her pocket and destroyed them. One was the cipher she had used to communicate with Manassas.

Captain Dennis rapped at her bedroom door. "Madam, madam," he cried, walking right in. Rose was half-undressed, and he stepped back. The clever matron took advantage of his split-second embarrassment and grabbed her revolver from a dresser drawer. She aimed it at his head. "Had he advanced one step, I should have killed him," Rose wrote later. "So steady were my nerves that I could have balanced a glass of water on my finger without spilling a drop."[15] But the detective regained his composure and seized her gun. Now Rose felt completely vulnerable. "I had no means of defense and for the first time in my life was exposed to the dread of personal violence," she wrote.[16]

A female detective named Ellen entered the room. "Her face reminded me of one of those India rubber dolls, whose expression is made by squeezing it," Rose wrote. The woman had weak gray eyes and looked as though she were going to cry. But her actions startled Rose, who realized she was about to be strip-searched: "I was allowed the poor privilege of unfastening my own garments, which one by one, were received by this pseudo-woman and carefully examined, until I stood in my linen." When the search was finished, she was permitted to dress herself.[17]

Throughout the evening, everyone, black or white, who tried to call on Rose was taken into custody. A former servant and his sister who walked past the house were held. The man was confined to a small closet under the stairs, the young woman to the parlor, where the men looked her up and down. "I was not aware of her being in the house until startled by a smothered scream," Rose wrote. "The girl was found in a state of great alarm from the rudeness to which she had been exposed and was sent below to her brother."[18] When Rose called out a warning to another couple approaching the house, Captain Dennis grabbed her arm and squeezed it so hard that he left bruises.[19]

Close to midnight, William J. Walker called on Rose, and Pinkerton had him shipped straight to prison, charged with engaging in contraband and treasonable correspondence with the rebels. Walker's influential friends in the city appealed to Secretary Seward, pleading there must be some dreadful mistake and attesting to his loyalty; but Pinkerton's insistence that he must be guilty of something and stubborn foot-dragging kept the man locked up for more than three months.

Surveying the scene, Rose realized her situation was more precarious than she had imagined initially. Detectives in the parlor began pouring themselves tumblers of rum and brandy. Rose overheard them bragging about the "nice times" they planned to have with the female prisoners. Rose took the opportunity while they drank and gabbed to destroy several more papers that she had hidden in drawers. Then, very quietly, she tiptoed into her library, lined with elegant books in many languages that Robert Greenhow had collected from all over the world. In the years since Robert's death, the room had become Rose's sanctuary.

After climbing to the top shelf, she took some papers from a dusty portfolio and stuffed them into the deep folds of her dress. There were more documents than she remembered, and she was unsure how to dispose of them. Thinking back to the detectives' search of her body earlier in the afternoon, she recalled that they had not removed her stockings and boots. After checking to make sure the guards were still drinking, Rose asked Lily Mackall to help conceal the papers in her shoes.

In the predawn darkness between 3:00 and 4:00 the following morning, the guards permitted their other prisoners to leave. The detainees were escorted out by detectives, who followed them home and watched their doors to check out their other contacts. Rose was allowed a few hours of sleep, but the doors to her bedroom were kept open and two guards with muskets were stationed inside. Local newspapers reported that guards erected a tall round tent in the yard, lending a circus atmosphere to the scene, and soldiers hung their blankets and blue uniform jackets on the fence and clothesline.[20] Several other women were arrested the same day Rose was, and they were soon transferred to her house, soon to be named "The House of Detention for Female Rebels." The press dubbed it "Fort Greenhow."

News of the detentions spread quickly. On August 26, the *National Intelligencer* ran a brief item headlined "Military Arrests" on page three: "Mrs. Phillips, wife of Philip Phillips, Esq., Ex-member of Congress, from Alabama; and Mrs. Greenhow, widow of the late Robert Greenhow, have been arrested on the charge of holding correspondence with the Confederates."[21] *The New York Times* and *New York Herald* also ran items. An article in the *Washington Chronicle* was reprinted in the *San Francisco Daily Bulletin,* near where Rose's daughter Florence was living with her husband, now a Union captain. "Mrs. Greenhow, a widow lady well known in this city, was arrested by the provost guard of the Brig. Gen. Porter," the reprint said. "Her secessionist proclivities have long been the subject of popular conversations. Doubtless the charge against her is of being in treasonable correspondence with the country's enemies now in arms."[22]

Word also sped south to Richmond, where Mary Boykin Chesnut, the wife of South Carolina senator James Chesnut Jr. and a close friend of Jefferson and Varina Davis, was uncharacteristically sympathetic. "They say Mrs. Greenhow furnished Beauregard with the latest news of the Federal movements, and so made the Manassas victory a possibility," the diarist wrote on August 26, only three days after the arrest. "She sent us the enemy's plans. Everything she said proved true, numbers, route and all."[23] Three days later, Mary Chesnut's diary entry shows how controversial Rose had become—and how mean-spirited were her enemies: "Some say Mrs. Greenhow had herself confined and persecuted so that we might trust her the more. The Manassas men swear she was our good angel, but the Washington women say she was up for sale to the highest bidder, always—and they have the money on us."[24]

ONE AFTERNOON NOT long after the arrest, President Lincoln's sons Willie and Tad arrived bursting with excitement at the home of their playmate Julia Taft. "They've got her shut up in her house with a lot of other spies," Tad Lincoln told Julia. "There's a guard at the door and they will probably shoot her at sunrise tomorrow."

In her memoirs, Julia Taft recalled "an official named Pinkerton" visiting her home to question the family about Rose, who had often been a guest. Julia's father told the detective that Rose seemed to enjoy the conversations she had with Union soldiers. Julia remarked also that Rose frequently asked her about the visits she and her younger brothers made to the White House and inquired as to what Mr. Lincoln had discussed. "My father remembered that she had asked him about the regiments that arrived," Julia later wrote of her White House memories. "But why did the gentleman ask these questions? What was wrong with Mrs. Greenhow?" After much begging, Julia's mother permitted her to accompany the Lincoln boys and her brothers to Rose's house. They found it surrounded by curiosity seekers and guarded by a detachment of Sturgis Rifles, who had been General McClellan's bodyguards.[25]

Detectives remained in Rose's home for a week, and each day they searched for more correspondence. They took every book off the library shelves and examined it, page by page. They seized newspaper articles describing the city's fear of attack, changes in the military budget, and Union troop movements. One newspaper clipping, dated August 20, 1861, was called "Onward to Washington" and reported, "The question for consideration . . . is, what measures ought to be taken to avert so fearful a catastrophe as the fall of the capital."[26]

The guards hauled out boxes of fine china and crystal that had been packed away for months. They pulled apart the furniture and took pictures from their frames. "My beds even were upturned many times as some new idea would seize them," Rose wrote.[27] In a final indignity, the detectives went into Gertrude's bedroom, where the dead girl's jewelry and toilet articles were displayed on the table as she had left them. They swept everything to the floor and pulled the sheets off the bed in which she had died. "My castle," wrote Rose, "has become my prison."[28]

The guards insisted on sitting at the dining room table with Rose when she took her meals, which The New York Times reported were catered by the same restaurateur who served General McClellan.[29] When several of the soldiers feigned sympathy for how she was being treated, Rose realized they were trolling for bribes and turned their game back on them. She offered food and laughed at their jokes, exuding her well-known Southern charm. "Two deserve special notice," the captive wrote. "One was a burly Irishman with a smooth tongue, professing the religion of my ancestors, that of the Holy Catholic faith. He marveled that so noble a lady should have been treated as a common malefactor." But the Irish detective didn't stop at flattering the prisoner. He also had his eyes on her maid, whom he hoped would shed light on her employer.

Lizzie, a witty Irish girl with a what-the-hell attitude, convinced herself that she was acting in the line of duty. "She entered keenly into the sport, and to use her own expressive words, 'Led Pat a dance,' " Rose wrote. "And under these new auspices, [she] performed some very important missions for me."[30] Very important missions? How tantalizing! What did Lizzie learn? Unfortunately, Rose did not write it down.

Rose noticed that another detective, a Scot named Robert, grew teary-eyed whenever anyone mentioned the "sublime fortitude" she had shown during the arrest. Seeking to ingratiate himself, he asked if she would autograph a document from McClellan. "Madam," he said in a voice choked with emotion, "there is no telling what may happen and I would like to look at your name and know that you had forgiven me."[31] Both men offered to sneak letters out of the house for her, but Rose suspected they were setting a trap and declined. She could imagine that Pinkerton would love to intercept a message and follow its trail to an informer.

She was right.

Sometime after Rose Greenhow's arrest, Mrs. Morris was summoned to the War Department to meet Secretary Edwin Stanton, a friend of her father's, but when she got there, she was astonished to find the president of the United States in Stanton's office.

"My dear little woman," Lincoln told her, "we wish to thank you for the great service you rendered unconsciously to our country." He explained that Rose had been planning to flee Washington for Richmond and from there escape to France. Mrs. Morris's chance encounter had enabled Federal agents to foil her scheme. As a souvenir, Lincoln gave her the pearl-and-ivory tablet on a silver chain that he said Rose had sewn into the thick lining of her skirt. "Be careful in the future how you make acquaintances, for this city is full of spies," Lincoln warned.[32]

CHAPTER 22

Fort Greenhow

ROSE WAS IMPRISONED in her house for five months. Wherever she went, a detective followed. If she wished to lie down, he sat a few paces from the bed. When she changed her dress, she was obliged to do so with the doors open. Inevitably, the lecherous guard peered inside. Rose was deeply offended at the treatment, but she had no alternative. "When I remonstrated with the detective, Captain Dennis," she wrote, "I was met with the answer that it was the order of the Provost-Marshall and that I was indebted to him that more disgusting severity had not been enforced."[1]

Rose learned that by sitting quietly, seemingly absorbed in her knitting and sewing, she could glean valuable information from the conversations of her guards. One mentioned that the government had offered a large reward for her cipher. She also heard that her friend Wilson and other top Republicans she didn't name had been summoned to a meeting of Lincoln's cabinet to explain themselves after they were implicated by information she sent south but that was intercepted by Federal agents. Once, she confessed, she was frightened when Lily Mackall spotted a sheet of blotting paper that contained a reverse image of her July 16 dispatch to Beauregard. Miss Mackall hastily retrieved it from a pile of papers before it was discovered.[2] Rose took considerable satisfaction at the incompetence of the detectives studying the pieces of paper they recovered. "The tables were filled with fragments of old letters, and scraps in cipher, in several languages, from early morn till late at night," she recounted. "For seven days they puzzled over them. I had no fear. One by one they had allowed the clue to escape them."[3]

Rose reported that a long letter she had sent to President Jefferson Davis about the political intrigues in Washington apparently had been intercepted by the Yankees and was discussed at a cabinet meeting. In it she described a scheme to replace the increasingly feeble General Winfield Scott by temporarily elevating McClellan. She boasted her information was so good, "I might almost be said to have assisted at Lincoln's Cabinet Councils, from the facilities I enjoyed, having verbatim reports of them as well as of the Republican caucus." She probably exaggerated, but there is clear evidence that some of her reports continued to reach Confederate headquarters and others were intercepted and studied by her captors.

In her letter to Davis, Rose said, she told of a proposition being considered to unseat her former friend Secretary of State Seward, who "has not the blood enough in him to entertain an honest opinion on any subject. . . . His genius," she added, "lay in his faculty of drawing to himself all the advantages of any successful measure, and of shuffling out of the way of an unpopular one." The ways of politicians have changed little over the years. "He wishes to be a great man and will buckle to anything for power," she said, noting in her book that when Seward learned of her remark, he "reddened to the roots of his hair."[4]

One of her dispatches, written in cipher, included drawings of fortifications and weak points that top Union officials "complimented as being equal to those of their best engineers—as well they might," she noted.[5]

She claimed they considered her so dangerous that they deliberated putting her on public trial for treason, but "my social position was such that they did not dare . . . for in their ranks I had many devoted friends who openly expressed their admiration for the position I took under circumstances of danger and difficulty."[6]

"I did not shrink from this trial," she wrote, "and when repeatedly warned that it might take place, said, 'Let it come. I will claim the right to defend myself and there will be rich revelations.' "[7] She undoubtedly knew then—and certainly by the time she wrote her memoir—that Lincoln had no intention of giving her the platform of a public trial or of making her a martyr.

On Friday morning, August 30, Rose was told that other prisoners would be brought to her house. Eugenia Phillips, two of her daughters, Fannie and Lena, and Mrs. Phillips's sister were escorted in. "These women were arrested the day after I was and subjected to the like, if not greater indignities from which the presence of the husband and father could not protect them," Rose wrote. The women exchanged a silent greeting with Rose as they passed her door. Another woman, Bettie Hasler, one of Rose's couriers, was confined to an adjoining room, and the door was nailed shut with a large wooden board. Like Rose, all had been arrested on August 23 and charged with "corresponding with the enemy." Mrs. Phillips was a sophisticated lady, but Mrs. Hasler was an uneducated woman who had delivered letters for Rose out of friendship and had no idea why she had been imprisoned. "She was brought in late at night and her convulsed sobs broke the stillness of the hour," Rose wrote. "Special care was taken to prevent this prisoner and myself from communicating, as they hoped, through her, to establish direct evidence against me." The morning after Bettie Hasler arrived, Rose distracted a guard while Lily Mackall slipped into the woman's room to warn her to deny all knowledge of Rose.[8]

Rose, Little Rose, and Lily Mackall were confined to one room. When Rose objected and threatened to complain to the secretary of war, the officer of the guard, Lieutenant Sheldon, relented and permitted the use of another small room for Little Rose and a maid. But Rose was not allowed to enter this room because it had a window with a shade opening onto the street. The detectives feared she would send signals to her ring of spies on the outside by adjusting the level of the shade.

Like prisoners everywhere, the women took to scribbling defiant messages on the walls, windowsills, and entryways to their rooms—any bare space they could find. Using lead pencils, they taunted their captors with parodies of national songs and rhymes, ridiculing their sordid conditions. One message read: "I had a vision last night. Me thought I saw Abe Lincoln, Wm. H. Seward, Simon Cameron, Andrew Porter and others praying to Almighty God, as Davis had done, for the mercy they denied to harmless women. And the Almighty God answers: 'Have I not said, as ye, mete it unto others, so shall it be measured unto you again? Depart from my sight, ye cursed, and take up your abode in the hell prepared for Abraham Lincoln and his government, and who assist him in his abominable persecutions.' "[9]

On the other side of the front doorway was another scrawled inscription: "We must sustain the Constitution of the United States: we must down Southern institutions that we may put the proceeds of all the negroes in our pockets. We must impress Southern women and children, and other such like chivalrous and magnificent acts—*Vide Seward.*"¹⁰

One morning one of the women sent a poem to Lieutenant Sheldon:

> I pray you, good Lieutenant Sheldon,
> Since I trouble you so very seldom,
> To send me cat or trap or vice,
> To catch these horrid little mice.
>
> These troublesome little government creatures
> Have tried to mar my southern features;
> They began the war against my clothes,
> And last night really bit my nose.¹¹

As the warm days of Indian summer faded and the afternoon shadows lengthened, Rose fought to keep her spirits from sagging. "The efforts of the Black Republicans had been persistently to make the term secessionist one of disgrace and reproach," she wrote, "and although they had with great assiduity courted the few Southern families who remained, there was no language too coarse for them to use in describing Secessionists." Defiant as ever, she complained that "every social element was brought to bear against the unhappy Southerner, and even her own relatives sided with the Union. No one suffered in this respect more than myself for many members of my immediate family sided with the despot and held high official position under him."¹²

More people learned of the arrest, and the guards made it increasingly difficult for Rose to communicate with friends. As a result, she devised clever ruses. She called one intermediary "my little bird,"¹³ later suspected by family members to be Little Rose. She used balls of yarn to weave tapestries with colors that followed a secret code sent to her from the outside. Her "vocabulary of colours," she said, was sufficient to convey basic information.¹⁴ Like her cipher, the code was probably quite simple, but it fooled the guards. Unfortunately, no records remain to show what information she conveyed with her needles or to whom she sent it.

Rose also wrote folksy letters to her correspondents with hidden meanings: "Tell Aunt Sally that I have some old shoes for the children, and I wish her to send someone down town to take them, and to let me know whether she has found any charitable person to help her to take care of them." The recipient understood she meant: "I have some important information to send across the river, and wish a messenger immediately. Have you any means of getting reliable information?"[15]

Rose's "reliable information" may have included details about troop strength and military plans learned from sympathetic visitors. She may also have overheard gossip about the inner workings of the Lincoln government from her chatty guards.

On September 7, two weeks after the arrest, Little Rose fell ill. Her mother wrote to Brigadier General Andrew Porter, provost marshal of the Washington district, asking that the family physician be permitted to pay a visit, but Porter refused, offering instead to send an army doctor. Rose was indignant and would not let the physician see her daughter. "I preferred to trust her life to the good Providence which had so often befriended me," she wrote.[16]

Each day, Rose's captors interrogated her. They continued to examine her letters and referred to her Southern correspondents as traitors. A doctor inspected the entire house daily, supposedly to check on the "sanitary conditions." Rose suspected that he enjoyed being able to tell people that he saw the city's most famous prisoner every day. On September 8, Edwin M. Stanton, a Democrat who would soon become head of Lincoln's War Department, visited the house to make arrangements for Mrs. Phillips to be sent south into exile. "What have you done to bring down the wrath of the abolitionists on your head?" he asked Rose, whom he had known when he handled California land claims cases for Jeremiah Black and later succeeded Black as attorney general in the Buchanan administration.

Rose replied that she was guilty of lèse-majesté, an affront to the crown, and did not know the charges against her. She asked Stanton to file a writ of habeas corpus on her behalf, insisting that the Union was violating the venerable right of a prisoner to be brought before a judge to determine whether or not she was being held legally. The former attorney general declined but offered to help her in any other way that he could. "I felt now that I was alone," she wrote, and that "the wall of separation from my friends was each hour growing more formidable."[17]

According to official records, Rose was charged with being a spy "and furnishing the insurgent generals with important information relative to the movements of the Union forces."[18] In one of the acts for which he has been most criticized since, Lincoln suspended the right of habeas corpus, first in certain trouble spots, then throughout the country, in 1862.

Pinkerton sought to further isolate her. On September 25, he ordered Rose's friend Lily Mackall out of the house and forbade her to have any communication with Rose. Anyone who even walked past Rose's house was threatened with arrest. Rose was growing weary of the new regime. According to her account, the rations for her and for Little Rose were reduced. "My food, which up to this time, though plain and often uneatable, had been sufficiently abundant, was now so reduced in quantity and quality, as to be inadequate often to satisfy the cravings of hunger," she wrote. Most meals consisted only of crackers and cheese, and she was allowed no exercise in her yard. The guards sent away Catholic priests who tried to visit and discussed nailing boards over Rose's windows to deprive her of light. Little Rose and the maid were permitted to attend church services, but a guard was instructed to sit in the pew with them and ordered them not to talk with anyone. Little Rose was permitted to play on the pavement in front of the house, under the watch of a guard, and neighbors sometimes gave her snacks. But some nights, she cried herself to sleep from hunger.[19]

On October 5, Rose bribed a guard to smuggle a letter to Thomas Jordan. Addressing her missive to "Thomas J. Rayford," the alias Jordan had instructed her to use, Rose wrote in cipher that she had been under house arrest since August "with 18 lions to guard me." She said that Mrs. Hasler, soon to be released, was allowed to go for walks and carriage rides, but that Rose was considered too dangerous for such privileges. Rose told Jordan that she had not received his last three dispatches—there is no indication of how she knew he sent them—and reported that her scouts were in place to carry out her plans. "I have signals," Rose wrote. "Take care that the cipher does not fall into their hands. I destroyed it and every paper of consequence, but oh my God, with what danger, with twenty detectives following every step." McClellan, Rose wrote, "is fast making the army efficient; it has been in a deplorable state. They look for an attack and are greatly puzzled to know what the plan is. They make blunders every day." She told him to destroy the cipher: "Thousands are offered for it. And for weeks the most skillful detectives are at work on it. As yet, nothing has been made of it." As for the military: "Artillery is constant and severe. About 60,000 troops are surrounding, including McDowell's command. They come in slowly and badly equipped. They ask for private contributions of blankets. You are losing golden moments. Bitter feuds in sections of the party. I am sorry to see that Lincoln is going with the strongest party, that which opposes interfering with slavery." In closing, Rose said: "Think of me with guards at my chamber door, with bayonet; how long is this to last? Enclosed is a list of the forts. It is a work of the wise."

Rose had trusted the wrong guard. He turned the message over to the provost marshal, and it was later used as evidence against her.[20] To further humiliate Rose, Pinkerton placed a guard in the room of Rose's deceased daughter Gertrude, which the mourning mother considered blasphemous.

On the evening of October 15, a Chicago prostitute with the alias Mary E. Onderdonk was arrested and brought to the female prison.[21] Mrs. Onderdonk was encouraged to talk with Rose, but when the two women were served meals together, Rose refused to eat. "It might have been supposed that my former social position and that which members of my immediate family still held in the Federal city, would have protected me from this attempt to degrade me," Rose sniffed. When high-ranking government officials began calling on Mrs. Onderdonk, Rose realized that the woman had been placed in her house as a spy: "Under the system established by Mr. Seward, there was a spy in every household. This means the sanctity of the home was invaded. Every unguarded expression uttered within its sacred precincts was sure to reach the ears of the secret police—those Thugs of America."[22] Lieutenant Sheldon had Mrs. Onderdunk moved to a different room.

When the prisoners' clothes were sent to the laundry, the head guard examined every article in the presence of another officer. Once, they went into a tizzy when a sprig of jasmine fell out of an undergarment, Rose reported. They were sure it had been smuggled to her as a hidden message.[23] When her faithful friend Lily Mackall fell seriously ill, Seward refused Rose's request to visit her dying friend, and she lashed out against her one-time dinner guest in her memoir: "I prayed that the God of Justice, in his hour of need, deny the heartless charlatan that mercy . . . which he had denied me."[24]

The newspapers reported regularly on the women's imprisonment, even when there was little to report. "Hotel Greenhouse, as the female prison is called, is still an existing institution in Washington," *The New York Times* wrote on November 5. "Mrs. Greenhow is still in close custody."[25]

On November 16, a Saturday, Rose's sister Ellen and Ellen's daughter, Adie Douglas, were permitted a fifteen-minute visit in the company of an army escort. It was an awkward meeting that underscored the divided loyalties of the family. Ellen's husband, James Madison Cutts, was serving as second comptroller of the Treasury, a position previously held by his father. Adie's husband, Senator Douglas, had died in June on a mission to Illinois to save the Union, and the president was advising Adie about her affairs. Adie's brother, James Madison Cutts Jr., had enlisted in the First Rhode Island Volunteers as a private in May, and Lincoln had later commissioned him as a captain in the Eleventh U.S. Infantry.[26] The army colonel assigned to attend the get-together took the opportunity to advise Rose to cooperate with the Federal government and offered to mediate open communications with Secretary of State Seward. Rose said she "declined this amiable counsel and proffer of aid as inconsistent with my own feelings and derogatory to my honour." She decided, however, to write Seward herself the next day, complaining bitterly about her arrest and treatment. She protested her loss of privacy and the guards' bad behavior, and she was adamant in defense of her constitutional rights. "Freedom of speech and of opinion is the birthright of Americans, guaranteed to us by our charter of liberty—the Constitution of the United States," she lectured the secretary of state. "I have exercised my prerogative, and have openly avowed my sentiments. During the political struggle I opposed your Republican party with every instinct of self-preservation. I believed your success a virtual nullification of the Constitution, and that it would entail upon us all the direful consequences which have ensued. These sentiments have doubtless been found recorded among my papers, and I hold them as rather a proud record of my sagacity."

Seizing equal opportunity from her dubious position, she said, "You have held me, sir, to a man's accountability, and I therefore claim the right to speak on subjects usually considered beyond a woman's ken. . . .

"You may prostrate the physical strength, by confinement in close rooms and insufficient food," Rose wrote. "You may subject me to harsher, ruder treatment than I have already received; but you cannot imprison the soul. Every cause worthy of success has had its martyrs. My sufferings will afford a significant lesson to the women of the South, that sex or condition is no bulwark against the surging billows of the 'irrepressible conflict.' "[27] She was throwing back at him his own words from an address in 1858 in which Seward said the North and South were embarked on a collision course, an "irrepressible conflict" between slavery and freedom.

Demonstrating she could still get some dispatches past her guards, Rose said she sent a copy of the letter to her "friends at Manassas," and it showed up in a newspaper in the Confederate capital of Richmond under the headline LETTER FROM A SOUTHERN LADY IN PRISON TO SEWARD—THE COWARDLY ATROCITIES OF THE WASHINGTON GOVERNMENT. *The Whig* newspaper claimed the letter came from one of Seward's confidential agents, and the rebels made the most of its propaganda value: "This letter of Mrs. Greenhow is the most graphic sketch yet given to the world, of the cruel and dastardly tyranny which the Yankee Government has established at

Washington. The incarceration and torture of helpless women and the outrages heaped upon them . . . will shock many natures and stamp the Lincoln dynasty everywhere with undying infamy."[28] Mary Boykin Chesnut
expressed sympathy of a sort at the indignities suffered by the widow
Greenhow. "Beautiful as she is, even in this time of her life, few women
like all the mysteries of their toilette laid bare to the public eye," Mrs.
Chesnut told her diary on December 6. "She says she was worse used than
Marie Antoinette, when they snatched a letter from the poor queen's
bosom."[29]

The *New York Herald* reprinted the article from Richmond with an editorial slap at Rose, calling her letter the sort of tirade "one would expect,
under the circumstances, from a spirited, dashing, active, and fearless female politician of the South Carolina school of Secession malignants."
The paper called her "a bright and shining light" of the "diluted rose-water
administration of Mr. Buchanan" and suggested she was supporting secession in hopes of returning to her earlier "reign of beauty and glory."[30]

A correspondent for another Northern newspaper went by for a look at
the supposed hellhole. His report on November 29 found little evidence of
mistreatment, at least from the outside: "Fort Greenhough [*sic*], as they
call it, where the secessionist women are shut up, is an ordinary brick
house of three stories," he wrote. "As I strolled by, I could see very little indications of its prison character. A lazy sentinel was standing in front of it,
but he held his musket like an umbrella and was busy chatting with some
gossiping friend. . . . The lower windows looked uncommonly dirty but
there were no bars at all. The women were restricted to the second floor,
and as I passed, some of them were visible."[31]

With private appeals from upstanding citizens and the public reports of
mistreatment of female prisoners, Pinkerton worried that Rose and her co-
conspirators would be released or exiled to the South, as many Southern
sympathizers had been, and he tried to head off any move to go easy on
her. In a report to the provost marshal in November and several follow-up
letters, Pinkerton painted Rose as an imminent threat to the Republic:
"Since the commencement of this rebellion, this woman from her long residence at the capital, her superior education, her uncommon social powers,
her very extensive acquaintance among and her active association with the
leading politicians of this nation has possessed an almost superhuman
power, all of which she has most wickedly used to destroy the Government. She has used her almost irresistible seductive powers to win to her
aid persons who were holding responsible places of honor and of profit

under the Government so that she might through them obtain information known only to the agents of the Government."

Pinkerton called Rose's house "the rendezvous for the most violent enemies of the government . . . a sort of focal center where treason found a resting place and where traitors were supplied with every needed care and where they were furnished with every possible information to be obtained by the untiring energies of this very remarkable woman."

Pinkerton said Rose had "secret and insidious agents in all parts of this city and scattered over a large extent of country," and following her arrest, "she has not ceased to lay plans, to attempt the bribery of officers having her in charge, to make use of signs from the windows of her house to her friends on the streets, to communicate with such friends and through them . . . to the rebels."[32]

Seward, enraged by Rose's defiant letter to him and the public embarrassment caused by its publication in both North and South, dismissed her complaint without replying directly. In a one-sentence order to Provost Marshal Porter, Seward instructed: "The Provost-Marshall will inform Mrs. Greenhow that her correspondence with the commanding general of the army besieging the capital renders all interference in her behalf with the regulations established by the military authorities for the prisoner's safety improper."[33]

According to Rose, however, she was not without her sympathizers in the government and had a visit a few days later from Colonel Thomas M. Key, an aide-de-camp to General McClellan. Key offered to negotiate her release and asked what terms she would accept. "My heart beat wildly, for even that chance gleam of freedom agitated me," she said. "I, however, crushed down the impulse—for I saw that he was watching me very narrowly—and answered, 'None, sir. I demand my unconditional release, indemnity for my losses, and restoration of my papers and effects.' " The meeting ended inconclusively, but Rose came away with the understanding the Union was ready to exile her to the South to be rid of her.

Christmas Day, Little Rose received a large cake and some small gifts from her cousin Adie Douglas, sent through the provost marshal's office. Lieutenant Sheldon broke the usual rules and let the little girl visit the homes of some young friends who were celebrating in the afternoon.[34]

The next day, Rose managed to sneak a message past her guards that reached Colonel Jordan at Beauregard's headquarters in Centreville, Virginia. "In a day or two 1200 cavalry supported by four batteries of artillery will cross the river above to get behind Manassas and cut off railroad and other communication with our army whilst an attack is made in front," she warned. "For God's sake heed this. It is positive. They are obliged to move or give up." It was to be part of McClellan's long anticipated offensive, and Confederate generals circulated Rose's intelligence report, along with several others identifying supposed Union objectives in Virginia, to commanders in the field.[35] The cautious McClellan fell ill, however, and his winter campaign was postponed, much to Lincoln's disappointment.

Rose told Jordan the Yankees found her "a hard bargain" and that she expected to be released in a few days on condition she agree to go south and not return to Washington until the war ended. "A confidential member of McClellan's staff came to see me and tell me that my case should form an exception," she informed her handler. "I only want to gain time. All my plans are nearly completed."[36]

Later the same day, however, she got word from her sources that plans were afoot to move her to a Northern prison. Key's mission had failed.[37]

On December 30, Catherine V. Baxley was arrested getting off a flag-of-truce boat in Baltimore, accused of spying, and sent to Fort Greenhow. She had been to Richmond to see President Jefferson Davis, had obtained a military surgeon's commission for her lover (who was promptly thrown in jail, too), and was returning to Washington with a packet of contraband letters, apparently including one intended for Rose. Pleading with Secretary of State Seward that she was nothing but a foolish Southern lady, Mrs. Baxley acknowledged she had gone to Richmond via the "underground railway" to see Davis, but she insisted that she "carried with me nothing in the world but a few friendly letters, packed it is true in my bonnet." She promised to go home and never to engage in such folly again and to "meddle no more with edged tools." Seeking to flatter Seward, she told him she didn't believe all those awful things people said about his being a "hard and heartless man, permitting nothing to stand in the way of his boundless ambition."

Rose was disgusted by the woman's performance, writing later that Mrs. Baxley got caught only because she boasted on the truce boat of her exploits and spoke openly of her wish to deliver a letter to Rose and establish communication with the notorious spy.

"The conduct of this woman on arriving at the prison confirmed the impression entertained at the time of her arrest, of her being non compos mentis," Rose wrote. "She raved from early morn till late at night, in language more vehement than delicate." The owner of the home-turned-prison complained that Mrs. Baxley and another of the female prisoners, a Miss Poole, took to "real or affected faints . . . , the premonitory symptoms being a loud cry, and heavy fall upon the floor." The spells would bring the guards running, an officer bringing up the rear, "conspicuously flourishing a brandy bottle, that being the masculine panacea for all the ills of life."[38]

When apology failed, Mrs. Baxley tried pity. A divorcée, she wrote to Secretary of War Stanton that her incarceration had thrown her fourteen-year-old son "upon the charities of a cold, unfeeling world." When the boy was brought to visit her, "I could scarcely recognize him—dirty, neglected, sick and so thin and careworn—every vestige of my once bright, happy boy gone. . . . Use your prerogative, sir; open these prison doors and send forth the women and infants." She didn't mention, though he doubtless knew, that while in Richmond, Mrs. Baxley had sought an appointment for her son as a Confederate military cadet.

Rose remained unimpressed. Miss Poole, she reported, had ingratiated herself with her guards by spying on Rose, after which she "took the oath of allegiance, and fifty dollars in gold from the Yankee Government, and went on her way rejoicing. The woman Baxley, also, applied to be released upon similar terms, which was refused."

Determined to extract a response from Seward—or annoy him further—Rose wrote a diatribe accusing him of brutal suppression and warning her countrymen would turn to guerrilla war rather than surrender. At the end of 1861, before the great and bloody battles that brought the South to its knees, she told Seward: "You have, Sir, brought about a mighty revolution, whose tide is even now surging towards your own homes. You have suspended the law throughout the land, and, by your secret police, hold the assassin's knife at the throats of your own people. The mist of fanaticism, which makes them for the present but blind instruments in your hands, will pass away; and he who raises the whirlwind does not always ride upon it into a harbour of safety. . . .

"We may not successfully compete with you in the open field, but we will then defeat you by stratagem," she said. "And beware lest you drive us to secret organization, or you in your day may experience that the vengeance of man is swifter than that of Heaven. No, Sir, you cannot subdue a people endowed with such a spirit of resistance; and, although we may yet wade through oceans of blood, we will achieve our independence, or leave our whole Southern land one howling wilderness, and a monument to all future time of the crimes of your party."[39]

Newspapers and magazines were having a heyday. *Frank Leslie's Illustrated Newspaper* reported that on New Year's Day, Rose received a cake containing several Confederate bills and an escape plan hidden between the layers: "Before delivering it to her, the sentinel, suspecting something wrong, cut it open and found inside a note informing the lady that arrangements had been made for her escape and conveyance to Richmond, naming the day and hour of her deliverance." The article claimed that Rose's anger was so uncontrollable that when Lieutenant Sheldon brought her a new cake, "she threw it down the stairs."[40] *Harper's Weekly* reported that Rose "has been detected in carrying on a secret correspondence with the enemy in spite of the close watch kept on her house in Washington" and predicted she would be sent to Fort Lafayette in New York, where there would be "no opportunity of communicating information to her Southern friends."[41]

The Federal government had had enough. On January 18, 1862, a Saturday, Pinkerton ordered that the windows of her house be boarded and all paper removed from the premises. Rose Greenhow and Mrs. Baxley were to be moved to a military prison on Capitol Hill, where they would be held under tighter rein.[42] "I was sitting in the library reading, with my little one playing at my feet with her dolls, prattling," Rose wrote. They gave the women two hours to pack, including the time it took for an armed guard to examine each article before it was placed in a bag.

Pinkerton wanted to move them in a covered wagon with military escort, but Lieutenant Sheldon, the officer of the guard who had insisted throughout on treating Rose like a lady, refused to permit that final indignity.[43]

At 4:00 P.M., a carriage pulled up in front of the house. Accompanied by Mrs. Baxley, Little Rose and her mother said good-bye to Lizzie, their faithful Irish servant. Little Rose wept bitterly. The other guards lined up on the street as Rose and her daughter walked slowly past the framed portrait of Gertrude hanging in the hallway and out the door.

Rose Greenhow was almost fifty years old. Her hair was streaked with gray and her face creased with deep lines, but she retained her strong presence, and her tongue was just as sharp. "Good by, Sir," Rose said to one soldier. "I trust that in the future you may have a nobler employment than that of guarding defenseless women."[44]

As she turned and looked up at her house for the last time, she saw several men hanging out of her bedroom windows and recognized reporters from the New York and Philadelphia papers. Pinkerton had undoubtedly tipped them off about the transfer to prison, ensuring that the event would get full news coverage and he would get credit for arresting and imprisoning the Confederacy's most notorious spy.

CHAPTER 23

The Old Capitol Prison

AS DARKNESS FELL, the carriage bearing Rose and Little Rose pulled up in front of the Old Capitol Prison, a dingy brick building on 1st Street, where the United States Supreme Court stands today.[1] Leased by the government for several years to house the Congress temporarily when the unfinished Capitol was burned by the British during the War of 1812, the building had served as a boardinghouse and school before the government converted it to a military prison early in the war. For Rose, it held many memories.

When she arrived in Washington as a teenager more than thirty years before, it had been Hill's Boarding House, her first home and the birthplace of her political awareness. Returning as a prisoner, Rose recalled sitting in the same room and listening to her hero and mentor Calhoun predict the breakup of the Union with his dying breath.

In the wide hallway, now only dimly lit by gas lamps, curious guards crowded around for a glimpse of the celebrity prisoner. Rose was met by the superintendent, William P. Wood, a generally good-humored man who had been commissioner of public buildings before he fell into disfavor and was made head of the prison—saved, no doubt, by his close friend William Seward. Wood, when he felt like it, treated the prisoners with respect.[2] He smiled when he greeted Rose, now his most famous charge. Little Rose stepped forward and looked up at the superintendent. "You have one of the hardest little rebels here you ever saw," the eight-year-old said. "But if you get along with me as well as Lieutenant Sheldon, you will have no trouble." Rose admonished her daughter: "Rose, you must be careful what you say here."[3]

The place was filthy. A tall wooden fence surrounded the yard. The once white walls were streaked with dirt; there were spiderwebs in the corners and half-eaten plates of cold rice and beans in the hall. The rooms reeked of burned mutton fat smoking in the mess, just off the hall.[4] The prison had been set up to house Confederate prisoners of war, but it soon collected a motley crowd of inmates: civilians suspected of disloyalty, Yankee deserters, blockade runners, and accused spies.

Rose and Little Rose were led to their quarters, one of five numbered rooms on the second floor that had once been the chambers of the U.S. House of Representatives.[5] The smaller rooms had three-tiered bunks along the walls. Federal officers who had disobeyed orders were locked in one room, suspect Virginians in others. Number 16, reserved for political prisoners called "suspects and enemies of the state," had a view of the east front of the Capitol, its dome still awaiting completion. The building had a large, arched window that looked out over the entrance, and flat, open land, woods, and fields stretched out behind. Confederate soldiers captured in battle were confined to the lower floor and basement.[6]

Rose and Little Rose were escorted to a room in the back with a view of the prison yard. Wood didn't want Rose looking for "secesh" sympathizers walking along the sidewalk out front. The room held a straw bed with unwashed cotton sheets, a dingy little feather pillow, wooden chairs, a wooden table, and a mirror.[7] Rose also had a pistol, though prisoners were not permitted to keep ammunition. Little Rose curled up in her mother's arms and fell asleep.

The next morning, a carpenter arrived to install bars on the windows. Wood told Rose that General Porter had personally made the drawings, placing the bars to exclude the most air and sunlight. When Wood protested that was unnecessary, Rose reported, the provost marshal warned him, " 'Oh, Wood, she will fool you out of your eyes.' "

Rose quickly found a new archenemy, the prison physician, and saw no reason to humor him. A portly army officer named Dr. Stewart, he had attempted to visit her cell soon after she arrived, but she had shown him a cold shoulder. The next morning, he entered the room without knocking and found Rose in bed.

"The customs of our people made this seem a great outrage to me," Rose wrote. Stewart was under orders to visit all prisoners, but Rose told him indignantly not to come back unless she called. "He spread himself like a Basha with three tails, discoursed fluently upon the dignity of his position and concluded by saying it was his pleasure to come."

Rose replied, "It is not mine to receive you."

As the doctor left the room, he said to the guard in a loud voice, " 'I am the first person who has made that woman feel that she is a prisoner, and I will yet reduce her to the condition of the other prisoners.' " Indignant, Rose called for the superintendent to protest.[8] It was not her last encounter with the prickly physician.

On January 20, two days after Rose's imprisonment, Secretary Seward's son Frederick, who served as his father's assistant secretary at the State Department, signed an order permitting the prisoner's niece and namesake, Adie Douglas, a single visit—but only in the company of "a proper officer."[9] Rose and Little Rose would sit alone in their room, hour after hour, day after day, waiting for their visitor.

The Old Capitol was jammed with prisoners, young and old, black and white. "What set the Old Capitol apart from all other prisons of war was not its location, background or facilities as much as it was the incredible heterogeneity of its prisoners," wrote historian James I. Robertson Jr. "No stranger conglomerate of people ever occupied the same compound . . . soldier and civilian, millionaire and vagrant, the brilliant, the retarded, the sadistic and the senile, as well as the guilty and the innocent."[10]

The stench was overwhelming. The latrines, or "sinks," as they were called, were located across the prison yard in a two-story wooden building that was also used for the hospital and apothecary.[11] At first, Rose, her daughter, and Mrs. Baxley were the only female inmates, but over the next weeks, others arrived. "Mrs. Rose Greenhow and myself were the first women brought to this old Union rat trap, but our number is gradually increasing," Catherine Baxley wrote on March 14. "The first accession was Mrs. [Mary] Morris, still with us; the second a Mrs. J. Barton, alias Mrs. McCarter, [she] still sports her male attire—can't help herself."[12] Even as a prisoner, Rose guarded her social station. She had no use for the other women, insisting that associating with them was "but a shade less obnoxious" than sharing a bench with the Negro prisoners, an indignity she could hardly contemplate.[13]

The prison yard, partially paved with cobblestones, was so crowded with captured Confederate soldiers that there was little opportunity for exercise. At first, Rose and Little Rose were not even permitted outside. They would stand at their second-story window, looking down on other prisoners in the yard playing dominoes and poker, using one-cent pieces for chips. Some prisoners were continually drunk, as whiskey was easy to come by, often procured by the guards. Southern matrons brought cakes and pies, as well as medicine, to Confederate soldiers. Favored prisoners received better cuts of meat from the kitchen.[14]

Rose demanded the attention of the officers of the guard and was not among the sentries' favored few. Her haughty manner and theatrics, coupled with her insistence on treating the guards as servants, antagonized her jailers. She made imperious demands, treated everyone with disdain, and flouted the regulations. "Mrs. Greenhow enjoys herself amazingly," wrote Mary Morris, a fellow prisoner. Even the detectives resented Rose's elitism. One insisted to everyone who listened that Rose's arrest had been the happiest day of her life.[15]

The guards watched her every move. They examined her letters and treated the paper and ink with chemicals to try to detect secret messages. The press had reported after she left her house that she had used invisible ink to pass secrets in her personal letters, but Rose claimed that had been a ruse. "I purposely left a preparation very conspicuously placed, in order to divert attention from my real means of communication, and they have swallowed the bait," she gloated in her memoir.[16]

Parts of her prison journal,[17] published later in her book, describe the treatment of prisoners as harsh, sometimes to the point of brutality, and Rose's spirits flagged after she had been incarcerated for months with no resolution of her case. Her defiance of Yankee authority nearly got her shot on one occasion, and she and Little Rose spent much of their time confined to their cell with almost nothing to eat. "I do not remember very much about our imprisonment except that I used to cry myself to sleep from hunger," Little Rose wrote in a letter many years later.[18]

At one point, Rose quietly pried loose a plank in their closet floor, large enough to slip Little Rose through. She would hold the child while POWs below caught her legs and lowered her to their room. "They were allowed to receive fruit, etc., from the outside, and generously shared with me," Little Rose wrote. "Also they would give mother news of the outside world."[19]

Rose was defiant as ever and refused to buckle. "To-day the dinner for myself and child consists of a bowl of beans swimming in grease, two slices of fat junk, and two slices of bread," she wrote in her journal on January 28. "Still, my consolation is, 'Every dog has his day.'"[20]

Occasionally, the guards allowed Little Rose to go down to the prison yard to play, but other prisoners teased the child about having a bad mother, and the little girl would return to their room in tears.

Little Rose soon inherited a measure of her mother's anti-Union spirit. A guard from the Ninety-first Pennsylvania Volunteer Infantry, which was assigned to the prison, recalled years later that the child sometimes played with Harry, the six-year-old son of another woman prisoner. "One morning while I was guarding the door of a room on the second floor occupied by a Confederate officer . . . a regiment with its band playing martial airs approached the prison," the guard, only sixteen himself at the time, remembered. "Little Harry ran down the stairway in front of me so he could see the troops and hear the music. The little girl called to him: 'Harry, I wouldn't go out to see those nasty Yankee soldiers.' But Harry's love for bright colors and music was so strong that he went on down and out."[21]

Rose took pride in Little Rose's spunk. "I was fearful at first that she would pine, and said, 'My little darling, you must show yourself superior to these Yankees,' " Rose wrote of her daughter. "She replied quickly, 'O mamma, never fear; I hate them too much. I intend to dance and sing "Jeff Davis is coming," just to scare them!' . . ."[22]

"I can conceive no more horrible destiny than that which was now my lot," the mother wrote. "At nine o'clock the lights were put out, the roll was called every night and morning, and a man peered in to see that a prisoner had not escaped through the keyhole."

Their straw cot swarmed with bedbugs, the walls with vermin. In order not to be eaten alive at night, Rose used precious hours of candlelight to burn bugs off the wall. The bed was so hard that she folded her clothes under the straw to act as a mattress, but they still were not comfortable. "Oh Mamma, the bed hurts me so much," Little Rose would cry.[23]

Of all the indignities she endured, Rose complained most bitterly about being held in a section of the prison with Negroes, an affront to her upbringing and passionate belief in slavery and white supremacy. "The tramping and screaming of Negro children overhead was most dreadful," she wrote at one point. "The prison-yard, which circumscribed my view, was filled with them, shocking both sight and smell—for the air was rank and pestiferous with the exhalations from their bodies; and the language which fell upon the ear, and sights which met the eye, were too revolting to be depicted—for it must be remembered that these creatures were of both sexes, huddled together indiscriminately, as close as they could be packed. Emancipated from all control, and suddenly endowed with constitutional rights, they considered the exercise of their unbridled will as the only means of manifesting their equality."[24]

Rose complained that her clothes were being stolen from the laundry and blamed "our free fellow-citizens of colour [who] felt themselves entitled to whatever they liked."[25] She was sure that Captain Gilbert of the Ninety-first Pennsylvania Volunteers drilled Negro soldiers below her window just to annoy her.[26] When a servant was sent in to clean her room or perform some small duty, guards immediately locked and bolted her door, and she would have to rap or call for five or ten minutes before the person was let out again. "When it is remembered that these servants were often Negro men who claimed perfect equality and would tauntingly tell me that 'Massa' Lincoln had made them good as me—that they would not be called Negroes but 'gem'men of colour,' some idea may be felt of the vague, undefined feeling of uneasiness that was constantly upon me."[27]

As word of her imprisonment spread, Rose was treated like a caged animal in a circus, expected to perform whenever people wanted to see her. Northerners requested passes from General Porter to visit the prison, which suddenly became a tourist attraction. Sometimes Rose engaged them in conversation in hopes of learning the latest about the Union army. She was amused when an editor from a Rochester journal told her that she had been locked up because of her writing talent, comparing her to the seventeenth-century French writer Madame de Sévigné. But on most occasions, she found the visitors boorish and intrusive. One woman helped herself to cake that had been a gift to Little Rose. A Boston woman broke into a tirade when she caught sight of the famous spy. "Confess that it was love of notoriety which caused you to adopt your course," the dowager yelled.[28]

Superintendent Wood told Rose he had daily visits from people "who would gladly give him ten dollars a-piece to be allowed to pass my open door, so as to obtain a view of the 'indomitable rebel,' as I was sometimes called in their papers. This was being 'damned to immortality.' "[29] If she tired of the notoriety, Rose nonetheless carefully copied into her journal news stories that carried her name.

She frequently protested her treatment and sometimes taunted her guards, as she reported in her journal on January 28: "This day, as I raised my barred windows, and stood before one of them to get out of the smoke and dust, the guard rudely called, 'Go away from that window!' and raised his musket and leveled it at me. I maintained my position without conde-scending to notice him, whereupon he called for the corporal of the guard. I called also for the officer of the guard, who informed me that I must not go to the window. I quietly told him that, at whatever peril, I should avail myself of the largest liberty of the four walls of my prison. He told me that his guard would have orders to fire upon me. I had no idea that such mon-strous regulations existed."

But they did. Three months later, an ex–U.S. Army officer being held on Rose's floor on suspicion of disloyalty defied a sentry's order to step away from the window of his cell. The sentry fired his musket from the yard out-side and killed the prisoner in his cell. Rose called the death of Jesse Wharton murder "in cold blood."

Little Rose came down with what her mother called camp measles dur-ing an outbreak of the disease in the prison, leading to another confronta-tion with the guard. Rose wanted a servant to help care for the child and rapped loudly on the door to draw their attention. She recorded the ex-change in her journal:

"What do you want?"

"Call the corporal of the guard."

"What do you want with him?"

"That is no business of yours. Call him!"

"I won't call him."

"You shall." (Rap, rap, rap.)

"G-d d——n you, if you do that again I will shoot you through the door."

"Call the corporal of the guard!" Then, without waiting for a response, Rose threw up her window and yelled into the yard at the top of her voice: "Corporal of the Guard!" The enraged guard echoed his prisoner's cry, and the corporal appeared at her door.

"I was seized with laughter," she wrote, "for there stood the Abolitionist, blubbering like a child, furious that he had 'not orders to shoot the d——d Secesh woman, who was not afraid of the devil himself.' "

Rose then sent for the corporal's superior, the officer of the guard, Lieu-tenant Carlton of Zanesville, Ohio. Carlton defended his men and told her they were not her servants.

"But my child is sick," Rose said. "I demand use of a servant."

The officer told her she was permitted use of a servant only in the morn-ing and at night. "Very well, sir," Rose told him. "I will resort to the window, then, as my only expedient." She got her servant—and promptly wrote the provost marshal to complain the guards were threatening to shoot her.[30]

Rose followed Washington social life from reports in the papers and chortled over the controversy that surrounded Mary Todd Lincoln, a temperamental woman whose extravagant White House spending during a time of war had become a subject of daily public criticism.

Mrs. Lincoln's lack of social skills and exaggerated pretense made her the butt of jokes in fashionable society. She came under further suspicion when it was learned that her family was split over the war. A brother and half-sister sided with the Union, another brother and three half-brothers with the South. Critics said she was "two-thirds slavery and one-third secesh."[31]

Rose, however, showed no sympathy for the woman, even if Mrs. Lincoln did have a bit of Southern blood in her family. "I saw Mrs. Lincoln once only, and paid a sixpence for the gratification of my curiosity," Rose wrote. "I was returning from the market-place, where I had gone to purchase some flowers and shrubs, one hot summer morning at an early hour, and in passing a small shop in the avenue saw, standing before it, the imperial coach, with its purple hangings and tall footmen in white gloves; so, yielding to the instinct of Mother Eve, I went into the shop and there beheld a little woman bargaining for some black cotton lace, very much seemingly to the disgust of the shop woman, who left her when I entered, and came to me. I enquired, 'Who is that?' for naturally I was curious to know which member of the family royal stood before me.

" 'Only Madam Lincoln.'

"I asked for some trifle, deposited my sixpence, and, feeling now that I had a legitimate right to look, made the most of the opportunity. She is a short, broad, flat figure, with a broad flat face, with sallow mottled complexion, light grey eyes, with scant light eyelashes, and exceedingly thin pinched lips; self-complacency, and a slightly scornful expression, characterise her bearing, as if to rebuke one for passing between the 'wind and her nobility.'

"Mrs. Lincoln, however, must be very tender-hearted, as she has been frequently known to express great compassion for the 'poor slaves whom God had made free, and the wicked Southerners had made this war to keep them in bondage.'

"Her dress, however, was very grand; yet I don't think that [Napoleon

III's Queen] Eugenie or Mrs. Davis would have selected it for that hour and occasion. The gown was composed of a rich silk, of light ground, with gaudy flowers embroidered over it, lying in voluminous folds full half a yard on the ground. Point Venise collar and sleeves, elaborately made up with pink ribands; white hat, adorned with feathers and flowers interspersed with tinsel balls; white parasol, lined with pink; white gloves, and a superb mantle of black lace, completed her costume. These items were all very deliberately noted; and, although not a very artistic description, it is nevertheless a precise inventory of Mrs. Lincoln's shopping toilet."[32]

Rose was right. The president's wife tried to disguise her insecurities with a queenly manner that offended friend and foe and threw the White House into disarray. Unlike her husband, who was known for his modest tastes, Mrs. Lincoln adorned herself in low-cut gowns of the finest satin, their bodices trimmed with rich velvets and black Chantilly lace. She made extravagant shopping trips by private railway car to Boston, New York, and the fashionable seaside resort of Long Branch, New Jersey, to purchase new furnishings for the White House: ornate rosewood tables with elaborate carvings and marble tops, curtains of purple satin with gold fringe, thick pile carpets à la française and gold lace draperies drawn back with cord and tassels. "Shots had been fired; blood had been shed. America was at war, and the President's wife was on a shopping spree," wrote White House historian William Seale.[33]

Rose snickered at a report that a congressional committee investigating corruption in the Lincoln administration learned Mrs. Lincoln had purchased new state china for the White House that should have cost about $800 but was billed to the government by a New York dealer at $2,500, supposedly infuriating the president and raising allegations that Mrs. Lincoln had taken a kickback on the deal.

Rose was also scathing in her review of a grand ball Mrs. Lincoln gave at the White House in February. Invitations had been issued a month in advance, with refreshments brought down from a fancy French caterer in New York and decorations in sugar commemorating Union warships and forts. James Gordon Bennett, the feisty and irreverent editor of the New York Herald, declined his invitation—but published it in his paper. "The description of the ball in its various phases, and the beautiful toilettes filled many columns of the papers for days after, to the exclusion of the exciting news from the seat of war," Rose wrote. "Mrs. Lincoln's costume received a large share of attention. She was described as being dressed in Court mourning—that is, with white and black, rose and white, and black lace intertwined and commingled, 'as a delicate compliment to Queen Victoria upon the death of Prince Albert.' "

Most appalling to Rose was that "this heartless pageant" went on despite the critical illness of the Lincolns' eleven-year-old son, Willie, whose disease, probably typhoid fever, worsened during the next several days. Willie died in the White House on February 20, casting the city in mourning and his parents into despair.[34] Little Rose was seriously ill at the same time, and her mother feared the worst. "Day by day I saw her fading away," Rose wrote. "Her round chubby face, radiant with health, had become pale as marble, the pupils of her eyes were unnaturally dilated, and finally, a slow nervous fever seized upon her." Rose appealed to the provost marshal to let her own physician, Dr. McMillen, treat the little girl, "unless it be the intention of your Government to murder my child."[35]

A few hours later, the door to her room was thrown open and the hated prison physician, Dr. Stewart, let himself in. Rose ordered him out, but he refused to leave, saying he was there by order of Brigadier General Porter, the provost marshal.

"Sir," Rose said, "I command you to go out; if you do not, I will summon the officer of the guard and the superintendent to put you out."

According to Rose's account, Stewart reached for the sick child, and Rose jumped between them.

"At your peril but touch my child," she warned. "You are a coward and no gentleman, thus to insult a woman."

"I will not go out of your room, Madam," Stewart said, by now livid and trembling himself.

"Call the Officer of the Guard," Rose shouted through the locked door. Lieutenant Carlton appeared, unsettled at having to deal with a confrontation involving a superior officer.

"Sir," Rose said, "I order you to put this man out of my room, for conduct unworthy of an officer and a gentleman, and I will report you for having allowed him to enter here."

The officer rubbed his hands nervously and replied, "I am sure Dr. Stewart will come out if you wish it."

"Sir," Rose snapped, "do your duty; order your guard to put him out." The sergeant, corporal, and guard, who Rose said also despised Stewart for his arrogance, were eager to obey, and the doctor "slunk out." Within a few hours, Dr. McMillen arrived, accompanied by an officer, and tended to Little Rose. He was under orders not to hold any conversation with Rose that was not strictly professional. Rose followed up with another letter to the provost marshal detailing her complaints against Stewart.

About three months after Rose's imprisonment, the female prisoners were let out of their rooms for a half hour of daily exercise in the yard. Rose almost scuttled the privilege with a prank. One afternoon, she went down to get some air just as a cart pulled in from the local market. She knew the driver, whose name was Charlie, and he jokingly offered her a ride. Rose jumped in the cart, and several of the other women piled in after her as Charlie circled the yard rapidly, with the women shouting, "I am off to Dixie!" The other prisoners rushed to their windows to watch the commotion, and the momentary merriment confused the guards, who dashed in to halt an escape.

"Stop that wehickle!" cried Captain Gilbert, the officer of the guard, as Rose mocked his Pennsylvania Dutch accent. After two or three times around, the cart finally drew to a stop in front of Gilbert, who "verily believed that an escape had been meditated and that his timely intervention had alone frustrated it."[36]

On March 3, Rose wrote a plaintive letter to her niece Adie Douglas, saying that Secretary of War Stanton had ordered that Rose's family be permitted to visit her in prison without official passes. She added that Little Rose had been very sick but that in the past two days, they had been permitted a half hour of exercise in the prison yard.

"We walk up and down, picking our way as best we can through mud and negroes, followed by soldiers and corporals with bayonet in hand, ready to cry 'Halt!' if we turn to the right or left," Rose wrote, adding sarcastically: "If I were not writing to so loyal a supporter of the Imperial Powers, I should say, may Heaven confound them. As it is, I shall only say, Goodby, with my love."

The provost marshal's office refused to let the letter pass, and when Rose protested, it was returned to her with a note saying it contained "improper matter and is improperly directed."[37] With that, Rose was cut off from her family. Angry, alone, and powerless, she had no one else of influence to whom she could turn.

CHAPTER 24

The Commission

MAJOR GENERAL JOHN Adams Dix had known Rose for many years, going back to the days when he and Robert Greenhow had worked on the Oregon boundary dispute. They had become friends more recently, when he served as a troubleshooting cabinet officer under President Buchanan and Rose was a grande dame of the society circuit. Dix went to see her in prison on Monday, March 17, 1862. It was an awkward meeting.

President Lincoln had named Dix to the two-man U.S. Commission Relating to State Prisoners, charged with resolving the cases of thousands of people who had been jailed on suspicion of disloyalty. After less than a year of war, Federal prisons were overflowing with political inmates, many of whom had never been formally charged or given an opportunity to defend themselves. Lincoln wanted to ease the burden on the system by freeing those who could be neutralized or exiled to the South, where they would be less of a threat to the Union. That also avoided the prospect of public trials that people like Rose could turn into propaganda platforms for the rebels.

"I had known General Dix formerly very well," Rose wrote. "He was one of the few Northern politicians in whose integrity I entertained any confidence, or for whom I felt any respect."

The general arrived at the Old Capitol Prison with his fellow commissioner, Edwards Pierrepont,[1] a secretary, and the hated Dr. Stewart, whom Rose said the inmates had taken to taunting by calling him "Cyclops." Dix told her he was there to try to settle her case, that he hoped a resolution could be achieved, and that he would do everything he could to help his old friend. Dix explained as plainly as he dared that if Rose cooperated with the commission and refrained from hurling insults at her captors, if she stopped the theatrics that served only to anger and embarrass the Lincoln administration, he would see that she and her daughter were quietly released.

Rose refused. "Thank you," she replied. "You have always had my profound respect. But in your capacity as minister of a tyrant, I could accept no service other than a simple demand for justice against your government." The response was pure Rose—stubborn, determined, too proud to let them see her bend. She put Dix, a seasoned deal maker, in an uncomfortable bind. He preferred a negotiated settlement to a complicated hearing. According to Rose, he expressed deep regret "to see my feelings so much embittered against the Government whose flag we had alike honoured in other days." It was Dix, after all, who in the days leading up to the war, had threatened to shoot anyone who hauled down the American flag.

Rose held firm. "I believe in the Mosaic law which exacts an eye for an eye and a tooth for a tooth," she responded. "I have been now nearly eight months a prisoner. I am not prepared to say whether I will appear before you in your capacity as a commissioner. I deny the power of your Government to lawfully deprive me of my legal rights. And as to that old flag, there was a time when I looked upon it as the proudest emblem of human freedom on earth, and have in other lands bowed before it in holy reverence. But now there is no pirate flag that floats upon the sea which is not more honorable in my eye, for none covers such infamy."[2]

The officer, who was also a gentleman, mumbled some reply and turned his attention to Little Rose, who was lying on the straw bed, her face deeply flushed. Dix put his hand softly on her forehead and said with alarm, "Why, she has a fever."

"Yes, Sir," Rose replied.

"Here is a physician," Dix offered, referring to Dr. Stewart.

"I have sent for one and decline the services of that gentleman," Rose said, infuriating the prison doctor as she had so many times before. Dix looked pityingly on Little Rose and her mother, and Rose silently thanked God that Lincoln had not chosen many agents as compassionate. It would have been impossible for her to hate John Dix as she did the others.[3]

As soon as the general and his entourage left the room, Dr. Stewart exploded in a bitter rage, furious that Rose had belittled him in the commissioner's presence. As Dix walked down the prison corridor, she cried out for him to protect her, and the general returned to see what was going on. When the obstinate physician tried to pursue his diatribe against Rose, Dix cut him off. "Stop, Sir, and retire, if you please," he ordered. Stewart retreated, crestfallen, and Rose gloated quietly at her victory.[4]

Rose refused to get her hopes up about being released, believing that the commission, in her case, was just "a pretext for still greater oppression."[5]

She hated everything about prison life—the food, the filth, the humiliating lack of privacy, the crude, uneducated Northern guards who never missed an opportunity to show her that they were in charge and she wasn't.

Almost two weeks after Dix's visit, Rose was summoned to appear at a commission hearing. Dix and Pierrepont, who had been a superior court judge in New York before the war, had been ordering the release of a stream of prisoners, on condition that they either take an oath of allegiance to the United States or sign a "parole of honor," a written pledge to keep out of the fight and refrain from providing aid or comfort to the enemy. A few refused and were recommitted; others were identified as enemy combatants and transferred to military custody as prisoners of war. The commissioners knew Rose's case would not be so easy.

Rose was the most notorious of political prisoners and regarded by the military as a serious threat. Considering the damage done to the Union forces at Bull Run and Rose's intrepidity in continuing to correspond with the enemy after her arrest, the government might have justified hanging her as a spy. It certainly could have gotten a conviction in a military court while Washington was under martial law. But Lincoln had no appetite for that. Women weren't for hanging, and he didn't need a rebel martyr to galvanize Confederate sympathies in Maryland and the other border states. He had enough problems keeping them in the Union. As Civil War historian James McPherson explains, hanging the mother of a young girl "would have been a public relations disaster for the Lincoln administration and the Union cause."[6]

In reluctantly surrendering the evidence he was holding regarding state prisoners for use by the commission, Brigadier General William Starke Rosecrans put Rose Greenhow at the top of his list. He cited her, unlike any of the other fifty-four prisoners, as a "dangerous, skillful spy."[7] But she had signaled to Colonel Key, back when she was still being held in her home, that she would not bow to federal authority, and she had told Dix and Pierrepont much the same when they went to her cell to bargain with her.

Heavy snow was falling on Saturday, March 29, when Rose boarded the black, horse-drawn carriage that would take her up Pennsylvania Avenue to the provost marshal's office at the other end of the city, where the commission held its hearings. "It was one of those raw uncomfortable days in which the cold penetrated to the marrow," she wrote of her first trip outside prison in more than three months. "The sun was obscured by clouds as dark as Yankee deeds."[8]

The commission met in the once elegant mansion that had belonged to her friend William Gwin, the senator from California, who had been arrested a few months earlier on suspicion of trying to go south to join the Confederacy. As Rose approached the building, she spotted the young army officer who had accused her of treason in the Senate gallery the previous August. He was waiting in the doorway, and Rose saw his face light up in triumph as she caught his eye. Unable to contain herself, she drew her finger across her throat and hissed, "Beware."[9]

When she entered the now filthy hallway where Mrs. Gwin had once welcomed her and Washington's finest, Rose pushed past a crowd of curious soldiers and spectators and climbed the staircase to the third floor, where she was left to wait alone in a freezing room. "My mind instinctively reverted to the gay and brilliant scenes in which I had mingled in that house, and the goodly company who had enjoyed its hospitality," she wrote. Only four years earlier, she had been "A Housekeeper of the Old School" for Mrs. Gwin's ball, which society ladies referred to decades later as the capital's "social gathering of the century."[10]

Rose sat shivering, her hands and feet completely numb. There was no fire in the fireplace. A guard rattled his musket outside the room to remind her of his presence.

Finally, the door of the hearing room was thrown open. Superintendent Wood cleared a path for Rose through a phalanx of soldiers jamming the hall. She was announced to the commission, and the commissioners, appearing ill at ease, stood to greet her. Acknowledging their respectful manner, Rose bowed and said: "Gentlemen, resume your seats."[11]

The scene resembled a makeshift courtroom. There was a long table in the middle of the room. General Dix sat at one end, Judge Pierrepont at the other. E. D. Webster, private secretary to Secretary of State Seward, sat at a small table to the general's left, acting as secretary to the commission. Two other men whom Rose didn't recognize sat at a small desk in the rear.[12] One, the hearing reporter, was in charge of transcribing the session. His bold, elegant script recorded the session verbatim.

Rose, who was not represented by counsel, seated herself at the long table between the two commissioners, in full view of everyone in the room. Her own account, although embellished in its rhetoric, is remarkably consistent with the official transcript of the proceeding, which is relied on here as the most accurate report of the session and a rare example of Rose's unedited voice. As in her testimony years before in the San Francisco courtroom, she yielded no quarter to authority.

Rose seized control of the proceeding immediately and did not relinquish it. "Mrs. Greenhow on entering the room remarked that she had been kept waiting so long that her patience was nearly exhausted," the reporter wrote.[13] The commissioners apologized, explaining defensively that they had not realized she had arrived in the building.[14]

As he waited for the hearing to begin, General Dix fiddled nervously with a pile of papers—a dozen pages of her letters and reconstituted messages rescued from her stove.[15]

Judge Pierrepont, who conducted the examination, got right to the point: "The charge that is brought against you is for aiding the enemy to military information."[16]

"I am a Southern woman, with Southern sentiments," Rose replied proudly. "I have a right to aid my cause in any manner that lies in my power—and I think I have a right to do it." She paused, then rose to her feet and turned to General Dix.

"Is this being taken down for the newspapers?" she asked. The commissioner assured her that it was not, that the transcript was to be kept strictly private.

"Very well, then," she said. "I did not know but what it would be published in the newspapers, and I should not be surprised at that, as every principle of decency has been outraged, and after people have been allowed to go through our place of confinement and gaze on us as though we were some public curiosity."

"It is not to be published in any of the newspapers," Judge Pierrepont insisted. "And whatever you like to say will be taken down as you give it and will then go to the War Department."

Rose did not wait for the next question. "You look upon me as having committed treason; and all because of the views I entertain. Is it not so?"

"You can say whatever you think best," Pierrepont replied. "You need not answer any questions which you do not want to." She was not under oath, and it was not, technically, a criminal proceeding.

"Go on with your questions," Rose said irritably. "Is this a kind of mimic court? Of course I am not obliged to commit myself. In fact, I have been cheated so much by this Government that I have no respect for it."

"You can make any reply you want to the charges," Pierrepont said.

"Charges! How many have you?" Rose asked. "Now isn't this a farce! Isn't it solemn! It's a perfect farce."

"You can make any reply you please to the charges," Pierrepont repeated.

In words alternately sarcastic and patronizing, Rose insisted that she had done nothing wrong. She was incensed that her private correspondence had been read by strangers and denied that she had destroyed any personal papers before her arrest. Told that she was accused of corresponding with the enemy and providing information about the force and position of Union troops, she grew indignant.

"Where is your proof?" she demanded. "This is a charge without any proof. I have corresponded on many occasions with my friends. This much is true. Cannot I write what I please? Must my private letters be torn open and laughed over, and my sentiments restricted? Besides, I am not in a position to get important information. None of those connected with the Government will give me any. All that has been good and glorious in this Government, I believe to have come from those who are now in the Confederate Government."

Judge Pierrepont repeated the accusation that she had "aided in giving information to the enemy, of the plans for our army, contrary to all the rules and articles of war prohibiting such communication."

"I want you to show me some proof of it," Rose insisted.

Pierrepont played into her hands, bringing up the letter protesting her treatment that she had written to Seward, a copy of which had subsequently shown up in a Richmond newspaper.

"Did you not send a letter to Richmond?" he asked.

"What was it?"

"One sent by you to the Secretary of State was afterwards published in a newspaper of the insurgent states."

"Yes," Rose said, conceding only authorship of the letter. "And I charge it upon Mr. Seward as an outrage to allow a private letter of mine to find its way into the public prints."

Pierrepont grasped for the reins. "The charge is that it was sent by you, to be published in the Richmond papers," he offered.

"I don't remember anything of the kind," Rose replied.

"How did it get into the Richmond papers?" Pierrepont pressed.

Rose refused to concede anything. "I have not the least idea," she responded. "I only know it was sent to Mr. Seward and got out through his office. [The newspaper had claimed its source of the letter was a Seward confidant.] I have no doubt but that you will charge me with counseling Mr. Davis how to lead his armies."

Exasperated, Pierrepont tried a different tack. "You are charged with corresponding with the rebels," he told her, "and particularly with giving them information of our army in relation to the battle of Bull Run."

"I am not aware of that," Rose replied. "It is certain that if I had the information, I should have given it. I should consider that I was performing a holy duty to my friends."

The commission was getting nowhere in its sparring match with the notorious "Mrs. G," as she was called in the record. Pierrepont cut to the chase.

"How would you like to better your condition by leaving your present place of confinement?" he asked.

Rose was cagey: "Seven months of imprisonment—with almost starvation sometimes—has not given me any relish for it."

"How would you like to go to the other side of the lines?"

"That would be a question."

"Suppose the government should conclude to let you go. Would you consider that you owed allegiance to it; and would you be willing to be bound by the rules of war?" Pierrepont was dangling an offer of releasing her to go south on a parole of honor.

Rose stiffened. "This is my home," she said. "I have been taken from my home and carried to prison, to be insulted and subjected to a treatment of the most outrageous kind. Every association of my home has been broken up and destroyed. If the government deigns to send me across the lines as an exile, I have no alternative but to go as such."

Pierrepont made clear the commission was not speaking only for itself, but that the Lincoln government was trying to get rid of her. "It has been proposed that we make this suggestion to you and to see if you would like to accept it," the judge said.

Rose pushed for more: "With the privilege of aiding and abetting my cause?"

"Yes, if that is your desire," Pierrepont replied.

"In other words, you mean to tell me that if I do not accept it, I will be forcibly exiled," she said.

"Would it be exiling you to send you South among your friends?" asked Pierrepont.

"It is exiling me to use any force, to send me South from my home," Rose responded.

"I merely made it as a suggestion," Pierrepont said.

Rose toyed with the mouse. "Is there any other charge of treason against me? It may be that I am charged with having spies in the government. It is really absurd to suppose that I could get important information of the Government's designs when I am not in the Government; or that I could get such information about the Government when no one in power would give it to me; or that if such information was my object, that I could get it unaided. If I gave the information that you say I have, I must have got it from sources that were in the confidence of the Government. I don't intend to say any more. I merely throw this out as a suggestion."

Judge Pierrepont looked wearily at the accused spy sitting at the table before him. Not yet fifty, she was a handsome woman—and stubborn as they came. "I suppose it is hardly worthwhile to ask you to take the oath of allegiance, or give your parole of honor," he said.

"You would blush to do that," she shot back, "because I belong to a religion and a section of the country which makes an oath binding. If I took an oath, I should consider myself bound by it. If I took the oath of allegiance—no matter how galling it might be—I should consider myself as being bound by that oath."

"Have you any particular religion?" Pierrepont inquired curiously.

"None but that which relies on the mercy and goodness of Providence," said the woman who had been raised a Roman Catholic.

The judge sighed and deferred to Dix: "General, I think you had better talk to Mrs. Greenhow. You are an old friend of hers." Dix was a professional problem solver. He had run two railroads, reformed the U.S. Post Office, stopped a financial panic, and won private backing to finance the Union war effort. But Rose Greenhow had him stymied.

"I don't know that I have anything to say," Dix muttered.

Rose drew a small measure of satisfaction from his obvious discomfort. "You both see how pleasant it is," she said.

"You might ask Mrs. Greenhow about the correspondence in cipher," Dix suggested to his colleague, trying to get back to the facts.

Rose quickly interrupted: "I am not obliged to answer that question."

"You are not obliged to answer any question that you do not please to," the general replied politely. "Those that you do answer will be recorded, so you see you have perfect freedom."

"Liberty of speech!" Rose retorted, her sarcasm spilling out.

"You have the privilege of putting the answer in your own form," Dix said patiently.

"Of course, General, I decline to answer questions of that sort," she said, getting back to the query about the cipher, then teasing him with it: "Although I believe your chief detective [Allan Pinkerton, alias E. J.] Allen found some cipher at my house while I was sick. It was a very good cipher and it might have been found useful, but I did not get an opportunity to use it. When Mr. Allen got it, I suppose he thought he had received the key of Beauregard's dispatches."

Pierrepont dropped the line of questioning Dix had suggested and tried a personal approach. "You have a son-in-law in the Union army?"

"I have a son-in-law and a nephew," Rose replied. "Unfortunately, I have a great many relatives who are benighted on the subject."

Pierrepont returned to the matter of exile: "You don't want to answer that question about going South now?"

"No, not now," the widow replied.

But General Dix was losing patience: "I want to ask you a question; of course you are not obliged to answer it. Yet the Judge and I would be much better pleased to see you exonerated from these charges or from a part of them."

Rose was not going to be pushed. "I consider that I have a perfect right, as an American citizen, to entertain any opinion that I desire," she warned.

Dix reached for a piece of paper in the pile before him. "I want to know in regard to this letter which was found in your house," he said, holding it in the air. "It reads: 'There are 45,000 on the Virginia side; 15,000 around the city, to wit, up the river above Chain Bridge, at Tenallytown, Bladensburg, across Anacostia Branch and commanding every approach to the city. If McClellan can be permitted to prepare, he expects to surprise you. . . .' Did you write this?"

"I have no recollection of it," Rose responded.

"There are other letters of the same sort," Dix said.

"Are those letters said to be found in my house?" Rose asked.

"Yes," the general replied.

"I think that is false. I think that is unequivocally false, I don't swear it is. I have been in the habit of entertaining guests at my house. So far as I am myself concerned, I pronounce it unequivocally false."

Judge Pierrepont: "The charge is not that you wrote these letters; but that it was through your agency that they were transmitted."

Rose: "That I pronounce to be false. No letters were left with Mrs. Greenhow to be transmitted through her agency. I say I am no one's agent. They might have been there, and they might not have been there. I am not to be made accountable for my guests."

Dix was scolding: "You know, Mrs. Greenhow, that in a context like this, while the very existence of the Government is in danger, the communication of such information as this, which tends to subvert the interests of the Government, should certainly be considered a very serious offense."

"I don't know about that," Rose replied, seeing an opening. "When the President, with his 100,000 men, has to hold in confinement a poor woman and children, I think he had better give up the ghost. Since his Black Republican party came into power—and I detest it in my very soul—I have kept entirely out of the world. I lost my child a short time before. I have not been in the world during that time; therefore any information I may have got must have been brought to my house, and brought to me. Brought to me by traitors, as you call them, in that party. Therefore I am to be held responsible for that? If Mr. Lincoln's friends will pour into my ear such important information, am I to be held responsible for all that? Could it be presumed that I could not use that which was given to me by others? If I did not, I would be unjust to myself and my friends. It is said that a woman cannot keep a secret. I am a woman, and a woman usually tells all she knows."

"If you got the information as a secret, what then?" Pierrepont asked.

"That doesn't make any difference," the prisoner replied. "I haven't any intention of working against my friends. I have written as much as any man against the party now in power; because I believe it is this party that has brought all the present trouble upon the country. This party has been the consequence of it. I believe it religiously." She went on a bit, then coyly apologized for "departing from the rule of rigid examination."

"We don't wish to limit you at all, Madame," Pierrepont told her, with Dix chiming in, "There is no restriction."

She asked the men to give her papers back, but Dix said the commission would decide about that.

Rose said she expected them to be returned because "I don't see any treason in all that you have told me."

"I don't think you are bent so much on treason as mischief," Pierrepont replied.

Mischief? Not treason but mischief?

"Let me tell you," the clever widow replied, "I have studied the Constitution and law of this country. I have informed myself about the Constitution as well as I have about my Bible. Your Government ought to be ashamed of itself for allowing me to be scandalously treated; in allowing such scoundrels as it did to get my letters, and read them and laugh over them. I have been made the victim of every kind of villainy. It has sent its emissaries to betray me; and persons who advised me to write letters but then betrayed them to the Government."

Pierrepont showed another card. "So you know J. S. Sheldon?" he asked, referring to the lieutenant who Rose thought had treated her so courteously while overseeing her imprisonment in her house.

"Yes, very well," Rose replied.

"There seem to be some letters here that passed through his hands," Pierrepont disclosed, indicating Sheldon had slipped them to Union authorities.

"Call him up and let him answer," Rose said indignantly. "Call him up and we will see what he has to say about that."

For the first time, Rose seemed rattled. So Lieutenant Sheldon had betrayed her. "I have no intention—I have no recollection of it at all," she began haltingly. "During the first month of my imprisonment I had perfect freedom to write what I pleased; and the letters were carried through the provost-marshal's office."

"The question is not as to whether you have written the letters," Pierrepont told her, "but, also, whether you have a right, knowingly, to try and subvert the purposes of the Government."

"I don't consider that I was," she replied. "I look at it in an entirely different light. I have a right to write what I please. I always did so."

Pierrepont cut her off: "It is wartime now."

General Dix picked out a letter written in Rose's distinctive hand on pink stationery and addressed to her daughter Florence in San Francisco. Dix held it up for Rose to see. He handed the pages to the witness and asked, "What have you to say about that letter?"

Rose read her words written only ten days before to her eldest child, whom she had not seen for more than two years. Florence had expressed her worry about Rose's safety, as well as the concern of her army officer husband, who was eager to fight for the Union. Rose now realized the guard she had bribed to sneak the letter out of prison had delivered it to the provost marshal instead of putting it in the post.

MARCH 15TH
OLD CAPITOL PRISON

My Darling,

All my letters must reach you through the underground as these despicable scoundrels, the detectives, now examine all letters and exercise their discretion about sending them. My last letters were returned to me, also a note to Adie Douglas.[17] My God, you cannot conceive the outrageous practices here. These Black Republican dogs have made a howl in Congress about the negroes that were confined to the jail, and they confined me and other ladies in a filthy room, the walls of which the few warm days were covered with vermin, and have lodged negroes in the same quarter, above, below and around. In fact we are confined in a negro quarter of the building. We cannot open our windows without the stench of over a hundred negroes, and if you have ever been in the neighborhood of a negro meeting house in summer, you can fancy what odors reach us when our door opens. I will have my revenge, and bear these outrages better on that account. I have no feeling but hate toward this detested, demoralized nation and I thank God that it is in its last throes. McClellan has gotten his congé, having served the purpose of killing off Scott. Stanton has been brought forward to get rid of McClellan, and he will be put aside in his turn. These men let their vanity blind them as to their real position, and content themselves with the applause manufactured in advance to suit the role they are intended to play and lose sight of what a light observation should point out to them: the necessity of making a party for themselves. Stanton is now fooled to the top of his bent. He writes magnificent orders for Lincoln and lords it in the most approved fashion; he does not see what others see, that his fall is not distant.[18]

Rose was incensed that her old rival John C. Frémont had been given yet another command in the Union army. The Pathfinder, having once been cashiered for insubordination, was awarded a star by Lincoln and put in command of the Western Department, including Missouri. After Frémont abolished slavery in that border state in 1861 without higher authority, Lincoln relieved him of his command, but the explorer's political friends in the Republican Party pressured the president to take him back and give him another chance. As Rose was writing her letter, Frémont had just been put in command of the Mountain Department, responsible for western Virginia, Kentucky, and Tennessee. "The abolition policy is now fully

avowed," Rose wrote. "Frémont has been again galvanized into prominence; if he was a man of talent and nerve, he would be the first American
dictator; as it is, he will be the cat's paw to draw the chestnuts out of the
fire for somebody else to eat."[19]

Rose confessed to Florence that other members of the family were
keeping their distance. "I do not care to speak of Mrs. Cutts," she said, referring to her sister Ellen. "When I tell you this, I am already seven months
a prisoner, but in that time, she and Adie have been three times to see me;
that only once during the whole period have they ever sent me the smallest
thing and this was on Christmas in an ostentatious display. But I am content. I shall send you some colored clothing for yourself and Leila. As for
myself, I shall never lay aside my mourning. God bless you, darling. My
love to dear Leila and Minnie. Your devoted mother."[20]

Rose dismissed the document after reading it. "This is of no account,"
she said haughtily. "There is nothing in it but what I have written often. It
contains my present feelings and sentiments."

"The letter is equal to declaring determined hostility to the Government," Dix insisted.

"I should have been the meekest, lowliest Christian in the world if, after
being smitten on one cheek by the Government, I should have turned the
other," Rose replied with no hint of remorse. "Well, now, have you any
other letters of mine?"

"I believe there are a great many others of the same purport," Dix said.

"The Government knew what my feelings have been, and always were,"
Rose said. "I have not changed them. I have no other feelings than those
now."

Dix gave up. "Judge," he said, addressing Pierrepont at the other end of
the table, "I don't know as we wish to ask Mrs. Greenhow any more questions."

But Rose Greenhow was determined to have the last word. "In these
war times, you ought to be in some more important business than holding
an inquisition for the examination of women," she said. "I look upon this
as nothing more than an inquisition." For the second time in a week, the
Union had tried to give her a way out. And for the second time, Rose refused to bow.

The clerk noted, "Further consideration of the case was postponed, and
the prisoner remanded."[21]

Rose Greenhow was escorted out of the room and sent back to the Old
Capitol Prison.

CHAPTER 25

A Martyr's Joy

ROSE HAD BEEN imprisoned now for almost seven months. She begged fruit and bread from other prisoners for Little Rose and picked vermin off their bed before curling up at night for a troubled sleep. The guards shot and killed a prisoner she knew, and Little Rose suffered from nightmares.

Superintendent Wood appeared at Rose's cell door the evening after the commission meeting to say the hearing reporter who had transcribed her session wished to have a word with her. Rose agreed and asked that he be brought to her room. The clerk told Rose that two newspapers, one in New York and another in Philadelphia, had each offered him $500 for a transcript of the proceeding. He tried to persuade Rose that with so much public interest in her case, it would be impossible to prevent leaks and that she would benefit from publication of an accurate account of her words. Rose didn't disclose whether or not the aide offered to share the potential windfall with her, claiming it was her wish was to avoid notoriety. "Besides, verbatim reports barely do justice to people's beliefs," she said.[1]

"On the contrary, madam, yours is calculated to make a great impression," she quoted the clerk as telling her in a flattering tone. "It has been read before the commissioners and official authorities, and the highest commendations bestowed upon it." He opened some papers and read some excerpts of what she had said at the hearing. Rose listened attentively as her words were read back to her and decided she had no objections to publication.[2]

Someone else did. Secretary of State Seward threatened to throw the commission clerk in prison and levy a heavy fine against him if he let the transcript get out to the press. Instead, according to Rose, the only stories that appeared in the newspapers claimed that "the arch-rebel Mrs. Greenhow had made a full confession of her accomplices, etc."[3]

Actually, the *National Intelligencer* reported the opposite. It carried an article on March 31, 1862, describing the appearance of Rose and Mrs. Morris before the commission: "The examination we learn resulted in nothing satisfactory. The ladies would confess nothing, promise nothing, give their parole for nothing, renounce nothing; and they were reconveyed to their quarters at the Old Capitol. Thus the examination ended in furnishing at least one instance of truth of the ungallant old sarcasm on female willfulness:

"If she will, she will, you may depend on't;

"If she won't, she won't; and there's an end on't."[4]

When Rose's favorite niece, Adie Douglas, read the *Intelligencer* report, she sat down and wrote a bitter note to her aunt: "I do believe you have a stern joy in your martyrdom, else you would embrace the opportunity to escape from it."[5]

Stern joy in your martyrdom. The words hit Rose like a slap in the face. The beautiful little girl Rose had helped raise and thought of almost as her own was now a highly regarded member of Washington society. She was grown, a widow like Rose. Her husband, Senator Douglas, who had championed compromise and popular sovereignty and campaigned for the Union after the outbreak of war, had died of typhoid fever in Chicago, with Adie at his side, two months before Rose's arrest. Now Adie had turned on her once beloved aunt.

Stung by the suggestion that she could possibly be enjoying life behind bars, Rose immediately wrote back to defend herself:

OLD CAPITOL PRISON; APRIL I.

My Dear Adie,

You seem to have received the idea that my imprisonment has been a voluntary thing on my part. Some one doubtless, my dear, has imposed upon your credulity, or endeavored to mislead you in regard to the facts of the case. . . .

Rose said she had complained to various military officials about the obscene abuses of the women in the prison. She conceded that Colonel Key had called on her and, in an unofficial capacity, brought up the subject of exile to the South, but she said nothing had come of it.

"No offer of release upon any terms has ever been made," Rose wrote:

I and my poor little child have been subject to barbarities which should call the blush to the cheeks of these people, if all sense of shame is not extinct. I will not shock your modesty by narrating the various experiences of my prison life; but in my future use of these facts, I shall require no adventitious aid to make the narrative effective, for the simple stern realities will throw into the shade the most extravagant efforts of imagination.

Rose told Adie that she had appeared before the commission, but "the examination was a farce, an amusing conversation, from which nothing was expected to be elicited." The commissioners were gentlemen, she conceded: "It is needless to tell you that the most high-bred courtesy marked the interview." Rose said that the prison superintendent informed her that evening that a sentence of exile had been passed, but she trusted not a word they said: "Until I have received the official notification, I of course cannot decide upon my future."

Rose admonished her niece for suggesting that by standing up for her beliefs, she was playing the role of martyr:

Do not, my dear, believe that I have any "stern joy in martyrdom." I am too keenly alive to the enjoyment of God's blessings to covet any such thing. I know now that hardships and severe trials are before me in the future. I am to be driven forth from my home by this magnanimous Government, in the midst of the bloodshed and carnage with which they are pursuing all who cherish my own political faith. I may witness the horrors of a sacked city, or sleep within sound of the cannon's roar on the battlefield. These probable frightful vicissitudes do not appall me, for a true woman has her mission.

Her mission, however, seemed to be driving her obsession: "I would to God I could obliterate the recollections of the outrages of the last eighteen months, for I fear now that my capacity of hate will overshadow every other feeling." Rose ended her letter asking Adie to visit her in the boardinghouse-turned-prison, "which was once my happy home. Yours affectionately, Rose O'N. Greenhow."[6]

That same day, Jesse Wharton was killed for standing in his prison window.[7] Rose did not exaggerate the "barbarities" she mentioned in her letter to Adie.

But the end appeared in sight. Two days later, Rose received formal notice that the commission would exile her to the South if she agreed not to return before the war was over.[8] She wrote in her journal that Superintendent Wood read her a copy of the commission's decree that evening, and she responded in a letter to General Wadsworth, the military governor, accepting her "banishment"—but added that she did so under protest and refused to promise not to return north. "I ask of your clemency time and freedom to make the necessary arrangements for clothes for myself and little child." Rose could not suppress a line of sarcasm: "Of course, if this is granted me, I shall bind myself for the period allotted not to blow up the President's house, equip a fleet, break open the treasury, or do any other small act which you may suppose comes within my limited powers to perform."[9]

The determined champion of the Southern cause still had spunk, but prison life and mothering her little girl through it sapped her emotionally and physically and bowed her spirit.

On April 14, Rose submitted: "Sir," she wrote to the military governor, "I am now ready to leave this prison to go South, according to the decree of the commissioners to that effect."[10]

The New York Herald learned about the commission's offer but apparently not that Rose decided to accept it: "Those distinguished and inextinguishable rebels in crinoline, the elegant Mrs. Greenhow and the fascinating Mrs. Morris . . . were offered their liberty on either of two conditions: the oath of allegiance to the government, or their retirement to some place within the temporary dominions of Jeff Davis, and that the two irrepressible feminines flatly refused to accept either proposition." The newspaper reported that the women refused to take the oath of allegiance: "They preferred imprisonment in Washington, under the flag of the Union, to liberty in Secessia. Napoleon Bonaparte, in his day of power, found an enemy in [novelist] Madame de Stael, and, annoyed by her political intrigues, and finding her otherwise unmanageable, he said, 'I will punish her with the extremest punishment she can bear. I will exile her from Paris.' "

Seward should have sent "Madame Greenhow" off to Richmond with his compliments, the Herald editorialized. "He would have made an example of her case which would have relieved him of any further annoyances from the fashionable lady secessionists of Washington—for Washington is their Paris—and beyond it they are in exile."[11]

When Rose read the piece, she was furious and dashed off a letter to James Gordon Bennett, editor of the *Herald*, complaining about the "stupid and ill-natured article." She told him that contrary to his newspaper's report, she had no intention of living in the same capital with Lincoln's boorish henchmen and *had* agreed to accept exile to the South.

OLD CAPITOL PRISON: TUESDAY NIGHT, APRIL 15.

SIR,

I should consider it a great trial to be obliged to live in this city under the present régime, for, according to my peculiar political ideas, all the refinement, all the intellect, which once constituted the charm of Washington society, has departed with my brethren of the South; and I shall only too gladly avail myself of the edict which banishes me from my whilom home to go amongst kindred spirits, and to a land made glorious by its heroic resistance of the invader.

I ask, Sir, of your sense of justice, the insertion of this my disclaimer in your paper.

Very respectfully,
Rose O'N. Greenhow.[12]

Another week went by with no response from the authorities to Rose's letter agreeing to the commission's terms. The trauma of Jesse Wharton's killing added to her distress. She was convinced—probably correctly—that the guards withheld the newspapers when there were any reports about the South. Rose wrote the military governor again, practically begging him to get her out of prison, saying further delay constituted "a wanton act of cruelty." She and Little Rose felt weak from hunger and listless from lack of exercise. And the tedium, Rose wrote in her memoir, was "greater than I can depict." Little Rose spent hours lying on her mother's lap, crying, "Mamma, tell me a story." Each night Rose made up endless legends for the child, holding her in her arms and talking quietly until she fell asleep. Rose herself had insomnia, heightened by her lack of anything to read. In a letter addressed to an unnamed "Mon Ami," Rose asked for French novels, "anything to wile away time."[13]

"My room swarmed with vermin, which the warm weather now caused to come out in myriads from their hiding-places," Rose wrote in her journal. She despised having to share the prison yard with "stolen negroes" during her daily half hour of exercise time, complaining that they "lay about, obstructing the walk, or engaged in boisterous practical jokes during the while, in utter disregard of social distinction, and even ventured to seat themselves on the same bench."

Rose reported that her fellow female prisoner Catherine Baxley got into a fight with a guard over being told to use a back staircase, bloodied his nose, and was knocked down and kicked for her insubordination. Rose stuck up for the guard.[14]

Occasionally, several members of Rose's family came to visit, although she said that prompted only tighter surveillance and made their lives more difficult. She heard from a congressman that her release was being held up by General McClellan, the cautious commander who had just begun his march up the Peninsula from the Virginia coast toward Richmond. She said she got the same story from Senator James Bayard of Delaware.

Those who did catch a glimpse of Rose were surprised that she did not look more haggard. A *New York Times* correspondent who toured the prison wrote that she was "about 48, but presents a much more youthful appearance and would readily pass for a person of 38 summers." He said she "has been a gay, dashing widow, rather tall, of small facial outline, and graceful in movement. We say she *has been* a gay, lively widow, as we understand that her vivacity is considerably reduced since her rebel plumage has been clipped with Union shears."[15]

The observation was astute, as Rose herself acknowledged. "This was the gloomiest period of my life," she wrote. "Time dragged most heavily. I had absolutely nothing to occupy myself with. I had no books, and often no paper to write on, and those who approached me appeared entirely oblivious of the mental as well as physical wants of a prisoner." Even with a reprieve in sight, she was losing hope, "chafing against my prison bars, with the iron of the despot eating into my soul."[16]

In some cases, the punishment for treason was death. In Richmond, on April 29, the Confederates hanged Timothy Webster, Pinkerton's favorite agent, who had been arrested twenty-six days earlier after two other Pinkerton men broke under interrogation and implicated Webster as a spy. According to Pinkerton's book *The Spy of the Rebellion,* President Lincoln and his cabinet deplored the planned execution, the first of an American spy since Nathan Hale, and authorized a message to President Davis warning that the Union would retaliate if the South resorted to such dire tactics.[17] Official records don't indicate whether or not the case jeopardized the deal to release Rose.

One would think that any prisoner hoping desperately for release would be on good behavior. Not Rose! She was implicated in an ill-fated effort to help other inmates escape—including one who had just learned he would be tried for espionage—and she gave another her pistol. Brazenly, Rose recorded the plan in her journal, though she claimed to have written the entry in cipher in case any of the guards tried to read it: "Captain Bryan and Harry Stewart are going to escape to-night—the attempt to be made when the guard whom they have bribed comes on at midnight." According to Rose's report, the prison guard had told Harry Stewart that he was charged with spying, and Stewart was desperate. The other prisoner was Captain Pliny Bryan, a captured Confederate Signal Corps officer. "I long for the morrow, and the 'All's well!' " Rose wrote. "A presentiment of evil weighs me down. I have a raging nervous headache. I have just bidden them both good-bye, and given Bryan my pistol. This continued anxiety is killing me."[18]

Sunday morning, May 11. "I was aroused at a little after five by the report of a rifle, and a cry enough to startle the dead: Harry Stewart had been shot by the guard whom he had bribed."[19] Stewart's shattered leg was amputated, but he died within hours from loss of blood. Bryan had backed out of the plan at the last minute.[20] Rose said she was interrogated about her suspected role in the escape attempt. Her punishment was to be denied visitors.

"My child is so nervous from a repetition of these dreadful scenes that she starts and cries out in her sleep," Rose wrote. "When will this end? I am nearly starved. I had a fowl served up to me to-day (or rather a small piece of one), which must have been the cock which crowed thrice to wake Peter; we could not get our teeth through it. Rose cried heartily, for she was very hungry. Captain Bryan, and the other gentlemen below, have just smuggled me a supper. I should starve but for the considerate kindness of these gentlemen."[21]

Rose reported that her old friend Senator Henry Wilson, with whom she supposedly was linked by love letters, visited the prison as part of a congressional committee and stopped in to see her. He told Rose he had learned that an order had been issued to send her south immediately but Seward and McClellan objected. Nonetheless, he told her, she would be freed soon because the rebellion was crumbling and Richmond had fallen.

If Wilson actually said this, he was wrong, but the news drove Rose further toward despair. "My existence is now a positive blank," she wrote on Friday, May 23. "Day glides into night with nothing to mark the flight of time, and hope paints no silver lining to the clouds which hang over me. . . . The chattering of a monkey would even break pleasantly on the monotony of my life."²²

While Rose was walking in the prison yard two days later, an inmate who had been captured in Virginia threw a tiny piece of paper at her feet. She scooped it up and stared at the message in disbelief: Stonewall Jackson had handed federal forces at Front Royal in the Shenandoah Valley an overwhelming defeat. "It made my heart leap with joy," Rose wrote.²³

The next evening, as she was searching for an item in her trunk, Rose placed a candle on her windowsill in order to have more light. Alarmed that she might be signaling someone on the street below, the guards ordered her to put out the flame. Defiantly, Rose lit another. "Damn you, I will fire into your room!" a guard yelled from the prison yard. Ignoring him, Rose ran down the corridor and collected candles from other prisoners and set them along her windowsill, lighting them one by one. Hearing a furious commotion in the hallway outside her room, she slipped a bolt into the lock. A guard rapped on her door. "What business do you have here?" she demanded.

"You are making signals and must remove your lights from the window," he replied.

"But it suits me to keep them there," she told him.

"We will break down your door if you don't open it," the guard shouted. Rose told him she kept a pistol on her mantel—they didn't realize she had no ammunition. The guard retreated, but the next day, the provost marshal ordered the pistol confiscated.²⁴

On Saturday, May 31, at 2:00 P.M., Superintendent Wood announced that Rose and Little Rose would finally be freed. They were to be exiled to the South and would leave for Baltimore that same afternoon. Mother and child had been imprisoned now for nearly ten months, five in confinement at their 16th Street house, more than four in a filthy room in the Old Capitol Prison. They were given an hour to pack, but when their departure time was delayed, the captain of the guard walked Rose through the prison, allowing her to bid farewell to the other inmates. With great compassion, she urged them to bear up and be brave.

As they reached the door of the prison, Rose and her daughter were turned over to a lieutenant at the head of a six-man detail in full uniform with swords and carbines in hand. A dozen mounted cavalrymen provided additional security. Seized by a last-second fear of a trick, Rose addressed the young officer: "Sir, 'ere I advance further, I ask you, not as Lincoln's officer but as a man of honour and a gentleman, are your orders from Baltimore to conduct me to a Northern prison or some point in the Confederacy?"

"On my honour, madam, to conduct you to Fortress Monroe [a Union stronghold on the Virginia coast] and thence to the Southern Confederacy," the officer replied. He showed her his orders. The two other female prisoners, Mrs. Baxley and Mrs. Morris, had already boarded the carriage. Reassured, Rose climbed in after them. The officer boosted Little Rose to a seat beside her mother.[25]

It was the last time Rose Greenhow would ride through Washington. She had walked the broad expanses many times over the years—with Cave Johnson and other suitors, with friends and neighbors and officials, with her late husband, Robert, and his sister, Mary Greenhow. For more than three decades, Rose had witnessed climactic political struggles from the Capitol to the White House. It was here that her heart was won and broken several times over, here that she had entertained Joe Lane and Henry Wilson, Buchanan, Seward, and Adams, and the cream of society. It was in this city that her eight children were born and where five of them died. Washington was her home, but now she was saying farewell.

CHAPTER 26

Crossing the Line

WHEN THEIR TRAIN arrived in the port city of Baltimore, Rose and Little Rose boarded one carriage, Mrs. Baxley and Mrs. Morris another. They were driven to Gilmor House on the corner of Calvert Street and Courthouse Lane. The former hotel had been seized by the federal government as a headquarters for the army provost marshal, who took control of the city's security after the police chief was jailed for fomenting rebellion.[1] As Rose prepared to sign the hotel register, she noticed that her name had been erased.[2] Lafayette C. Baker, the nation's top detective, wanted to avoid any demonstrations of sympathy for the Maryland native Rose Greenhow in this rebel-prone city.

It was Sunday, June 1, 1862, a critical moment for the Confederacy. The day before, 150 miles to the south, General Joseph E. Johnston had attacked McClellan's advancing forces in the first serious attempt to halt the Union army's march up the Peninsula to take Richmond. At the Battle of Seven Pines, Johnston himself was seriously wounded and carried off the field, leaving the defending Confederate army without a strong leader. On Sunday afternoon, with the battle having ended in a bloody draw barely seven miles from the Confederate capital, Jefferson Davis handed General Robert E. Lee command of the army defending the city. As Rose prepared to cross the line to her beloved South and head up that same Peninsula, the citizens of Richmond could hear the Yankee guns pounding in the distance.[3]

At 5:00 P.M., an officer announced it was time to board the boat for Fort Monroe, a Federal stronghold at the eastern end of the Peninsula formed by the James and York rivers in Virginia. The vessel would steam south about two hundred miles through Union-held waters, down the Chesapeake Bay toward Norfolk, now abandoned by the Confederates, along with its naval base. The boat's departure was delayed several hours to wait for General Dix, one of the commissioners who had conducted Rose's hearing. He was headed south also to take command of Fort Monroe as McClellan's Army of the Potomac with its one hundred thousand men advanced from there toward Richmond. Rose wrote that Southern sympathizers jammed the Baltimore wharf, waving handkerchiefs to say good-bye.

At 8:00 P.M., General Dix boarded, and the order was given to weigh anchor. *The New York Times* reported that as the boat steamed out of the harbor, soldiers at the fort on Federal Hill fired thirteen guns in salute to their departing general.[4]

In the early morning hours of June 2, the craft reached Fort Monroe, McClellan's first toehold on the Peninsula and a key logistical base for his campaign toward Richmond. Upon arrival, each of the three women signed the parole they had promised to obey as a condition for release:

> We, the undersigned, late prisoners of the Old Capitol at Washington, do pledge our word of honor that in consideration of our being set at liberty beyond the lines of the U.S. Army, we will not return north of the Potomac River during the present hostilities without the permission of the Secretary of War of the United States.

Rose O'N. Greenhow
Mrs. C. V. Baxley
Mrs. Augusta Morris[5]

Rose was about to cross over to another country—*her* country—and finally, in writing, she agreed not to return to her home in the North until the war was over. The commissioners had kept their word.

After General Dix went ashore to assume his new command, the ship's captain surprised everyone by ordering a fine luncheon with iced champagne. Holding her glass in the air, Rose audaciously toasted Jefferson Davis "under the bristling guns of the enemy." Their Union guard, she claimed, "behaved very well and discreetly got out of hearing." As the luncheon ended, the provost marshal boarded the ship to ask where Rose wished to be taken.

"To the capital of the Confederacy, wherever that may be," the spy answered, uncertain how the war was going.

"It is still Richmond," the officer replied. "The city has not yet fallen. But it will have before you have a chance to get there."[6]

"I will take my chances," she said. "Let us waste no time." The officer ordered a small launch from the USS *Monitor* to escort Rose, her daughter, and the other prisoners up the James to City Point, a port twenty miles south of Richmond and occupied by Union forces since May 19.[7] Maneuvering carefully through the dark waters, the boat passed the hulks of the USS *Congress* and the USS *Cumberland*, sunk in Hampton Roads three months earlier by the ironclad CSS *Virginia*, better known by her previous name, USS *Merrimack*. They also steamed near the *Monitor* herself, the squat, revolutionary armored gunboat that had stopped the *Virginia*'s rampage. "I had a good view of the low black ugly thing," Rose wrote. She watched it while she waited for the boat's skipper to get instructions from the *Monitor*'s captain for putting her ashore upstream.[8]

As they made their way up the winding, rain-swollen river, thousands of McClellan's blue-coated troops were slogging through mud somewhere off to their right. The spring rains had turned the roads to sloughs that swallowed caissons and wagons up to their axles, washed out bridges, and slowed the Union army to a crawl. Yankee gunboats controlled the James almost as far as Richmond, but they had been turned back under heavy artillery fire from the bluffs within sight of the city two weeks before. Rose was holding her breath. "I was under intense excitement," she recalled, "for after nearly ten weary months of imprisonment, I was in sight of the promised land."

Standing in the bow of the boat, the widow took a large Confederate battle flag from the folds of a shawl around her neck.[9] She and other prisoners had secretly sewn the banner for General Beauregard. "I felt strongly tempted to unfold it and cast it to the breeze, as a parting defiance to the Yankees," Rose wrote. But for once, she thought better of the idea.[10] Instead, Rose watched intently while the Yankee crew hoisted a white flag of truce into a brooding sky and turned toward shore at City Point.[11]

The boat docked at a pier jutting into the river where the Appomattox joined the James, and Rose was welcomed to her new country by Colonel W. S. Ashe, "whose bold and soldierly bearing contrasted most strikingly with the Vandal race whom I had seen, I hope, for the last time," she wrote.[12] City Point, run-down, shelled, and largely abandoned after the first Federal gunboats appeared offshore, consisted of only twenty-five dwellings and a few rickety old wharves. It was nothing but a dying port town.[13] To Rose, it was paradise.

The women and Little Rose boarded a dockside freight train that took them, still under a truce flag but now with Confederate escort, to Petersburg, a small city just south of Richmond. "Upon these cars, Mrs. Greenhow, Mrs. Baxley and Mrs. Morris, who were not a little humiliated at the carriage prepared for them, took passage for Secessia," reported the *Washington Evening Star.* "As they mounted the cars, the rebels gave three cheers for Mrs. Greenhow and her company."[14] The former prisoners and their military escort transferred to more comfortable accommodations on the regular Petersburg-Richmond line and rolled into the capital of the Confederacy on the morning of June 4, five days after their release from Old Capitol Prison.

They went straight to Ballard House, the city's premier hotel on the corner of 14th and Franklin streets. The weather was ghastly, the roads slippery with mud. It rained so hard, according to the *Daily Dispatch,* that "shrubbery and small undergrowth was nearly all beaten down. Important military operations were said to be on foot."[15] That night, Brigadier General John H. Winder, commander of Richmond, went to Rose's hotel to welcome her. The next evening, President Davis paid her a visit. Davis had just celebrated his fifty-fourth birthday and was more confident than he had been that the danger to Richmond had abated. He was pleased to see that Rose had made the journey safely and thanked her profusely for her efforts. "But for you, there would have been no Battle of Bull Run," Davis said.[16] Later he wrote privately to his wife, Varina, that he was shocked to see how much Rose had aged: "The Madam looks much changed and has the air of one whose nerves were shaken by mental torture."[17]

Rose's long, silky black hair was still wound elegantly into a chignon, but there were dark hollows under her eyes, and her face was etched with deep lines. Davis was right. She *had* aged. But his words helped ease the pain and sorrow she had endured over the last months, and the still-handsome widow held her head high. This was, as Rose wrote afterward, the proudest moment of her life.[18] She didn't know the Confederate president had an even bigger challenge in mind for her.

dwellings and a few nearby lots whatever. It was nothing but a dying port
town. To Rose it was paradise.

The women and Little Rose boarded a stockade freight train that took
them, still under a truce flag now with Confederate escort, to Petersburg, a small city just south of Richmond. Upon these cars, Mrs. Greenhow, Abe, Bayley and Mrs. Morris, who were not a little humiliated at not
carriage prepared for them, [...] for Secession, [...] and the Washington [...] back. As they [...] the rebels gave three
cheers for Mrs. Greenhow and her company. The former prisoners and
their military escort transferred to more comfortable accommodations on
the regular Petersburg-Richmond line and rolled into the capital of the
Confederacy on the morning of June 4, five days after their release from
Old Capitol Prison.

They were brought to Ballard House, the city's premier hotel on the corner of 14th and Franklin streets. The weather was ghastly, the rainfall slippery with mud. It rained so hard, according to the Daily Dispatch, that
shrubbery and small undergrowth was nearly uprooted down. Important
military dignitaries were said to be on foot. That night, Brigadier Gen-
and John H. Winder commandant of Richmond, went to Rose's hotel to
welcome her. The next evening, President Davis paid her a visit. Davis had
just celebrated his fifty-fourth birthday and was more careful of how he
had been that day despite to Richmond had abated. He was pleased to see
that Rose had made the journey safely, and thanked her profusely for her
efforts. But for you there would have been no Battle of Bull Run, Davis
said. Later he wrote privately to his wife, Varina, that he was shocked to
see how much Rose had aged. The Madam looks much changed and has
the air of one whose nervous system has been shattered by mental torture.

Rose's long, inky black hair was still wound elegantly into a chignon,
but though age and its hollows under her eyes, and her face was etched with
deep lines. Davis was right. She had aged. But her words helped ease
the pain and sorrow she had endured over the last months, and she still,
high-born widow held her head high. This was, as Rose wrote afterward,
the proudest moment of her life. She didn't know the Confederate president had an even bigger challenge in mind for her.

Part Five

CONFEDERATE
EMISSARY

CHAPTER 27

Richmond

A Dreadful Year

ROSE ARRIVED IN Richmond on the heels of railcars and wagons, ox-carts, buggies, and hacks bearing the bloodiest cargo the war had yet seen. Newspapers called for citizens to help carry Confederate dead and wounded pouring into the city from the battles at nearby Southern Pines and Fair Oaks, filling the hospitals and cemeteries that would see no end of the fighting's brutal toll for three long years.

Rose was welcomed as a heroine who had defied her captors and proved the mettle of Dixie womanhood. "If the tyrant has released her, it was because that even he quailed before the might of her power as a representative of the feelings of every true Southern lady," the *Daily Dispatch* wrote on June 5. "She never hesitated to let the abolition horde of Washington know her sentiments. Mrs. Greenhow will be ever welcome in her native South."[1]

The *Richmond Whig* was even more effusive: "Arrived—Mrs. Green-how, whose name has been rendered historic by the barbarous imprison-ment she has been subjected to for nearly a year in Washington, and the heroism with which she has endured its hardships, and defied the monsters who imposed it, arrived in this city yesterday, by flag of truce, through the enemy's lines."[2]

But it was not a time for celebration. McClellan had been stopped—for the moment—but the Confederates had lost eight thousand, killed or wounded, in two days. The Union lost nearly six thousand. The plateau atop Chimborazo, one of Richmond's picturesque hills that rise from the banks of the James, was now capped by a forty-acre hospital of long, narrow, white-painted pine huts lined up row by row with military precision to treat three thousand wounded at a time.

Most of the captured Yankee soldiers went to Libby Prison, the former Libby & Sons warehouse down by the canal, now overflowing with wounded prisoners of war. More than half the sick and wounded Union soldiers brought there died before they could be exchanged. Many succumbed to the slow, fatal rot of gangrene.[3]

As hospitals overflowed—and there were forty-two listed in the 1862 *City Intelligencer,* or *Stranger's Guide*—the ladies of Richmond set up cots for the wounded in empty warehouses, vacant buildings, private homes, any place they could find. Some men were simply placed on boards. "There was not enough soap, not enough bandages, drugs, equipment, help—not enough of anything a hospital needed," wrote Civil War historian Ernest B. Furgurson.[4] Desperate nurses used green persimmon juice to stop bleeding, hemlock for opium, and wild cherry for digitalis.[5]

People talked of nothing but war, and they hated the Yankees with a bitterness that deepened by the day. Richmonders had not rushed toward secession; many of the city's oldest families were sorry that it came to that, but with Federal soldiers on their doorstep, they united to defend their land, their honor, and their way of life. It was a war for survival.

The proper ladies of Richmond would not have welcomed Rose under any circumstances, despite her late husband's pedigree, which tied her to Virginia's oldest families. They would have been polite—Richmonders were invariably polite—but they disapproved of women as strong-willed, independent, and outspoken as Rose. What's more, the women had heard the Washington gossip about late-night callers and trading favors for information. Of course, they didn't know what she *really* did in her bedroom—nobody ever does—but they knew they didn't approve. "She must not come handicapped with her old life," wrote Mary Chesnut.[6]

But President Davis cared not a whit for gossip. He wasn't a Virginian, either, and his Mississippi-born wife had been snubbed as well by the ladies of Richmond, who regarded her as a coarse Westerner with a suspiciously dark complexion. Davis showed remarkable respect for Rose and gratitude for her service. She, in turn, eagerly sought his company, and correspondence suggests she saw him often. Davis wrote to his wife, Varina, who had fled Richmond with her children, that Rose presented him with a gift of jelly and three oranges. He said he accepted them gratefully and gave one of the precious oranges to the wounded General Johnston. Davis also noted that Little Rose "had inquired very affectionately for [their daughter] Maggie and asked if there were any Yankees where she was."[7]

The *Richmond Enquirer* reported three weeks after Rose reached the city that forty coffins had piled up at the Oakwood Cemetery outside the grounds of Chimborazo because the keeper did not have enough grave-diggers. The heat caused many bodies to swell and burst the coffins, creating a putrid stench that permeated the city.[8] The tall chimneys of Tredegar Iron Works belched endless streams of thick, sooty smoke into the Southern sky. "The Works," which had cast the armor for the *Merrimack,* was running seven days a week to rush armored plate, guns, cannonballs, torpedoes, and railroad tracks to Confederate forces.[9]

But even in crisis, the city provided a freedom that Rose and Little Rose had not known since shortly after the war began. Despite shortages of food, clothing, and medicine, there were at least four Richmond theaters operating, and the nightly entertainment ranged from Shakespeare to a production of the folktale *Beauty and the Beast.*[10] To keep up morale, there were "starvation balls," where water was served instead of punch, but the music was gay, the atmosphere inviting, and soldiers were welcome. Matrons like Rose Greenhow, no longer belles of the ball, were more likely to be included as chaperones, but the events offered everyone a brief respite from the grief and anxiety that surrounded them.

With throngs from farms and plantations on the Union-occupied Peninsula and elsewhere flooding into the small city, housing was impossible to find. The Chesnuts, he a former United States senator now working for the Confederate president, could not do better than a room in a boardinghouse for what Mary Chesnut called "decayed ladies."[11] The Federal-style brick mansions on Church Hill, named for the old church where Patrick Henry cried, "Give me liberty or give me death," were almost certainly beyond the dreams of Rose and Little Rose. Another female spy lived there, though. Elizabeth Van Lew, a Richmond native who despised slavery and secession, hid fugitive Union soldiers in her family's Grace Street mansion and ran a spy ring right under the noses of her proper Church Hill neighbors.[12]

Van Lew was only one of many Yankee spies in Richmond. A week after the Greenhows arrived, Little Rose spotted one of McClellan's officers disguised in a Confederate uniform at dinner in the American Hotel on Main Street, just off Capitol Square. The *Daily Enquirer* reported that "when he discovered her eyeing him very suspiciously, he cut out and disappeared before information was given in time to capture him."[13]

Almost no records of Rose's year in Richmond survive. Her memoir, *My Imprisonment and the First Year of Abolition Rule at Washington*, ends with her arrival in the Confederate capital—but she and Little Rose probably walked along Franklin Street, where the city's upper class lived in fine houses with small, narrow porches and fences covered with starry white blossoms of native clematis. If tired, or the day particularly hot, they could sit unobserved under the shade of the old sycamore trees in Capitol Square, where Jefferson Davis took the oath of office as president of the Confederacy on February 22, Washington's birthday. Davis chose the date because he believed the first president of the United States—a Virginian—would have supported the South in its struggle, and he kept a portrait of Washington in his study.

The houses were beautiful, but Richmond's streets, like those of Washington and other cities of the time, were filthy. The horses that were the primary means of locomotion dropped their manure as they walked, and people threw garbage and the contents of their chamber pots into the gutters. Richmond's steep hills offered natural drainage, but in the wet weather that accompanied Rose's arrival, even the streets paved with cobblestones could swallow boots in muck. Women pinned a fragrant purple calycanthus flower on their dresses to ward off the smell.[14]

The Greenhows probably went to St. Peter's Roman Catholic Church on Grace Street, just off Capitol Square. Parishioners included Rose's friends General Beauregard, navy secretary Stephen Mallory, and Julia Gardiner Tyler, widow of Robert Greenhow's cousin President Tyler, whom Rose had known in Washington. On Sunday, April 21, 1861, four days after Virginia seceded, Father John Teeling, St. Peter's parish priest, had dropped the traditional prayer for the president of the United States. He was said to be the first pastor in the city to do so.[15]

With most able-bodied men off to war, Southern women took over households and plantations, managed slaves, and ran stores that law and tradition in the antebellum South had always left to men. Lower-class and immigrant women worked as seamstresses, free black and slave women as laundresses in hospitals, and some educated women took government jobs.[16] Lucy Parke Chamberlayne, who would soon marry popular Richmond journalist George William Bagby, went to work in the Confederate Treasury Department. "There were about 30 of us girls in the room together," she wrote later. "It was called 'Angels Retreat' in the Department."[17]

Rose spent much of her time writing a book based on journal entries she had kept of her arrest and imprisonment in Washington. But given her passionate support of the cause and her recent personal experience, it is likely she joined hundreds of other ladies in Richmond who cared for sick and wounded soldiers in hospitals, homes, and wherever they lay. The women made beds and bedding, wrapped bandages, changed dressings, wrote letters home, and comforted the boys however they could.

A month after Rose's arrival, General Lee, in his first strategic move as commander of the Army of Northern Virginia, staged an audacious series of attacks on Union positions outside the capital, convincing McClellan (wrongly) that the Yankees were heavily outnumbered. Like brushfires jumping from ridge to ridge, Lee's divisions hit the Yankees at crossroads and villages from Mechanicsville to Gaines's Mill, then Savage's Station and White Oak Swamp to Frayser's Farm. On July 1, the Union army turned and made a stand on Malvern Hill, cutting down row after row of Confederate attackers. But the Seven Days' Battle had saved Richmond. McClellan retreated down the Peninsula.

When the fighting began, Richmonders not only heard cannon and musket fire in the distance, they could also see flashes of artillery light the night sky. President Davis, joined by Secretary of War George W. Randolph and Secretary of the Navy Stephen Mallory, rode out to watch the start of the attack and were sent away by Lee. A soldier was killed at Davis's feet.

The adventurous Elizabeth Van Lew went to visit friends out the Mechanicsville Turnpike and stumbled onto the battle's opening day. She watched the galloping riders, saw the flash of bursting shells, and heard the roar of the guns. "No ball could ever be so exciting as our ride this evening," she wrote in her diary. "I realized the bright rush of life, the hurry of death on the battlefield."[18]

One week later, McClellan's army had fallen back from within five miles of Richmond to twenty. Lee had unnerved the Union army and established himself as a fearsome and cunning leader.[19] In a July 7 letter published in a local newspaper, the general credited his soldiers and said, "The immediate fruits of our success are the relief of Richmond from a state of siege. The service rendered to the country in this short but eventful period can scarcely be estimated."[20]

For the South, it was the biggest victory since Manassas, but Richmond again paid the price. The city was inundated with many of the twenty thousand Confederate dead and wounded, its prisons packed with thousands more Yankees.[21] Civil war historian James M. McPherson noted the bitter irony of Lee's triumph: "If McClellan's campaign had succeeded, the war might have ended," he writes. "The Union probably would have been restored with minimal destruction to the South. Slavery would have survived in only slightly modified form, at least for a time. By defeating McClellan, Lee assured a prolongation of the war until it destroyed slavery, the Old South and nearly everything the Confederacy was fighting for."[22] A similar hypothesis holds the same could be said of Rose's secret messages to Beauregard the year before. Had she not warned him in time to prepare and strengthen his forces, the North would have won the First Battle of Bull Run and Lincoln might have clipped the insurrection in its bud.

Like many Southerners whose lives were upended by the war, Rose was struggling financially. She had lost her house and belongings in Washington and had no apparent means of support. On August 1, Davis ordered Confederate secretary of state Judah P. Benjamin to send her a check for $2,500 from a small secret service fund he had "as an acknowledgment of the valuable and patriotic service rendered by you to our cause," according to official Confederate records. Another letter showed that Mrs. Baxley received $500. There was no mention of Mrs. Morris.[23]

The funds would have been most welcome. With prices rising and engravers cranking out Confederate money, residents had trouble keeping up with inflation. Richmond was the most expensive city in the Confederacy, and when the military tried to cap prices, the supply of goods quickly dried up. Boardinghouses, which served breakfast and dinner, charged an average of $75 a month per person,[24] less for a child. That would have left Rose more than $1,000 for other expenses, which probably included having a few dresses and bonnets made from whatever material she could scare up. Women in city jobs made half that amount.

Rose was also speculating in cotton and tobacco. U.S. judge advocate general Joseph Holt reported to Secretary of War Stanton that she had given a power of attorney to William T. Smithson, a prominent Washington banker and Confederate sympathizer, who was buying and selling Southern securities. Rose empowered him "to sell, collect &c., as her agent, all stocks, securities, dividends, &c, which she may hold in the United States." Holt wrote that when Smithson was arrested earlier in the war, government agents found a certificate for 120 shares of railroad stock in his bank belonging to Rose Greenhow. "She also advises him to join her in cotton and tobacco speculations in Richmond which she represents as promising large profits," Holt wrote.[25] Smithson was arrested a second time on a charge of corresponding with the enemy and sentenced to five years in prison.[26]

Nor had Rose lost her taste for spycraft. The same day Davis rewarded her for past service, she penned a note to Confederate major E. Porter Alexander, a former signal officer on General Beauregard's staff and chief of ordnance on General Johnston's staff who had recently been put in charge of a reconnaissance balloon. Alexander's craft was similar to those used by Thaddeus S. C. Lowe during the Peninsula Campaign to spy on Richmond and Lee's army for the North, but Rose and Alexander had something more audacious in mind than local aerial reconnaissance. Rose asked Alexander to call on her as soon as it was convenient. "The right man has turned up for the duty we spoke of the other day," she wrote.[27] Years later, Alexander sent the letter to a friend who collected autographs, explaining that he and Rose had been making arrangements to send a spy north by balloon.[28] At a time when military commanders were still arguing over whether or not aerial reconnaissance had a meaningful role in warfare, Rose and Alexander were collaborating in a scheme to use the new technology to plant spies behind enemy lines!

During the summer, Lincoln had been considering a move to free the slaves in the states that had seceded, and in July, he presented a draft proclamation to his cabinet. Secretary of State Seward convinced the president to wait for a significant victory on the battlefield to avoid the appearance that he was acting out of desperation.[29] He soon got his chance. Lee took the war to the North in early September, crossing the Potomac above Washington and driving deep into western Maryland. McClellan's army met him at Sharpsburg, near Antietam Creek, and, on September 17, 1862, stopped the Confederate offensive in the bloodiest day in American history. Lee's battered forces withdrew across the Potomac, and on September 22, Lincoln issued the preliminary version of the Emancipation Proclamation, declaring all slaves in territory still in rebellion on January 1 "forever free."

Southerners, of course, were outraged, but the move also alienated moderates in Lincoln's own party who didn't want to fight a war to free the slaves. Democrats began thinking of the engagement as a Republican war. In Washington, where slaves already had been freed by law the previous April, crowds of rejoicing blacks surrounded the White House, and mothers named their babies after the president. For many, however, it was far from certain just what freedom would mean.[30]

One provision opened the Union army and navy to slaves freed by the proclamation, a step one of General Grant's field commanders predicted would be "terrible on the enemy."[31] Secretary of War Stanton ordered that two Negro regiments be raised from Massachusetts. "The enlistment of black soldiers to fight and kill their former masters was by far the most revolutionary dimension of the emancipation policy," wrote historian McPherson.[32]

The Emancipation Proclamation "became a crucial part of northern military strategy, an important means of winning the war," according to McPherson.[33] The policy also added moral force to the Yankee cause. It was no longer a war to hold the Union together, but a war to end slavery.

Spring and summer victories had brought Lee international recognition, and Lord Palmerston, the British prime minister, was considering a plan for a negotiated end to the war based on separation. Lee had hoped his offensive into the North would win British support for the South. Now England and France were much less likely to intervene.

In January 1863, a smallpox epidemic swept Richmond. The *Daily Enquirer* announced that a white flag must be displayed in front of every house where the disease existed or the inhabitants would be fined $10.[34] Temperatures dropped to ten degrees below zero, unheard of in the city. February and March each brought a foot of snow. Shops were closed, streets and bars deserted. Food, clothing, and medicine were scarce, Confederate soldiers cold and hungry.[35] Clover Hill coal was selling for $20 a load—when people could find it, flour for $17.50 a barrel.[36] Rose would certainly have been concerned for her daughter, whose health had been compromised by months in prison.

With their fathers off at war, the boys of Richmond joined unruly street gangs that fought a class war between the young gentlemen of the Shockoe Hill neighborhood, where the White House of the Confederacy stood, and the ragged children of immigrants and freed blacks from Butchertown, the old slaughterhouse district in the lowland valley between Shockoe Hill and Church Hill. The Hill Cats and Butcher Cats, as the gangs were known, fought a protracted territorial battle that went on for years. Stone throwing was the most common means of warfare, but knives and even pistols came into play on occasion. An infant was nearly killed when hit in the head by a wayward rock early in the war.[37]

Jeff Davis Jr. and his brother Joe were Hill Cats, and at one point, their father tried to mediate the dispute, as recounted after the war by Mrs. Davis: "He descended the hill and, relying on his popularity with children, he made a little speech to the Butcher Cats, in which he addressed them as the future rulers of their country. They listened attentively, nudging their approval to each other, but when he concluded, the tallest boy said, 'President, we like you, we didn't want to hurt any of your boys, but we ain't never going to be friends with them Hill cats.' So the President, like many another self-appointed peacemaker, came back without having accomplished anything except an exhausting walk."[38]

In early April, several hundred poor women marched on Capitol Square, demanding food from government warehouses at cost. They were led by Mrs. Jackson, the widow of a butcher in the Old Market, who carried a large meat cleaver in her hand and a pistol only partly concealed in her belt.[39] The women paraded through the muddy streets shouting, "Bread!" and marched on the governor's home. When he did not appear, the angry women rioted, smashing store windows and stealing anything they could grab—groceries, candles, cloth, hats, pants, cavalry boots, ladies' slippers, embroidered children's dresses. They proceeded to the Exchange Hotel and Ballard House, where President Davis told the women that soldiers would begin firing into the crowd in five minutes if they did not disperse.[40] "[They] robbed them of everything but bread, which was just the thing they wanted least," the Richmond Examiner wrote in an editorial condemning the women.[41]

East of the city, where Union soldiers still camped on the Peninsula awaiting a new commander and orders for another offensive, Private Josiah Garrison, a thirty-two-year-old farmer and mason from Port Jervis, New York, tried to liberate a Southern bull and slaughter it for meat to feed the troops. The huge animal tossed him against a post, and the soldier spent part of the war in a Union field hospital near Falmouth, Virginia. The bull was recaptured and tied to a supply wagon, but according to the commander of the company of New York volunteers, "he roared, and he tore at the ground, and pulled the wagon around to such an extent that night that somebody deemed it expedient to cut his lordship loose, and at an early hour of the morning, he elevated his tail, shook and then lowered his head between his fore-legs, gave us a farewell roar, and struck a beeline for his home . . . carrying away as he bounded through the neighboring camps a dozen or more tents."[42]

May, with its fragrant blossoms and warm weather, brought a return of the dreaded Army of the Potomac, now under the command of General Joseph Hooker, on yet another march to take Richmond. Lee, outnumbered more than two to one, confounded a fundamental rule of military tactics and divided his army before a superior force, sending Stonewall Jackson to hit Hooker's right flank in a surprise attack while Lee kept the main force occupied in what quickly became known as the Battle of Chancellorsville, a crossroads sixty miles north of Richmond. Jackson's force burst out of a tangled forest of underbrush near Fredericksburg called the Wilderness with rebel yells and guns blazing, hurling back the off-guard Yankees. But that evening, Jackson rode out ahead of his troops to reconnoiter for the next day's battle. The great hero of the Confederacy was shot by his own men, who mistook him and his staff for a Yankee cavalry patrol. Jackson lost his left arm, then developed pneumonia, and by May 10, he was dead. "The bell at the station on 3rd Street tolled and tolled, and I knew our hero had died," Lucy Bagby wrote in her Richmond diary. "What misery and what despair we felt."[43]

The Confederate victory on the battlefield sent Hooker back across the Rappahannock River, and once again the Confederate capital was spared. The Southern armies were proving themselves superior in the field, and the South's prospects brightened for a moment. But that changed at Vicksburg, where a scruffy, determined general named Ulysses S. Grant directed a deafening, demoralizing, six-week siege that broke the heavily fortified Confederate defenses guarding a strategic bend in the Mississippi. On July 4, 1863, as the Confederate defenders surrendered at Vicksburg, General Lee ordered a retreat from Gettysburg, the climax of another daring drive into the North. The three days of fighting in the rolling hills of Pennsylvania had engaged more men—and cost more lives—than any battle in the war. Lee fell back toward his beloved Virginia with his caravan of wounded stretching fourteen miles.[44] Davis's and Lee's perpetual dream of winning international recognition and support by showing military superiority in the field flickered in the gloom of defeat.

But not everyone had lost hope. Jefferson Davis had a plan.

"Stroke of Genius"

JEFFERSON DAVIS WAS a West Pointer and Mexican War veteran who micromanaged the war and frequently second-guessed his own commanders, cabinet officers, and diplomats. He had conceived a long-shot diplomatic ploy to gain European support. Davis would send Rose Greenhow across the Atlantic as his emissary to woo the French and British elite. They were sure to receive her, for as Lincoln biographer Carl Sandburg wrote later, she possessed "a gaunt beauty, education, manners and resourceful speech. Her proud loyalty to the south and her will and courage set her apart as a woman who would welcome death from a firing squad if it would serve her cause."[1]

It was a unique mission. The wives of United States officials had occasionally joined their husbands on foreign postings, but it was highly unusual, perhaps unprecedented, for a president to send a woman to represent her country in a foreign land, even in an unofficial capacity. "Not only would Davis *not* have worried about sending a woman to Europe on a diplomatic mission," said Civil War historian James McPherson when asked about the unusual assignment. "Davis would have been convinced that this particular woman was the best person for the job because her imprisonment in a Union 'Bastille' had evoked indignation and sympathy abroad, especially among the upper classes in Britain and France, where it was seen as an example of Yankee oppression and vulgarity. Sending Greenhow was a stroke of genius by Davis."[2]

Rose took her new assignment seriously and wrote regular, detailed reports to Davis about her observations and what people around her were saying. As she traveled south into fierce fighting on her way to find passage to Europe, she wrote long, newsy letters describing the progress of the war. Unlike some of Davis's generals, Rose had no compunction about telling him what she thought he needed to hear, even if the news was bleak.

Rose decided to use "white gold" to pay her expenses. "I shall take out as much cotton as I can," she wrote on June 19 to Alexander R. Boteler, a Confederate congressman who had represented Virginia in Washington and had roomed at the Ballard House when Rose was staying there.[3] President Davis's "King Cotton" policy limited exports to Britain and France under a theory that the shortage would make European countries better appreciate the South's resources and encourage them to come to the aid of the Confederacy. As a result, cotton had become a prized commodity in Britain and was sure to bring a hefty sum. Before leaving Richmond, Rose met with General Lee and wrote Davis that she was impressed with "his calm, confident tone."[4]

Rose originally planned to go straight to Wilmington, North Carolina, where she intended to catch a blockade runner leaving for Bermuda on Friday, June 26. She was delayed, however, and was still in Richmond when Vicksburg fell and Lee retreated from Gettysburg. She set out the next week, just as the Confederates suffered another setback. Port Hudson, Louisiana, the last Confederate stronghold on the Mississippi, surrendered to the Union on July 9, giving the North control of the great river from its source to New Orleans and effectively cutting the Confederacy in two. Rose reached Wilmington but told Davis in a letter that growing fears for the fate of the besieged city of Charleston caused her to continue her journey 170 miles south to see the situation for herself. The "Palmetto City"—so named, she told Davis, because it had only one such tree—had been holding out against the Union navy, which had been trying to regain Fort Sumter since the war began.

As Rose rode down the coast, she passed train cars laden with cotton and even carriages and horses being sent inland, "showing the sense of insecurity which very generally prevailes . . . hand bills were distributed along the route setting forth the imminent peril of Charleston and calling upon the people for 3,000 negroes to work on the defenses."[5] In a detailed report to Davis on July 16, Rose said as she neared the city, "the booming of the heavy guns was distinctly heard." The worst still lay ahead.

Rose took a room at Miles House, where she received a visit from her old friend General Beauregard, whose imperious attitude had estranged him from Davis and got him sent back to Charleston, where he had led the firing on Fort Sumter to start the war. Beauregard, wrote Rose, was "deeply impressed with the gravity of the position." In a sixteen-page letter, Rose passed along Beauregard's request for heavy guns and mortars to dislodge enemy forces from their fortifications on Morris Island, insisting: "Without them, Charleston will fall." In an ironic twist of fortune, the military commander who credited Rose Greenhow with giving him the information that enabled him to win Bull Run was now using her to deliver a message to the Confederate president.

Rose fed Davis detailed accounts of the military situation, not just from Beauregard, but from local officials and Governor Milledge Luke Bonham, the former general who had first received Rose's fateful message before Bull Run and passed it on to Beauregard. She gave dispassionate accounts about Beauregard's command and even told Davis which officials were preoccupied with speculating in cotton instead of tending to their duties: "I think it right that you should know all that is said, and that it is not idle street gossip but comes to me from men in high position."[6]

Rose reached Charleston only days before the Yankees' spectacular and costly assault on Fort Wagner, spearheaded by the Fifty-fourth Massachusetts, the first black combat regiment raised in the North to fight the South. On the afternoon of the attack, after the Union army and navy's daylong bombardment of the Confederate battery at Fort Wagner, Rose climbed to the observatory in the steeple of St. Michael's Church for a commanding view of the assault on the fort protecting Morris Island, a barrier island that controlled southern approaches to the harbor. "The battle then began with great animation and the Island and Sea was like one continuous lightning flash and the atmosphere became heavy with smoke," she wrote Davis after the assault. "At about six, the enemy began to storm Batry Wagner, their line being described by a line of smoke. It was then that the scene became terrifically grand. All at once Fort Sumpter which had remained dark and quiet seemed one blaze of fire and smoke."[7]

Colonel Robert Gould Shaw, the white commanding officer of the Fifty-fourth, was killed in the attack, as were sixty-one of his men. Some of the attacking troops succeeded in scaling the parapet and planting an American flag inside the fort, but they were driven back with heavy losses.

Despite the Union navy's determination to seal off the port, Charleston was home to many companies engaged in the lucrative business of running the North's blockade to keep up trade and communication with Europe.

The docks were crowded with sleek, modern vessels designed to outrun all challengers, just the sort of transport Rose needed for her mission.[8] But the battle for Charleston effectively shut down the port for more than two months, and George A. Trenholm, who owned several blockade runners, advised her to go back to Wilmington, where many shipping firms had relocated. Rose asked Davis to send the order for her travel, as well as cotton, to Wilmington and telegraph her in Charleston when it was done, "as I must either go by the 24th on account of the tide or wait for another moon."

She didn't tell her president, but all the bad news of late left her uncharacteristically dispirited. "Finding it impossible to get out of this port, I have remained here," she wrote to an unknown male friend, probably Boteler, on July 23. "Eagerly looking for some lifting of the clouds which hang over us and have finally concluded to put off my trip for another month for the reason that I cannot make up my mind to leave until things look less gloomy. . . .

"We are retreating everywhere and everywhere sorely pressed," she wrote. "I have never felt so little hopeful in my life. The Yankees have attacked with a determination to take it, and however long we try [to] keep them in check, I believe they will eventually take it." Rose closed her letter, as she had with other men over the years, by flirtatiously questioning his intentions: "I shall hope to hear from you and see you, that is, if you still retain a desire to take a little trouble to see me."[9] Once again, Rose was bidding for a man's attention.

Despite the ravages of war, Rose found Charleston "too luxurious a place for an army to rest in long without becoming demoralized—the markets are filled with every delicacy to tempt the palate and the temperature delightful, a continuous sea breeze rendering the atmosphere cool."[10]

But she didn't stay to enjoy it. Rose got to Wilmington about ten days later to leave on August 5 with Little Rose on the blockade runner *Phantom*. The night before, she sat down to write a farewell letter to Davis. The envelope, marked "Private," was addressed "To the President, Richmond, Va." Rose told Davis she would board the *Phantom* in a few hours and was anxious about reports that they would face a double line of blockades and "unusually vigilant" guns from Forts Warren and Delaware, which remained under Union command. But she added, "I think I should brave any fate rather than remain here two days longer." Unlike Charleston, with its cooling sea breezes, Wilmington "is the hottest and most disagreeable place in the world, and the very atmosphere seems laden with disease."[11]

Rose told Davis that "the better class" of citizens had fled Wilmington, but that her old friends from California, former senator William and Mary Gwin, were waiting to leave on the blockade runner *Ella and Annie* for France. Gwin hoped to persuade Napoleon III to join a plan to colonize New Mexico with settlers from the Confederacy. Rose said that she had met the previous evening with Brigadier General Henry Chase Whiting, commander of Wilmington's defenses. Whiting had served as chief engineer on General Johnston's staff at First Manassas, commanded a division at Fair Oaks, and fought under Stonewall Jackson at the Seven Days' Battle. He had accepted a transfer to Wilmington the previous year to supervise the building of an extensive line of fortifications around Fort Fisher to protect the main approach to the Cape Fear River.[12] "In the course of the conversation," Rose wrote, "[Whiting] said he thought that he could raise a brigade of cavalry among persons about here whom he knew if he were able to promise that the officers selected would be commissioned." Whiting, like Beauregard, was using Rose to send a message to the Confederate president.

Rose closed her letter to Davis on a grateful note:

> And now, my dear sir, I must say goodbye. I can never sufficiently thank you for your goodness to me. May He ever guard you, sir, and keep you in health, is my most fervent prayer.

Rose O'N. Greenhow[13]

The political operator was again at center stage, still thriving in the company of powerful men. They listened to her counsel and treated her with respect. Rose had spent almost a year in the heart of the Confederacy, and while it had been a dreadful year for the South, a year of heartache, death, and despair, she had established herself as one of its key players. At the request of her president, she was about to embark on another risky mission.

CHAPTER 29

Flight of the *Phantom*

AS THE CLOCK struck noon on Wednesday, August 5, 1863, Captain Stephen G. Porter, a furloughed naval officer assigned to the Confederate Ordnance Bureau,[1] escorted Rose and her daughter aboard the *Phantom*, one of the fastest vessels in the Confederate service.[2] They were his only passengers on a daring mission to slip past Yankee blockaders and cross the Atlantic. Porter had nine hours until darkness and high tide would enable him to make a run for it.

The captain showed Rose and Little Rose to a small stateroom furnished, as she described it, "with everything good taste could suggest." Rose spent the afternoon arranging her toilet articles "with a distinct foreshadowing of the inutility of such preparation." Knowing her penchant for seasickness, she wanted to be back on deck and breathing fresh air before *Phantom* put to sea.

After the crew fumigated the ship and port officers made a final sweep for stowaways, Captain Porter eased his vessel away from the pier and down the Cape Fear River "to be in readiness for the tide and the friendly screen of night to get over the bar and through the blockading squadron out at sea," Rose wrote.[3] He had more than twenty miles of uncontested water before he had to decide which route to take around Smith Island[4] at the mouth of the river to make his break for the open ocean.

Built in England, the *Phantom* was one of five swift steamships designed to slip in and out of Southern ports through the tightening net of the

Union blockade. She was 193 feet long, only 22 feet wide on deck, and could travel at 17 nautical miles per hour.[5] Rose described her as "steel clad sharp and narrow like a needle." Painted light gray to make her almost invisible on moonless nights, she had two engines for speed and two hinged masts that could be dropped on deck to lower her profile for the dash past the federal gantlet. Her minimal seven-foot draft helped her glide over the shallow bar at New Inlet that kept out larger vessels, including the Union's heavier-laden warships. The *Phantom* burned hard, smokeless anthracite coal instead of cheaper, more readily available bituminous coal, whose billowing smoke was easier to spot in harbor and at sea. Even the funnels could be "telescoped" close to the deck to reduce her silhouette, and sailors wrapped her paddles with tarps to muffle the sound of churning water. Exhaust pipes were rigged to channel steam from the boilers under water, where it would dissipate and bubble to the surface instead of rising in clear white puffs. Sailors and passengers were not permitted to smoke their pipes or carry on conversations on deck.

In addition to Porter, described by Captain James Bulloch as "a seaman and man of courage and judgment,"[6] the *Phantom* carried two mates, a carpenter, steward, cook, six seamen, three engineers, eight firemen, two ordinary seamen, and two boys.[7] Most of them were foreigners, who were likely to be released if captured by the U.S. Navy. She was unarmed, relying entirely on speed and stealth to elude her pursuers. The cargo was stowed both in the hold and on deck, where it offered some protection from gunfire. If conditions remained favorable, they could make the 674-mile run to Bermuda in three or four days.

It was a new command for Porter, and he was entrusted with a valuable cargo of turpentine and Rose's 540 bales of cotton, which weighed five hundred to seven hundred pounds each. Two other vessels, the *Pet* and the *Hebe*,[8] planned to run the blockade that night as well and steamed out ahead of the *Phantom*, quietly signaling the traditional greeting of good luck and Godspeed.

"There they go ahead of me," Captain Porter remarked, his voice filled with worry.[9]

"Oh, never mind, wait 'til the full tide is in," Rose replied. The woman never tired of advising a man about his own business.

The captain, watch in hand, floated downriver as the last lingering rays of light disappeared over the horizon. Rose said that before dark they could see the dreaded Yankee ships offshore, watching them. When the hands of the captain's timepiece pointed to 9:00, Porter gave the order to swing the ship toward New Inlet, the northernmost passageway to open water. He still had two hours before moonrise and a chance to slip out undetected on a rising tide.[10] Rose went below to put Little Rose to bed. The child was nearly asleep, and Rose returned quickly to watch the captain work his way through the inlet, over the bar, and through the cordon of blockading ships.

As the *Phantom* gathered speed with a full head of steam, she passed the *Pet* and the *Hebe*. Both vessels, bound for Nassau,[11] had run aground because they left too early. "Our anxiety was too great on our own account to bestow much thought upon friends," Rose wrote. The 321-ton *Phantom* was picking her way through a shallow channel with only a few feet of water under her keel.[12] Everyone on board was on edge.

A picket boat from the Union blockader *Niphon* was posted near New Inlet to signal gunboats north of the bar if a Confederate vessel tried to get through. At forty minutes after midnight, Lieutenant James Trathen aboard the *Mount Vernon,* another Union blockader with the Cape Fear Squadron, saw the *Phantom* cross over the bar unobserved by the picket boat and pass his ship's stern. "We immediately stood for her at full speed, but soon found that she was fast leaving us," Trathen reported afterward. "She passed so close to us before discovering us that we fired two broadsides at her, with what effect is unknown."[13]

"The Yankees threw up rockets which revealed to us the fact that we were in the midst of five of her 'blockaders,' " Rose wrote in her diary, reporting the encounter from the perspective of the prey, "but right gallantly, we went through them at the rate of sixteen knots the hour. Three of them followed in pursuit, but we distanced and finally lost sight of them."[14]

Lieutenant Trathen recorded that the *Mount Vernon* finally gave up the chase at 3:00 A.M., "the speed of the steamer being so much greater than our own that she had run out of sight."[15]

"We then relaxed our speed," Rose reported, "and gradually resumed our regular course. By this time I had become very sea sick." Acting Rear Admiral Samuel Phillips Lee, commander of the North Atlantic Blockade Squadron on board his flagship *Minnesota,* complained in a letter to navy secretary Gideon Welles that many of its ships were "dull" in the water and in need of repairs. Lee asked for fifteen to eighteen more steamers and proposed that an ironclad or two wooden vessels with plenty of guns be stationed at each entrance to the Cape Fear harbor.[16]

Throughout the next year—from August 1863, when she steamed out of Wilmington, until August 1864, when she boarded the *Condor* to return home—Rose kept a personal diary of her life abroad. In it, she recorded her moods, observations, travels, gossip, discussions with British and French political leaders and the elite members of European society, the progress of the war, and her delight in Little Rose, who was her closest companion. An examination of other available records, such as the Union navy's account of *Phantom*'s escape, shows that Rose was a diligent reporter of events, although she also candidly expressed her prejudices and political opinions. The 128-page diary was found among her personal effects in a trunk on the blockade runner *Condor* after the vessel went aground on October 1, 1864. Inside the cover is a rough pencil sketch of a cat and a note, probably written by Rose: "My pen is so scratchy that I am barely able to write with it."[17]

From the outset of the war, the Union had been trying to choke the South's agricultural economy by cutting off its access to markets and manufactured goods from abroad. Blockade runners supplied 60 percent of the South's arms, one-third of its lead for bullets, much of its powder, and nearly all of its paper for cartridges, as well as leather and cloth for uniforms.[18] Many ships operated by private firms carried government supplies as well as expensive wartime luxuries: silks, linens, woolens, hosiery, dried fruit, drugs, liquors, and medicines that were otherwise unobtainable in the Confederacy. The U.S. Navy's North Atlantic Blockade Squadron patrolled the Virginia and North Carolina coast. Other squadrons stationed warships off Charleston, Savannah, Mobile, and New Orleans, as well as in rivers and sounds used as ports of refuge, to stop the frequent attempts to strike for the open sea. As Rose rode the *Phantom* out of Wilmington, the Yankees had eleven blockaders off New Inlet: four near the bar, four in a second line farther out, and three outside cruisers. Twelve more warships were guarding the Old Inlet west of Smith Island to catch ships trying to get out that way.[19]

When a Federal ship captured a Confederate vessel, the government gave the captain and crew half the value of the ship and cargo as its share of the "prize." When Federal vessels spotted a blockade runner, they were expected to fire a rocket in the direction the ship was traveling to signal other gunships, but the financial incentive to make the capture was so strong, they sometimes fired in the opposite direction to throw their competition off the trail.[20]

Nonetheless, running the blockade was a lucrative gambit for British and Confederate shipping companies as the price of cotton soared in Europe and speculators got several times prewar prices for imported commodities in the South. A vessel could clear as much as $150,000 in gold on a successful round trip,[21] but it was dangerous and controversial work. Ships, many of which were built in England and captained by British naval officers, frequently sailed under false names and registration to conceal their ownership, and captains often used several aliases.

The Confederate defeats at Gettysburg and Vicksburg in early June 1863 shook Europe's confidence in the South's solvency, wrecked the Confederate bond market, and forced Jefferson Davis's government to take over the blockade-running operation.[22] Charleston was under attack and tightly blockaded, and as Rose discovered, companies were shifting their operations to Wilmington.

The *Phantom,* operated by the Confederate Ordnance Bureau out of Wilmington, ran to and from Bermuda. The government-owned vessel normally didn't take passengers, but Rose was granted passage because she was on official business.[23] After New Orleans and a succession of Southern ports fell under Federal control, Wilmington rose to prominence as a vital harbor. Situated twenty-seven miles from the mouth of the Cape Fear River, it was the state's largest city and principal seaport, with rail connections to Charleston and strategic depots in Virginia. The two outlets around Smith Island, more than five miles apart, made it difficult for the blockaders to close the port. The entrances were guarded by Confederate batteries at Fort Fisher to the north and Fort Caswell and Fort Holmes to the south, forcing the Yankees to keep their distance offshore.[24] Colonel William Lamb, commander at Fort Fisher, helped devise a system of red and white shuttered lanterns as signal lights to help guide blockade runners through New Inlet.[25] Before entering the inlet, the ship would show a small light from the inshore side of the vessel, and it would be answered by two lights a short distance apart on the beach. When the lights lined up, the vessel's pilot knew he was in the channel that led to the river.[26]

Once the *Phantom* reached the Gulf Stream currents, "our little ship was tossing and dancing upon the waters in the most phantastic and irregular way," Rose recounted. Captain Porter had a crewman spread a mattress on deck between the cotton bales, and the widow lay on it, staring at the light of a waning three-quarter moon, retching into a bucket at her side, "the victim of that most unfortunate infirmity." Little Rose stumbled on deck and crouched at her mother's side. "Mamma, I can't stand to have my head bumped from side to side," the child cried. Rose twined her fingers in the bagging of the cotton bales to hang on and fell into a feverish sleep with Little Rose cradled in her arms.

At first light, the ship changed course abruptly and got up speed, jolting Rose awake. Captain Porter appeared to inform her that they were being chased by a Federal cruiser. They outran it, but Rose was incensed. "How my blood boils to think that even in the wide ocean we are not free from that despicable foe who seeks by numerical strength to crush us," she wrote. "Yet God is just."[27]

The water turned from deep blue to turquoise, and flying fish sparkled in the sun as they jumped through waves. Captain Porter kept a sharp lookout for Yankee vessels, Rose wrote, because—borrowing from Andrew Jackson—"eternal vigilance is the price of freedom in a blockade runner."[28]

On Saturday, August 8, their fourth day at sea, Captain Porter announced that they would reach Bermuda by early evening. The port of St. George was a regular stopping point for vessels crossing the Atlantic, but the Federal navy stood off the island to try to catch Confederate vessels before they reached the safety of British waters. Just as Bermuda came within sight, Porter spotted another Federal blockader behind him and turned away from the island, running four hours in another direction. Porter approached the town of St. George again, this time in darkness, but he dared not try to thread the treacherous coral reefs around St. George harbor without local knowledge and anchored offshore.

At daybreak, he picked up a pilot, and by 6:00 A.M., the ship was safely inside the harbor. Bermuda's emerald water ran deep and clear.[29] Rose could see the picturesque town, its houses built with soft limestone and whitewashed roofs. Each building had its own catch basin to collect rainwater from the roof, the island's only source of fresh water. A British flag flying over the Governor's House signaled that England's chief representative was in residence.

Captain Porter escorted Rose to Mrs. Haywood's, the only lodging house on the island, where the guests included a number of Southern ladies who had fled their homes in the Confederacy and were waiting out the war on the island. They assembled in the parlor to welcome the famous patriot. It was Sunday morning, and the peal of church bells called people to worship, but Rose was still feeling queasy and went directly to her room.[30]

Bermuda, a British colony since 1612, was a neutral port that provided safe harbor to Confederate ships carrying cargo to England. The Confederacy had agents on the island to transfer goods from the comparatively small blockade runners to larger British ships bound for Great Britain.

Union vessels were barred from firing on Confederate ships in Bermuda waters to avoid antagonizing the British, who already showed some sympathy for their Confederate trading partners.

Rose and Little Rose remained in Bermuda for more than three weeks. At first, they enjoyed the tropical trees, formal gardens, and warm, dry island breezes, finding Bermuda not nearly as hot as Wilmington or Richmond. Rose dined frequently with Major Norman S. Walker, the Confederate agent in charge of military shipments, who operated a perpetual open house for supporters of the South. He and his wife lived in a pretty little cottage surrounded by tropical trees and plants, "which you reach," Rose explained, "by tortuous and devious wanderings through crooked allies and lanes."

In a cryptic letter to Boteler, she indicated that she had recruited Walker for a secret mission "to render service to the country of a magnitude that would be startling if it were prudent to speak yet." Later it became apparent she was using Walker to forward dispatches to her from Richmond, possibly in code. Walker's role in the Confederate secret service toward the end of the war remains a tantalizing mystery.[31]

She liked the Walkers but was particularly impressed by the British, especially the governor, whom she described as "a fine looking man hansome enough to be a Southern planter of cultivated manners and pleasing address." His wife, she said, "without being hansome is fine looking, and like her husband has charming manners with that entire absence of pretense common to all high bred people."[32]

As days turned to weeks, the island lost its charm for Rose, who was accustomed to a more sophisticated city life. It reminded her, she wrote, "of an interior village in the Confederacy." Her racial prejudice dripped from her pen: "The Negroes are lazy, vicious and insubordinate . . . constantly encroaching on the prerogatives of the white settlers," she told her diary. "The negroes seem to have no idea of moral or religious restraint, and like the beasts of the fields, unconscious that they offend against the laws of God or Man . . . few negro women reach the age of puberty without becoming mothers and it is an established etiquette that the first child shall be white in order to make incontestable the claim of the mother to 'good' society. After that it does not damage her position, should her succeeding progeny be black.

"The proportion who can read and write compare very unfavorably with our slave population. In fact I have not met a single negro here who can read & write, and I mention this with no disposition to censure the omission—for nature has gifted this race with none of the higher intellectual at-tributes of her Caucasian race. They have imitation qualities which under the influence of constant contact with the white men approximates to rea-son and intelligence qualities shared in a lesser degree with the aurang-otang and the ape."[33] She complained that since their emancipation by the British Empire in 1834, blacks had been buying up the best property on Bermuda and that a black man had even been elected to the island's legis-lature. "The Beecher Stowes and the English philanthropists generally who have interested themselves in the destruction of the wise and benefi-cent system of servile labor at the South would here find ample field for the exercise of Christian humanities."

Rose could not wait to leave for England. "Time hangs heavily," the for-mer prisoner wrote. "I am impatient to be gone. The narrow bounds of this island oppress me, and I chafe at the detention."

Finally, at noon on Sunday, August 30, the Greenhows sailed out of St. George harbor aboard the *Harriet Pinckney,* a fast new British brig with an iron frame and a ninety-horsepower auxiliary steam engine. *HP,* as she was frequently called, ran at an impressive eighteen knots during her tri-als,[34] prompting the Confederate navy to purchase her secretly. On this voyage, there were seven passengers, including one other woman and a young boy.[35]

The captain was a jolly Englishman who took pride in making his pas-sengers comfortable, and Little Rose enjoyed the trip. But once again, Rose suffered terribly from seasickness and spent the first few days in her cabin. The weather was clear, and *HP* encountered no Federal vessels; but three days out of Liverpool, the captain told his passengers that to avoid Yankee cruisers in the Irish channel, he would put into the port of Fal-mouth on the south coast of Cornwall. "This was unexpected to us all and everyone set to work to know where Falmouth was and what sort of a place— but the captain could give us little information," Rose wrote.[36]

The *Harriet Pinckney* steamed into Falmouth harbor early Sunday morning, September 13, 1863, and Rose saw the jagged granite headlands and curving beaches of the English coast for the first time. An officer from the Custom House boarded the ship to inspect the cargo, looked through Rose's soiled clothes, and let her pass with a prized box of Southern to-bacco she had brought for James Murray Mason, the Confederate envoy in London.

Falmouth was charming. The warm waters of the Gulf Stream encour-aged English gardeners to create dramatic landscapes with tropical plants.

Rose admired the old castle of Pendennis, part of a chain of castles built along England's south coast by Henry VIII. But after nearly six weeks since she left North America, she was anxious to get to work. She had business in Liverpool, where there was considerable sympathy for the Southern cause, and although the war was going badly back home, she was determined to win support in this new land.

CHAPTER 30

The Messenger

London, 1863

IN ENGLAND, ROSE seized every opportunity to meet important people and press her case for recognition of the Confederacy, even after her government had officially given up trying. One evening not long after her arrival, she was invited to discuss politics over tea at the Cheyne Row residence of the eminent British essayist, historian, and philosopher Thomas Carlyle, "the Sage of Chelsea." Carlyle had outraged his peers fourteen years earlier with an article in *Fraser's Magazine* fiercely attacking the notion of racial equality and holding that Britain's purchase of emancipation, especially in the British West Indies, where sugar was grown with slave labor, had been an economic disaster. Although first published anonymously, the essay was widely reprinted and attributed to Carlyle, who acknowledged his authorship and printed it again in 1853 as a pamphlet entitled *Occasional Discourse on the Nigger Question.* In it, he called economics "the dismal science," a tag that survives 150 years later. When Rose met him, Carlyle was probably the most outspoken defender of slavery in Britain.

Carlyle's redbrick house, his home for forty-seven years, was built in the early 1700s, and he entertained in a bright and spacious drawing room with a bookcase crammed from floor to ceiling, often receiving his guests in a dressing gown and slippers.[1] "Found him entirely different from what I had expected," Rose noted. "He is erect, tall, 5 feet 8 or 10 inches, little sinewy figure, full brown beard and slightly grizzled hair—has a strong

Scotch accent . . . talks a great deal, is deeply interested in American affairs and a most noble advocate of the South. . . .[2]

" 'I will do anything for your Country,' " she said Carlyle told her when she finally rose to leave as the hour approached midnight. She asked him to write another article that "from you Sir will carry weight and will be deeply gratifying to our President and people." He promised to consider it[3] and, indeed, did write another unapologetic defense of slavery, "Shooting Niagara—And After?" but not until the war in America was over.

Having landed unexpectedly near the southwest tip of England, Rose had to crisscross the country to sell her cotton in Liverpool some 350 miles to the north, then hurry to London to deliver a letter she was carrying from President Davis to James Murray Mason, the senior Confederate official in Great Britain.

"In four hours, 'did Liverpool,' in Yankee parlance," Rose told her diary. Then she and Little Rose caught a train and were out of there.

It is not certain the letter Rose carried contained Mason's walking papers, but five days after she delivered it, the commissioner notified the British government that he had been ordered to give up his post and leave the country. President Davis, Mason said, had concluded it was hopeless to expect establishment of normal relations between the two countries.[4] The Confederate leader was too proud to play mendicant.[5]

If Rose knew what was in the dispatch she carried, she didn't let on, even to her diary. "Drove to Mr. Masons, and gave him my letter from the President," she wrote. "He was very kind—and we had a long talk. The next morning he came and asked me to dinner and to bring Rose. Several persons there. In the evening Mr. [James] Spence of Liverpool, [a prominent businessman,] came in. I was glad to meet him as he has written a very clever book upon the American question."[6]

Mason soon left for Paris, where he concluded sadly that relations with both England and France were stalled and his London commission could not be salvaged. That left Rose Greenhow in an unusual and envious position as perhaps Davis's closest confidante in England. If there was any chance of persuading the British government to change its position, she was determined to try.

Lord Palmerston's Liberal government held a slim majority in Parliament over the Conservatives, led by Benjamin Disraeli and Edward George Stanley, fourteenth Lord Derby. A small group of MPs adamantly opposed to slavery wielded the balance of power in Palmerston's government, complicating the Confederacy's efforts to win British support. Rose was undeterred. She spent much of the next year in England, ferrying back and forth to Paris to meet Confederate colleagues and press her cause with the nobility.

She had written a memoir about her imprisonment and now sought a publisher. It was good propaganda and sure to attract attention to the Southern cause. She probably had an introduction to Richard Bentley, "Publisher in Ordinary to Her Majesty," because four days after her arrival in London, he signed a contract to bring out a book entitled *My Imprisonment and the First Year of Abolition Rule at Washington.* Rose and Bentley agreed to split the profits for all sales in Great Britain, on the Continent, in the United States, or elsewhere, but Rose reserved "to herself alone the right of publication within Confederate States." She signed the document "Rose Greenhow" and pointedly struck out her Irish maiden name: O'Neale.[7]

The memoir, dedicated to "the brave soldiers who have fought and bled in this our glorious struggle for freedom,"[8] appeared three months later to considerable publicity in Europe as well as the United States. The *Index,* a British weekly journal of politics, literature, and news sympathetic to the Confederate cause, described Rose as a woman "of warm southern sympathies and of a spirit and talent not common even among women of the south." The article said her book was "calculated to amuse almost as much as to interest us."[9] The staunchly pro-Union *New York Times* called the book "as bitter as a woman's hate can make it. Perhaps it is rather too spiteful to serve its object. People do not pity one who seems to take her own part, and many may wonder, not that she was treated with such severity, but that she got off so easily."[10]

During the next year, Rose met with the highest officials in the British and French governments, dined with top leaders of European society, and buttonholed anyone who would listen to her arguments for recognition and her defense of slavery. She even successfully negotiated the release of a Confederate naval officer with Charles Francis Adams, the United States minister to the Court of St. James's. That Adams agreed to see her—and treated her with respect—was remarkable in itself. He certainly knew his government had imprisoned her as a spy and sent her into exile.

That fall, Rose braved the raw London weather to visit Westminster Abbey and wandered among the "Tombs of the Mighty Dead," a legion of British monarchs and their consorts and such luminaries as Geoffrey Chaucer, Samuel Johnson, Sir Isaac Newton, and William Pitt. She dined with old friends, met many new ones, and held forth on world politics. "All

Europeans I have met are ignorant about Mexico and Mexican politics," she wrote on November 10. "They fancy that the Mexicans trouble themselves about Constitutions and governments, where as in reality, a few vandals get together and wage war for plunder upon the country."[11] Lady Georgiana Fullerton, a novelist and philanthropist, became one of her closest friends. Like Rose, Lady Fullerton suffered the death of a child in the prime of life and was still in mourning. She often invited Rose to accompany her to charity events.

London was a diverse, sprawling city where rich and poor coexisted uneasily at its center, and the growing numbers of Victorian middle class were buying property in the suburbs. The London underground railway system was in its infancy, and the cobbled roads were congested with carriages, horse-drawn carts, and hansom cabs. Children in tatters, beggars, prostitutes, and tradesmen seeking employment roamed the city streets, while the social life of prominent men centered around their clubs, which provided a place for good conversation and dining. To be seen in the city in late summer or autumn suggested that one did not have a country residence or other resources for comfortable living. Rose rented modest rooms over commercial premises, but they were located in Mayfair, an elegant section known for its fine old houses with silk-lined drawing rooms and liveried footmen.

In December 1863, three months after her arrival in England, Rose begged her old friend Alexander Boteler of Virginia for war news from home to counter what she assumed were exaggerated reports of Yankee victories in the pro-Union press. She said she was finding a great deal of public sympathy for the Confederate cause but that the news of reverses on the battlefield back home was depressing. She had just heard about a defeat at Lookout Mountain, and while she may have gotten a slanted version, the war in Tennessee was, indeed, going badly for the South. She dismissed the hostility shown by "Lord John," referring to British foreign secretary Lord John Russell, saying he had not been "more civil to the Yankee emissaries than to our own. . . .

"I would write you many interesting particulars," she told Boteler, but she feared her information would be intercepted and used to embarrass the South. Rose asked him to obtain a cipher from Secretary of State Benjamin, using her name as a key, and she would encrypt her letters to him. "I can tell you many things," she promised, adding that his letters to her would not need similar protection, as they could be sent directly to Major Walker in Bermuda, who would get them to her in confidence. "I wish I could write fully and freely but the fear of seeing myself in the NY Herald restrains my desire," she wrote. "I trust that I should be at home before the winter is over."[12]

It is not clear whether or not Boteler took her advice. If he did, her secret correspondence has not been found. More likely, based on her complaints that she almost never heard from him, her plan was not implemented, and she therefore reported only what she believed would help the cause if it was intercepted. There are also gaps in Rose's diary that suggest she censored her own work. Many pages were torn from the volume between her entries for September 16 and November 1, 1863.[13]

Rose, who had kept Little Rose at her side through house arrest, imprisonment, exile, and running the Union blockade under fire, decided it was time to put the ten-year-old in a school where she would live with other children and get a proper education. The Greenhows had sent their older daughters to the Patapsco Female Institute in Maryland. For Little Rose, Rose selected a Catholic convent school in France, where the young girl would be well away from the horrors of civil war. The child, who had never been far from her mother's side, dreaded the prospect.

On December 12, the Greenhows set off for Paris just after dawn. They took the Dover, Chatham, and Kent Railway and passed the great Canterbury Cathedral towering over the city and countryside of Kent on their way to the English Channel. "In a short time we left the smoky and murky atmosphere of London behind," Rose wrote. They arrived in Dover in time to catch the 9:40 A.M. ferry for a daylight crossing on the Royal and Imperial Mail Steam Packet. Rose had picked the route from Dover to Calais because it meant she would be on the water only about ninety minutes; the short passage seemed to afford the best defense against her perennial seasickness, which she said "rises before me as the greatest evil to which poor human nature can be exposed." She remained on deck throughout the trip, hoping the strong sea breeze would ward off "my enemy, mal de mer." But no sooner had the white cliffs of Dover faded in the distance than she was crouched on her knees, covering her face with her hand, "for one who has been much at sea has always the comfortable assurance of being laughed at by all who are not found to pay the same tribute to Neptune."[14]

As they approached Calais, a neutral harbor, Little Rose spotted a warship anchored with a Confederate ensign "flaunting gracefully" in the breeze, and the child danced with delight. "Oh Mama, here is our flag," she cried. Walking to the train, they saw a Confederate naval officer in uniform and stopped to speak to him about his ship, being fitted out in the harbor, before they caught a train operated by the Chemin de Fer du Nord to get to Paris by evening. The journey had taken about eleven hours.

Rose booked rooms at the Grand Hotel on the rue Scribe in central Paris, across from the new opera house still under construction. The Grand Hotel had been opened the previous year by Louis-Napoleon, the pleasure-loving Emperor Napoleon III, and was, Rose wrote, "more magnificent than imagination can conceive." She described an entrance like a fairy-land, with a great square court filled with orange trees and other tropical plants sitting in immense tubs covered with moss.

The city was in the midst of a makeover by Napoleon III's architect, Baron Georges-Eugène Haussmann. Paris was being transformed from an old European city with a maze of narrow streets and foul alleys into a mag-nificent metropolis of long, broad boulevards, blocks of new apartment buildings with symmetrical, wrought-iron balconies, and modern gas lamps lighting the Champs-Élysées.[15] The grand avenues, vast parks, and imposing new public buildings were more regal than anything Pierre L'En-fant had envisioned in his ambitious design for the new capital of Wash-ington seventy years earlier. Rose was bowled over. They drove past the Louvre, the Place Vendôme, and the Place de la Concorde, where she noted that Marie-Antoinette and King Louis XVI were beheaded during the French Revolution. "The magnificence of Paris dawned upon me," Rose wrote.[16]

They visited the formal gardens of Tuileries Palace, home of the em-peror, and the exquisite groves of the Bois de Boulogne, once the royal hunting forest, which Napoleon III had turned into an expansive public park modeled after London's Hyde Park. Rose declared it "imposing be-yond description." At the ancient Hôtel de Cluny on the Left Bank, they examined relics of tapestries, lace, and court dresses. A few days later, they drove through "the most filthy terrible place in this world . . . the only link with the bloody days of revolution," which was scheduled for demoli-tion the following year. They were on their way to see where the elegant Gobelin tapestry was made and when they got there had to slip a franc to a guard because they didn't have a permit. At night, they went to the Théâtre Impérial de Châtelet to see *Aladdin* from *Arabian Nights* and to the Théâtre de l'Opéra de Paris to see *La Sonnambula,* Bellini's outstand-ing musical production.

Confederates in the city welcomed her. Mason, still in Paris after being ordered to leave London, and his counterpart in France, John Slidell, came by her hotel. Slidell brought his wife and daughters. Returning from one of her first days of touring, Rose found the calling cards of several friends, including her old Washington neighbor William W. Corcoran, and was sorry to have missed them. But she did not hurry to resume her social and political duties while she still had her daughter in tow.

Rose had studied French for years and was charmed by the ambience of Paris, its boutiques filled with fineries—clothes, perfume, jewelry, and, for Little Rose, chocolates of every variety. They lingered over afternoon coffee at the Café Anglais, Café de Paris, Maison d'Or, and Café Cardinal. An innovative department store on the Left Bank called Bon Marché was a good place to find bargains and novelties. One evening, Rose waited until the dining room of the Grand Hotel was filled before she made her entrance. "My eyes were fairly dazzled by the blaze of light reflected from glasses for the whole walls were covered with gilding," and mirrors were mounted over the doors, she wrote.

On December 24, after ten days' seeing the sights, Rose took her daughter to visit the Convent du Sacré Coeur on the Left Bank.[17] The convent operated a Catholic boarding school with two hundred students, mostly from France but also from Belgium, Spain, Brazil, Cuba, and Ireland, as well as North America. Rose presented a letter of introduction from an Irish friend to Adèle Davidoff, head of the primary school. "My little one was very shy as she does not like the idea of being placed here," Rose wrote in her diary. "Never the less, it is her destiny."[18]

On Saturday, January 2, 1864, Rose wrote Jefferson Davis a twelve-page letter from the Hôtel de l'Amiraute in Paris saying that her New Year's Day was the most dismal she had ever spent. She seemed to know it wasn't much better for Davis after a terribly bloody month in November in which Grant took command of Union forces in Tennessee and drove the Confederates east, chasing them deep into Georgia. "It would be a mockery to pay you, Sir, the compliment of a day considered a festive one, and I can only hope that God will protect you through another year of trial and difficulty and that the next New Year will open more auspiciously for us."[19]

Rose also acknowledged that sentiment had turned against the South in France as well as in England. "I have come to the conclusion that we have nothing to hope from this side of the Channel," she wrote. "The French emperor will slightly give us sympathetic words for they want tobacco now quite as much as the English want cotton—it is now a pressing demand—and I believe that if we were to stop the going out of either cotton or tobacco, it would have more effect than anything else."

She advised Davis to withdraw Slidell from Paris as he had pulled

Mason out of London. The Confederate commissioner wasn't doing any better than any private individual would, she said, and Mason, who was languishing in Paris, ought to return to London, not as a commissioner but as a private agent of the government. "As a private person he would do us more good than in his official capacity, for then even friendly officers of the Gov. were obliged to be guarded in their intercourse," she wrote. Rose was almost certainly unaware that a new commission had already been prepared for Mason and would be approved by the Confederate Senate on January 18.[20] It would give him a role similar to that Rose envisioned for him.

Rose also told Davis that she planned to request an audience with Napoleon III, hoping to persuade him to provide ships, rifles, and cannons for the Southern cause, but she was not hopeful of seeing him. She concluded on a somber note: "I long more than I can tell you to get home and I remain abroad a short time longer only that I believe I can do some good."[21]

CHAPTER 31

An Imperial Welcome

Paris, 1864

NAPOLEON III INVITED Rose to a meeting to discuss foreign affairs, knowing she was in Paris as an agent of Jefferson Davis. It was probably the first time in history the emperor of France had agreed to see an American-born woman for a policy talk.

This was not Rose's first glimpse of Louis-Napoleon. She and Little Rose had seen the emperor and his Spanish-born wife, Empress Eugénie, skating in the Bois de Boulogne with their seven-year-old son, the prince imperial. The empress was dressed entirely in black—a black velvet petticoat with a black dress lopped over it, a black bodice drawn to the waist, black pantaloons, and a black hat with a heron's plume.[1] She was a handsome woman, but living with a wayward husband for years had left her with a severe look, and she was on the heavy side.

A day after that sighting, Rose sent Napoleon III a formal request for an audience. It was typical Rose, showering her subject with flattery and, at the same time, calling attention to her own influential position. "It would fill me with great grief to be obliged to return to the Confederacy and tell President Davis that I had not seen the only man in Europe who was his peer, and who has filled my mind with wonder as the originator of this Wonderful City which has become the Centre of Civilization of the World," she wrote.[2] An exchange of messages with the palace followed, and Rose was told the emperor would receive her.

When she arrived at the Tuileries Palace on January 22, 1864, Rose was passed from one official to another as they escorted her through wide halls and up and down several flights of winding staircases until she reached the Audience Chamber, where the Duc de Bassano, an imperial aide, greeted her and asked that she sit down: "His Majesty will receive you in just a few moments." Seconds later, Bassano returned and bowed low: *"Entrez, Madam, dans la cabinet de l'Empereur."* The duke ushered her in, bowed again, and closed the door behind her.

Napoleon III, a medium-size man with dark eyebrows, a waxed mustache, and a chin beard, was standing in the middle of the room. Rose made a deep curtsy, and the emperor extended his hand.

"Vous parlez Francais, Madam?" he asked.

"No Sire," Rose responded. *"Je ne parle pas assez pour me faire comprendu, mais je connais que votre majesty parle parfaitment Englais."* Rose said—in almost perfect French—that she didn't speak good enough French to make herself understood but knew that His Majesty (who had lived briefly in the United States, as well as in Britain) spoke excellent English. The emperor took her hand, led her to a velvet chair, and seated himself directly across from her.

"You are from the South," he said.

"Yes, Sire, from that unhappy country," Rose responded. Napoleon III expressed sympathy for the Southern cause and asked Rose several questions. "When my opinions came in conflict with his preconceived opinions, he admitted the force of my reasons as only a great man could," she wrote afterward in her diary.

Rose lost no time getting to the point. "I urged the question of recognition with great earnestness, showing that we considered ourselves entitled to it—and the moral strength it would give us," she wrote. "He said that he hoped to render us efficient aid but that he could not do so alone—that he had frequently made overtures to England on the subject—but that she had either evaded or rejected his overtures."[3]

Earlier in the war, Napoleon III had hinted privately to Confederate commissioner Slidell that he wished to help the South, but no official aid had been forthcoming. Now the emperor told Rose to assure Jefferson Davis of his sympathy and again promised to make every effort to help. Rose reported, however, that the emperor was critical of Southern military strategy, a subject certain to get Davis's attention. "If instead of throwing all your strength upon Vicksburg, you could have left that to its fate, and strengthened Lee so as to have taken Washington, the war would have ended," she quoted the emperor as saying. "England would have been obliged to recognize you, and should, of course."

Not even an emperor could criticize the Confederate military in front of Rose Greenhow and get away with it. "The President is fully convinced of the wisdom of such a movement," she snapped, "but there are grave political reasons for pursuing the course we have pursued—in order to prevent the alienation of our own territory." Rose even dared to patronize the emperor. "Besides," she said, "you can have no conception of the vast area of our military operations. The State of Virginia is as great as this mighty empire—and to show disregard to any portion of the Country would excite feelings injurious in a crisis like this."

After much conversation, Napoleon III asked about General Lee. "Sir," Rose responded with pride and flattery, "he is worthy to be one of your marshals."[4]

Rose did not linger. She had said what she had to say and stood to leave. Napoleon III, charmed by the Southern widow, took her hand. "I wish you would remain in France," he said.

"Even the attractions of your mighty Capital cannot keep me," Rose replied.

"I know your history," said the emperor. "The women of the South have excited the admiration of the world. I wish you a prosperous voyage. Tell President Davis that my admiration and sympathy are with him and his people."

Rose tried one last time. "I wish you would have me tell him that you would recognize us as one," she said.

"I wish to God I could," Napoleon III answered. "But I cannot do it without England . . . but you may assure the president that I will make renewed efforts to serve him."[5] With that, the emperor escorted Rose to the door and shook her hand. "So much for my interview with this ruler of the destiny of Europe," she wrote after the meeting.[6]

Back at her hotel, Rose found both Mason and Slidell waiting to debrief her, and she sat down to write Jefferson Davis a verbatim account of her audience, describing the emperor's "friendly policy and feeling," but "indulging in no exaggerated speculations as to what might be the result."[7] She was right not to raise false hope. The next month, Napoleon III concluded that it was not in the long-term interest of France to support the South, and he closed French ports and other facilities to the Confederates.

A few weeks later, after some time for reflection, Rose sent a harsh assessment to her friend Boteler. She "was treated with great distinction great kindness," she said, "and my audience in Court Circles was pronounced 'une grande success'—and altho the Emperor was lavish of expressions of admiration of our President and cause there was nothing upon which to hang the least hope of aid unless <u>England acted simultaneously</u>—the French people are brutal, ignorant and depraved to a degree beyond description and have no appreciation of our struggle. They believe it is to free the slaves and all their sympathies are really on the Yankee side. The Emperor sympathises with us but altho ruling with despotic power he is obliged to be watchful and wary as any false step would be his ruin and he dare not take a step unless England joins him."[8]

Regardless of the feelings about the French expressed in her letter, Rose thoroughly enjoyed being welcomed to the imperial court. On Sunday, January 31, she was a guest at a masked ball at the Tuileries Palace. Napoleon III loved big, flashy events and often appeared as a seventeenth-century Venetian noble. The occasions were dazzling, each a world of fantasy more extravagant than the last.[9]

Rose, finally emerging from nearly a decade of mourning, had begun to wear red roses in her hair again, and bright jewels sparkled at her breast.[10] The evening, she wrote, was like a scene from the play *Arabian Nights* that she had seen with Little Rose at the Théâtre Impérial. Guards in ceremonial armor lined the grand staircase "like so many petrified steel-clad warriors." The salon was crowded with people in elegant attire: gentlemen in embroidered court dress carrying swords, foreign diplomats in brilliant sashes and military decorations, women with low-cut necklines and skirts held to an exaggerated width by a new frame of ten steel rings called a crinoline. The emperor and empress were seated on a throne outlined with crimson and gold tassels.

At midnight, doors to the opulent dining room were thrown open, but only foreign ambassadors were invited to dine with the imperial family. One ambassador asked Rose to accompany him, and she quickly accepted. "I had a good opportunity to see the Empress & Court," she wrote. "She was standing near me for some time. She is not at all pretty nor distinguished in appearance." The empress, who at the time was distressed over an affair that her husband was conducting with a dancer, wore a dress of white tulle garnished with brown butterflies and velvet. There were great plumes in her hair, fastened in the front with diamonds, and around her neck was "an immense quantity" of large pearls, also fastened with diamonds. The emperor wore a plain dark suit with a broad red sash across his chest. Princess Mathilde, the emperor's cousin and onetime fiancée, was dressed in white and wore a magnificent tiara of diamonds, but in Rose's view, she was "fat and vulgar looking." Rose didn't mention that the princess was reputed to have the nicest cleavage in Europe. Princess Clotilde, the wife of Prince Napoleon, Mathilde's brother, was dressed in red gauze and also wearing a tiara of diamonds: "She was thin with sharp features, a turned up nose and an unnatural way [of] looking," Rose wrote.[11] The ladies did not impress her: "I saw no handsome woman in the circle, altho blazing in jewels, the toiletry did not strike me as very pretty."[12]

Rose also attended the last state ball of the season, and the *Index,* in a society report from Paris, mentioned "among the strangers present, Rose Greenhow lately Mr. Lincoln's prisoner." Afterward she boasted to Boteler, "I had almost forgotten to tell you that I went to the grand state ball at the Tuileries, and was the only stranger mentioned in the description of the ball."[13]

Little Rose started school at the convent in early February, and both mother and daughter dreaded the parting. The two had never been separated, and ten-year-old Little Rose was miserable. Rose left for England on February 6, noting, "I left my little one behind and my heart was heavy. It is no pleasant thing traveling alone at any time, but in a strange country it is something very disagreeable."

Captain James Bulloch, a Confederate agent in Europe in charge of purchasing military equipment, took Rose to the train station in Paris and found her a place in a boat cabin reserved for women traveling alone marked "*Dames Seules.*" The weather was awful. Heavy rain and a fierce wind churned the sea. "A rough trip we had across the channel," Rose wrote. "Everyone on board was seasick and huddled as close as could be packed in the cabin as the sea dashed over the deck which was several feet in the water. At last we were over—and once more in the train for London. I cannot say how glad I was to be in England once more. I had a warm feeling which quite irritated me for I could not help remembering my own dear land and the bloody struggle which was desolating her all on account of the selfish policy of this Country."

At Dover, a customs agent examined Rose's formally unrecognized Confederate passport and allowed her bags to pass unopened as she slipped two shillings into his hand. When she reached Victoria Station in London, she was met by her maid, Elizabeth, "a most faithful creature," who arranged for Rose's carriage ride to temporary quarters, where a good supper awaited. Two days later, she moved into new lodgings at 157 New

Bond Street, a house owned by a tailor named Henry Browne.[14] Confederate friends began calling on her almost immediately, but she fell ill with a severe cold, "la grippe as it is called in France," and she didn't go out for two weeks.

The remarkable trip to Paris had sapped much of her spirit and energy, but her friend Lady Georgiana Fullerton noticed that the cloud over Rose's head seemed to lift after her return to England. The hollows in her cheeks began to fill, and when she was presented with a compliment, tears welled in her eyes.[15] Once recovered, she attended grand dinner parties almost every evening and did her best to persuade British officials to support her Southern cause. After a discussion over dinner one night with Lord Derby, formerly prime minister but now a member of the opposition, she wrote: "He was bitterly ignorant of everything save that we once formed a part of the old United States government," and he had no "clear idea of the grounds upon which we claimed the rights of secession."[16]

Rose loved these society events because they gave her an opportunity to make her case, but she had little attraction for the formality of European society. At a charity ball held at the Grand Hotel in March, all the men were on one side of the ballroom and the women on the other, not at all the sort of party Rose enjoyed. "It seemed dull and lifeless," she wrote in her diary. "No conversation going on between the sexes."

Other occasions were just "stupid." While staying at the Grand, she noted: "Dined at the Table d'Hotel—found it very stupid and disagreeable." She would meet Carlyle again in May and make him four cups of tea during a delightful talk about the South, but it was followed by "3 stupid visits."[17]

In late March Rose returned to Paris to spend ten days with Little Rose. The child had been in the convent for six weeks, and Rose was annoyed when she showed up on Sunday morning and the nuns wouldn't release her daughter until after Mass. As soon as Little Rose saw her mother, she burst into tears. "They were soon dried," Rose wrote. "We came home, dressed and went out to dine."[18]

After six months hopscotching between London and Paris, Rose finally began to relax. She apparently developed at least one openly romantic relationship in England, but she didn't write about it. The tantalizing clue is that years later, Rose's European address book was found with a note scrawled next to the name "Wharncliffe," apparently by one of Rose's daughters. "If your grandmother had not died," it said, "you would have been his granddaughter. He was mummy's chum and [unintelligible] marry him."[19]

The writer of the note most likely mistook the third Baron Wharncliffe, whose full name was Edward Montagu Granville Stuart-Wortley, for another British lord in the address book, George Granville Lleveson-Gower. (Wharncliffe's grandfather James Archibald Stuart-Wortley-Mackenzie took the name Baron Wharncliffe in 1826.) Lord Granville was a widower and brother of Rose's friend Lady Georgiana Fullerton and was mentioned frequently in Rose's diary. Leader of the House of Lords, Granville lost his wife in 1860 and was actively seeking a new mate. His personal correspondence showed he weighed various candidates and contemplated the importance of money versus social position in the selection of a partner.[20]

Wharncliffe, on the other hand, was more than ten years younger than Rose and married to someone else. Rose saw both Wharncliffe and his wife frequently. In Victorian London, divorce would have undermined his social position. A letter Wharncliffe wrote to Rose a month after her departure focused on his admiration for the Confederate leaders and contained no suggestion of an affair.[21] If Rose was engaged to marry—as the note in the address book suggests—it more likely would have been to Lord Granville.

Rose's diary, however, drops few hints of a love life. She seemed more interested in being remembered for her devotion to the Confederacy. Her personal diversions show she soaked up details of the historic castles and churches she visited, signed the register book at Shakespeare's Stratford birthplace (guessing she was the first Confederate to do so), and called by mistake at the cottage of "the greatest ornithologist in the world." He was Professor Richard Owen, actually a famed anatomist and paleontologist whom she described as a great friend of the late Prince Albert. They chatted about some curious antediluvian remains he had just discovered on the coast of France. Rose also visited Dr. Edward Headlam Greenhow in Upper Berkeley Square, a prominent physician and relative of her husband, still known for his pioneering research on Addison's disease.[22]

Her writing rarely displayed a melancholy side—disgust and anger were more common negative emotions—but one evening in Paris, she sat in her hotel room and cried uncontrollably as she wrote in her journal: "What trifles colour life and make it dark as night. Blessed are they who let no human feeling stir their souls. I know I ought not to be miserable, and yet I am. And tears which I try to keep back flow down my cheek and blind me." As if to scold herself for revealing the agony of a long, losing struggle, she hastily halted such introspection. "Well, I will put down my paper and hope that tomorrow's sun will disperse the cloud which is now heavy upon my soul. Je suis très misèrable ce soir. Au revoir, Mrs. Greenhow, vous êtes un très mal companion." ("I am so miserable this evening. Good-bye, Mrs. Greenhow, you are a very bad companion.")[23]

As the sun broke through the next day, Rose's mood recovered. Her friends from home—former senator and Mrs. Gwin; William Corcoran, who had fled Washington when the war began; and John Slidell, the Confederate envoy to France—called on her at her hotel. Gwin, like Rose, had been thrown in prison for suspected disloyalty early in the war and reached Paris about the time she got there.[24] Little Rose did not like it when her mother's attention was directed at anyone else. "My little one is quite happy, but quite jealous that I should smile on anyone," Rose wrote. Friday, March 31, brought mail she had been anxiously awaiting. "News from home still good."

Rose came back to her apartment one evening to put Little Rose to bed and found Captain James Bulloch waiting for her to say good-bye. Bulloch, who masterminded the surreptitious construction of warships for the Confederate navy in the supposedly neutral shipyards of Britain, spent much of the war living in Liverpool with his family. "I am very sorry he is going," she wrote, "for it is a pleasant thing to feel that a true friend is near, and such he is to me."

Rose celebrated her daughter's eleventh birthday on April 2 and returned to London five days later. She was in the crowd that witnessed Italian patriot Giuseppe Garibaldi's triumphant visit to London, watching as he crossed Westminster Bridge and proceeded slowly down Whitehall past Downing Street to Trafalgar Square. She described him standing in his carriage, hat in hand, and bowing to the crowd. "Not that I had any respect for the old brigand," she wrote, "but I felt curious to see an English Crowd. It was a popular demonstration by the Mobocracy for its idol. The expression on his face is benevolent but indicative of a low order of intellect."[25]

On April 29, she lunched with Mary Hargreaves at Silwood Park, the estate of Lancashire cotton mill owner John Hargreaves adjacent to Windsor Castle. Afterward, Rose drove down the stately "Avenue of Elms" carriage path that links Windsor Great Park with Windsor Castle. She found the royal residence outside London unimpressive. "Was very much disappointed with the interior," she wrote after touring the huge castle. "Far inferior to Versailles or the Tuileries in France." She stood on the spot where

Herne's Oak had been blown over or cut down the previous year. The famous tree was memorialized by Shakespeare in *The Merry Wives of Windsor.*

Rose never missed an opportunity to proselytize. She was traveling on a train with James Spence of Liverpool when "a high dignitary of the Church of England" climbed aboard. Rose buttonholed him and preached the Confederacy until he jumped off at the next stop. "He got out—shook me heartily by the hand and said I pray that God will prosper your cause and give success to your countrymen," she wrote. "At this point another person Bishop of Windsor I think got in—and precisely the same thing happened. . . . Mr. Spence said in all his experiences of traveling in England he had never seen anything like it."[26]

At a large party in May, a guest she didn't recognize approached her and asked a single question: Which man was superior, President Lincoln or President Davis?

"Sir," Rose replied, "if you accept the scientific origin rather than the religious one—and believe man in the beginning was a baboon or an ouranotang—and that successive ages of improvement has brought him to his present high state of perfection—almost equaling the God head—I will assume Mr. Lincoln is at the beginning of the species, Mr. Davis at the end."[27]

The guest, Reverend Newman Hall, a prominent abolitionist and supporter of the Union, tried to lecture Rose about slavery, but she stood up to him and rudely dismissed his arguments. "Your remarks are so absurd that I could almost suppose that you could have derived your argument from the romance of Mrs. Beecher Stowe," she replied. When the man conceded that the abolitionist author was his source, Rose said she considered him a subject for "compassionate toleration rather than argument, a candidate for the straight jacket." They squabbled over recent news reports of a battle at Fort Pillow in Tennessee, where Confederate cavalry troops were said to have massacred the white commander and more than two hundred soldiers of the U.S. Colored Troops, among the Union's first black combat units, who were overrun in an attack on the fort.

"If I were a Negro, I would have taken arms," he told her.

"Then I would have shot you with as little compassion as I would a dog," Rose snapped. "You must excuse me but I do not consider the opinions of a man who confessed Mrs. Stowe as his Authority worthy of refutation."

"The sympathy of England is worth something," said Hall.

"The sympathy of the enlightened Classes are all with us," she shot back. "When it is in your interest to recognize us, you will. Our destiny is entirely in our own hands and the events of this war have removed from us all anxiety upon the slavery question. The fate of the slave rests with his Southern Master—as the Masters with God! But will you free him? Never, either extermination or eternal slavery is his lot according to the lights before me."[28]

The room fell silent. Guests crowded around their Confederate friend, according to Rose, united in their support. She was exhausted. Once again, the patriot had spoken from the heart.

CHAPTER 32

A Chance for Peace

London, 1864

"SICK WITH ANXIETY," Rose wrote on May 21. "Refused to see anyone. News by steamer. Thank God that it is good. Lee repulsed the enemy."[1] She must have received the first reports of the spring campaign that initially went well for the South. In reality, it was the beginning of the end.

General Ulysses S. Grant, who had recently been put in command of the U.S. Army, crossed the Rapidan in early May 1864 "to get possession of Lee's army"[2] in Virginia and press on to Richmond. The two armies met in a furious battle in the Wilderness. Lee's brigades were outnumbered, but they were fighting on their home ground and slaughtered the Yankees. Rose had been hoping for a Lee victory over Grant to budge the British and had reason to be elated.

At a party given by her friends the Wharncliffes, Rose met an ally in William Schaw Lindsay, a member of Parliament and aide to the prime minister, Lord Palmerston. At dinner, Lord Wharncliffe toasted "a sentiment which will be acceptable to everyone here, the success of the Confederate Cause and Mrs. Greenhow."

"All bowed low to me," Rose told her diary. "I was glad, embarrassed and could only say, 'I thank you all for my Country and for myself.' "[3]

Rose was in her element, basking in the approving glow of British high society. Later in the evening, Lindsay, a merchant and shipowner, approached her to say he was interested in trying to broker a cease-fire between the Union and Confederate states. He told her that Palmerston wanted to stop the war and that Lindsay would agree to drop his resolution proposing diplomatic recognition of the South and introduce one that would call instead for England, France, and other nations to mediate a suspension of hostilities. Rose readily accepted the proposal. A cease-fire would amount to a victory for the South because it would preserve separation.

Lord Palmerston thought the approach "perfectly acceptable," but Lord Russell, the foreign secretary, "violently opposed it," Rose reported. Yet Russell agreed to meet with Lindsay to discuss the issue. In her diary, Rose described a succession of political maneuvers in which she and Lindsay tried to lure Confederate emissary James Murray Mason back from Paris to meet with Palmerston. But Mason declined to go because he had no instructions from his government or a direct invitation from the British leader.

Rose had little patience for diplomatic protocol. She had already written Mason "to say that I thought he was wrong in his refusal[,] that extraordinary circumstances warranted a departure from the rules applicable to warring times—that a feather might now turn the tide in our favor; and that any chance should be seized with avidity for stopping this dreadful war, where our gallant Countrymen were falling like ripe grain in a harvest."

Before leaving the Wharncliffe party, Rose apologized to her British friends if they thought she was too outspoken. "I cannot be calm when I talk of this war," she said. "I hope you will all pardon me if I seem unwomanly in my denunciation of the vandals who now lay waste our land[,] violate our women and murder our kindred."

"Madam," she said the noble Lord Wharncliffe responded, "you have earned your right to paint these deeds in burning languages as you do, and it would not be human if you could speak calmly on this subject."[4]

Lindsay told Rose he would come to see her after his meeting with Russell, and he called at her home on June 3. By her account, Lindsay warned the foreign minister that a Northern victory could bring guerrilla war, that the South would even arm its women and its slaves if need be: "Can anyone picture then the horrors which will follow?"[5]

Russell "admitted that it would be dreadful" and recounted a discussion he had with Charles Francis Adams, the U.S. minister to Britain, who is largely credited with heading off Britain's recognition of the Confederacy. According to Lindsay, Russell told Adams he did not believe the South could be vanquished or the Union restored and that Adams laid out the

Union's strategy for capturing all the major Southern cities: Richmond, Charleston, Mobile, and others, forcing the South to lay down its arms and accept the U.S. government's terms. Lindsay was said to argue that even if the North succeeded, it "would be obliged to hold [the South] by a military despotism greater than was ever exercised by Austria or Russia in the dark ages—the people would be unconquered and would still resist," Rose wrote. "Lord Russell said that is the very argument which I used with Mr. Adams."

Lindsay told Rose his discussion with Lord Russell showed the foreign secretary understood the difficulty of conquering a determined, resistant population and that "very sharp language must have passed" between the British foreign secretary and the U.S. minister.

Lindsay showed Russell his cease-fire resolution and said he was willing to substitute it in Parliament for his proposal to recognize Richmond and would incorporate any changes Russell requested. Rose copied the words into her diary: "That this House deeply regretting the great loss of life & suffering of the people of the United States and of the Confederate States of North America by the continuance of the war which has been so long raging between them, trust that Her Majesty's Govt will avail itself of the earliest opportunity of mediating in conjunction with other Powers of Europe to bring about a cessation of hostilities."

Lindsay met with Palmerston to discuss whether or not to invite Mason to London. "Shall I tell Mr. Mason that you wish to see him?" the aide reportedly asked.

"Yes!" Palmerston replied.

"So," Rose's diary says, "Mr. Mason agreed to come." But she worried that Lindsay lacked "such weight and influence as I would like for the man who is to take so prominent a part."[6]

Meanwhile, a pro-Confederate gentleman identified only as "Mr. Devaux" tried to recruit Rose to go to Rome to ask the pope to use his influence to stop the war. He was working with one of Napoleon III's ministers, the Duc de Persigny, "who considers the thing worth trying," Rose reported, and she contemplated seeking another audience with the emperor of France, "that master mind of Europe. . . .

"I have already enlisted high Catholic influence here in our behalf," she noted.[7]

Rose, however, was also making plans to return home. But on June 9, she received a letter from her daughter Florence with surprise word that Florence would be arriving in England—the next day—by ship from New

York. Rose had not seen her eldest daughter since before the war and flew into preparations for the most welcome visit.

"Hunted apartments all day," Rose wrote. "Gave up mine Tuesday. My landlady is a fury at my going. I am very sorry, always frightened at a tempest—an angry woman is a frightful object."[8] Rose went to Mass and to a dentist for a toothache and worried when the steamer did not arrive on time.

While waiting for Florence, she had a long meeting with Mason, who ignored his standing instructions from home and did return to England, still skeptical but assured by his friend Lindsay that Palmerston wanted to see him. The Virginian was normally a gregarious man, but this time his tone was serious. Grant's army was within twelve miles of Richmond, and they expected him to get closer before Lee made a stand.

"Confederate loss is heavy," Rose wrote. "God grant that this is the last of the bloody fighting."[9] Her information was less than three weeks old, but by the time she met Mason, the war had grown bloodier still. On June 3, 1864, Grant hurled his army at Lee's entrenched defenders at Cold Harbor east of Richmond, and the Confederates chewed up the blue-coated attackers in mindless slaughter.[10] Grant's superior force of more than one hundred thousand men suffered some twelve thousand casualties, the Confederates far fewer. It was Grant's worst defeat—but Lee's last victory. The Union's new commander showed he had the men and matériel to keep chasing Lee and was willing to absorb staggering losses to catch him.

After the meeting with Mason, Rose received a telegram from Florence that she had arrived in Liverpool but was too fatigued from the crossing to leave immediately for London. "I am nervously anxious for time to meet my Child whom I have not seen for so long a time," Rose wrote. "I fear that she is ill. O how sad has been this terrible war in its effect upon families. Mine has been torn asunder."[11]

When Rose met Florence at the train station on the afternoon of June 13, she was shocked by her daughter's gaunt appearance. "She is ill," Rose wrote, "but this climate, I trust, will bring her up." Florence had come to England alone on the fifth anniversary of the death of her son. Her husband, Captain Tredwell Moore, having finally gotten his wish to be sent east to join the war, was then serving with the Union army as chief quartermaster of the military supply depot in Wheeling, West Virginia.[12] "Florence is very much fatigued," Rose noted the next day. "Looks very pale and thin—but still very lovely." Rose kept up her busy social schedule, trying to use Confederate successes on the battlefield to get her agenda back on the table, but Florence wasn't well enough to accompany her. Rose took her to a doctor, and after a few days Florence was on the mend.

Rose was still working on the plan to seek papal intervention, but she decided not to tell Mason about it until she had seen the Duc de Persigny about getting French assistance for the venture. Then she would ask Mason for his advice. She met several times with Cardinal Nicholas Wiseman, the first Catholic cardinal in Britain since the Reformation. He expressed personal sympathy for her position but said it could be a disaster if he overstepped his bounds and was seen as meddling in politics. "He urged me to go to Rome as he thought this a fortunate moment," she wrote.

Rose had become a regular at morning Mass in London and had another reason to meet with the cardinal. Although she had been born into a Catholic family and attended Catholic services throughout her life, she had never been confirmed in the church. Cardinal Wiseman performed the ceremony on Wednesday, June 29, in the little chapel attached to his country residence, Etloe House, in East London. The Marchioness of Lothian, wife of the voluble pro-Confederate activist, acted as her sponsor, and the Marchioness of Londonderry, a daughter of the Earl of Roden, attended.[13]

While attending a luncheon, Rose learned that the Confederates' most famous cruiser, the CSS *Alabama,* had been trapped by a Union sloop-of-war, the USS *Kearsarge.* The *Alabama,* which had captured more than sixty Union merchant ships and sunk at least one Federal warship, was being refitted in the harbor at Cherbourg, France, when the *Kearsarge* arrived and took up station at the entrance to the port. The Confederate cruiser put to sea for a duel in international waters and was quickly outgunned and sunk, leaving her surviving crew to swim for their lives. The victor captured some; others made it to a British yacht.

Rose met some of the young Confederate officers at a garden party thrown by Lady Jane Franklin. One told the story of abandoning his sinking ship, being rescued by a boat from the *Kearsarge,* then jumping overboard and swimming to a French vessel to avoid being taken prisoner by the Yankees.

"Should we make this man a belted knight?" Rose playfully asked Lady Caroline Owen.

"He should certainly be K-C-B," Mrs. Owen replied. "Knight of the Cold Bath."

Rose mixed meetings with members of Parliament and introducing

Florence to her friends. They attended the horticultural show at South Kensington and found the roses "magnificent" but sniffed that the grapes were inferior to those they had seen in California.[14]

On July 8, Rose heard of more Confederate battlefield victories that she interpreted—erroneously—as a sign the Confederates had the Yankees on the run. "Thank God it foreshadows the end," she wrote. "God grant that those vandals may be destroyed, exterminated. . . . Impatiently I want to see the bitter chalice placed at their lips, the assassin's knife at their throats and the torch of the incendiary applied to their homes."[15]

Mason's long awaited meeting with Palmerston took place at the prime minister's home on July 14. Mason did most of the talking and came away optimistic that, although "the Ministry fears to move under the menaces of the North," Palmerston was satisfied "the independence of the South [is] an accomplished fact."[16]

Despite what the British said privately, none of the news of battlefield successes had the desired effect of moving the government toward recognition or intervention for a cease-fire. The hard-nosed U.S. minister, Charles Francis Adams, had Palmerston's ear, and he countered every Confederate attempt to advance on the diplomatic front. On one small field, however, Rose won a noteworthy victory.

Commissioner Mason and Captain Raphael Semmes of the *Alabama* were concerned about the mental state of Third Lieutenant Joseph D. Wilson, one of the *Alabama*'s officers taken prisoner by the *Kearsarge,* and they were discussing what to do when Rose arrived to see them in early July.

"The very person we want," Mason was quoted as saying in an account of the incident published by *The New York Times.* "She can get him off if anybody can. Good morning, Madam. We want somebody to do something!"

"I'll do it—what is it?" the lady responded with characteristic willingness.

"We want you to go to Mr. Adams and get this poor fellow off his parole so that he can be taken care of."[17]

Adams certainly would not have seen Mason or Semmes, who held official positions in the Confederacy, but Rose had no title, which worked in her favor. Adams agreed to meet with her on July 11. The U.S. minister's wife, Abigail, had once caused a stir at a dinner party in Rose's home when she lionized John Brown as a "holy saint and martyr." Rose was calling in a favor.

When she sent up her card at Portland Place, which served as the American embassy, Adams received her immediately. According to the *Times'* account, which is quite similar to that in Rose's diary, Rose argued that Captain Semmes had freed scores of Federal officers to be exchanged for Confederate counterparts, and this case would be seen as an act of Union kindness. Adams said Captain John Winslow of the *Kearsarge* controlled the fate of the young officer. A flurry of meetings and correspondence followed, and four days later, Wilson was released. It was not the last time he and Rose would cross paths.

Rose insisted that most of the British aristocracy supported her, but she encountered opposition as well and never shrank from a debate. She and Lord Granville were deep in conversation one evening when they were approached by William Gladstone, then chancellor of the Exchequer. "I always thought it as best for the interest of England that the old Government of the U.S. should stand as it was with its strong sectional antagonistic interest," she quoted the future prime minister as telling them. "Quarrelling among themselves kept them from endangering the peace of other countries."

"The Mexican war should have disabused you of that idea," Rose snapped. The United States had been divided over going to war with Mexico, she said, but once the shooting started, the populace united behind its government and wound up with California.

According to Rose's journal, Lord Granville told her Napoleon III had proposed a joint intervention with England to stop the fighting "and if peace did not follow, to recognize us at once." The British government, however, wanted all the European powers, especially Russia, to participate or "it would do no good."[18]

On the evening of July 23, Rose attended a "brilliant party" given by Lord and Lady Palmerston at their imposing London residence on Piccadilly and, for the first time, talked at length with the prime minister. Palmerston was the most important person she had met in England and the only one whose support could really make a difference to the Confederate army. He was nearly eighty years old but still robust.

"He asked me how I got over," Rose wrote afterward.

"I ran the blockade."

"Was it not dangerous?"

"Only so because your government chooses to respect it," Rose replied tartly.[19]

They launched into a conversation about recognition but broke no ground. Palmerston gave her the party line that it would only unite the North and wouldn't help the South. She told the prime minister she disagreed. She didn't flatter. She didn't cajole. She didn't try to change his mind, as she had with the French emperor and so many others. Perhaps she had grown weary and knew the fight for Palmerston's government was lost.

Rose was getting ready to return to North America. She went to Paris one more time to visit Little Rose and meet the Duc de Persigny about the advisability of going to Rome. When she got there, she learned the duke was out of town and scrapped the plan to see the pope. The weather in Paris was hot and disagreeable, but Little Rose was overjoyed to see her mother, and Rose picked up compliments about her daughter from Madame Davidoff, the head of the primary school, and Mrs. Slidell, wife of the aging Confederate commissioner. Slidell himself, she jotted in her diary, was "as Civil as his rude nature will admit of." On Saturday, July 30, after four days together, Rose took Little Rose back to the Convent du Sacré Coeur and left the child sobbing bitterly. "It was a heavy trial to say goodby," Rose wrote. "God bless her. My heart is very Sad." It was the last time mother and daughter would embrace.

Accompanied by her maid, Elizabeth, Rose boarded the Channel steamer for England. The emotional farewell with her daughter left her exhausted, and now the rolling sea made her stomach turn. She lay on a bench on the deck, her head on Elizabeth's lap. Rain began to fall, washing down Rose's cheeks like tears, but she was so close to being sick that she couldn't even turn her head.

Rose's mission and the South's prospects were slipping away. Nothing had come of Mason's meeting. Lindsay had withdrawn his resolution, and Parliament had adjourned. By the beginning of August, Rose's wealthy friends shut up their houses and left for the country. Rose had arranged for Florence to spend the season at a resort hotel called Oatlands, the former estate of the Duke of York in Weybridge, Surrey.

Rose gathered supplies for her own journey, buying much-needed clothes and welcome gifts for family and friends whose lives had been shattered by the war. She went to dinner at the home of Alexander Collie, a merchant and shipowner who commissioned vessels to run the Yankee blockade, and met Captain William Hewett, commander of the ship Collie had selected to take the Southern patriot back to the Confederacy. "I like his looks," Rose wrote on August 2, "and am quite sure he will not lose his vessel if caution and coolness will save it."[20]

She was frustrated when she learned her departure was delayed and the itinerary changed. "Not going to Havana—on account of yellow fever but again to that nasty little island of Bermuda,"[21] she noted. It was even harder to say good-bye to Florence. How often mother and daughter had been separated—by the trip Rose and Robert took to Mexico and California, by Florence's marriage to Tredwell Moore, by this bitter, brutal war. They had spent years apart and barely three months together in London, hardly enough time to become reacquainted. "My heart is sorely tried when I look upon her lovely face and pleading eyes, until the last moment she had hoped that I would not go—but alas, inexorable destiny seems to impel me on."

Rose could not bear to be gone any longer. She belonged to the South, to the land and its people and its proud traditions. "The desperate struggle in which my people are engaged is ever present," she wrote, "and I long to be near to share in the triumph or be buried under the ruins . . . without home, without nationality."[22]

Rose saw Lord Palmerston one more time: "Had a long talk with him and I think rather startled him by some of my ideas. He said he did not think recognition would do us much good—it would unite the Yankees and make them bitter &c., besides it would involve G.B. in hostilities. . . . I said does it never occur to you that you probably bring upon yourself the very evil which you deprecate."[23] It was her parting shot at the British government.

But Rose's role as a power broker for wealthy men was not over. Collie, the shipping merchant, sat down at his desk in London on August 9 to write a letter asking Rose to speak to President Davis about blocking the exile of his Wilmington agent, who had gotten in some sort of trouble and was being ordered to leave the country. The merchant said that loss of his agent in Wilmington, the only Confederate port the Union blockade had not been able to close, would hurt trade with the South and end his distribution of $10,000 a month to Southern charities. "If you can aid me privately at Richmond, you will oblige me and I know that you will benefit many of your countrymen," Collie told Rose.[24]

The next day, Collie and Mason accompanied Rose by train from London to the Scottish port of Greenock to put her aboard the *Condor,* now set to leave for Bermuda, Halifax, and Wilmington. After a year in England that began with her delivering a letter from Davis to Mason, she was heading home with one from Mason to Davis attesting to the breadth of the contacts she had made and her seizing every opportunity to promote the cause "in quarters where it could not but be of value."[25]

Wednesday, August 10, 1864, found Rose in a reflective mood as she prepared to leave. "A sad sick feeling crept over me, of parting perhaps forever, from many dear to me," she wrote that night. "A few months before I had landed a stranger—I will not say in a foreign land—for it was the land of my ancestors—and many memories twined around my heart when my feet touched the shores of Merry England—but I was literally a stranger in the land of my fathers and a feeling of cold isolation was upon me."[26]

It was Rose Greenhow's last entry in her European diary. She was weary and sad. Her impossible mission was at an end. She had not succeeded in persuading the European powers to recognize the Confederate States of America, but she had won the respect of a remarkable collection of women—and men. It was time to go back.

CHAPTER 33

The *Condor*

A LIGHT WIND rippled the inky waters of the Atlantic as the *Condor* approached the entrance to the Cape Fear River in the early morning hours of Saturday, October 1, 1864. At 3:00 A.M., the breeze freshened slightly, and it started to drizzle. A powerful swell from an offshore storm somewhere heaved the ship and let her down gently before rolling on toward shore and breaking on the shoals that ran along the coast.[1] The tide was rising, and the *Condor* was about to make her run through the Union blockade. Rose Greenhow had every reason to believe she was in good hands.

The *Condor* was a fast, three-stack iron steamer on the last leg of her maiden voyage to the Confederate states. Built in Scotland for Alexander Collie & Company expressly to run the Union blockade, she was more than seventy feet longer than the *Phantom,* which had taken Rose out of Wilmington the previous year.[2] Intelligence reports from the U.S. consul in Halifax, Nova Scotia, called her a superior vessel of rakish build with two short, schooner-rigged masts, a crew of forty, and a "very large and valuable cargo."[3] She was painted "elusive white" to make her difficult to spot from a distance. "Swift as a sea swallow," reported the *London Evening Mail.*[4]

The hull color was not her only camouflage. The captain was listed in some records as Samuel S. Ridge and "Captain Wright." His real name was William Nathan Wrighte Hewett, a thirty-year-old British naval officer furloughed on half pay while awaiting a new command. At twenty,

Hewett had won the Victoria Cross, Britain's highest award for gallantry, in the Crimean War, and he later served on Queen Victoria's yacht. Like many British officers who changed their colors like chameleons during the Civil War, Hewett knew the North Atlantic, was accustomed to danger, and stood to make big money running the Federal blockade. Many Royal Navy men used pseudonyms to protect their government's veil of neutrality.[5]

Carrying a valuable cargo of military uniforms and supplies, the *Condor* had arrived in Bermuda on August 19. She continued on to Halifax, Nova Scotia, where the U.S. consul reported nine blockade runners were waiting "for the moon to change and the nights to become dark" before leaving for Wilmington.[6] The *Condor* took on coal and picked up additional passengers, including Judge James P. Holcombe, the Confederate commissioner to Canada, and Lieutenant Joseph D. Wilson, the young officer from the CSS *Alabama* Rose had helped free from imprisonment aboard the *Kearsarge*.[7] In a quick message to Secretary of State Seward, the U.S. consul reported that the *Condor* left port on September 24 and was on her way to the South.[8] Rear Admiral S. P. Lee aboard the blockading squadron flagship USS *Malvern*, alerted that more swift ships were en route, ordered the *Niphon*, the USS *Alabama*, and the *Kansas* to finish refueling and return to stations off New Inlet "with all dispatch."[9]

As the *Condor* approached New Inlet, two lines of blockaders were waiting, patrolling just out of range of the Confederates' heavy guns guarding the inlet from batteries at Fort Fisher.

At 3:30 A.M., the crew of the *Niphon*, standing south of New Inlet, spotted a ship creeping noiselessly into the river off to her port and fired a broadside at her but missed. She turned around and stood along the beach to the northward, driving aground on Swash Channel Bar. Ten minutes later, the *Niphon*'s lookout saw another vessel, a low, three-pipe sidewheel steamer, heading for the inlet.[10] It was the *Condor*.

The fast runner carrying Rose Greenhow was only three hundred yards from shore, almost in the shadow of Fort Fisher. A Confederate shore battery opened fire with its Whitworth long-range rifled guns to warn the Yankee ship to keep her distance. As a burst of rockets lit up the night sky, the pilot aboard the *Condor* saw the looming silhouette of another vessel dead ahead. Trying to negotiate the narrow passage without the red and white range lights that usually guided ships through the channel, the *Condor*'s pilot swerved to starboard to avoid what he thought was a Federal ship in deep water. It was a fateful mistake. The ship he saw was the wreck of the

Night Hawk, another blockade runner the *Niphon* had driven onto the bar two nights before. As she turned, the *Condor* rode up onto the Federal shoals and jolted to a sickening stop, hard aground and helpless.

Rose panicked. Having been imprisoned once by the Yankees, she had no intention of letting that happen to her again. She demanded to go ashore. Captain Hewett resisted. Experience told him the shoal water and guns of Fort Fisher would keep the blockaders at bay, and he hoped his new ship would float free on the rising tide. The captain insisted it was safer to remain on board. "He was most energetic in his efforts to dissuade her," wrote Thomas E. Taylor, a friend of Hewett's who had been wounded in the Federals' firing on the *Night Hawk* two nights earlier.[11] But Rose was a persuasive woman, all too accustomed to getting her way. Hewett finally relented.

The crew lowered a lifeboat on the leeward side with Rose, Lieutenant Wilson, Judge Holcombe, the pilot, and two seamen assigned to row the party ashore.[12] Rose wore a heavy black silk dress and carried a leather pouch with dispatches for Secretary of State Benjamin from Commissioners Mason and Slidell along with four hundred British sovereigns, quarter-ounce gold coins worth, at the time, about $2,000. The money came from sales of her book, and she planned to give it to a Southern relief fund. The heavy bag was attached to a chain fastened around her neck.

Swells broke over the bar as the boat touched the water, and the small craft scarcely cleared its davits before it was caught broadside and swamped by a breaker, washing everyone into the pounding surf. The other passengers—Wilson, Holcombe, the pilot, and both seamen—struggled back to the capsized boat and clung to the keel. All were rescued. But in the predawn darkness, the anxious *Condor* crew found no trace of Rose Greenhow.[13]

A few hours later, a sentry named J. J. Prosper For Me D. Doctor Duval Connor—said to be the shortest man with the longest name in the Confederate army—was patrolling the beach in front of Fort Fisher, keeping an eye out for Federal sailors who sometimes slipped ashore from the blockaders for a night on the town. At three feet eleven inches, "Doc" Connor was barely able to shoulder his musket, an indication of how desperate the Confederate army was for recruits. As the sun crept above the horizon, he spotted something glistening at the water's edge—the metal buckle of a leather pouch "tossed up on the beach like a bit of seaweed," the *Daily Mail* reported.[14]

Opening the bag, Connor saw handfuls of gold sovereigns and checks written on the Bank of England. Connor family legend holds the sentry worried that if he kept the bag, he would be accused of stealing it, so he buried it in the sand under a partly burned log and sprinkled the area with ocean water to make it appear undisturbed. But then he had second thoughts and worried that his commanding officer would learn what he had done and punish him. He returned to the buried treasure, dug it up, and turned it in to his unit, which rewarded him with a $20 gold piece.[15] Other accounts say that when Connor learned the gold had belonged to a heroine of the Confederacy and was meant for the cause, he felt guilty and turned it in.[16]

At daylight, Thomas Taylor, who was supervising the salvage of his company's grounded and burned blockade runner *Night Hawk,* found Rose's body washed up on the beach. "A remarkably handsome woman, she was, with features which showed much character," Taylor wrote.[17]

Taylor or, more likely, some of the three hundred slaves he had doing salvage work, carried the corpse to Colonel William Lamb, commander of Fort Fisher, who wrote in his diary: "Her lifeless body was soon found, the cruel waves having cast it up on the cold, wet sands, as the flowing tide came in. It was a sad, a touching sight; that lovely face, that graceful form in pure development of womanhood, that well-poised head with its luxuriant hair falling below the knees, with the indomitable spirit flown beyond all human recall." Lamb's wife, Daisy, prepared the body to be sent up the river to Wilmington aboard the steamer *Cape Fear.*[18]

Hundreds of ladies lined the wharf when the steamer approached. Eliza Jane De Rosset, wife of a prominent physician in the city and president of the Soldier's Aid Society, had the body brought to her elegant river-view mansion to be prepared for funeral and burial.[19] "I cut off her hair and will keep it for her daughters, in case we ever hear from them," wrote Mrs. De Rosset, who sent six sons to fight for the cause and saw five return. "She was an elegant woman, not at all changed by death."[20]

Rose's body was carried to the chapel of Hospital Number 4, where an honor guard was stationed at the door. It lay on a bier, draped in a magnificent Confederate flag, her exposed face "so unchanged as to look like a calm sleeper, while above all rose the tall ebony crucifix—emblem of the faith she embraced in happier hours."[21] The report in the newspaper said a profusion of candles burned around the corpse, and the choicest flowers of the North Carolina autumn were woven into crosses, garlands, and bouquets. Sable-robed mourners stood silently at the head and foot as a tide of

THE *CONDOR* • 301

visitors who knew her only for her service to the Confederacy filed past, "women and children, with streaming eyes, and soldiers, with bent heads and hushed steps."[22]

Captain Hewett and his crew, who had remained aboard ship until the seas subsided, got to shore safely the next day. "The brave sailor was almost unmanned at the pitiful fate of his passenger," Colonel Lamb wrote.[23]

On Sunday afternoon, Rose's body was taken to St. Thomas the Apostle Roman Catholic Church, where the Reverend Dr. James Andrew Corcoran conducted the funeral Mass. Corcoran, a South Carolinian, offered "a touching tribute to the heroism and patriotic devotion of the deceased, as well as a solemn warning, on the uncertainty of all human projects and ambition, even though of the most laudable character."[24]

A flag-draped coffin, "as richly decorated as the resources of the town permitted," was borne through Wilmington with high-ranking officers representing army and navy, a special agent of the War Department, and local dignitaries bearing the pall. They were followed by an immense cortege that included eight carriages and many townspeople on foot as the procession made its way through the rain to a grassy slope under towering oaks and magnolias in Oakdale Cemetery.

Torrents of rain fell throughout the day, the newspaper reported, but as the coffin was being lowered into the grave, the sun burst forth and a rainbow of vibrant colors spanned the horizon. An anonymous scribe for the local paper wrote, "Let us accept the omen, not only for her, the quiet sleeper, who, after many storms and a tumultuous and checkered life, came to peace and rest at last, but also for our beloved country, over which we trust the rainbow of hope will ere long shine with brightest dyes."[25]

Mrs. De Rosset called it "a sad, sad sight." Not a tear of affection was shed at the grave, for no one in the midst of all the trappings of sacred honor and cherished tradition really knew Rose Greenhow. The mourners understood only that she had died in service to her country. Like so many in that terrible time, the proud patriot had no family or close friends around her when she died.

The local obituary, however, gave her full measure: "At the last day, when the martyrs who have with their blood sealed their devotions to liberty shall stand together, firm witnesses that truth is stronger than death, foremost among the shining throng, equal with the Rolands and Joan d'Arcs of history, will appear the Confederate heroine, Rose Greenhow."[26]

The lady would have loved it.

Epilogue

ROSE GREENHOW LEFT no will. The property found on her body or aboard the grounded *Condor* was turned over to William A. Wright on November 22, 1864, to sell at public auction.[1] On July 14, 1866, the Orphan's Court in Washington, D.C., valued her estate at $374.36.[2] The following year, a bill of complaint was filed against Wright by Rose's three daughters and her son-in-law, Tredwell Moore, stating that they had never received money or an accounting for what they described as "a large amount of gold, English bank notes, jewelry and other valuable property, including a magnificent wardrobe of female attire."[3]

Moore, who rose to the rank of brevet brigadier general in March 1865, a month before Lee's surrender at Appomattox, was accused of defrauding his mother-in-law's estate. Yet according to a letter he wrote on June 18, 1870, she died owing him more than $10,000. Moore said that when he agreed to administer her estate, he believed that the sale of gold and valuable property that she brought from Europe, as well as her shares of Chicago & North West Rail Road Company stock, would cover her debts. But the "so-called Confederate Government," Moore wrote, claimed that there was nothing belonging to Mrs. Greenhow, except for a small amount of jewelry valued at less than $100 that he gave to Leila and Little Rose. He sold the railroad stock for $4,327. That, he said, "was all that was ever received from her Estate."[4]

Little Rose was inconsolable after her mother died. "Les larmes de la pauvre enfant ne tarissaient pas," wrote Mère Prévost, Mother Superior of the Convent du Sacré Coeur. ("The poor child's tears never stop.") According to school records, Little Rose asked to be baptized in order to better pray for her mother. "Si j'étais baptisée," Little Rose wrote to the Mother Superior, "je pourrais gagner des indulgences pour ma chère maman. Ah! Madame, vous qui êtes maintenant deux fois ma bonne Mère, faites-moi baptiser!" ("If I were baptized, I could pray for my dear mother. Oh, Madam, you who are my mother now twice over, baptize me.")[5] Her wish was granted on November 21, 1864, by Bishop Henri Faraud, a missionary from Alberta, Canada. She was eleven and a half years old.[6]

After the war ended, Little Rose returned to the United States and, like her older sister, married a dashing young army officer, Lieutenant William Penn Duvall, a West Pointer, on November 30, 1871, in Newport, Rhode Island. She was eighteen years old. Penn later distinguished himself in the Spanish-American War in 1898, rose to commandant of U.S. forces in the newly won Philippines, and retired as a major general in 1911, before World War I. At some point, Rose and Duvall divorced. They had one daughter, Lee Duvall, born October 1, 1872, at West Point. Lee apparently took the name Mary Lee, the name she used when she married Louis A. Marié, a prominent Philadelphia architect, in Fort Monroe, Virginia, on September 19, 1894.[7]

After her first child died, Florence Greenhow Moore had a second son, Tredwell Jr. Her husband, Tredwell Sr., died in 1876. The 1880 census showed Florence living as a widow in Schenectady, New York. Tredwell Jr. was away at college. The *Wilmington Messenger* of May 12, 1892, noted that "Mrs. Tredwell Moore of Washington, D.C., stopped over here on her way home from Augusta, Georgia," and "came to visit the grave" of her mother.[8] Florence died three months later, on September 4, 1892, at Narragansett Pier, Rhode Island.[9] She was fifty-six.

Leila Greenhow married Alexander Craven, and they lived in Jefferson County, Indiana. They appear to have had a number of children who died before reaching adulthood. Leila died in 1887 and is buried in Fairmount Cemetery in Jefferson County, Indiana.[10]

Bettie Duvall, the daughter of a Maryland family that lived in Washington, D.C., married John Converse Webb in 1866, and the couple moved to St. Paul, Minnesota. She died on July 3, 1891, in Baltimore and is buried in the Oak Hill Cemetery in Washington, D.C.[11]

In 1888, the Ladies Memorial Association marked Rose Greenhow's grave with a simple marble cross on which is carved: "Mrs. Rose O'Neal Greenhow. A Bearer of Dispatches to the Confederate Government."[12] It is there to this day.

The wreck of the *Condor* still lies on the bar where she ran aground off Fort Fisher.

Assessing Rose's Spycraft

MILITARY HISTORIANS HAVE debated for more than a century whether or not Rose Greenhow's espionage changed the course of the Civil War. General Beauregard, who received two critical messages from Rose about Union troop movements toward Manassas in July 1861, credited her with the information that led him to request reinforcements that arrived in time to defeat the Union army at Bull Run. The Confederate victory turned an insurrection that the North regarded as a nuisance into four years of carnage whose bitter residue still wells in the throats of black and white Americans. Beauregard's most detailed account, published nearly twenty years after the war ended, was based on contemporaneous records and is supported in key respects by the known movements of the opposing armies. Beauregard makes clear that Rose's coded dispatches were not the only intelligence he received—indeed, he sought her confirmation of Union brigadier general Irvin McDowell's plans after capturing and debriefing a Union agent. Nor does a wise commander make monumental decisions based on single pieces of information. Yet there is abundant evidence beyond her own self-laudatory account and that of her nemesis Allan Pinkerton to show the Confederate command gave Rose's secret correspondence the highest priority.

After McDowell's pickets and advance columns interrupted the "underground mail" route from Washington to Manassas that Bettie Duvall had taken with Rose's first message concealed in her hair, Beauregard dispatched another courier, George Donnellan, to go to Rose with his un-signed, encrypted "Trust bearer" message and bring back confirmation of McDowell's marching orders. Author William A. Tidwell, a retired brigadier general with a career in military intelligence, obtained what he described as Donnellan's cover letter for Rose's second message to Beau-regard. It was addressed to Colonel Daniel Ruggles, who was on the Vir-ginia side of the Potomac, and bears the instruction "This must go thro' by a lightning express to Beauregard. Incur any expense upon authority of my instructions and I'll certify to the bills when I return. G. Donnellan."[1] Rug-gles would not have gone to those lengths, scrambling riders with relays of fast horses, unless he thought the dispatch was critical.

Nor would Rose's handler, Colonel Thomas Jordan, have continued to request information from Rose and relay it to Beauregard and other senior commanders if he did not think she had valuable sources.

Edwin C. Fishel, a retired intelligence officer noted for his discovery of Union intelligence documents from later in the war, conceded that Rose provided "an extremely valuable nugget of information" before First Ma-nassas, but in his book *Secret War for the Union*, he claimed her achieve-ments were exaggerated, even fabricated, by Rose's admirers. To make his case, however, Fishel relied on tests such as whether or not Rose's infor-mation was as fresh or complete as it might have been, dismissing the ev-idence at hand that the Confederates relied on her reports, which were generally accurate and contained useful notes about the numbers and movements of Union forces around Washington. Recent investigations of the far more sophisticated intelligence apparatus employed by the United States in modern times show that political leaders and military comman-ders frequently rely on less accurate intelligence than Rose supplied to Beauregard.

Stooping to a bit of salacious rumormongering, Fishel suggests that Robert Greenhow could not have been the father of Rose's last child, born nine years before the war. He attempts to justify his digression into spuri-ous arithmetic by claiming, "The point has some importance because if Mrs. Greenhow maintained her high social position in the face of a rather public illegitimacy, we are that much better able to understand the brazen drive that made her the leader of a spy ring."[2] Not really.

Fishel was right in one respect: Rose *was* brazen. But he apparently was unaware that her husband, Robert, joined her in Warrenton Springs, Vir-ginia, in July 1852, which is when she became pregnant with her eighth child, Little Rose. While ship records of Greenhow's complete journey east that summer are missing—as are many passenger lists of the period—there is evidence he returned to San Francisco in August.[3] It is both logical and likely that he was vacationing with his wife and family before he returned to California. Had Little Rose been the product of an extramarital affair when Robert was out west, Jessie Benton Frémont and other of Rose's rivals and detractors undoubtedly would have found such gossip too delicious not to mention in their letters and diaries.

Rose never pretended to be a highly trained spy; she begged her handlers for instruction. When she didn't know what was required, she reported apologetically that "not being a military man I can only trust to my untutored judgment as to what is of value." She assured them, however, "All that I sent is reliable." And she sent everything she could.

Rose was not cautious or careful or subtle about her work. In a spy's world of shadows and secrets, she remained outspoken about her views and did nothing to conceal her identity. Nor did she offer excuses or apologies. She didn't believe she had done anything wrong. But President Lincoln thought she was threatening enough to warrant locking her up. His generals never doubted the threat she posed. They called her clever and dangerous and dragged their heels when told to let her go.

After Rose was released from prison and sent south, a grateful Jefferson Davis rewarded her handsomely, then asked that she take on another longshot assignment—an extraordinary mission to Europe—to try to save their beloved Confederacy.

It was too late. Yet Rose Greenhow—courageous, independent, adventurous woman that she was—gave it all she had.

APPENDIX II

Court Records of
Black Washingtonians

Records of the District of Columbia Circuit Court
1828–1850

DECEMBER TERM 1828[1]

Civil Appearances

131 *Susan Wilson v. William Addison*	petition for freedom
177 *Sylyia Lee v. Elizabeth Smallwood*	petition for freedom
180 *Negro Gerrard v. Zachariah Cox*	petition for freedom
181 *Ann Williams and Children v. George Miller*	petition for freedom
451 *Negro Mary and child v. Lewin Talburt*	petition for freedom

Civil Trials

92 *Walter B. Beale v. Lambert S. Beck*	"took . . . one negro slave named William . . . and unjustly detained him against sureties & pledges . . . whereby [Beale] saith that he is injured & hath damage to the value of a thousand dollars"
95 *Jesse A. Dollerude v. George Milburn*	"one negro or mulatto girl . . . about fifteen years of age" $206.25

Criminal Appearances

24 *U.S. v. Alexander Young*	assault & battery on constable
72 *U.S. v. John Sanders*	assault & battery

127 *U.S. v. James Colbert*	stole a spade worth $1.00 and a clothesline worth 50 cents
129 *U.S. v. Ann Talbutt*	stole three pairs of shoes worth $4.00
132 *U.S. v. Ann Talbutt*	stole two quilts worth $1.50 and one chest worth $3.50
148 *U.S. v. Nancy Ashton*	stole one cloak worth $1.00
156 *U.S. v. Caroline Calvert*	cut Nancy Ashton with an axe
159 *U.S. v. Thomas Rollins*	stole one pair of shoes worth $1.12
161 *U.S. v. William Chubb*	stole eight dozen herrings worth 80 cents
172 *U.S. v. Jim Davis*	stole $50 in banknotes and $3 in silver money
175 *U.S. v. John Barnes*	stole one cheese worth $1.00
176 *U.S. v. Horace Gales*	same theft as Jim Davis, #172
177 *U.S. v. Thomas Johnson*	stole one blanket worth $1.25
187 *U.S. v. Rezin Barker*	stole one overcoat worth $15; 1 pr gloves worth 50 cents

Records of the District of Columbia Circuit Court
1828–1850

NOVEMBER TERM 1835

Civil Appearances

36 *Sally Robertson v. Henry Robertson*	petition for freedom
37 *Negro Joseph v. Basil Hatton*	petition for freedom

Criminal Appearances

83 *U.S. v. John Proctor (free negro)*	stealing clothing worth $7.00
93, 145 *U.S. v. Washington Henning*	"For kidnapping, and attempting to sell a free coloured boy called Thea Key— in the City of Washington"
102 *U.S. v. Arthur (alias John Arthur Bowen)*	"attempting to murder his mistress"
104 *U.S. v. Edward Peters (free negro)*	stealing goods worth $4.12½
111 *U.S. v. Lewis Lee (free negro)*	stealing a watch worth $15.00
113 *U.S. v. Elizabeth Custis (free negress)*	stealing 1 pr shoes worth $1.00
116 *U.S. v. Henry Simms (free negro)*	stealing 1 silver watch worth $10[2]

Records of the District of Columbia Circuit Court
1828–1850

MARCH TERM 1837

Criminal Appearances

31 *U.S. v. Negro Kitty Berry*	larceny (cotton cloth worth $3); nol pros

35 *U.S. v. Negro William Talbert*	assault on Ann Royal nol pros
36 *U.S. v. Negro James Kennedy*	assault on Maria Williams (negress); $5 fine
61 *U.S. v. Negro John Butler*	larceny (four bars soap worth 56 cents); $1 fine, 1 mo jail
62 *U.S. v. Negro Martha alias Judy Nokes*	larceny (goods worth $6.47); $1 fine, 1 day jail
67 *U.S. v. Negro William Williams*	larceny (goods worth $66.50); 3 yrs penitentiary
68 *U.S. v. Negro James Collins*	larceny (lumber worth $2); $2 fine, 1 mo jail
71 *U.S. v. Negro Henry Brown*	larceny (meat worth $1.50); not guilty
72 *U.S. v. Negro (?) William Atkins*	larceny (lumber worth 50 cents); not guilty
74 *U.S. v. Nace Cole (the younger)*	a & b on his mother; $1 fine
75 *U.S. v. Nace Cole (the younger)*	stealing clothing worth $1.50; $1 fine, 1 day jail
77 *U.S. v. Ellen Lindsey*	stealing clothing worth $5.50 from Duff Green, slave $3 fine, 1 mo jail
81 *U.S. v. Negro William Thompson*	stealing a silver watch worth $8; nol pros
82 *U.S. v. Negro William Thompson*	stealing a penknife worth 50 cents; nol pros[3]

Records of the District of Columbia Circuit Court[4] 1828–1850

NOVEMBER TERM 1837

Civil Appearances

109 *Ann Bell and Children v. Gerald T. Green*	petition for freedom
120 *George Kean v. Olivia Kean*	petition for freedom
126 *Lidia Haines v. William M. Lewis*	petition for freedom
132 *Susan Wilson v. William Addison*	petition for freedom

Criminal Appearances

59 *U.S. v. Elizabeth Johnson*	stealing table cloth worth $2; $1 fine, 1 mo jail
60 *U.S. v. Gustavus Dunlop*	stealing silver tablespoon worth $2.50; $2 fine
62 *U.S. v. Joseph Hornsbery*	stealing a leather apron worth $7; ½ yr penitentiary
64 *U.S. v. Joseph Fletcher*	stealing a crowbar worth $3; $1 fine, 1 mo jail
67 *U.S. v. Charles Ford*	stealing clothing, cash worth $5.75; $2 fine, 2 mos jail

70 *U.S. v. James Conner*	stealing two wagon wheels worth $14; 1 yr penitentiary
71 *U.S. v. William Carpenter*	stealing goods worth $79; 3 yrs penitentiary
72 *U.S. v. Gustavus Dunlop*	stealing one pair pantaloons worth $5; not guilty
74 *U.S. v. David Granderson et al.*	receiving stolen goods; not guilty
75 *U.S. v. Teresa Granderson*	receiving stolen goods; 1 yr penitentiary
76 *U.S. v. Mary Jenifer*	receiving stolen goods; 1 yr penitentiary
79 *U.S. v. John Simpson*	stealing one cord wood worth $1.33; not guilty

Records of the District of Columbia Circuit Court[5]
1818–1840

NOVEMBER TERM 1840

Civil Appearances

102 *George Crowner & David Over v. Peggy Barnes*	petition for freedom
223 *John & Ann M. Lee v. William Aiken*	petition for freedom
305 *Eliza Johnson v. Thomas J. Belt*	petition for freedom

Civil Trials

271 *Henrietta Hanson v. Mary Ann Cox*	petition for freedom

Judicials

1 *John M. Woodgate v. Sedley Woodward*	"one negro woman named Belinda, aged about 35 years" $400 "one negro girl named Martha, aged about 7 years" $150 "one negro boy named Isaac, aged about 2 years" $100
31 *John B. Morgan v. William L. Bent*	"one negro boy named William Henry aged 23 years" $1000
65 *Fielder B. Poston v. Francis Lowndes*	"one negro man named Charles Ford aged about 17 years" $400 "one negro woman named Sally aged about thirty years of age & her son named Robert aged about six years" $300
85 *Patriotic Bank v. Mathias Jeffers*	"one negro boy named John, aged about 15 years (dark)" $500

141 *William Brent v. Richard B. Mason*   eight slaves, various ages, both
                                                           sexes—appraised at $2500,
                                                           three of the men actually sold
                                                           for $785.

Records of the District of Columbia Circuit Court[6]
1828–1850

MARCH TERM 1850

Civil Appearances

62 *William H. McKenny v. Isaac Buckingham*	petition for freedom
63 *William Taylor v. Isaac Buckingham*	petition for freedom
66 *Letty Lucas v. John R. Ratcliff*	petition for freedom
67 *Benjamin Qualls v. Jane W. Stevenson*	petition for freedom
89 *Margaret & Alfred Atkins v.*	
J. Bowling & C. Gardner	petition for freedom
103 *Betsy Burke v. Ann Turner*	petition for freedom
106 *Louisa Woodward v. Jane Mumoe*	petition for freedom
116 *Allen Seymour v. Nathan Seymour*	petition for freedom
126 *Lucy Williams formerly known as*	
Lucy White v. George Hope	petition for freedom
139 *Negro William Scott v. William H. Williams*	petition for freedom
319 *Lucy Bosy v. Ann Maria Fitzhugh*	petition for freedom

Richard Ellis, at the National Archives, who compiled these records, writes that at about this time, the clerk began to give up specifying black defendants by race in the docket books and printed forms, but "negro" and "negress" continue to appear in small, handwritten notes in most files. The court record ends here.

Acknowledgments

WRITING A HISTORICAL biography is like putting together pieces of a giant jigsaw puzzle. There may be a handful of colorful pieces, but others are faded, ripped, burned, disintegrating, or missing altogether. And as with every puzzle, there were many people who have contributed to this portrait of Rose O'Neale Greenhow.

First, I offer H. G. Jones at the University of North Carolina at Chapel Hill my sincere thanks for identifying and transcribing Rose Greenhow's diary forty years ago and generously lending it to me for this manuscript. He is in every way a scholar and a gentleman.

I received encouragement all along the way from my thoughtful agents, Lane Zachery and Todd Shuster, at Zachery Shuster Harmsworth in New York; my editor at Random House, Kate Medina, whose creativity, enthusiasm, and flawless sense of focus helped me bring Rose alive; and Kate's editorial assistant, Danielle Posen.

Pulitzer Prize–winning Civil War historian James M. McPherson was generous with his time and analysis. Senate historian Donald A. Ritchie was a patient adviser and read countless chapter drafts. Patricia Hass, herself an editor and a proud Richmond native, introduced me to her city. Novelist Ann McMillan helped me understand how Rose would have been received by proper Richmond society. Stephen R. Wise, curator of South Carolina's Parris Island Museum, added his expertise on blockade running and confirmed that the *Condor*'s captain, often misidentified in naval histories, was William Nathan Wrighte Hewett. Janet K. Seapker, architectural historian and former director of the Cape Fear Museum in Wilmington, N.C., was a superb guide and tireless detective. North Carolina State underwater archaeologist Richard W. Lawrence and historic interpreter Ray Flowers at Fort Fisher helped with navigation detail of Rose's dramatic blockade-running sea voyages. Fred Voss, senior historian emeritus at the National Portrait Gallery in Washington, helped identify and select images. Peter Earnest at Washington's International Spy Museum offered generous counsel. William Ferris at the University of North Carolina's Center for the Study of the American South provided much-needed reassurance that a Jersey girl could write about the South. Michael J. Crawford, head of the Early History Branch of the Naval Historical Center, advised on USS *Princeton* research.

Several books have been mainstays. The most important was Rose Greenhow in her own words: *My Imprisonment and the First Year of Abolition Rule at Washington,* published in 1863 in London and now available on the Internet at the University of North Carolina's digital history project, Documenting the American South. I also drew from Allan Pinkerton's own account of his arrest of Rose Greenhow. It was reassuring to find that while both Greenhow and Pinkerton were inveterate self-promoters, their detailed accounts were not only similar, but largely backed up by the Official Records of the Union and Confederate Armies and Navies, also online.

Of the few previous biographies written about Rose Greenhow, Ishbel Ross's *Rebel Rose,* published in 1954, served as an excellent guide. Others include Margaret Leech's *Reveille in Washington;* Ernest B. "Pat" Furgurson's *Ashes of Glory: Richmond at War;* and Stephen R. Wise's *Lifeline of the Confederacy: Blockade Running During the Civil War.* The David Rankin Barbee Papers at Georgetown University Library's Special Collection gave me a good start. My model for how a biography *should* be written is Pulitzer Prize winner David McCullough, whose masterpiece *John Adams* has not been out of reach for three years.

One person whose help could not be duplicated is Sheila Evans, in London, who dug deeply into Rose Greenhow's important year in Europe, found long forgotten documents in the British museums and offered invaluable guidance; Tim Walsh, my principal researcher in Washington, D.C., performed all kinds of magic tricks to find material buried in the Library of Congress. I also thank Jean Russo in Annapolis, Maryland; Trina Lopez and Sara Ellberg in San Francisco; and Jill Cairns-Gallimore, David

Rohrbach, and Anne King in Washington, D.C., all of whom helped with the research.

A special bow to the superb archivists at the National Archives: DeAnne Blanton, Robert Ellis, Milton Gustafson, Charles Johnson, Rebecca Livingston, Rick Peuser, and Trever Plante. Thanks also to Jeffrey M. Flannery in the Manuscript Division of the Library of Congress; Lynda L. Crist, editor of the Papers of Jefferson Davis at Rice University; and Haskell M. Monroe Jr., former editor of the Papers of Jefferson Davis, who collected material about Rose Greenhow for four decades and generously shared his files. Wendy Schnur at the Mystic Seaport Museum located ships' histories and passenger lists. Historian Catherine Clinton helped me understand Rose Greenhow's personality. James M. Burgess Jr., a museum specialist at the Manassas National Battlefield Park, pored over Civil War detail; James H. Blankenship Jr., a historian at the Petersburg National Battlefield, weighed in on the Peninsula Campaign. Historian Edward C. "Ted" Keefer at the State Department provided department history.

Local historical societies have been invaluable: Gail Redmann at the District of Columbia's City Museum deserves a large bouquet. I also thank Jane Sween and Pat Andersen at the Montgomery County Historical Society; Nelson Lankford, Frances Pollard, and Gregory Stoner at the Virginia Historical Society; Dean Knight and Ruth Ann Coski at the Museum of the Confederacy; Laura E. Beardsley at the Pennsylvania Historical Society; Stephen Becker at the California Historical Society; Susan Riggs at the Swem Library at the College of William and Mary; Melinda Linderer Huff at Tudor Place in Washington, D.C.; Debbi Blake at the North Carolina State Archives; Elizabeth Proffen at the Maryland Historical Society.

Also, thanks to T. Stephen Whitman at Maryland's Mount St. Mary's College and Patrick Rael at Bowdoin College for help on slavery issues; Anna Nelson at American University, who guided me through the war with Mexico; Chris E. Fonvielle Jr. at the University of North Carolina, Wilmington, who provided invaluable help with detail on Rose's death; Jean Baker at Goucher College for a James Buchanan tutorial; Jack Myer at State University of New York, Plattsburgh, for insight into Senator Henry D. Wilson; Jules Bernstein, who interpreted nineteenth-century law; Ford Rowan for help with the history of Native Americans; Knight Kiplinger for sharing his personal library on Washington history and adding nuance to the chapter on Washington society; Marian Horn for guidance on the Limantour case; Kenneth A. Boulier, a navy codebreaker during World War II, for analysis of Rose Greenhow's cipher; and Sheila

R. Phipps, author of *Genteel Rebel: The Life of Mary Greenhow Lee.* Thanks as well to Wilber E. Meneray, Libraries for Special Collections at Tulane University; David Kessler, Bancroft Library, University of California, Berkeley; and Darlene Ramey Freeman of Urbandale, Iowa, for research on Bettie Duvall.

John O'Neal II and Beverly Ann Crowe of the O'Neal Genealogy Association in Amherst, Ohio, shared years of detective work. Franklin Jamison, a real estate agent in Poolesville, Maryland, drove me around the O'Neale plantation, Conclusion. Thanks to Sister Maryvonne Duclaux, RSCJ, at the Sacred Heart Convent in Paris; Agnès Bardou, also in Paris; Jacque Galke at the Patapsco Female Institute in Maryland; Shelley Brody and Al Kilborne at the Maret School in Washington; Tina and Neil Diver in San Francisco; and Patricia Rowan in Annapolis.

Special thanks to my *Wild Rose* copy editor, Sona Vogel, and to Random House associate copy chief Dennis Ambrose.

Whatever errors remain are my own.

I wish to thank Ivy E. Broder, dean of academic affairs at American University, who gave me the title of scholar-in-residence in the School of Communication, which gave me invaluable access to the university library.

Friends in my old girls' network listened patiently, as they have for so many years: Linda Lipsett kept me laughing; Margaret Dalton kept me walking; Viveca Novak, Karen Tumulty, Martha Brant, Ellen Goodman, Patricia O'Brien, Diane Cross, Lynn Hart, Ann Van Dusen, Beverly Jackson, and Brooke Shearer held my hand.

Special thanks to Estrella Damaso for keeping our life organized.

And finally, our family. My sister and brother-in-law, Carolyn and Glenn Jacoby, were encouraging from the start and provided documentation on our cousin David Garrison, a Union soldier. Henry Putzel Jr. pored over the manuscript with a meticulous eye. Henry "Pete" Putzel III added his usual flair to Rose Greenhow's legal trials. Helen Putzel Belliard found holes that would trip a horse.

Our children, Leila and Christof, were once again patient and supportive while Mom was deep in the "book zone." I have new appreciation for Leila's exhaustive efforts in helping to revitalize downtown Washington. And Christof's celebration of documentary film has helped me look for small, selective details to make a story sing. My pride in their lives and accomplishments—and my love for them—know no bounds.

My husband, Michael Putzel, is my lifeline and compass, as he has been for more than thirty years. His imprint is on every draft, every chapter, every paragraph, of this book. Mike not only located many pieces of the puzzle and helped me interpret them, but sustained me throughout the painstaking process of fitting it all together. His influence on my work—and my life—is without parallel. I dedicate *Wild Rose* to Mike, with my love.

Bibliography

Manuscripts and Collections

British Library (London)
British National Archives (London)
> Papers of the Phantom, *Public Record office, FO5/12415*
> Private correspondence of Lord Granville, *Public Records Office 30/29/18/19*

California Historical Society (San Francisco)
> *José Yves Limantour Biography Collection*

City Museum of Washington, D.C.
> *John C. Proctor* Sunday Star *newspaper clipping file*

Clemson University (Clemson, S.C.)
> *John C. Calhoun Papers*

College of William and Mary (Williamsburg, Va.)
> *Maupin-Washington Papers, Special Collections*
> *Travel Account of Robert Greenhow, Manuscript and Rare Books Department*

Duke University (Durham, N.C.)
> *M. J. Solomon Scrapbook, Rose O'Neal Greenhow Papers, Digital Scriptorium Special*
>   *Collections Library*
> *Jefferson Davis Papers, Digital Scriptorium Special Collections Library*
> *Alexander Robinson Boteler Papers, Special Collections Library*

Georgetown University Library (Washington, D.C.)
> *David Barbee Collection, Special Collections*
> *Jesuit Plantation Project, Maryland Province Archive*

Historical Society of Pennsylvania (Philadelphia, Pa.)
> *James Buchanan Papers*

Library of Congress (Washington, D.C.)
James Barbee Papers
Diary of Michael Shiner ("His Book, 1814–1869")
Papers of Martha Elizabeth Wright Morris
Cutts family collection of papers of James and Dolley Madison, 1794–1845
Papers of Mary Greenhow Lee, 1837–1845

Manassas National Battlefield Park Library
John C. Tidball Papers

Martin Luther King Library, Washingtoniana Collection (Washington, D.C.)
General Land Records, District of Columbia
Washington City Directory
Records of the Columbia Historical Society

Maryland Historical Society (Baltimore, Md.)
Mary Greenhow Papers
Passano Historic Buildings File, H. Furlong Baldwin Library

Maryland State Archives (Annapolis, Md.)
Governor and Council (Pardon Papers), 1817–1818

Miami University (Oxford, Ohio)
Samuel W. Richey Confederate Collections, Walter Havighurst Special Collections

Montgomery County Historical Society (Rockville, Md.)
Montgomery County Register of Wills
Manuscript of "Dr. Wootton"

Museum of the Confederacy (Richmond, Va.)
Eleanor S. Brockenbrough Library
Papers of Alice Cary Ball Duvall

Mystic Seaport Museum (Mystic, Ct.)
G. W. Blunt White Library
Louis J. Rasmussen San Francisco Ship Passenger Lists

National Archives (Washington, D.C., and College Park, Md.)
Dispatches from the United States Ministers to Mexico 1823–1906 (Diplomatic Dispatches, Department of State)
Proceedings of the Commission Relating to State Prisoners, Records of Department of State
Records of the District Court of the United States for the District of Columbia, Old Series Administration Case Files, 1801–78
Records of the Department of the Navy, Logs of U.S. Naval Ships
Seized Correspondence of Rose O'Neal Greenhow

New Hanover County Library (Wilmington, N.C.)
New Hanover County Administrator's Bonds, Book A, 1856–1865, p. 334
New Hanover Court of Pleas and Quarter Sessions

North Carolina State Archives (Raleigh, N.C.)
European Journal of Rose Greenhow, 1864–1865
Rose O'Neal Greenhow Papers, 1863–1864

Rice University (Houston, Texas)
Papers of Jefferson Davis, Jefferson Davis Association

Richmond Court House (Richmond, Va.)
Civil Court Records, Richmond, Va.

St. Mary's Catholic Church (Barnesville, Md.)
Book of Baptism, 1815

St. Patrick's Church (Washington, D.C.)
Baptismal Registry, 1844

Sheffield Archives (Sheffield, England)
Wharncliffe Muniments M 461/8–10.

Tulane University (New Orleans, La.)
Special Collections, Tulane University Library

United States Senate (Washington, D.C.)
Papers of Isaac Bassett

University of California (Berkeley)
Limantour (José Y.) Papers, Bancroft Library

University of Michigan (Ann Arbor)
Papers of James M. Mason, William L. Clements Library

University of Michigan (Bloomfield Hills)
Charles Haydon Civil War Journal, Bentley Historical Library

University of North Carolina (Chapel Hill)
Rose Greenhow's European Diary, transcribed by H. G. Jones
De Rosset Family Papers, Southern Historical Society

Virginia Historical Society (Richmond, Va.)
Bagley Family Papers, 1824–1960
Papers of Thomas Jefferson

Westminster City Archives (London)

Newspapers and Periodicals

American Review: A Whig Journal of Politics, Literature, Art, and Science (New York)
Baltimore Sun (Baltimore, Md.)
Berkshire County Eagle (Berkshire, Mass.)
Boston Saturday Evening Gazette (Boston, Mass.)
Cambridge Chronicle (Cambridge, Mass.)
Charleston Advertiser (Charleston, Mass.)
Chelsea Telegraph and Pioneer (Chelsea, Mass.)
Congressional Globe (Washington, D.C.)
Daily Alta California
Daily Dispatch (Richmond, Va.)
Daily Globe (Washington, D.C.)
Daily National Intelligencer (Washington, D.C.)
Frank Leslie's Illustrated Newspaper (New York)
Harper's Weekly (New York)
The Index (London)
Journal of Commerce

Liberator (Boston)
London Evening Mail
Lowell Daily Courier (Lowell, Mass.)
Madisonian (Washington, D.C.)
Maine Farmer (Augusta, Me.)
National Catholic Reporter (Kansas City, Mo.)
National Tribune (Washington, D.C.)
North Bridgewater Gazette (North Bridgewater, Mass.)
New York Herald
The New York Times
New York Shipping & Commercial List
Overland Monthly (San Francisco)
Petersburg Republican (Petersburg, Va.)
Republican Compiler (Gettysburg, Pa.)
Richmond Enquirer (Richmond, Va.)
Richmond Examiner (Richmond, Va.)
Richmond Times-Dispatch (Richmond, Va.)
Richmond Whig (Richmond, Va.)
Roxbury City Gazette (Roxbury, Mass.)
San Francisco Daily Evening Bulletin
San Francisco City Directory, 1854
Southern Literary Messenger (Richmond, Va.), 1848
Sunday Star (Washington, D.C.)
Telegraph and Democratic Review (Alton, Ill.)
Temple Bar Magazine (London)
The Times (London)
The Washington Post (Washington, D.C.)
The Washington Post Magazine (Washington, D.C.)
Woburn Journal (Woburn, Mass.)

Books and Articles

Abdy, E. S. *Journal of a Residence and Tour in the United States of North America, from April 1833, to October 1834,* volume 2. London: J. Murray, 1835.

Allgor, Catherine. *Parlor Politics, In Which Ladies of Washington Help Build a City and a Government.* Charlottesville and London: University Press of Virginia, 2000.

Arnett, Ethel Stephens. *Mrs. James Madison: The Incomparable Dolley.* Greensboro, N.C.: Piedmont Press, 1972.

Bakeless, John. *Spies of the Confederacy.* Philadelphia/New York: J. B. Lippincott Co., 1970.

Baker, Jean H. *James Buchanan.* New York: Henry Holt & Co., 2004.

Baker, Richard Allan. *The Senate of the United States: A Bicentennial History.* Malabar, Fla.: Robert E. Krieger Publishing Company, 1988.

Barbee, David Rankin. "Robert Greenhow," *William and Mary Quarterly* 2, vol. 13 (1933).

Barry, T. A., and B. A. Patten. *Men and Memories of San Francisco in the Spring of '50.* San Francisco: A. L. Bancroft & Co., 1873.

Bartlett, Irving H. *John C. Calhoun: A Biography.* New York: W. W. Norton, 1993.

Bastian, Beverly E. "Henry Wager Halleck, the *Californios,* and the Clash of Legal Cultures." *California History* 72, no. 4 (Winter 1993–1994).

Bayard, Samuel John. *A Sketch of the Life of Com. Robert F. Stockton.* New York: Derby & Jackson, 1856.

Bayne, Julia Taft. *Tad Lincoln's Father.* Lincoln: University of Nebraska Press, 2001.

Beauregard, G. T. "The First Battle of Bull Run." Undated manuscript, accessible at www.civilwarhome.com/bullruncampaign.htm.

Bennett, John. "Chelsea Link with the Confederacy." Accessible at www.americancivilwar.org.uk/articles/linkchelsea.htm.

Beymer, William Gilmore. *Famous Scouts and Spies of the Civil War.* Alexandria, Va.: Time-Life Books, 1985.

———. *On Hazardous Service: Scouts and Spies of the North and South.* New York: Harper & Brothers, 1912.

Bierman, John. *Napoleon III and His Carnival Empire.* London: John Murray, 1989.

Birkner, Michael J., ed. *James Buchanan and the Political Crisis of the 1850s.* Selinsgrove, Pa.: Susquehanna University Press, 1996.

Boaz, Thomas. *Guns for Cotton: England Arms the Confederacy.* Shippensburg, Pa.: Burd Street Press, 1996.

Bryan, Wilhelmus Bogart. *A History of the National Capital—From Its Foundation Through the Period of the Adoptation of the Organic Act.* New York: Macmillan, 1916.

Burger, Nash R. *Confederate Spy: Rose O'Neale Greenhow.* New York: Franklin Watts, 1967.

Bushell, T. A. *Royal Mail: A Centenary History of the Royal Mail Line 1839–1939.* London: Trade and Travel Publications, 1939.

Byrd, Robert C. *The Senate, 1789–1989: Addresses on the History of the United States Senate.* Washington, D.C.: Government Printing Office, 1989–1994.

Callahan, James Morton. *Diplomatic History of the Southern Confederacy.* New York: Frederick Ungar Publishing Co., 1964.

"Captain Roberts, Running the Blockade." *Civil War Times Illustrated* 6 (December 1967).

Chesnut, Mary Boykin. *A Diary from Dixie.* Boston: Houghton Mifflin Co., 1905.

Clay-Clopton, Virginia. *A Belle of the Fifties: Memoirs of Mrs. Clay of Alabama, Covering Social and Political Life in Washington and the South, 1853–66.* New York: Doubleday, Page & Co., 1905.

Clinton, Catherine. *The Plantation Mistress.* New York: Pantheon, 1982.

Cohen, Anthony M. "The Underground Railroad in Montgomery County," in *The Montgomery County Story* (Montgomery County, Maryland, Historical Society), February 1995.

Cooper, John S. "Presidents and First Ladies." October 8, 1999. Accessible at www.suite101.com/article.cfm/presidents_and_first_ladies/26544.

Corrigan, Mary Beth. "Imaginary Cruelties?: A History of the Slave Trade in Washington, D.C." *Washington History* (Fall/Winter 2001–2002).

———. "Making the Most of an Opportunity: Slaves and the Catholic Church in Early Washington." *Washington History* (Spring/Summer 2000).

———. "A Social Union of Heart and Effort: The Afro-American Family in the District of Columbia on the Eve of Emancipation." PhD dissertation, University of Maryland, College Park, 1996.

Cutts, Lucia B., ed. *Memoirs and Letters of Dolly [sic] Madison, Wife of James Madison, President of the United States, Edited by Her Grand-Niece.* Boston: Houghton Mifflin, 1886.

Dabney, Virginia. *Richmond: The Story of a City.* Garden City, N.Y.: Doubleday & Co., 1976.

Dalzell, Robert F., Jr. *Daniel Webster and the Trial of American Nationalism 1843–1852.* Boston: Houghton Mifflin Co., 1973.

Davis, Jefferson. *The Papers of Jefferson Davis.* Edited by Haskell Monroe, James McIntosh, Lynda Lasswell Crist, and Mary Seaton Dix. 10 volumes to date. Baton Rouge: Louisiana State University Press, 1971–.

Davis, William C. *Battle at Bull Run: A History of the First Major Campaign of the Civil War.* Baton Rouge: Louisiana State University Press, 1977.

"The Day Journal of Milton S. Latham." *Quarterly of the California Historical Society* (March 1932).

DeGregorio, William A., and Connie Jo Dickerson. *The Complete Book of U.S. Presidents.* New York: Random House, 1997.

DeLeon, T. C. *Four Years in Rebel Capitals: An Inside View of Life in the Southern Confederacy from Birth to Death.* Mobile, Ala.: The Gossip Printing Company, 1890.

Dorman, James H. "Thespis in Dixie." *Virginia Cavalcade* (Summer 1978).

Douglass, Frederick. *Narrative of the Life of Frederick Douglass.* Boston: Anti-Slavery Office, 1845. Accessible at docsouth.unc.edu/douglass/douglass.html.

Drayton, Daniel. *Personal Memoir of Daniel Drayton, for Four Years and Four Months a Prisoner (for Charity's Sake) in Washington Jail, Including a Narrative of Voyage and Capture of the Schooner Pearl.* 2nd ed. New York: American and Foreign Anti-Slavery Society, 1855.

Dunbaugh, Edwin L., and William du Barry Thomas. *William H. Webb: Shipbuilder.* Glen Cove, N.Y.: Webb Institute of Naval Architecture, 1989.

Ellet, E. F. *The Court Circles of the Republic.* New York: J. D. Dennison, 1869.

Fishel, Edwin C. *The Secret War for the Union: The Untold Story of Military Intelligence in the Civil War.* Boston: Houghton Mifflin Co., 1996.

Fleischner, Jennifer. *Mrs. Lincoln and Mrs. Keckly.* New York: Broadway Books, 2003.

Foote, Shelby. *The Civil War: A Narrative.* New York: Random House, 1958–1974.

"Frederick's Chief Justice, Roger Brooke Taney," *Journal of the Historical Society of Frederick County, Maryland* (Spring 2004).

Friedlander, Amy. *Natural Monopoly and Universal Service: Telephones and Telegraphs in the U.S. Communications Infrastructure, 1837–1940.* Reston, Va.: Corporation for National Research Initiatives, 1995.

Froncek, Thomas, ed. *An Illustrated History of the City of Washington by the Junior League of Washington.* New York: Alfred A. Knopf, 1977.

Furgurson, Ernest B. *Ashes of Glory: Richmond at War.* New York: Alfred A. Knopf, 1996.

———. *Not War but Murder: Cold Harbor 1864.* New York: Alfred A. Knopf, 2000.

———. *Freedom Rising: Civil War in Washington.* New York: Alfred A. Knopf, 2004.

Gaither and Addison. *Washington Directory and National Register for 1846.* Washington, D.C.: John T. Towers, 1846.

Gallagher, Gary W., ed. *The Richmond Campaign of 1862: The Peninsula and the Seven Days.* Chapel Hill: University of North Carolina Press, 2000.

Garidel, Henri. *Exile in Richmond: The Confederate Journal of Henri Garidel.* Charlottesville: University Press of Virginia, 2001.

Genovese, Eugene D. "Getting States' Rights Right." *Atlantic Monthly* (March 2001). Accessible at www.theatlantic.com/issues/2001/03/genovese-p1.htm.

Green, Constance McLaughlin. *The Secret City: A History of Race Relations in the Nation's Capital.* Princeton: Princeton University Press, 1967.

Greenhow, Robert. *The History of Oregon and California and the Other Territories on the West Coast of North America.* Boston: C. C. Little & Brown, 1844.

Greenhow, Rose. *My Imprisonment and the First Year of Abolition Rule at Washington.* London: Richard Bentley, 1863. Also accessible at docsouth.unc.edu/greenhow/menu.html.

Harrold, Stanley. *The Abolitionists and the South, 1831–1861.* Lexington: University of Kentucky Press, 1995.

———. *Subversives: Antislavery Community in Washington, D.C., 1828–1865.* Baton Rouge: Louisiana State University Press, 2003.

Hart, V. *The National Road.* Rockville, Md.: Montgomery County Historical Society.

Haws, Duncan. *Merchant Fleets: Royal Mail & Nelson Lines.* Brighton, Eng.: Planet Press Limited, 1982.

Henson, Josiah. *The Life of Josiah Henson, Formerly a Slave, Now an Inhabitant of Canada, as Narrated by Himself.* Boston: Arthur D. Phelps, 1849.

Herr, Pamela. *A Biography: Jessie Benton Frémont.* New York: Franklin Watts, 1987.

———, and Mary Lee Spence, eds. *The Letters of Jessie Benton Frémont.* Urbana-Chicago: University of Illinois Press, 1993.

Hiebert, Ray Eldon, and Richard MacMaster. *A Grateful Remembrance.* Rockville, Md.: Montgomery County Historical Society, 1976.

Horne, Alistair. *The Seven Ages of Paris.* New York: Alfred A. Knopf, 2003.

Hoslett, Schuyler Dean. "Southern Expectation of British Intervention in the Civil War." *Tyler's Quarterly Magazine* 22 (1940–1941).

Huffman, Alan. "Tumult and Transition in 'Little America.' " *Smithsonian Magazine* (November 2003).

Inglis, Frances Erskine (Mme. Calderon de la Barca). *Life in Mexico During a Residence of Two Years in That City.* New York: E. P. Dutton & Co., 1931.

Jackson, Andrew. Farewell Presidential Address, March 4, 1837. Accessible at www.search.eb.com/elections/pri/Q00050.html.

Jennings, Paul. "A Colored Man's Reminiscences of James Madison," 1865. Accessible at www.whitehousehistory.org/08/subs/08_b01.html.

Johnson, Kenneth M. *José Yves Limantour v. the United States.* Los Angeles: Dawson's Book Shop, 1961.

Kemble, John Haskell. *The Panama Route, 1848–1869.* Berkeley: University of California Press, 1943.

Kennedy, Randall. *Interracial Intimacies: Sex, Marriage, Identity, and Adoption.* New York: Vintage Books, 2003.

Keyes, Erasmus D. *Fifty Years' Observation of Men and Events, Civil and Military.* New York: Scribner's, 1884.

Klein, Philip Shriver. *President James Buchanan: A Biography.* University Park: Pennsylvania State University Press, 1962.

Kohl, Clayton Charles. *Claims as the Cause of the Mexican War.* New York University Series of Graduate School Studies, no. 2. New York: Faculty of the Graduate School, New York University, 1914.

Lamb, William. *The Life and Times of Colonel William Lamb, 1835–1909: Patriot, Benefactor, Statesman.* Austin: University of Texas Press, 2000.

Leech, Margaret. *Reveille in Washington.* New York: Harper & Brothers, 1941.

"The Liedesdorff-Folson Estate." *California History* 2, no. 2 (June 1928).

Little, Ann Courtney Ward, ed. *Recollections and Records.* Published for the Columbus County Bicentennial Commission, 1976.

Lomax, Elizabeth Lindsay. *Leaves from an Old Washington Diary, 1854–1863.* New York: E. P. Dutton, 1943.

Lowe, Thaddeus. *Memoirs of Thaddeus S. C. Lowe, Chief of the Aeronautic Corps of the Army of the United States During the Civil War: My Balloons in Peace and War.* Lewiston, N.Y.: Edwin Mellen Press, 2004.

March, Charles W. *Reminiscences of Congress.* New York: Baker & Scribner, 1850.

Marryat, Frank. *Mountains and Molehills, or Recollections of a Burnt Journal.* London: Longman, Brown, Green, 1855.

Marszalek, John E. *The Petticoat Affair: Manners, Mutiny and Sex in Andrew Jackson's White House.* New York: The Free Press, 1997.

Mason, Virginia, ed. *The Public Life and Diplomatic Correspondence of James M. Mason.* Roanoke, Va.: Stone Printing & Manufacturing Co., 1903.

Mayer, Henry. *All on Fire: William Lloyd Garrison and the Abolition of Slavery.* New York: St. Martin's Press, 1998.

McKay, Ernest. *Henry Wilson: Practical Radical: A Portrait of a Politician.* Port Washington, N.Y.: Kennikat Press, 1971.

McLaughlin, Andrew C. *Readings in the History of the American Nation.* New York: D. Appleton & Co., 1914.

McPherson, James M. *Battle Cry of Freedom: The Civil War Era.* New York: Oxford University Press, 1988.

———. *Abraham Lincoln and the Second American Revolution.* New York: Oxford University Press, 1990.

———. *Antietam: The Battle That Changed the Course of the Civil War.* New York: Oxford University Press, 2002.

Melder, Keith, ed. *City of Magnificent Intentions: A History of the District of Columbia.* Washington, D.C., History Curriculum Project, 1983.

Meriweather, Robert L., ed. *The Papers of John Calhoun.* 28 volumes. Columbia: University of South Carolina Press, 1959–2003.

Miller, William Lee. *Arguing About Slavery: The Great Battle in the United States Congress.* New York: Alfred A. Knopf, 1996.

Mitchell, Mary. *Divided Town: A Study of Georgetown D.C. During the Civil War.* Barre, Mass.: Barre Publishers, 1968.

Moore, Virginia. *The Madisons: A Biography.* New York: McGraw-Hill, 1979.

Muscatine, Doris. *Old San Francisco: The Biography of a City.* New York: Putnam's, 1975.

Nash, Howard P., Jr. "The Princeton Explosion." *American History Illustrated* 5, no. 5 (August 1969).

Nelson, Anna K. *Secret Agents: President Polk and the Search for Peace with Mexico.* New York: Garland Publishing, 1988.

Neville-Singleton, Pamela. *Fanny Trollope: The Life and Adventures of a Clever Woman.* New York: Viking, 1997.

Niven, John. *Martin Van Buren: The Romantic Age of American Politics.* New York: Oxford University Press, 1983.

Norfleet, Fillmore. *Saint Mémin in Virginia: Portraits and Bibliographies.* Richmond, Va.: The Dietz Press, 1942.

Northup, Solomon. *Twelve Years a Slave: Narrative of Solomon Northup, a Citizen of New-York, Kidnapped in Washington City in 1841, and Rescued in 1853.* Accessible at www.docsouth.unc.edu/northup/northup.html.

Osborne, John. *Guide to the West Indies, Madeira, Mexico, Northern South-America, Comp. from Documents Specially Furnished by the Agents of the Royal Mail Steam Packet Company, the Board of Trade, and Other Authentic Sources [. . .]* London: Royal Mail Steam Packet Co., 1845.

Osbun, Albert G. *To California and the South Seas: The Diary of Albert G. Osbun 1849–1851.* Edited by John Haskell Kemble. San Marino, Calif.: The Huntington Library, 1966.

Papenfuse, Edward C., Jr. "An Act Concerning Religion, April 21, 1649: An Interpretation and Tribute to the Citizen Legislators of Maryland." Accessible at www.mdarchives.state.md.us/msa/speccol/sc2200/sc2221/000025/html/titlepage.html.

————, Alan F. Day, David W. Jordan, and Gregory A. Stiverson, eds. *A Biographical Dictionary of the Maryland Legislature, 1635–1789.* Baltimore: John Hopkins University Press, 1985.

Pearson, Lee M. "Princeton and the Peacemaker." *Technology and Culture* 7, no. 2 (Spring 1966).

Phipps, Sheila R. *Genteel Rebel: The Life of Mary Greenhow Lee.* Baton Rouge: Louisiana State University Press, 2004.

Pinkerton, Allan. *The Spy of the Rebellion.* Lincoln: University of Nebraska Press, 1989.

Poore, Ben: Perley. *Reminiscences of 60 Years in the National Metropolis.* Philadelphia: Hubbard Brothers, 1886.

Rasmussen, Louis J. *San Francisco Ship Passenger Lists.* Colma, Calif.: San Francisco Historic Records, 1966.

Rawick, George P., ed. *The American Slave: A Composite Autobiography.* Westport, Conn.: Greenwood Press, 1972.

"Redecoration and Willie's Death." 2004. Accessible at www.mrlincolnswhitehouse.org/templates/display.search.cfm?ID=208.

Rehnquist, William. "Civil Liberty and the Civil War: The Indianapolis Treason Trials." October 28, 1996. Accessible at www.law.indiana.edu/ilj/v72/no4/rehnquis.html.

Reiff, William Coffin. "A Federal Prison Guard." *Confederate Veteran* 19 (1911). Accessible at freepages.military.rootsweb.com/~pa91/cc23001.html.

Remini, Robert V. *Daniel Webster: The Man and His Times.* New York: W. W. Norton & Co., 1997.

Rippy, J. Fred. *Joel R. Poinsett: Versatile American.* New York: Greenwood Press, 1968.

Rives, George Lockhart. *The United States and Mexico, 1821–1848: A History of the Relations Between the Two Countries from the Independence of Mexico to the Close of the War with the United States.* New York: Charles Scribner's Sons, 1913.

Robbins, Peggy. "Allan Pinkerton's Southern Assignment." *Civil War Times Illustrated* (January 1977).

Robertson, Dr. James I., Jr. "Prison for the Capital City." *UDC Magazine* (August 1990).

Ross, Ishbel. *Rebel Rose*. Simons Island, Ga.: Mockingbird Books, 1954.

Russell, William Howard. *My Diary, North and South*. New York: Harper & Brothers, 1863.

Russo, Jean. "The Early Towns of Montgomery County." *The Montgomery County Story* 34, no. 2 (May 1991).

St. Mary's Catholic Church, Barnesville, Md.: The Official Shrine of Our Lady of Fatima for the Archdiocese of Washington. Tappan, N.Y.: Custombooks, 1985.

Sandburg, Carl. *Abraham Lincoln: The War Years*. New York: Harcourt, Brace & Company, 1938.

Seale, William. *The President's House: A History*. Washington, D.C.: White House Historical Association, 1986.

Sears, Stephen W., ed. *For Country, Cause and Leader: The Civil War Journal of Charles B. Haydon*. New York: Ticknor & Fields, 1993.

Sigaud, Louis A. "Mrs. Greenhow and the Rebel Spy Ring." *Maryland Historical Magazine* (September 1946).

Sioussat, St. George L., ed. "The Accident Aboard the USS *Princeton*, February 28, 1844: A Contemporary Newsletter." *Pennsylvania History* (July 1937).

Smith, Margaret Bayard. *The First Forty Years of Washington Society*. New York: Charles Scribner's Sons, 1906.

Stephenson, Mary A. *The General Store, 18th Century*. Williamsburg, Va.: Colonial Williamsburg Foundation Library Research Report Series, 1954.

Stern, Philip Van Doren. *Secret Missions of the Civil War: First-hand Accounts by Men and Women Who Risked Their Lives in Underground Activities for the North and South*. New York: Wings Books, 1959.

Stowe, Harriet Beecher. *Uncle Tom's Cabin*. New York: Modern Library, 2001.

Taylor, Thomas E. *Running the Blockade*. Introduction by Stephen R. Wise. Annapolis, Md.: Naval Institute Press, 1995.

Tidwell, William A. *April '65: Confederate Covert Action in the American Civil War*. Kent, Ohio: Kent State University Press, 1995.

Trask, David F. "A Short History of the U.S. Department of State, 1781–1981." U.S. Department of State, Office of the Historian, January 1981.

United States District Court, Northern District of California. *The United States vs. José Y. Limantour*. n.p., n.d.

U.S. Naval History Division, *Civil War Naval Chronology, 1861–1865*. Washington, D.C.: Government Printing Office, 1971.

United States Naval War Records Office. *Official Records of the Union and Confederate Navies in the War of the Rebellion*. 30 volumes. Washington, D.C.: Government Printing Office, 1894–1922. Accessible at cdl.library.cornell.edu/moa/browse.monographs/ofre.html.

United States War Department. *The War of the Rebellion: A Compilation of the Official Records of the Union and Confederate Armies, Published Under the Direction of the Secretary of War*. 70 volumes. Washington, D.C.: Government Printing Office, 1880–1901. Accessible at cdl.library.cornell.edu/moa/browse.monographs/waro.html.

Vandiver, Frank. *Confederate Blockade Running Through Bermuda*. Austin: University of Texas Press, 1947.

Varon, Elizabeth R. *Southern Lady, Yankee Spy: The True Story of Elizabeth Van Lew, a Union Agent at the Heart of the Confederacy*. New York: Oxford University Press, 2003.

Webster, Donald B., Jr. "The Beauty and Chivalry of the United States Assembled." *American Heritage* 17, no. 1 (December 1965).

Wentworth, John. *Congressional Reminiscences: Adams, Benton, Calhoun, Clay, and Webster*. Chicago: Fergus Printing Co., 1882.

"White House History in James Buchanan's Time." *Journal of the White House Historical Association* 12 (Winter 2003).

Wilson, Charles Reagan, and William Ferris, eds. *Encyclopedia of Southern Culture*. Chapel Hill: University of North Carolina Press, 1989.

Wise, Henry A. *Seven Decades of the Union.* Philadelphia: J. B. Lippincott & Co., 1872.

Wise, Stephen R. *Lifeline of the Confederacy: Blockade Running During the Civil War.* Columbia: University of South Carolina Press, 1988.

Young, James Sterling. *The Washington Community, 1800–1828.* New York: Columbia University Press, 1996.

Young, Robert W. *Senator James Murray Mason: Defender of the Old South.* Knoxville: University of Tennessee Press, 1998.

Online Resources

johnoneal@onealwebsite.com.

"John Brown's Raid." Accessible at www.civilwarhome.com/johnbrown.htm.

Bartleby.com. Accessible at www.bartleby.com.

Cave's Cove. Accessible at www.cavescove.com.

Cook, Gynger. *"The Richmond Theater Fire, compiled in 2000." Accessible at jshaputis.tripod.com/ClayArticles/richmond_theater_fire.htm.*

"Documenting the American South." University of North Carolina at Chapel Hill. Accessible at docsouth.unc.edu/greenhow/menu.html.

Encyclopedia Britannica, 11th ed. (1911). Accessible at www.1911encyclopedia.org.

"Flags of the Confederate States of America." Fact Index. Accessible at www.fact-index.com/f/fl/flags_of_the_confederate_states_of_america.html.

Gale Literary Databases. Accessible at library.concordia.ca/collections/gld.html.

Gettysburg. PBS. Accessible at www.pbs.org/wnet/goingplaces2/civil_war/hilite1.html.

"The Historic Congressional Cemetery" website. Accessible at www.congressionalcemetery.org.

"Letters of the Civil War." Accessible at www.letterscivilwar.com.

Making of America. Accessible at cdl.library.cornell.edu/moa.

Mystic Seaport. Accessible at mysticseaport.org.

Suite101.com. Accessible at www.suite101.com.

Virtual Reality Moon Phase Pictures. Accessible at tycho.usno.navy.mil/vphase.html.

David Rumsey Map Collection, Cartography Associates. Accessible at www.davidrumsey.com.

Notes

Legend

ROG—Rose O'Neale Greenhow
RG—Robert Greenhow
STM—S. Tredwell Moore
FGM—Florence Greenhow Moore
JB—James Buchanan
JCC—John C. Calhoun
JD—Jefferson Davis
JL—Joe Lane
HDW—Henry D. Wilson
JF—John Forsyth
WHS—William Henry Seward
EJP—Edward J. Pringle
JYL—José Yves Limantour
SPC—Salmon Portland Chase
HSP—Historical Society of Pennsylvania (Philadelphia)
LOC—Library of Congress, Washington, D.C.
MOC—Museum of the Confederacy, Richmond, Va.
MCHS—Montgomery County Historical Society, Rockville, Md.
MHS—Maryland Historical Society, Baltimore
MLK—Martin Luther King Library, Washington, D.C.
MSA—Maryland State Archives, Annapolis, Md.
MSM—Mystic Seaport Museum, Mystic, Conn.
VHS—Virginia Historical Society, Richmond
CHS—California Historical Society, San Francisco

Preface: Searching for Rose

1. Mallory to Mrs. Clement Clay, wife of a Confederate commissioner in Canada, October 28, 1864, Clement C. Clay Manuscripts, William R. Perkins Library, Duke University.
2. Author interview with H. G. Jones, March 25, 2004, Chapel Hill, N.C.
3. Book contract between Richard Bentley and Rose Greenhow, September 19, 1863. British Library Collections, 03 BU 327C, Add. 46617, folio 334.
4. European address book of Rose Greenhow (hereafter "ROG"), found among her possessions after she died, contained a notation by a daughter, probably Little Rose, saying that as she was "leaving America this last time," she burned many of her mother's letters, including those from friends in Britain. North Carolina State Archives. Transcription by Debbi Blake, archivist, North Carolina Office of Archives and History.
5. ROG, *My Imprisonment and the First Year of Abolition Rule at Washington* (London: Richard Bentley, 1863), 59. Electronic edition available on Documenting the American South website, University of North Carolina at Chapel Hill, docsouth.unc.edu/greenhow/menu.html.

Chapter 1: Rose's Game

1. Diary of Allen Alonzo Kingsbury, Medfield, Massachusetts, of Company H, First Massachusetts Infantry, July 7, 1861, Letters of the Civil War website (www.letterscivilwar.com).
2. Letter from Allen to his parents, Camp Banks, July 10, 1861, Letters of the Civil War website.
3. Letter to the Editor, signed "Hal," *Chelsea Telegraph and Pioneer*, July 13, 1861, 2, col. 3, Letters of the Civil War website.
4. Diary of Allen Alonzo Kingsbury, July 9, 1861, Letters of the Civil War website.
5. Letter dated July 12, 1861, *Roxbury City Gazette*, July 18, 1861, Letters of the Civil War website.
6. Stephen W. Sears, ed., *For Country, Cause and Leader: The Civil War Journal of Charles B. Haydon, 2nd Michigan Infantry* (New York: Ticknor & Fields, 1993), 24. National Battlefield Park Library (Manassas, Va.).
7. Sears, *For Country, Cause,* 40.
8. Ibid., 36–42.
9. Journal of John C. Tidball ("Bull Run"), Tidball Papers, National Battlefield Park Library (Manassas, Va.), 214–96.
10. Letter to the Editor, signed "Hal," *Chelsea Telegraph and Pioneer,* July 13, 1861.
11. This is Route 193 today.
12. John Bakeless, *Spies of the Confederacy* (Philadelphia, New York: J. B. Lippincott Co., 1970), 21. Alice Cary Ball Duvall, *Recollections of the War by Grandmama.* Eleanor S. Brockenbrough Library, Museum of the Confederacy (hereafter MOC), Richmond, Virginia.
13. William Howard Russell, *My Diary, North and South* (New York: Harper & Brothers, 1863), 165–66.
14. Ibid., 166.
15. Seized Correspondence of ROG, RG 59, National Archives (College Park, Md.).
16. The slip of paper with Beauregard's name on it still exists, but the message accompanying it was lost. William C. Davis, *Battle at Bull Run: A History of the First Major Campaign of the Civil War* (Baton Rouge, La.: State University Press, 1977), xi.
17. William Lamb, *The Life and Times of Colonel William Lamb, 1835–1909: Patriot, Benefactor, Statesman* (Austin, Texas: 2000), 167.
18. STM to Major General E. D. Townsend, June 18, 1870, Records of the District Court of the United States for the District of Columbia, Book 84, Record Group 21, Entry 115, Old Series Administration Case Files, 1801–78, National Archives (Washington, D.C.).
19. Jean H. Baker, *James Buchanan* (New York: Henry Holt & Co., 2004), 20.

Chapter 2: Grande Dame

1. Virginia Clay-Clopton, *A Belle of the Fifties: Memoirs of Mrs. Clay of Alabama, Covering Social and Political Life in Washington and the South, 1853–66* (New York: Doubleday, Page & Co., 1905), 126.
2. "Fashionable Intelligence," *The New York Times*, April 12, 1858, 1.
3. E. F. Ellet, *The Court Circles of the Republic* (New York: J. D. Dennison, 1869), 488.
4. Clay-Clopton, *A Belle of the Fifties*, 132.
5. Ibid., 35–126.
6. "Fashionable Intelligence."
7. Clay-Clopton, *A Belle of the Fifties*, 35–133.
8. Ibid.
9. Ellet, *The Court Circles of the Republic*, 488.
10. "Fashionable Intelligence."
11. Clay-Clopton, *A Belle of the Fifties*, 35–134.
12. Ibid., 128. The galop was a lively dance in double time.
13. Seward's speech on March 3, 1858, caused a national sensation and provided ammunition for similar charges by Abraham Lincoln in his debates against Douglas.
14. Clay-Clopton, *A Belle of the Fifties*, 35, 87.
15. William Seale, *The President's House: A History*, Volume 1 (Washington, D.C.: White House Historical Association, 1986), 347.
16. ROG to F. D. Cleary, Deed of Trust Recorded January 31, 1857, General Land Records, District of Columbia, J.A.S. 127, 236. The *Washington City Directory of 1858* also lists ROG at this address.
17. Ibid.
18. The *Washington City Directory of 1858* lists Rose as living in a house at 206 G Street North. The *Directory of 1860* lists her at 398 16th Street. Also, an obit for her grandson in June 1859 says that she was holding the funeral service in her home at 398 16th Street. Today this is the site of the St. Regis Hotel.
19. Erasmus D. Keyes, *Fifty Years' Observation of Men and Events, Civil and Military* (New York: Scribner's, 1884), 330.
20. Ibid., 330–31.
21. "Statement Concerning Secret Affairs relating to the Mexican War" dated late December 1884, in Pamela Herr and Mary Lee Spence, eds., *The Letters of Jessie Benton Frémont* (Urbana, Chicago: University of Illinois Press, 1993), 504. There is no evidence that there were any letters from Keyes in Rose's possession when she was arrested.
22. ROG, *My Imprisonment*, 109.
23. Brown's ghost would later march into battle with Northern soldiers, who put his name to music in the marching song "John Brown's Body Lies A'Mouldering in the Ground." Poet Julia Ward Howe heard it at a troop parade in Washington in the fall of 1861 and wrote new words to the tune. It became "The Battle Hymn of the Republic." See www.pbs.org/wgbh/amex/brown/sfeature/song.html.
24. ROG, *My Imprisonment*, 190.
25. Ibid., 190–92.
26. Ibid., 192.
27. Ibid.
28. Ibid.
29. "The Day Journal of Milton S. Latham," *Quarterly of the California Historical Society* 11 (March 1932).
30. JL to ROG and from HW to ROG, undated, Seized Correspondence of ROG, RG 59, National Archives (College Park, Md.).
31. JL to ROG, undated, Seized Correspondence of ROG, RG 59, National Archives (College Park, Md.).
32. Ibid.

33. The poem was found in Rose's house when she was arrested. Seized Correspondence of ROG, RG 59, National Archives (College Park, Md.).

Chapter 3: "The Coming Storm"

1. Seale, *The President's House*, 358.
2. Elizabeth Lindsay Lomax, *Leaves from an Old Washington Diary, 1854–1863* (New York: E. P. Dutton & Co., 1943), 138.
3. *Frank Leslie's Illustrated Newspaper*, January 19, 1861.
4. Biographical sketch of John Adams Dix, *Encyclopedia Britannica*, 11th ed. (1911), accessible at www.1911encyclopedia.org.
5. Jefferson Davis, farewell speech to the U.S. Senate, January 21, 1861, accessible at www.americancivilwar.com/south/jdexit.html.
6. E-mail from John Wilson Myers, Wilson biographer, December 3, 2003.
7. *Congressional Globe*, January 30, 1861, 638–39.
8. Undated letters, Seized Correspondence of ROG, RG 59, National Archives (College Park, Md.). Classified as "supposed to have been written to Rose Greenhow by Henry Wilson, U.S. Senator from Massachusetts."
9. Ernest A. McKay, *Henry Wilson: Practical Radical: A Portrait of a Politician* (Port Washington, N.Y.: Kennikat Press, 1971), 154. Myers e-mail to author, December 2, 2003; November 12, 2004.
10. Margaret Leech, *Reveille in Washington, 1860–1865* (New York: Harper & Brothers Publishers, 1941), 137. Fish attributed his information to newspaper owner and diplomat James Watson Webb, who said he got it in confidence from Jordan himself.
11. Letter from Commission Relating to State Prisoners to John W. Forney, secretary of the Senate, March 31, 1862, *The War of the Rebellion: A Compilation of the Official Records of the Union and Confederate Armies*, series 2, volume 2, 576, accessible on Cornell University's Making of America website, cdl.library.cornell.edu/moa/browse.monographs/waro.html.
12. Pringle to ROG, Seized Correspondence of ROG, RG59, National Archives (College Park, Md.).
13. Ernest B. Furgurson, *Ashes of Glory: Richmond at War* (New York: Alfred A. Knopf, 1996), 51.
14. Clay-Clopton, *A Belle of the Fifties*, 151.
15. Mary Greenhow Lee to ROG, January 14, 1861, Seized Correspondence of ROG, RG 59, National Archives (College Park, Md.).
16. Peggy Robbins, "Allan Pinkerton's Southern Assignment," *Civil War Times Illustrated*, January 1977, 6–11, 44–47.
17. Shelby Foote, *The Civil War, A Narrative: Fort Sumter to Perryville* (New York: Vintage Books, 1958), 36–37.
18. Lomax, *Leaves from an Old Washington Diary*, 145.
19. ROG, *My Imprisonment*, 196.
20. *National Intelligencer*, March 18, 1861, 1, col. 6.
21. Bill for Service, March 19, 1861, in Records of the District Court of the United States for the District of Columbia, Record Group 21, Entry 115, Old Series Administration Case Files, 1801–78, National Archives (Washington, D.C.).
22. Foote, *The Civil War*, 39.
23. STM to ROG, June 23, 1861, Seized Correspondence of ROG, RG 59, National Archives (College Park, Md.). Historical Register and Dictionary of the U.S. Army; Biographical Register of the Officers and Graduates of the United States Military Academy.
24. Pamela Herr, *Jessie Benton Frémont: A Biography* (New York: Franklin Watts, 1987), 33, 219.
25. STM to ROG, March 11, 1861, Seized Correspondence of ROG, RG 59, National Archives (College Park, Md.).
26. ROG to WHS, April 9, 1861, William Henry Seward Papers, Department of Rare Books & Special Collections, University of Rochester Library.

27. Letter dated May 13, signed "Bunker Hill," *Charleston Advertiser,* May 18, 1861, 1, col. 3, Letters of the Civil War website.
28. Leech, *Reveille in Washington,* 72–73.
29. Cutts would later win the Medal of Honor for gallantry.
30. STM to ROG, April 20, 1861, Seized Correspondence of ROG, RG 59, National Archives (College Park, Md.).
31. FGM to ROG, April 28, 1861, Seized Correspondence of ROG, RG 59, National Archives (College Park, Md.).
32. William Rehnquist, "Civil Liberty and the Civil War: The Indianapolis Treason Trials," October 28, 1996, accessible at www.law.indiana.edu/ilj/v72/no4/rehnquist.html.
33. Letter dated July 3, 1861, *Berkshire County Eagle,* July 11, 1861, 2, col. 6, Letters of the Civil War website.
34. Letter signed "Bunker Hill," *Charlestown Advertiser,* May 18, 1861, Letters of the Civil War website.
35. Letter signed "M.H.," *North Bridgewater Gazette,* May 28, 1861, 1, col. 2, Letters of the Civil War website.
36. Letter signed "Bunker Hill," *Charleston Advertiser,* May 18, 1861, Letters of the Civil War website.
37. Letter from Captain J. A. Sawtell, *Lowell Daily Courier,* May 9, 1861, 2, col. 3, Letters of the Civil War website.
38. Letter signed "H.F.R.," *Chelsea Telegraph and Pioneer,* May 11, 1861, 2, col. 5, Letters of the Civil War website.
39. Thaddeus S. C. Lowe, Official Report to the Secretary of War, June 4, 1863, in *Memoirs of Thaddeus S. C. Lowe, Chief of the Aeronautic Corps of the Army of the United States During the Civil War: My Balloons in Peace and War* (Lewiston, N.Y.: Edwin Mellen Press, 2004).
40. Ernest B. Furgurson, *Freedom Rising: Washington in the Civil War* (New York: Knopf, 2004), 106.
41. Letter signed "H.F.R.," *Chelsea Telegraph and Pioneer,* May 18, 1861, Letters of the Civil War website.
42. Letter dated May 24, 1861, signed "Bunker Hill," *Charlestown Advertiser,* May 29, 1861, Letters of the Civil War website.
43. Lomax, *Leaves from an Old Washington Diary,* 157.
44. Letter dated May 24, 1861, signed "Bunker Hill," *Charlestown Advertiser,* May 29, 1861, Letters of the Civil War website.
45. Ibid.
46. Letter dated June 9, 1861, signed "Bunker Hill," *Charlestown Advertiser,* June 15, 1861, 2, col. 4, Letters of the Civil War website.
47. Letter dated July 1, 1861, signed "W.D.G.," *Cambridge Chronicle,* July 6, 1861, 2, col. 2, Letters of the Civil War website.
48. Letter from an unknown soldier, *Roxbury City Gazette,* July 25, 1861, 3, col. 1, Letters of the Civil War website.
49. Letter signed "L.," *Lowell Daily Courier,* May 9, 1861, Letters of the Civil War website.
50. FGM to ROG, May 16, 1861, Seized Correspondence of ROG, RG 59, National Archives (College Park, Md.).
51. STM to ROG, April 29, 1861, Seized Correspondence of ROG, RG 59, National Archives (College Park, Md.).
52. STM to Major General E. D. Townsend, June 18, 1870, Records of the District Court of the United States for the District of Columbia, Book 84, Record Group 21, Entry 115, Old Series Administration Case Files, 1801–78, National Archives (Washington, D.C.).
53. ROG to SPC, May 1861, in David Barbee Collection, Georgetown University Library, Special Collections, Box 8, Folder 246.
54. SPC to ROG, May 30, 1861, Seized Correspondence of ROG, RG 59, National Archives (College Park, Md.).

55. The Fourth Alabama Regiment.
56. Mary Greenhow Lee to ROG, May 20, 1861, Seized Correspondence of ROG, RG 59, National Archives (College Park, Md.).
57. FGM and STM to ROG, June 23, 1861, Seized Correspondence of ROG, RG 59, National Archives (College Park, Md.).

Chapter 4: The Making of a Spy

1. Leech, *Reveille in Washington*, 137. Fish attributed his information to newspaper owner and diplomat James Watson Webb, who said he got it in confidence from Jordan himself.
2. Letter from Thomas Jordan to J. P. Benjamin, October 29, 1861, *War of the Rebellion*, series 1, volume 5, 928.
3. Author interview with Ken Boulier, a navy code breaker during World War II, May 26, 2004.
4. This code was reportedly found on ROG's body when she died on October 1, 1864. North Carolina State Archives, Rose O'Neale Greenhow Papers, Raleigh, N.C.
5. Leech, *Reveille in Washington*, 94–95.
6. Author interview with Jim Burgess, Manassas National Battlefield Park Museum specialist, April 7, 2004.
7. ROG, *My Imprisonment*, 26–27.
8. Pass dated August 3, 1861, Seized Correspondence of ROG, RG 59, National Archives (College Park, Md.).
9. EJP to ROG, January 10, 1861, Seized Correspondence of ROG, RG 59, National Archives (College Park, Md.).
10. EJP to ROG, undated, Seized Correspondence of ROG, RG 59, National Archives (College Park, Md.).
11. Ibid.
12. Ibid.
13. EJP to ROG, June 21, 1861, Seized Correspondence of ROG, RG 59, National Archives (College Park, Md.).
14. Edwin C. Fishel, *The Secret War for the Union* (Boston, New York: Houghton Mifflin, 1996), 58–59.
15. G. T. Beauregard, "The First Battle of Bull Run," undated manuscript, accessible at www.civilwarhome.com/bullruncampaign.htm.
16. E. J. Allen to Provost Marshal Andrew Porter, January 9, 1862, *War of the Rebellion*, series 2, volume 2, 1308–9.
17. Beauregard, "The First Battle of Bull Run."
18. ROG, *My Imprisonment*, 15.
19. William A. Tidwell, *April '65: Confederate Covert Action in the American Civil War* (Kent, Ohio, and London, Eng.: Kent State University Press, 1995).
20. Beauregard, "The First Battle of Bull Run."
21. G. T. Beauregard to Miss Augusta J. Evans, March 24, 1863, *War of the Rebellion*, series 1, volume 55, part 2, 688.
22. Leech, *Reveille in Washington*, 97.
23. ROG, *My Imprisonment*, 16.
24. Letter dated July 20, signed Chas. A. Jackson, *Chelsea Telegraph and Pioneer,* July 27, 1861, 1, col. 1, Letters of the Civil War website.
25. These were soldiers from the First Massachusetts, Twelfth New York, and Third and Fourth Michigan.
26. Brevet Major General James B. Fry, "McDowell's Advance to Bull Run," The Battle of Bull Run (First Manassas) website, www.civilwarhome.com/advancetobullrun.htm. At Bull Run, Fry was captain and assistant adjutant general on McDowell's staff.
27. E-mail correspondence with Jim Burgess, Manassas National Battlefield Park Museum specialist, April 7, 2004.

28. Leech, *Reveille in Washington*, 100.
29. Mary Mitchell, *A Divided Town* (Barre, Mass.: Barre Publishers, 1968), 53.
30. Russell, *My Diary, North and South*, 162.
31. Ibid., 168.
32. Leech, *Reveille in Washington*, 101–3.
33. Letter dated July 22, 1861, marked "Camp Sprague," *Boston Daily Courier,* July 27, 1861, 1, col. 3, Letters of the Civil War website.
34. Letter dated July 24, 1861, marked "Washington, D.C., Camp Clark," *Boston Daily Courier,* August 3, 1861, 1, col. 3, Letters of the Civil War website.
35. Letter dated July 25, 1861, signed "Allen," Letters of the Civil War website.
36. Davis, *Battle at Bull Run*, 245.
37. Letter dated July 20, marked "Camp Banks," *Roxbury City Gazette,* July 25, 1861, 2, col. 8, Letters of the Civil War website.
38. Letter dated July 27, 1861, *Boston Herald,* August 23, 1861, 1, col. 6, Letters of the Civil War website.
39. Thaddeus S. C. Lowe, Official Report to the Secretary of War, June 4, 1863, in *Memoirs of Thaddeus S. C. Lowe.*
40. ROG, *My Imprisonment*, 16–17.
41. John Kemble, *The Panama Route, 1848–1869* (Berkeley: University of California Press, 1943).
42. ROG, *My Imprisonment*, 19.
43. Ibid., 18.
44. Ibid., 19.
45. Ibid., 20.
46. Lowe, *Memoirs of Thaddeus S. C. Lowe.*
47. ROG, *My Imprisonment*, 24.
48. Tidball, "Bull Run," 294.
49. Leech, *Reveille in Washington*, 106.
50. ROG, *My Imprisonment*, 22.

Chapter 5: "A Dangerous Character"

1. ROG, *My Imprisonment*, 39.
2. After ROG's arrest, these letters were pieced together from fragments. The Dix-Pierrepont Commission used xxx to indicate missing words. Proceeding of the Commission Relating to State Prisoners, Records Department of State, RG59 E962, National Archives (College Park, MD).
3. Letter dated August 26, 1861, signed "A.K.J.," *Cambridge Chronicle,* September 7, 1861, 1, col. 4, Letters of the Civil War website.
4. O'Malley was a member of the Ninth Massachusetts. Letter dated August 5, 1861, marked "Arlington Heights," *Boston Saturday Evening Gazette,* August 10, 1861, 2, col. 4, Letters of the Civil War website.
5. ROG, *My Imprisonment*, 36.
6. Ibid., 43.
7. Ibid., 29–30.
8. Ibid., 31.
9. Allan Pinkerton, *The Spy of the Rebellion* (Lincoln: University of Nebraska Press, 1989), 245.
10. Letter dated August 8, 1861, signed "Hal," marked "Fort Albany, Arlington Heights," *Chelsea Telegraph and Pioneer,* August 17, 1861, 2, col. 4, Letters of the Civil War website.
11. *Roxbury City Gazette,* August 8, 1861, 2, col. 5, Letters of the Civil War website.
12. Letter from David Garrison, November 30, 1861, in possession of a Garrison descendant.
13. These three letters from Proceeding of the Commission Relating to State Prisoners.
14. ROG, *My Imprisonment*, 37.
15. Ibid., 38.
16. Ibid.

17. Pinkerton, *The Spy of the Rebellion,* 252.
18. Ibid., 253–57.
19. ROG, *My Imprisonment,* 209.
20. Ibid., quoting undated *Philadelphia Press* story.
21. Pinkerton, *The Spy of the Rebellion,* 256–57.
22. Ibid., 257.
23. Ibid.
24. Ibid.
25. Ibid., 258.
26. Ibid., 259.
27. Ibid., 260–62.
28. Ibid., 263.
29. Ibid., 266.
30. Ibid., 267–68.
31. Martha Elizabeth Wright Morris, *Memories,* an unpublished memoir in Martha Elizabeth Wright Morris Papers, Manuscripts Division, LOC.

Chapter 6: Death of a Master

1. Book of Baptism, St. Mary's Catholic Church, Barnesville, Maryland. The book was started in 1815. Mary Ann and John Eliza O'Neale are the only O'Neale children to be included. Mary Ann's birthday is listed as October 17, 1816—which meant that John Eliza would have been born after her father died on April 22, 1817.
2. Jean Russo, "The Early Towns of Montgomery County," *The Montgomery Country Story* 34, no. 2 (May 1991).
3. Handwritten, undated manuscript by "Dr. Wootton" of the Historical Society of Frederick County to the Maryland Historical Society, Montgomery County Historical Society, Rockville, Maryland. Dr. Wootton is thought to be Dr. William Turner Wootton, who knew the O'Neale family.
4. Author interview with Frank Jamison, December 27, 2002. Jamison drove around Conclusion property with author on April 18, 2003.
5. Manuscript of Dr. Wootton.
6. Ibid.
7. The slave was referred to derisively as "Jim Crow," a stereotypical caricature of a black-faced minstrel singer that appealed to white audiences receptive to the idea of blacks as lazy and inferior.

"Helloa, Jim Crow!" said Mr. Shelby, whistling and snapping a bunch of raisins towards him, "pick that up, now!"
The child scampered, with all his little strength, after the prize, while his master laughed.
"Come here, Jim Crow," said he. The child came up, and the master patted the curly head and chucked him under the chin.
"Now, Jim, show this gentleman how you can dance and sing." The boy commenced one of those wild, grotesque songs common among Negroes, in a rich, clear voice, accompanying his singing with many comic evolutions of the hands, feet and whole body, all in perfect time to the music.
"Bravo," said Haley, throwing him a quarter of an orange.
—From Harriet Beecher Stowe, *Uncle Tom's Cabin*
(New York: Modern Library, 2001), 6

8. Excerpts on N. Jacob Case, Governor and Council (Pardon Papers), 1817–1818, MSA, S 1061-18-5, Box 18, Folder 5.

9. "My master's habits were such as were common enough among the dissipated planters of the neighborhood. One of their frequent practices was to assemble on Saturday or Sunday, which were their holidays, and gamble, run horses, or fight game-cocks, discuss politics, and drink whiskey, and brandy and water, all day long. Perfectly aware that they would not be able to find their own way home at night, each one ordered a slave, his particular attendant, to come after him and help him home. I was chosen for this confidential duty by my master; and many is the time I have held him on his horse, when he could not hold himself in the saddle, and walked by his side in darkness and mud from the tavern to his house." From Josiah Henson, *The Life of Josiah Henson, Formerly a Slave, Now an Inhabitant of Canada, as Narrated by Himself* (Boston: Arthur D. Phelps, 1849), 20–21.

10. Excerpts on N. Jacob Case, Governor and Council (Pardon Papers) 1817–1818, MSA.

11. Death Warrant and Letters Asking for Pardon for N. Jacob, Governor and Council (Pardon Papers) 1817–1818, MSA, Box 18, Folder 5.

12. Henson, *The Life of Josiah Henson*, 22.

13. Excerpts on N. Jacob Case, Governor and Council (Pardon Papers) 1817–1818, MSA.

14. Death Warrant and Letters Asking for Pardon for N. Jacob, Governor and Council (Pardon Papers) 1817–1818.

15. E-mail correspondence with Stephen T. Whitman, January 7, 2003. See also Stephen T. Whitman, *The Price of Freedom: Slavery and Manumission in Baltimore and Early National Maryland* (Lexington: University Press of Kentucky, 1997); and *Challenging Slavery in the Chesapeake, 1775–1865* (Maryland Historical Society Press, forthcoming).

16. Whitman e-mail with author, January 7, 2003.

17. Anthony M. Cohen, "The Underground Railroad in Montgomery County," *The Montgomery County Story* (Rockville, Md.: Montgomery County Historical Society, 1995).

18. O'Neale Genealogy Association (Amherst, Ohio).

19. "Frederick's Chief Justice, Roger Brooke Taney," *Journal of the Historical Society of Frederick County, Maryland* (Spring 2004), 7.

20. Edward C. Papenfuse Jr., archivist of Maryland, "An Act Concerning Religion, April 21, 1649: An Interpretation and Tribute to the Citizen Legislators of Maryland," accessible at www.mdarchives.state.md.us/msa/speccol/sc2200/sc2221/000025/html/titlepage.html.

21. Peter Kenney, Society of Jesus, "Temporalities," Report to Corporation Leadership, 1820: Maryland Province Archive, Georgetown University, Document MdP XT1.

22. Mary Beth Corrigan, "Making the Most of an Opportunity: Slaves and the Catholic Church in Early Washington," *Washington History* 12, no. 1 (Spring/Summer 2000), 92.

23. Randall Kennedy, *Interracial Intimacies: Sex, Marriage, Identity and Adoption* (New York: Vintage Books, 2003).

24. Editorial, *National Catholic Reporter,* November 24, 2000.

25. Author interview with Fr. George B. Reid, pastor emeritus, St. Mary's Catholic Church (Barnesville, Md.), March 12, 2003.

26. *St. Mary's Catholic Church, Barnesville, Md., The Official Shrine of Our Lady of Fatima for the Archdiocese of Washington* (Tappan, N.Y.: Custombook Inc., 1985).

27. Two of Lawrence O'Neale's children left money to the Roman Catholic Church in their wills: see biography of Lawrence O'Neale, *A Biographical Dictionary of the Maryland Legislature, 1635–1789,* edited by Edward C. Papenfuse, Alan F. Day, David W. Jordan, and Gregory A. Stiverson (Baltimore: Johns Hopkins University Press, 1985).

28. Ibid.

29. Catherine Clinton, general statement, *The Plantation Mistress* (New York: Pantheon, 1982), 77.

30. William O'Neale booklet, Montgomery County Register of Wills, MCHS.

31. John O'Neale Sale, Montgomery County Register of Wills (Estate Record), MSA, C1138-13, L/357.

32. Ibid.

33. Ibid.

34. Ray Eldon Hiebert and Richard MacMaster, *A Grateful Remembrance* (Rockville, Md.: Montgomery County Historical Society, 1976), 116.

35. William O'Neale booklet, Montgomery County Register of Wills, MCHS.
36. John O'Neale Sale, Montgomery County Register of Wills.
37. Clinton, *The Plantation Mistress*, 51.
38. H. V. Hill is listed as "carpenter" in the *Washington City Directory of 1830*, Washingtoniana Room, MLK Library.
39. It is not known exactly when Rose and Ellen came to live at the Hill's Boarding House. Rose refers to the period briefly in her memoir, *My Imprisonment and the First Year of Abolition Rule at Washington*, 281.

Chapter 7: Washington Society

1. V. Hart, *The National Road*, Montgomery County Historical Society, 91–93.
2. Judith Beck Helm, *Tenleytown, D.C.: Country Village into City Neighborhood* (Washington, D.C.: Tennally Press, 1981), 81.
3. Jean B. Russo, "The Early Towns of Montgomery County, 1747–1831," *The Montgomery County Story* 34, no. 2 (May 1991), 155.
4. Richard P. Jackson, *The Chronicles of Georgetown, D.C., 1751–1875* (Westminster, Md.: Willow Bend Books, 2001), 45.
5. These are M and K streets today.
6. W. B. Bryan, *A History of the National Capital*, volume 2 (1815–1878) (New York: Macmillan Co., 1916), 32.
7. *An Illustrated History of the City of Washington* by the Junior League of Washington, edited by Thomas Froncek (New York: Alfred A. Knopf, 1977), 47.
8. ROG, *My Imprisonment*, 281.
9. James M. Goode, *Capital Losses: A Cultural History of Washington's Destroyed Buildings* (Washington, D.C.: Smithsonian Institution Press, 1979), 290–92.
10. James Sterling Young, *The Washington Community, 1800–1828* (New York: Columbia University Press, 1996), 100.
11. "Quaint Old Days of Capital," *The Washington Post*, November 1, 1939, City Museum (Washington, D.C.).
12. John Clagett Proctor, "Historic Site of the Supreme Court," *Sunday Star* (Washington, D.C.), April 15, 1945. City Museum, Washington, D.C.
13. *Full Directory for Washington City, Georgetown and Alexandria for 1834*, Washingtoniana Room, MLK Library.
14. Handwritten, undated manuscript by "Dr. Wootton" of the Historical Society of Frederick County to the Maryland Historical Society, MCHS.
15. Catherine Allgor, *Parlor Politics, In Which Ladies of Washington Help Build a City and a Government* (Charlottesville, London: University Press of Virginia, 2000), 119, 146.
16. Margaret Bayard Smith, *The First Forty Years of Washington Society* (New York: Charles Scribner's Sons, 1906), 256.
17. Ibid., 281.
18. Records of St. Mary's Catholic Church (Barnesville, Md.).
19. Diary of Mary Greenhow, Mary Greenhow Papers, MHS. This diary was kept between 1837 and 1838 by Rose's sister-in-law, Mary Greenhow, who lived in Washington for much of 1837. Mary made repeated references to dinners and parties with the Peter family. She is introduced in depth later in the story.
20. Author interview with Melinda Linderer Huff, curator, Tudor Place, Washington, D.C., January 3, 2003.
21. Diary of Mary Greenhow, Mary Greenhow Papers, MHS.
22. Ishbel Ross, *Rebel Rose* (Simons Island, Ga.: Mockingbird Books, 1954), 7. Ross cites no source for her assertion, unsupported by other records, but Ross's research was generally accurate.
23. Biography of Cave Johnson, *Dictionary of American Biography*, volume 10, from Cave's Cove website, www.cavescove.com.

24. Allgor, *Parlor Politics,* 105.
25. Ibid., 121.
26. Diary of Mary Greenhow, Mary Greenhow Papers, MHS, MS. 534, 11, 13.
27. Ibid., 13.
28. Diary of Mary Greenhow, separate list of visits for 1837, Mary Greenhow Papers, MHS. There are several of Rose Greenhow's formal calling cards in her file at the National Archives.
29. Smith, *The First Forty Years of Washington Society,* 324.
30. Diary of Mary Greenhow, MHS, MS. 534, 19.
31. Ethel Stephens Arnett, *Mrs. James Madison: The Incomparable Dolley* (Greensboro, N.C.: Piedmont Press, 1972), 272.
32. *Records of the Columbia Historical Society* 3 (1900).
33. Smith, *The First Forty Years of Washington Society,* 134.
34. *National Intelligencer,* December 25, 1833, 3, col. 5, LOC.
35. Virginia Moore, *The Madisons: A Biography* (New York: McGraw-Hill, 1979), 456.
36. Ross, *Rebel Rose,* 9.
37. Diary of Mary Greenhow, MHS, MS. 534, 24.
38. Irving Bartlett, *John Calhoun: A Biography* (New York: W. W. Norton & Company, 1993), 210.
39. Clyde N. Wilson and W. Edwin Hemphill, eds., *The Papers of John C. Calhoun,* volume 10 (Columbia: University of South Carolina Press, 1959), 239.
40. J. Kingston Pierce, "Andrew Jackson and the Tavern-Keeper's Daughter," *American History Magazine,* June 1999.
41. Ibid.
42. Smith, *The First Forty Years of Washington Society,* 252–53.
43. John F. Marszalch, *The Petticoat Affair: Manners, Mutiny and Sex in Andrew Jackson's White House* (New York: The Free Press, 1997), 54.
44. Smith, *The First Forty Years of Washington Society,* 305.
45. John S. Cooper, "Presidents and First Ladies," October 8, 1999, accessible at www.suite101.com/article.cfm/presidents_and_first_ladies/26544.
46. Marszalch, *The Petticoat Affair,* 198.
47. Pierce, "Andrew Jackson and the Tavern-Keeper's Daughter."

Chapter 8: Slavery in Washington: "A Tale of Woe"

1. W. C. Clephane, "Local Aspect of Slavery," *Records of the Columbia Historical Society* 3 (1900), 239; Mary Beth Corrigan, "Imaginary Cruelties?: A History of the Slave Trade in Washington, D.C.," *Washington History* (Fall/Winter 2001–2002), 12. Ironically, two of the slave pens were located near the ground where the Smithsonian Institution's National Museum of African Art stands today.
2. W. C. Clephane, "Local Aspect of Slavery," 239.
3. E. S. Abdy, *Journal of a Residence and Tour in the United States of North America, from April, 1833, to October, 1834,* volume 2 (London: J. Murray, 1835).
4. Corrigan, "Imaginary Cruelties?," 7.
5. Jennifer Fleischner, *Mrs. Lincoln and Mrs. Keckly* (New York: Broadway Books, 2003), 24.
6. George P. Rawick, ed., *The American Slave: A Composite Autobiography,* Texas Narratives, volume 5 (Westport, Conn.: Greenwood Press, 1972), 62–65.
7. Letitia Woods Brown, *Free Negroes in the District of Columbia, 1790–1846* (New York: Oxford University Press, 1972).
8. William Lee Miller, *Arguing About Slavery: The Great Battle in the United States Congress* (New York: Alfred A. Knopf, 1996), 13, 16.
9. Author interview with Stephen T. Whitman, author of *Challenging Slavery in the Chesapeake, 1775–1865* (Baltimore: The Press at the Maryland Historical Society [forthcoming]), January 6, 2003.
10. Br. Joseph Mobberly, Society of Jesus, "Slavery, or Cham," Jesuit Plantation Project, Georgetown University Library.

11. Fleischner, *Mrs. Lincoln and Mrs. Keckly*, 78.
12. LeeAnn Whites, "The Civil War as a Crisis in Gender," in Catherine Clinton and Nina Silber, eds., *Divided Houses: Gender and the Civil War* (New York: Oxford University Press, 1992), 6.
13. Pamela Neville-Singleton, *Fanny Trollope: The Life and Adventures of a Clever Woman* (New York: Viking, 1997).
14. Diary of Martha Elizabeth Wright Morris ("Memories"), in Martha Elizabeth Wright Morris Papers, Manuscript Division, LOC. Mrs. Morris later made friends with Rose when she moved back to Washington after Lincoln was elected, but her husband intervened and ordered her to end the relationship.
15. Constance Green, *The Secret City: A History of Race Relations in the Nation's Capital* (Princeton: Princeton University Press, 1967), 33.
16. Ibid., 35.
17. Corrigan, "Imaginary Cruelties?," 17.
18. Stanley Harrold, *Subversives: Antislavery Community in Washington, D.C., 1828–1865* (Baton Rouge: Louisiana State University Press, 2003), 5.
19. Corrigan, "Imaginary Cruelties?," 6.
20. Corrigan, "A Social Union of Heart and Effort: The Afro-American Family in the District of Columbia on the Eve of Emancipation" (PhD thesis, University of Maryland, 1996).
21. Frederick Douglass, *Narrative of the Life of Frederick Douglass* (Boston: Anti-Slavery Office, 1845), 14, accessible at docsouth.unc.edu/douglass/douglass.html.
22. E-mail from Patrick Rael, associate professor of history, Bowdoin College, May 5, 2003.
23. Harrold, *Subversives*, 78.
24. Ibid.
25. Ibid. The month in question is March 1843.
26. Ibid., 64, 93.
27. Diary of Michael Shiner, 31–32, Manuscript Division, LOC.
28. Henry Mayer, *All on Fire: William Lloyd Garrison and the Abolition of Slavery* (New York: St. Martin's Press, 1998), 112.
29. Fleischner, *Mrs. Lincoln and Mrs. Keckley*, 79.
30. Green, *The Secret City*, 36.
31. Corrigan, "A Social Union of Heart and Effort," 53.
32. *National Intelligencer,* September 27, 1836, LOC.
33. Record Group 21, Records of the District Courts of the United States, District of Columbia, Circuit Court for the District of Columbia, Entry 6, Case Papers Containing Appearances, Trials, Imparlances, Judicials, etc., 1802–86. Compiled by Robert Ellis, archivist, Old Military and Civil Branch, National Archives and Records Administration. (Partial list for this term.)
34. Ibid.

Chapter 9: John C. Calhoun

1. John Wentworth, *Congressional Reminiscences: Adams, Benton, Calhoun, Clay, and Webster* (Chicago: Fergus Printing Co., 1882).
2. ROG, *My Imprisonment*, 59.
3. Tudor Place Exhibition Brochure, "Splendors of Georgetown: 25 Architectural Masterpieces,"April 13–December 31, 2001, 9.
4. Ben: Perley Poore, *Reminiscences of 60 Years in the National Metropolis* volume 1 (Philadelphia: Hubbard Brothers, 1886), 64.
5. Bassett served in the Senate from 1831 to 1861.
6. Isaac Bassett Papers, United States Senate, Office of the Senate Curator, Box 1, Folder 6, 95.
7. ROG, *My Imprisonment*, 59.
8. Bartlett, *John C. Calhoun*, 281.
9. Ibid., 282.

10. Eugene D. Genovese, "Getting States' Rights Right," *Atlantic Monthly* (March 2001), accessible at www.theatlantic.com/issues/2001/03/genovese-p1.htm.

11. Bartlett, *John C. Calhoun,* 139–50.

12. U.S. Congress, Senate, *Register of Debates in Congress,* Twenty-first Congress, first session, 5–28. Accessible at www.senate.gov/artandhistory/history/resources/pdf/HaynesReply.pdf.

13. Charles W. March, *Reminiscences of Congress* (New York: Baker and Scribner, 1850), 132–33.

14. Poore, *Reminiscences,* 118.

15. Ibid.

16. U.S. Congress, Senate, *Register of Debates in Congress,* Twentieth Congress, first session, 58–80.

17. Robert V. Remini, *Daniel Webster: The Man and His Times* (New York: W. W. Norton, 1997), 327.

18. Smith, *The First Forty Years of Washington Society,* 310.

Chapter 10: Romance in the Wind

1. Mary A. Stephenson, *The General Store, 18th Century,* Colonial Williamsburg Foundation Library Research Report Series, 1954, 17.

2. George M. West, *Richmond in By-Gone Days; Being Reminiscences of an Old Citizen* (privately published by George M. West in Richmond, 1856), 181–85; accessible at www.webroots.org/library/usahist/ribgdvao.html.

3. Correspondence between RG and Thomas Jefferson in 1825, VHS.

4. Gynger Cook, "The Richmond Theater Fire, compiled in 2000," accessible at jshaputis.tripod.com/ClayArticles/richmond_theater_fire.htm.

5. Fillmore Norfleet, *Saint Mémin in Virginia: Portraits and Bibliographies* (Richmond, Va.: The Dietz Press, 1942), 168. VHS.

6. "Black History, Virginia Profiles," *Richmond Times-Dispatch,* February 1, 2002.

7. In her memoir, Rose wrote scornfully of John C. Frémont and his father, Charles: "Like many of the soldiers of fortune whose names have been emblazoned on the scroll of fame in the Old World, [Charles Frémont] is entitled to the bar sinister on his shield. This worthy son of la belle France was not content with the golden harvest he could legitimately reap in the exercise of his professional skill, but essayed his talents in another field, and soon made himself master of the situation, and bore off in triumph a Mrs. Pryor, the wife of an old and respectable citizen of Richmond. . . . The romantic pair had winged their flight to Charleston, in which city he resumed the practice of his profession; and our hero, John Charles Frémont, was the fruit of this auspicious conjunction. Some of the citizens of Charleston took great interest in young Frémont, who was educated at their expense and afterwards sent to West Point, where he graduated, without, however, giving any indications of extraordinary capabilities, and was, some years afterwards, appointed as assistant to Mr. Nicholet, in his scientific explorations and surveys; and here even he was regarded more for his methodical industry than for genius. He was a good draftsman, and, after Mr. Nicholet's death, was employed to work out the result of his labours, which he did with accuracy and skill. Frémont had meanwhile married the daughter of the Honourable Thomas Hart Benton, who after a few years assumed his guardianship, and launched him on his career." ROG, *My Imprisonment,* 142–44.

8. Biography of RG, *Dictionary of American Biography,* volume 7 (New York: Charles Scribner & Sons, 1931), 580. Columbia University letter dated March 3, 2003, verifying Greenhow graduated from its medical school in 1821.

9. David Rankin Barbee, "Robert Greenhow," *William and Mary Quarterly* 2, vol. 13 (1933), 182–83.

10. Letter from RG to Dr. Watson in Richmond, Virginia, July 18, 1823, VHS.

11. RG to Thomas Jefferson, June 16, 1825, Thomas Jefferson Papers, VHS.

12. *Daily Alta California,* March 28, 1854, 2, col. 1, CHS.

13. Some biographies show Greenhow starting at the State Department in 1828, but the State Depart-

ment Index of Commissioned Employees shows him listed as of 1831. He is not listed in the Official Registers for 1828–1831.

14. Clyde N. Wilson, ed., *The Papers of John C. Calhoun*, volume 18, 1844.
15. In 1815, U.S. senators had an annual salary of about $1,500.
16. The Official Register of State Department Employees, National Archives, September 1831.
17. Edward Livingston began his term as secretary of state on May 24, 1831. Louis McLane took over the job on May 29, 1833.
18. Livingston is quoted in David F. Trask, "A Short History of the U.S. Department of State, 1781–1981," U.S. Department of State, Office of the Historian, January 1981.
19. RG to Livingston, March 14, 1832, Records of Department of State, National Archives (College Park, Md.).
20. *Richmond Inquirer,* June 2, 1835, 3, col. 6, LOC.

Chapter 11: Journey to Mexico

1. Registered on May 20, 1844, Baptismal Registry, St. Patrick's Church (Washington, D.C.).
2. Land Records of the District of Columbia, W.B. 61, 235.
3. David F. Trask, "A Short History of the U.S. Department of State, 1781–1981," U.S. Department of State, Office of the Historian, 37.
4. John Niven, *Martin Van Buren: The Romantic Age of American Politics* (New York: Oxford University Press, 1983), 443–44; George Lockhart Rives, *The United States and Mexico, 1821–1848: A History of the Relations Between the Two Countries from the Independence of Mexico to the Close of the War with the United States,* volume 1 (New York: Charles Scribner's Sons, 1913), 429.
5. JF to RG, May 27, 1837, in *Despatches from the United States Ministers to Mexico 1823–1906,* volume 9, National Archives (College Park, Md.).
6. There are frequent references in the diary of Mary Greenhow about Rose and Robert Greenhow attending dinner parties at the Forsyth residence.
7. Travel Account of RG, 1837, Manuscripts and Rare Books Department, Earl Gregg Swem Library, College of William and Mary, McV, Tr5.
8. *National Intelligencer,* May 29, 1837, LOC.
9. Gene M. Brack, *Mexico Views Manifest Destiny, 1821–1846: An Essay on the Origins of the Mexican War* (Albuquerque: University of New Mexico Press, 1975), 82–83; *Pensacola Gazette,* May 13, 1837, 3, col. 3.
10. Travel Account of RG. There are no records of any correspondence between Robert and Rose.
11. Letter from RG to JF, August 12, 1837, *Despatches,* volume 9, Roll 10.

Chapter 12: Life on K Street

1. Mary Greenhow Papers, MHS, MS. 534, 1.
2. Mary Greenhow was born September 9, 1819.
3. Mary Greenhow's List of Visits, Mary Greenhow Lee Papers, LOC.
4. The U.S. Census 1840 shows the Greenhows owned two slaves.
5. Mary Greenhow Papers, MHS, MS. 534, 22.
6. Benjamin Disraeli, *Venetia: The Works of Benjamin Disraeli, Earl of Beaconsfield,* volume 11 (New York: M. Walter Dunne, 1976, 1904), 212.
7. Mary Greenhow Papers, MHS, MS. 534, 3.
8. Ibid., 4.
9. Ibid.
10. Ibid., 7.
11. Ibid., 71.
12. Ibid., 42.

13. Ibid., 24.
14. Ibid., 13.
15. Ibid., 6–7.
16. Ibid., 9.
17. J. Fred Rippy, *Joel Poinsett, Versatile American* (New York: Greenwood Press, 1968), 171.
18. Mary Greenhow Papers, MHS, MS. 534, 12. The chiefs were actually speaking the Sioux language.
19. Rippy, *Joel Poinsett, Versatile American,* 185.
20. Mary Greenhow Papers, MHS, MS. 534, 21.
21. Ibid., 29.
22. Ibid., 21.
23. Ibid., 16.
24. Ibid.
25. Ibid., 17.
26. Ibid., 23.
27. Ibid., 17, 20, 27.
28. Ibid., 43.
29. Ibid., 20.
30. Recount of Estate Sales of RG, June 13, 1854, National Archives #3481 (Washington, D.C.).
31. Mary Greenhow Papers, MHS, MS. 534, 14.
32. Ibid., 27.
33. Ibid., 10.
34. Ibid., 37.
35. U.S. Census 1840.
36. *National Intelligencer,* September 28, 1836, LOC.
37. ROG European Diary, 1864–1865 (North Carolina State Archives, transcribed by H. G. Jones), 8–9.
38. Mary Greenhow Papers, MHS, MS. 534, 42.
39. Ibid., 47–48.
40. Letter from RG to JF, June 12, 1837, *Despatches,* volume 9.
41. Mary Greenhow Papers, MHS, MS. 534, 51.
42. Ibid.
43. Ibid., 56.
44. Ibid., 58.
45. Ibid., 68.
46. Ibid., 65.
47. Ibid., 62.
48. Sir Edward Bulwer-Lytton, *Leila: or, The Siege of Granada* (Philadelphia: J. J. Lippincott Co., 1888), 29–30.
49. In the transcribed version of Mary Greenhow's diary, Mary Ann married Dr. John Howard. The District of Columbia Marriage Licenses 1811–1858, compiled by Wesley E. Pippenger, show the marriage of John R. Rowand and Mary O'Neile [*sic.*] on March 24, 1838. On March 30, 1838, the *National Intelligencer* reported: "Married—at St. Patrick's Church, in this city on Tuesday evening, the 27th instant, by the Rev. J. P. Donellan, John Randolph Rowland, M.D. of Philadelphia, to Miss Mary O'Neile, of Montgomery County, Md."
50. Mary Greenhow Papers, MHS, MS. 534, 74.
51. Ibid., 77.
52. Ibid., 79.

Chapter 13: Reversal of Fortune

1. Baptismal Registry, St. Patrick's Church (Washington, D.C.), May 20, 1844, shows Gertrude was born August 21, 1838. Robert honored his friend and mentor Edward Livingston, who had brought him to State, by giving her the middle name Livingston.

2. Deed of Trust, Land Records of the District of Columbia, #7 W.B. 84, 1840–1841, 50 (RG and wife to Richard Smith, October 5, 1840). Robert Ellis, an archivist at the National Archives and Records Administration, who studied the documents, says that it appears Greenhow was behind on his mortgage payments and that the bank was going to take him to court.
3. *National Intelligencer,* July 1, 1840, 3, col. 6.
4. Mary Greenhow Lee Papers, LOC.
5. Will of Robert Greenhow Sr., July 15, 1840, Richmond Court House, Civil Court Records (Richmond, Va.); Sheila R. Phipps, *Genteel Rebel: The Life of Mary Greenhow Lee* (Baton Rouge: Louisiana State University Press, 2004), 56.
6. D.C. Recorder of Deeds, General Index Land Record #8, W.B. 104. 1843, Square 284 (RG to W. Orme and wife).
7. Land Records of the District of Columbia, W.B. 104, 31.
8. The Greenhows apparently rented the F Street house, as tax records don't show them owning any real estate in the city during that time.
9. Baptismal Registry, St. Patrick's Church (Washington, D.C.), May 20, 1844.
10. *National Intelligencer,* October 12, 1846, 1, col. 6; and June 26, 1847, 3, col. 5, LOC.
11. RG to JCC, April 30, 1849, John C. Calhoun Papers, Clemson University.
12. ROG, *My Imprisonment,* 59.
13. Speech by JCC to the U.S. Senate, February 6, 1837, reprinted in Andrew C. McLaughlin, *Readings in the History of the American Nation* (New York: D. Appleton & Co., 1914), 206–12.
14. Greenhow, *My Imprisonment,* 59.
15. Author interview with Donald A. Ritchie, Senate historian, July 8, 2003.
16. Corrigan, "Imaginary Cruelties?," 8.
17. Solomon Northup, *Twelve Years a Slave: Narrative of Solomon Northup, a Citizen of New-York, Kidnapped in Washington City in 1841, and Rescued in 1853* (Auburn: Derby & Miller, 1853), 38. Electronic text available at Documenting the American South website, University of North Carolina at Chapel Hill, docsouth.unc.edu/northup/northup.html.
18. Northup, *Twelve Years a Slave,* 43.
19. ROG European Diary, 82.
20. Bartlett, *John C. Calhoun,* 299.
21. "Robert Greenhow," Gale Literary Databases.
22. *The American Review: A Whig Journal of Politics, Literature, Art and Science* 2, no. 2 (August 1845), Critical Notices, 220. Cornell University Library Making of America website, cdl.library.cornell.edu/moa.
23. "Statement Concerning Secret Affairs Relating to the Mexican War," in Herr and Spence, eds., *The Letters of Jessie Benton Frémont,* 504–5. The young scholar was Josiah Royce, and his history was entitled *California: From the Conquest in 1846 to the Second Vigilance Committee in San Francisco* (Boston, New York: Houghton Mifflin, 1892).
24. "Statement Concerning Secret Affairs Relating to the Mexican War," in Herr and Spence, eds., *The Letters of Jessie Benton Frémont,* 504–5.
25. Britain was on the side of the Mexicans in trying to stop the U.S. acquisition of more territory, whether in Mexico (including Texas and California) or the Northwest (Oregon Territory). Robert's boss, Calhoun, favored annexation of Texas as a slave state, and Robert argued for uncontested U.S. control of the Oregon Territory to give the United States unbroken land from sea to shining sea.
26. ROG, *My Imprisonment,* 141–60.

Chapter 14: Explosion of the Peacemaker

1. Howard P. Nash Jr., "The *Princeton* Explosion," *American History Illustrated* 5, no. 5 (August 1969).
2. St. George L. Sioussat, ed., "The Accident Aboard the USS *Princeton,* February 28, 1844: A Contemporary Newsletter," *Pennsylvania History* (July 1937).

3. Description of cannon firing and ability are from Donald B. Webster Jr., "The Beauty and Chivalry of the United States Assembled," *American Heritage* 17, no. 1 (December 1965).

4. From the *Journal of Commerce*, February 28, 1844, reprinted in the *Liberator*, March 8, 1844.

5. Ellet, *The Court Circles of the Republic*, 355–56.

6. From the *Journal of Commerce*, February 28, 1844, reprinted in the *Liberator*, March 8, 1844.

7. Samuel John Bayard, *A Sketch of the Life of Com. Robert F. Stockton* (New York: Derby & Jackson, 1856).

8. Ellet, *The Court Circles of the Republic*, 355–56.

9. William A. DeGregorio and Connie Jo Dickerson, *The Complete Book of U.S. Presidents* (New York: Random House, 1997), 157. Slave's name from the *Journal of Commerce*, February 28, 1844, reprinted in the *Liberator*, March 8, 1844.

10. Lee M. Pearson, "Princeton and the Peacemaker," *Technology and Culture* 7, no. 2 (Spring 1966).

11. From the *Journal of Commerce*, February 28, 1844, reprinted in the *Liberator*, March 8, 1844.

12. *The Madisonian*, February 28, 1844, reprinted in the *Maine Farmer*, March 7, 1844; the *Liberator*, March 8, 1844, 3.

13. Webster, "The Beauty and Chivalry of the United States Assembled."

14. Lucia B. Cutts, ed., *Memoirs and Letters of Dolly [sic] Madison, Wife of James Madison, President of the United States, edited by her Grand-Niece* (Boston: Houghton Mifflin, 1886), 205.

15. Henry A. Wise, *Seven Decades of the Union* (Philadelphia: J. B. Lippincott & Co., 1872), 220.

16. Sioussat, "The Accident Aboard the USS *Princeton*."

17. *National Intelligencer*, March 4, 1844, LOC.

18. Maxcy, a well-known political figure and close friend of Calhoun, would nonetheless be represented in the funeral procession through the capital.

19. *National Intelligencer*, March 4, 1844, LOC.

20. Sioussat, "The Accident Aboard the USS *Princeton*."

21. Ibid.

22. *National Intelligencer*, March 4, 1844, LOC.

23. Nash, "The *Princeton* Explosion."

24. Wise, *Seven Decades of the Union*, 211–23.

25. Bartlett, *John C. Calhoun*, 306–7.

26. Ibid., 308.

27. Ibid., 323–24.

28. Gaither and Addison, *Washington Directory and National Register for 1846* (Washington, D.C.: John T. Towers, 1846), 28. City Museum, Washington, D.C.

Chapter 15: Pursuit of the *Pearl*

1. RG to JB, December 11, 1846, James Buchanan Papers, Roll 10, HSP and National Archives (College Park, Md.).

2. Bartlett, *John C. Calhoun*, 348.

3. Ibid., 348–49.

4. RG to JB, March 14, 1848, James Buchanan Papers, Roll 14, HSP and National Archives (College Park, Md.).

5. RG to the Virginia Historical Society, May 3, 1848, VHS, Mss 2:G 8386561-2. Greenhow had discovered and translated a Spanish document to support his case, noting the Spanish explored the whole southeastern coast of North America and "even attempted to form a settlement near the mouth of the great bay."

6. Walter C. Clephane, "The Local Aspect of Slavery in the District of Columbia," *Columbia Historical Society Records* 3 (1900), 247–48; Mary Kay Ricks, "A Passage to Freedom," *The Washington Post Magazine*, February 17, 2002.

7. Paul Jennings, "A Colored Man's Reminiscences of James Madison" (1865), accessible at www.whitehousehistory.org/08/subs/08_b01.html.

8. Daniel Drayton, *Personal Memoir of Daniel Drayton, for Four Years and Four Months a Prisoner*

(for Charity's Sake) in Washington Jail, Including a Narrative of Voyage and Capture of the Schooner Pearl, 2nd ed. (New York: American & Foreign Anti-Slavery Society, 1855).
9. Ricks, "A Passage to Freedom."
10. RG to Robert Evans, September 20, 1848, D.C. Recorder of Deeds.
11. Keith Melder, ed., City of Magnificent Intentions: A History of the District of Columbia (Washington, D.C.: D.C. History Curriculum Project, 1983), 97.

Chapter 16: End of an Era

1. ROG to JCC, April 3, 1849, John C. Calhoun Papers, Clemson University.
2. "Died on Sunday evening, April 29, Morgan Lewis, the only son of Robert and Rose Greenhow, age 13 months," Washington Union, May 1, 1849, LOC.
3. RG to JCC, April 30, 1849, John C. Calhoun Papers, Clemson University.
4. RG to JCC, July 6, 1849, John C. Calhoun Papers, Clemson University.
5. The infant died. National Intelligencer, October 11, 1849, 3, col. 6, LOC.
6. RG to JCC, July 6, 1849, John C. Calhoun Papers, Clemson University.
7. RG to JCC, August 12, 1849, John C. Calhoun Papers, Clemson University.
8. ROG to JCC, August 29, 1849, John C. Calhoun Papers, Clemson University.
9. RG to JCC, August 12, 1849, John C. Calhoun Papers, Clemson University.
10. ROG to JCC, August 29, 1849, John C. Calhoun Papers, Clemson University.
11. National Intelligencer, October 11, 1849, 3, col. 6, LOC.
12. Ibid., February 20, 1850, 3, col. 3.
13. Robert Byrd, The Senate, 1889–1989: Addresses on the History of the United States Senate, volume 1 (Washington, D.C.: U.S. Government Printing Office, 1989–1994), 189. See also Robert F. Dalzell Jr., Daniel Webster and the Trial of American Nationalism 1843–1852 (Boston: Houghton Mifflin Co., 1973), 178–79.
14. ROG, My Imprisonment, 59; Bartlett, John C. Calhoun, 370.
15. Isaac Bassett Papers, U.S. Senate, Office of the Curator.
16. Bartlett, John C. Calhoun, 371–72; Dalzell, Daniel Webster, 174–75.
17. Byrd, The Senate, 1889–1989, 194; Bartlett, John C. Calhoun, 374.
18. ROG, My Imprisonment, 59.
19. Ibid., 212.
20. Ibid., 60.

Chapter 17: Leaving Washington

1. Congressional Globe, April 17, 1850, 762–64.
2. Herr, Jessie Benton Frémont, 217.
3. State Department Index of Commissioned Employees, National Archives (College Park, Md.).
4. Article reprinted in Telegraph and Democratic Review (Alton, Ill.), May 10, 1850, CHS.
5. John M. Clayton to RG, April 22, 1850, Special Missions, National Archives (College Park, Md.), volume 1, 306.
6. Ibid.
7. Nash R. Burger, Confederate Spy: Rose O'Neale Greenhow (New York: Franklin Watts, 1967), 30. This could not be confirmed, but ship records show the Greenhows did not travel with their children, and Burger's report that they remained with their aunt in Washington is probably correct.
8. The Rasmussen San Francisco Ship Passenger List (MSM) shows "R. Greenhow and lady" on one leg of the trip.
9. New York Shipping & Commercial List, June 5, 1850. See also John Osborne, Guide to the West Indies, Madeira, Mexico, Northern South-America, &c., &c., Comp. from Documents Specially Furnished by the Agents of the Royal Mail Steam Packet Company, the Board of Trade, and Other Authentic Sources [. . .] (London: Royal Mail Steam Packet Co., 1845), 105, MSM.

10. Duncan Haws, *Merchant Fleets: Royal Mail & Nelson Lines* (Brighton, Eng.: Planet Press Ltd., 1982), 26, 28. G. W. Blunt White Library, Mystic Seaport, Mystic, Conn.

11. Osborne, *Guide to the West Indies,* 105. MSM.

12. Virtual Reality Moon Phase Pictures, tycho.usno.navy.mil/vphase.html.

13. Osborne, *Guide to the West Indies,* 106. MSM.

14. T. A. Bushell, *Royal Mail: A Centenary History of the Royal Mail Line 1839–1939* (London: Trade & Travel Publications, 1939), 34. MSM.

15. John Haskell Kemble, *The Panama Route, 1848–1869* (Berkeley, Los Angeles: University of California Press, 1943), 164.

16. Bushell, *Royal Mail,* 34.

17. Osborne, *Guide to the West Indies,* 109.

18. Description of the city from Frances Erskine Inglis (Mme. Calderon de la Barca), *Life in Mexico During a Residence of Two Years in That City* (New York: E. P. Dutton & Co., 1931), 27, 34, 35. Originally published in 1843. Inglis lived in Mexico from December 1839 to January 1842.

19. Osborne, *Guide to the West Indies,* 114.

20. Edward Bosqui, quoted in Kenneth M. Johnson, *José Yves Limantour v. the United States* (Los Angeles: Dawson's Book Shop, 1961), 74. CHS.

21. "Limantour," *Overland Monthly* 2, no. 2 (February 1869), 154. CHS

22. United States District Court, Northern District of California, *United States v. José Y. Limantour,* n.p., n.d., 442–43, CHS.

23. E. E. Albertson, "The Most Stupendous Fraud," *National Motorist for May–June 1953,* 6, in José Yves Limantour Biography Collection, CHS. U.S. attorney general Black estimated in 1860 that Limantour's claims were worth $150 million.

24. United States District Court, *United States v. José Y. Limantour,* 445, CHS.

25. Ibid., 445.

26. Ibid., 443.

27. "Special Agents of the Department of State 1794–1906," from RG, in Mobile Bay. Erroneously dated October 9; at Mexico City, June, August 12; National Archives (College Park, Md.), October 23, microfilm, Roll 37, Roll 9, volume 18.

28. Inglis, *Life in Mexico,* 34.

29. Rasmussen, San Francisco Ship Passenger Lists, 1966, San Francisco Historic Records, MSM. Edwin L. Dunbaugh et al., *William H. Webb: Shipbuilder* (Glen Cove, N.Y.: Webb Institute of Naval Architecture, 1989), 171–72.

30. Rasmussen, San Francisco Ship Passenger Lists, 1966, San Francisco Historic Records, MSM. See also Kemble, *The Panama Route,* 164.

31. Ibid.

32. Herr, *Jessie Benton Frémont,* 33, 219.

33. Rasmussen, San Francisco Ship Passenger Lists, 1966, San Francisco Historic Records, MSM.

Chapter 18: San Francisco: City of Dreams

1. Doris Muscatine, *Old San Francisco: A Biography of a City* (New York: G. P. Putnam's Sons, 1975), 110.

2. Ibid., 129, 225.

3. Ibid., 242.

4. Ibid., 106.

5. Ibid., 123.

6. Ibid.

7. Herr and Spence, eds., *The Letters of Jessie Benton Frémont,* 33, 51.

8. ROG, *My Imprisonment,* 147.

9. T. A. Barry and B. A. Patten, *Men and Memories of San Francisco in the Spring of '50* (San Francisco: A. L. Bancroft & Co., 1873), 72. CHS.

10. Ibid.

11. Herr, *Jessie Benton Frémont,* 221.
12. Frank Marryat, *Mountains and Molehills, or Recollections of a Burnt Journal* (London: Longman, Brown, Green, 1855).
13. Kemble, *The Panama Route,* 166; Herr, *Jessie Benton Frémont,* 188–89.
14. David Rumsey Map Collection, Cartography Associates (e-mail address www.davidrumsey.com).
15. Kemble, *The Panama Route,* 231.
16. *New York Herald,* October 19, 1851, MSM.
17. ROG to John Y. Mason, Washington, November 12, (probably 1851), VHS, Mss 1:M3816a 1294.
18. Baker, *James Buchanan,* 55–56.
19. ROG to Peter G. Washington, Maupin-Washington Papers, College of William and Mary Special Collection, Williamsburg, Va., 65, M44, Box 1, Folder 4.
20. JB to ROG, August 28, 1852, Records of Department of State, National Archives (College Park, Md.).
21. Rasmussen San Francisco Ship Passenger Lists, June 17, 1852, to January 6, 1853, 83–84, San Francisco Historic Records, MSM.
22. *Quarterly of the California Historical Society* 1, no. 1 (July 1922), 9. The society was incorporated April 29, 1852.
23. Hubert H. Bancroft, *The Works of Hubert Howe Bancroft,* volume 23: *History of California, Vol. VI 1848–1859* (San Francisco: The History Company, 1888), chapter 20, "Mexican Land Titles," 542. Reprinted at Santa Barbara by Wallace Hebberd in 1970. See footnote 12, CHS.
24. RG to Caleb Cushing, December 15, 1853, quoted in Beverly E. Bastian, "Henry Wager Halleck, The *Californios,* and the Clash of Legal Cultures," *California History* 72, no. 4 (Winter 1993–94), 317–18. Quote originally from California Attorney General's Office, Letters Received, Record Group 60, Box 6, Folder 4, National Archives (College Park, Md.).
25. Johnson, *José Yves Limantour vs. the United States,* 29, CHS.
26. Ibid., 35.
27. Limantour himself had been called to France in late 1850 and did not appear in San Francisco until November 1852. United States District Court, *United States v. José Y. Limantour,* 445, CHS.
28. JB to ROG, March 21, 1853, Records of Department of State, National Archives (College Park, Md.).
29. "The Liedesdorff-Folson Estate," *California History* 2, no. 2 (June 1928), 111. CHS.
30. "Montgomery Block," *San Francisco City Directory, 1854,* San Francisco Public Library.
31. Recount of Estate Sales of RG, June 13, 1854, National Archives #3481 (Washington, D.C.).
32. Records of the Convent du Sacré Coeur, Maryvonne Duclaux e-mail, October 3, 2003.
33. *Daily Alta California,* March 28, 1854, 2, col. 1, CHS.
34. Ibid.
35. Baltimore *Sun,* April 27, 1854, LOC.
36. *Daily Globe,* April 28, 1854, LOC.
37. Amy Friedlander, *Natural Monopoly and Universal Service: Telephones and Telegraphs in the U.S. Communications Infrastructure, 1837–1940* (Reston, Va.: Corporation for National Research Initiatives, 1995), 11–17.
38. A Swem librarian found this letter in a volume of Greenhow's book, *The History of Oregon and California and the Other Territories on the West Coast of North America* (1846), located in Earl Gregg Swem Library, College of William and Mary (Williamsburg, Va.).

Chapter 19: Widow

1. Richard Allan Baker, *The Senate of the United States: A Bicentennial History* (Malabar, Fla.: Robert E. Krieger Publishing Co., 1988), 49. See also Philip Shriver Klein, *President James Buchanan: A Biography* (University Park: Pennsylvania State University Press, 1962), 286–90.
2. "Continuation of the Annals of San Francisco, June 1854," *California Historical Society Quarterly* 15, no. 1 (1936), 172.

3. A Century of Lawmaking for a New Nation: U.S. Congressional Documents and Debates, Thirty-third Congress, Sess. 1, Ch. 60, 1854.
4. ROG to JB, December 23, 1855, James Buchanan Papers, HSP, Roll 25.
5. Thomas Fromcek, ed., *The City of Washington: An Illustrated History* (New York: Alfred A. Knopf, 1977), 165.
6. Barbee Papers, Box 7, 398, Georgetown University Library (Washington, D.C.).
7. Leech, *Reveille in Washington*, 8.
8. Baker, *James Buchanan*, 22.
9. Ibid., 67.
10. ROG to JB, December 23, 1855, James Buchanan Papers, HSP, Roll 25.
11. JB to ROG, November 23, 1855, Records of Department of State, National Archives (College Park, Md.).
12. Lomax, *Leaves from an Old Washington Diary*, 47–48.
13. ROG to JB, December 23, 1855, James Buchanan Papers, HSP, Roll 25.
14. Keyes, *Fifty Years' Observation of Men and Events*, 330–31.
15. Baker, *James Buchanan*, 68.
16. ROG to JB, December 23, 1855, James Buchanan Papers, HSP, Roll 25.
17. Herr, *Jessie Benton Frémont*, 238–41.
18. ROG to JB, February 11, 1856, James Buchanan Papers, HSP, Roll 25.
19. ROG to JB, June 5, 1856, James Buchanan Papers, HSP, Roll 26.
20. Ibid.
21. ROG to JB, September 27, 1856, James Buchanan Papers, HSP, Roll 29.
22. *New York Herald*, September 28, 1856, 1, MSM.
23. ROG to JB, September 27, 1856, James Buchanan Papers, HSP, Roll 29.
24. Michael J. Birkner, ed., *James Buchanan and the Political Crisis of the 1850s* (Selinsgrove, Pa.: Susquehanna University Press, 1996), 39.
25. ROG to JB, November 11, 1856, James Buchanan Papers, HSP, Roll 30.

Chapter 20: A Lady of Influence

1. ROG to JB, November 30, 1856, James Buchanan Papers, HSP, Roll 30.
2. Ibid.
3. Baker, *James Buchanan*, 27.
4. Ibid., 26.
5. Klein, *President James Buchanan*, 263.
6. Ibid., 267.
7. ROG, *My Imprisonment*, 76. Buchanan was never critically ill. Either Rose was exaggerating or thought it was worse than it was.
8. Ibid.
9. Notation by Buchanan historian Jean H. Baker, May 14, 2004.
10. Lomax, *Leaves from an Old Washington Diary*, 66.
11. Clay-Clopton, *A Belle of the Fifties*, 74.
12. James Buchanan Inaugural Address, March 4, 1857, accessible at www.bartleby.com/124/pres30.html.
13. Klein, *President James Buchanan*, 271.
14. Lillie to Eugene B. Cook, March 4, 1857, quoted in Klein, *President James Buchanan*, 272.
15. Taney, forever remembered for his infamous decision in the Dred Scott case, had not always defended slavery. In 1818, he successfully defended an abolitionist Methodist minister against charges of inciting slaves to riot. In his closing argument, he discussed "the evil of slavery" and called it "a blot on our national character," insisting that "every real lover of freedom confidently hopes that it will effectively, though it must be gradually, be wiped away." *Journal of the Historical Society of Frederick County, Maryland* (Spring 2004), 21. During the Civil War, Taney

staunchly defended the right of habeas corpus when the military was locking up citizens without charge or trial. Lincoln ignored his rulings.

16. *Scott v. Sanford* 19 How. (60 v.s.) 393 (1857) Justices McLean and Curtis dissented.
17. Clay-Clopton, *A Belle of the Fifties,* 35–36.
18. Baker, *James Buchanan,* 88–89.
19. Senator William M. Gwin, Rose's friend and a key figure in California and Washington at the time, said in his memoirs that "the spread of the wings of the eagle on each differed from an eighth to a sixteenth of an inch, and it was demonstrated that the seal on the Limantour grants was counterfeit." "Memoirs of Hon. William M. Gwin," *California History* 19 (June 1940), 163.
20. ROG to JYL, May 17, 1857, Limantour Papers, University of California Bancroft Library (Berkeley, Calif.).
21. United States District Court, *United States v. José Y. Limantour,* 159, CHS.
22. Ibid., 154–58.
23. Johnson, *José Yves Limantour vs. the United States,* 73.
24. ROG to JYL, December 4, 1857, Limantour Papers, University of California Bancroft Library (Berkeley, Calif.).
25. Johnson, *José Yves Limantour vs. the United States,* 68. The legal historian added that Judge Hoffman "found fraud in every area suggested by the United States. . . . All of the documentary evidence on the part of Limantour was found to be false and the majority of the witnesses to be perjurers."
26. Johnson, *José Yves Limantour vs. the United States,* 74.
27. ROG to JYL, January 25, 1859, Limantour Papers, University of California Bancroft Library (Berkeley, Calif.).

Chapter 21: Downfall

1. Undated Letters, Seized Correspondence of ROG, RG 59, National Archives (College Park, Md.). Classified as *"supposed* to have been written to Rose Greenhow by Henry Wilson, U.S. Senator from Massachusetts."
2. Beauregard, "The First Battle of Bull Run."
3. Morris, *Memories.*
4. Pinkerton, *Spy of the Rebellion,* 252. His memoir, a lively defense of his wartime years, was produced largely from memory and published in 1883. The account contains numerous inaccuracies and frequently relates conversations at which he wasn't present. In key respects, however, his description of his investigation and arrest of Rose Greenhow dovetails with her own.
5. Ibid., 268, 269; Brigadier General Porter from E. J. Allen (Pinkerton), November 1861, *War of the Rebellion,* series 2, volume 2, 566–69.
6. Seized Correspondence of ROG, RG 59, National Archives (College Park, Md.). Wilson remained in the Senate and at the head of the military committee throughout the war and later was elected vice president.
7. ROG, *My Imprisonment,* 52–54.
8. Ibid., 53–54.
9. Ibid., 55–56.
10. Julia Taft Bayne, *Tad Lincoln's Father* (Lincoln: University of Nebraska Press, 2001), 62.
11. Seized Correspondence of ROG, RG 59, National Archives (College Park, Md.).
12. ROG, *My Imprisonment,* 57.
13. Ibid., 58.
14. Lomax, *Leaves from an Old Washington Diary,* 168.
15. ROG, *My Imprisonment,* 61.
16. Ibid., 70.
17. Ibid., 62.
18. Ibid., 64.
19. Ibid., 69.

20. Unidentified news clipping, November 29, 1861, M. J. Solomon Scrapbook, Rose O'Neal Greenhow Papers, Digital Scriptorium Special Collections Library, Duke University, accessible at scriptorium.lib.duke.edu/greenhow.

21. *National Intelligencer*, August 26, 1861, 3, col. 3, LOC.

22. *San Francisco Daily Evening Bulletin*, September 17, 1861, 1, col. 3, CHS.

23. Mary Boykin Chesnut, *A Diary from Dixie* (Boston: Houghton Mifflin Company, 1905), 121.

24. Ibid., 124. From February 1861 to July 1865, Mary Chesnut kept a series of diaries filled with astute observations about the leading figures of Richmond society—Jefferson Davis, his cabinet, the military, and their families. Writing with intelligence, wit, and a keen sense of irony, she painted a vivid portrait of the Confederacy during the war.

25. Bayne, *Tad Lincoln's Father*, 60–61.

26. Seized Correspondence of ROG, RG 59, National Archives (College Park, Md.).

27. ROG, *My Imprisonment*, 68.

28. Ibid., 86.

29. *The New York Times*, September 28, 1861.

30. ROG, *My Imprisonment*, 69–70.

31. Ibid., 71–72.

32. Morris, *Memories*.

Chapter 22: Fort Greenhow

1. ROG, *My Imprisonment*, 72. Under President Lincoln's order putting Washington under martial law, General Porter had absolute authority over prisons and law enforcement.

2. Ibid., 77.

3. Ibid., 76–77.

4. Ibid., 78–79.

5. Ibid., 81.

6. Ibid.

7. Ibid., 96.

8. Ibid., 88–89.

9. *Wilmington Journal*, February 26, 1862. Article courtesy of Wilmington historian Robert Cook. New Hanover County Library microfilm, Wilmington, N.C.

10. Ibid.

11. Ibid.

12. ROG *My Imprisonment*, 90.

13. Ibid., 110.

14. Ibid., 92.

15. Ibid.

16. Ibid., 94.

17. Ibid., 101.

18. *War of the Rebellion*, series 2, volume 2, 561.

19. ROG, *My Imprisonment*, 102.

20. Roster of Evidence, Proceedings of the Commission Relating to State Prisoners, RG 59 E962, Records of Department of State, National Archives (College Park, Md.).

21. Letter from E. J. Allen to Brigadier General A. Porter, U.S. Army, Provost Marshal, November 11, 1861, *War of the Rebellion*, series 2, volume 2, 135.

22. ROG, *My Imprisonment*, 104.

23. Ibid., 107.

24. Ibid., 136.

25. *The New York Times*, November 5, 1861.

26. Louis A. Sigaud, "Mrs. Greenhow and the Rebel Spy Ring," *Maryland Historical Magazine* (September 1946), 185, MHS.

27. ROG, *My Imprisonment*, 124.

28. M. J. Solomon Scrapbook, Duke University Special Collections.
29. Chesnut, *A Diary from Dixie,* 169.
30. ROG, *My Imprisonment,* 164.
31. Unidentified news clipping, November 29, 1861, M. J. Solomon Scrapbook, Rose O'Neal Green-how Papers, Digital Scriptorium Special Collections Library, Duke University.
32. *War of the Rebellion,* series 2, volume 2, 567.
33. Ibid., 572.
34. ROG, *My Imprisonment,* 167.
35. Letter from Jordan to Beauregard on December 28, 1861, containing Rose's letter of December 26, 1861, *War of the Rebellion,* series 1, volume 5 (West Virginia), 1019, 1038.
36. Ibid., 1038.
37. ROG, *My Imprisonment,* 167.
38. Ibid., 207.
39. Ibid., 179–89.
40. *Frank Leslie's Illustrated Newspaper,* January 18, 1862. LOC.
41. *Harper's Weekly,* January 18, 1862. LOC.
42. Baxley to Dr. Septimus Brown, March 14, 1862, *War of the Rebellion,* series 2, volume 2 (West Virginia), 1319–20.
43. ROG, *My Imprisonment,* 203.
44. Ibid., 204; *The New York Times,* January 22, 1862.

Chapter 23: The Old Capitol Prison

1. ROG, *My Imprisonment,* 205.
2. Leech, *Reveille in Washington,* 147.
3. ROG, *My Imprisonment,* 207.
4. Leech, *Reveille in Washington,* 141.
5. ROG, *My Imprisonment,* 207.
6. Dr. James I. Robertson Jr., "Prison for the Capital City," *UDC Magazine* (August 1990), 18–19, City Museum (Washington, D.C.).
7. ROG, *My Imprisonment,* 213–14.
8. Ibid., 215.
9. *War of the Rebellion,* series 2, volume 2, 575.
10. Robertson, "Prison for the Capital City," 18–19.
11. Ibid.
12. Baxley to Dr. Septimus Brown, March 14, 1862, *War of the Rebellion,* series 2, volume 2 (West Virginia), 1319–20.
13. ROG, *My Imprisonment,* 291.
14. Leech, *Reveille in Washington,* 142.
15. Ibid., 149.
16. ROG, *My Imprisonment,* 216.
17. Rose quoted several daily entries from what she described as her journal in her memoir, *My Imprisonment and the First Year of Abolition Rule at Washington,* but the journal itself was never published, and the original has been lost.
18. William Gilmore Beymore, *On Hazardous Service: Scouts and Spies of the North and South* (New York: Harper & Brothers, 1912), 202–3.
19. Ibid.
20. ROG, *My Imprisonment,* 216–17.
21. William Coffin Reiff, "A Federal Prison Guard," *Confederate Veteran* 19 (1911), 526, reprinted at freepages.military.rootsweb.com/~pa91/cc23001.html.
22. ROG, *My Imprisonment,* 216.
23. Ibid., 221–22.
24. Ibid., 222.

25. Ibid., 223.
26. Ibid., 224.
27. Ibid., 220.
28. Ibid., 230.
29. Ibid.
30. Ibid., 216–20.
31. Foote, *The Civil War,* 252.
32. ROG, *My Imprisonment,* 201–2.
33. Seale, *The President's House,* 384.
34. ROG, *My Imprisonment,* 238; "Redecoration and Willie's Death," 2004, Mr. Lincoln's White House, accessible at www.mrlincolnswhitehouse.org/templates/display.search.cfm?ID=208.
35. ROG, *My Imprisonment,* 243.
36. Ibid., 257.
37. Ibid., 251.

Chapter 24: The Commission

1. Rose apparently had never met Pierrepont, misidentifying the New Yorker in her memoirs as "Governor Fairfield."
2. ROG, *My Imprisonment,* 261. Rose undoubtedly knew Dix's own love of flag and country. While secretary of the Treasury just before the outbreak of war, Dix, a navy veteran of the War of 1812 whose father had died in battle, got word that Southern sympathizers might try to seize one of his department's revenue cutters in the port of New Orleans. "If anyone attempts to haul down the American flag, shoot him on the spot," Dix ordered. The message made him famous.
3. ROG, *My Imprisonment,* 262.
4. Ibid., 260–63.
5. Ibid., 263.
6. James M. McPherson e-mail to author, February 16, 2004.
7. "Suspected and Disloyal Persons," *War of the Rebellion,* series 2, volume 2, 271.
8. ROG, *My Imprisonment,* 268.
9. Ibid., 30.
10. Clay-Clopton, *Belle of the Fifties,* 126–37.
11. Proceeding of the Commission Relating to State Prisoners, Records of Department of State, RG 59, E962, National Archives (College Park, Md.); ROG, *My Imprisonment,* 269–70.
12. ROG, *My Imprisonment,* 270.
13. Proceeding of the Commission Relating to State Prisoners, Records of Department of State, RG 59, E962, National Archives (College Park, Md.).
14. ROG, *My Imprisonment,* 270.
15. Ibid. The documents are now held in a file of seized correspondence of ROG at the National Archives (College Park, Md.).
16. The entire court scene was written directly from the Proceeding of the Commission Relating to State Prisoners, Records of State Department, RG 59, E962, National Archives (College Park, Md.); ROG, *My Imprisonment,* 269–70.
17. Rose spelled her niece's nickname "Adie." The commission transcript, which spelled it "Addie," has been changed to conform.
18. Proceeding of the Commission Relating to State Prisoners, Records of Department of State, RG 59, E962, National Archives (College Park, Md.).
19. Rose certainly took great satisfaction when Confederate general Thomas J. "Stonewall" Jackson gave Frémont's forces a drubbing in the Shenandoah Valley two months later and the Pathfinder was relieved of command for a third and final time.
20. Proceeding of the Commission Relating to State Prisoners, Records of Department of State, RG 59, E962, National Archives (College Park, Md.).
21. Ibid.

Chapter 25: A Martyr's Joy

1. ROG, *My Imprisonment*, 277.
2. Ibid., 276.
3. Ibid., 277.
4. *National Intelligencer,* March 31, 1862, 3, col. 2, LOC.
5. ROG, *My Imprisonment*, 277.
6. Ibid., 277–81.
7. In her memoir, Rose confused the date with the fatal shooting a few weeks later of another prisoner who was shot trying to escape.
8. Dix and Pierrepont wrote to Brigadier General James S. Wadsworth on April 1, 1862, telling him to "convey Mrs. Rose O'N. Greenhow [and other prisoners] . . . beyond the lines of the U.S. forces into the State of Virginia and release them upon them giving their written parole of honor that they will not return north of the Potomac River during the present hostilities without permission of the Secretary of War." *War of the Rebellion,* series 2, volume 2, 577.
9. ROG, *My Imprisonment*, 282–83.
10. Ibid., 284.
11. *New York Herald,* April 15, 1862, 6, cols. 5–6, LOC.
12. ROG, *My Imprisonment*, 285.
13. Undated letter to "Mon Ami," Seized Correspondence of ROG, RG 59, National Archives (College Park, Md.).
14. ROG, *My Imprisonment*, 292.
15. "The Old Capitol Prison and Its Inmates," *The New York Times,* April 15, 1862.
16. ROG, *My Imprisonment*, 298–99.
17. Pinkerton, *The Spy of the Rebellion*, 546–48.
18. ROG, *My Imprisonment*, 302.
19. Ibid.
20. Bryan was eventually released, returned to combat, and won a citation for extraordinary courage and daring, sinking four Union ships with underwater explosives. Sensitive to the conditions of prisoners of war, he reported to superiors the "shocking" conditions he found among Negro POWs in a Confederate prison in Charleston. Bryan died of yellow fever in November 1864. *War of the Rebellion,* series 2, volume 6, 843; series 1, volume 42, 1220.
21. ROG, *My Imprisonment*, 303–4.
22. Ibid., 298–310.
23. Ibid., 331.
24. Ibid., 311–13.
25. Ibid., 315.

Chapter 26: Crossing the Line

1. Passano Historic Buildings File, H. Furlong Baldwin Library, MHS; *War of the Rebellion,* series 1, volume 2, 140–41.
2. ROG, *My Imprisonment*, 317.
3. Furgurson, *Ashes of Glory,* 136–38.
4. *The New York Times,* June 2, 1862, 1.
5. *War of the Rebellion,* series 2, volume 2, 577.
6. ROG, *My Imprisonment*, 319.
7. Ibid., 319–20. The reference to the patrol boat from the *Monitor* comes from *The Washington Post,* January 12, 1913. See also William Gilmore Beymer's *Famous Scouts and Spies of the Civil War* (Alexandria, Va.: Time-Life Books, 1985). Petersburg National Battlefield historian James H. Blankenship Jr. pinpoints City Point in Federal hands (e-mail to author, May 17, 2004).
8. ROG, *My Imprisonment*, 320–21.

9. The Confederacy did not adopt the Battle Flag of Northern Virginia with its Southern Cross on a field of white until May 1863. See "Flags of the Confederate States of America," Fact Index website, www.fact-index.com/f/fl/flags_of_the_confederate_states_of_america.html.

10. ROG, *My Imprisonment*, 321.

11. *Richmond Whig*, June 5, 1862, Letters of the Civil War website.

12. ROG, *My Imprisonment*, 321.

13. E-mail from James H. Blankenship Jr., historian, Petersburg National Battlefield, May 17, 2004.

14. *Washington Evening Star*, June 7, 1862, LOC.

15. *Daily Dispatch*, June 5, 1862, Civil War Richmond website.

16. ROG, *My Imprisonment*, 322.

17. JD to Varina Davis, June 13, 1862, Jefferson Davis Papers, volume 8, 1862.

18. ROG, *My Imprisonment*, 320–22.

Chapter 27: Richmond: A Dreadful Year

1. *Richmond Daily Dispatch*, June 5, 1862, Civil War Richmond website.

2. *Richmond Whig*, June 5, 1862, Civil War Richmond website.

3. *Richmond Examiner*, July 25, 1862, Civil War Richmond website.

4. Furgurson, *Ashes of Glory*, 150–53.

5. Virginius Dabney, *Richmond: The Story of a City* (New York: Doubleday & Co., 1976), 177.

6. Chesnut, *A Diary from Dixie*, 311.

7. JD to Varina Davis, June 12, 1862, and June 19, 1862, Jefferson Davis Papers, volume 8.

8. *Richmond Enquirer*, June 24, 1862, Civil War Richmond website.

9. Furgurson, *Ashes of Glory*, 187.

10. James H. Dorman, "Thespis in Dixie," *Virginia Cavalcade* (Summer 1978).

11. Furgurson, *Ashes of Glory*, 160–61.

12. Elizabeth R. Varon, *Southern Lady, Yankee Spy: The True Story of Elizabeth Van Lew* (New York: Oxford University Press, 2003), 33–34.

13. *Richmond Enquirer*, June 16, 1863, Civil War Richmond website.

14. Author interview with Coal Culver, Henrico County master gardener, April 2, 2004.

15. Henri Garidel, *Exile in Richmond: The Confederate Journal of Henri Garidel* (Charlottesville, London: University Press of Virginia, 2001), 54.

16. "Southern Women's History Collection," MOC.

17. Lucy Bagby Memoir, Bagley Family Papers, 1824–1960, VHS.

18. Varon, *Southern Lady, Yankee Spy*, 79.

19. James M. McPherson, *Antietam: The Battle That Changed the Course of the Civil War* (New York: Oxford University Press, 2002), 47.

20. Newspaper article pasted into the Lucy Bagby Memoir, Bagby Family Papers, 1824–1960, VHS.

21. Furgurson, *Ashes of Glory*, 150. Perspective on the Seven Days' Battle also comes from Gary W. Gallagher, ed., *The Richmond Campaign of 1862: The Peninsula and the Seven Days* (Chapel Hill: University of North Carolina Press, 2000), chapter 1.

22. James M. McPherson, *Battle Cry of Freedom: The Era of the Civil War* (New York: Oxford University Press, 1988), 490–91.

23. *Official Records of the Union and Confederate Navies*, series 2, vol. 3, 504.

24. Garidel, *Exile in Richmond*, 55.

25. Holt to Stanton, May 25, 1863, *War of the Rebellion*, series 2, volume 5, 699.

26. Leech, *Reveille in Washington*, 275.

27. ROG to Alexander, August 1, 1862, Eleanor S. Brockenbrough Library, MOC.

28. Alexander to Mrs. DeRenne, June 11, 1886, Eleanor S. Brockenbrough Library, MOC.

29. Furgurson, *Ashes of Glory*, 169.

30. Leech, *Reveille in Washington*, 248–50.

31. James M. McPherson, *Abraham Lincoln and the Second American Revolution* (New York: Oxford University Press, 1990), 35.

32. Ibid.
33. Ibid., 85.
34. *Richmond Enquirer*, January 23, 1863, 2, Civil War Richmond website.
35. Dabney, *Richmond: The Story of a City*, 178, 180.
36. *Richmond Sentinel*, March 3, 1863, Civil War Richmond website.
37. *Richmond Whig*, September 4, 1861, Civil War Richmond website. Dean Knight, MOC.
38. Varina Davis, *Jefferson Davis, Ex-President of the Confederate States of America: A Memoir by His Wife* (New York: Belford Co. Publishers, 1890), 198–99.
39. *National Tribune*, August 17, 1899, Civil War Richmond website.
40. Varon, *Southern Lady, Yankee Spy*, 102–4.
41. *Richmond Examiner*, April 4, 1863, Civil War Richmond website.
42. From *History of the 124th Regiment of New York State Volunteers: The Orange Blossom Regiment* by Lieutenant Colonel Charles H. Weygant (Originally published in 1877, unknown publisher; current reprint by Ironclad Publishing, Celina, Ohio, 2002), 56.
43. Lucy Bagby Memoir, Bagley Family Papers 1824–1960, VHS.
44. See, for instance, *Gettysburg*, PBS website, www.pbs.org/wnet/goingplaces2/civil_war/hilite1.html.

Chapter 28: "Stroke of Genius"

1. Carl Sandburg, *Abraham Lincoln: The War Years* (New York: Harcourt, Brace & Co., 1938), volume 1, 327.
2. James M. McPherson, e-mail to author, March 16, 2004.
3. Boteler appears to have been her principal contact at home during her foreign travels.
4. ROG to JD, July 16, 1863, Jefferson Davis Papers, Digital Scriptorium Special Collections Library, Duke University.
5. Ibid.
6. Ibid.
7. ROG to JD, July 19, 1863, Special Collections, Tulane University Library.
8. Stephen R. Wise, *Lifeline of the Confederacy: Blockade Running During the Civil War* (Columbia: University of South Carolina Press, 1988), 122.
9. ROG to [unknown], July 23, 1863, M. J. Solomon Scrapbook, Rose O'Neal Greenhow Papers, Digital Scriptorium Special Collections Library, Duke University.
10. ROG to JD, July 19, 1863, Special Collections, Tulane University Library.
11. ROG to JD, August 4, 1863, "Confederate Veteran," May 1932, William L. Clements Library, University of Michigan (Ann Arbor).
12. Wise, *Lifeline of the Confederacy*, 129–30.
13. ROG to JD, August 4, 1863, "Confederate Veteran," May 1932, William L. Clements Library, University of Michigan (Ann Arbor).

Chapter 29: Flight of the *Phantom*

1. Letter from Stephen R. Wise to author, May 20, 2004.
2. Wise, *Lifeline of the Confederacy*, 94–100.
3. ROG European Diary, 1.
4. Now known as Bald Head Island.
5. Thomas H. Dudley to Charles Francis Adams, March 24, 1863, National Archives (London), FO 881/2001.
6. James D. Bulloch to S. R. Mallory, August 4, 1862, *War of the Rebellion*, series 2, volume 2, 232–33. Mallory, then secretary of the navy, sent Bulloch to England in June 1861 to purchase military supplies and acquire ships for the Confederate fleet.
7. *Phantom* papers, Public Record Office, British National Archives, FO5/12415.
8. Rose or her informant mistook the *Pet* for the *Elizabeth*, which ran aground and was burned on

September 26, 1862. The *Pet* and the *Hebe* cleared Wilmington on August 6, 1863. Wise, *Lifeline of the Confederacy*, 138, 243, 304.

9. ROG European Diary, 2.

10. Fred Espenak, Planetary Systems Branch, NASA/Goddard Space Flight Center, communication with author.

11. Wise, *Lifeline of the Confederacy*, 243.

12. Richard W. Lawrence, branch head, Underwater Archaeology Branch, North Carolina Office of Archaeology, e-mail to author, May 28, 2004.

13. Acting Volunteer Lieutenant James Thathen to Acting Rear Admiral S. P. Lee, August 7, 1863, *Official Records of the Union and Confederate Navies in the War of the Rebellion*, series 1, volume 9, 150, accessible on Cornell University's Making of America website, at cdl.library.cornell .edu/moa/browse.monographs/ofre.html.

14. ROG European Diary, 3.

15. Acting Volunteer Lieutenant James Thathen to Acting Rear Admiral S. P. Lee, August 7, 1863, *Official Records*, series 1, volume 9, 150.

16. S. P. Lee to Secretary of the Navy Gideon Welles, August 7, 1863, *Official Records*, series 1, volume 9, 150.

17. ROG European Diary.

18. Wise, *Lifeline of the Confederacy*, 7.

19. Stephen R. Wise, e-mail to author, May 14, 2004.

20. Author interview with Ray Flowers, historic interpreter at Fort Fisher, Cape Fear River, March 2, 2004.

21. Lamb, *The Life and Times of Colonel William Lamb*, 165.

22. Thomas E. Taylor, *Running the Blockade* (Annapolis: Naval Institute Press, 1995), Introduction by Stephen R. Wise, xxii.

23. Wise, *Lifeline of the Confederacy*, 94–100.

24. "Captain Roberts," "Running the Blockade," *Civil War Times Illustrated* 6 (December 1967), 10–16.

25. Lamb, *The Life and Times of Colonel William Lamb*, 75, 164.

26. "Captain Roberts," "Running the Blockade," 10–16.

27. ROG European Diary, 4.

28. Ibid.; Farewell Presidential Address by Andrew Jackson, March 4, 1837, accessible at www.search.eb.com/elections/pri/Q00050.html. Jackson's exact words were "Eternal vigilance by the people is the price of liberty."

29. Wise, *Lifeline of the Confederacy*, 95.

30. ROG European Diary, 6–7.

31. ROG to Boteler, August 13, 1863, and December 10, 1863, M. J. Solomon Scrapbook, Rose O'Neal Greenhow Papers, Digital Scriptorium Special Collections Library, Duke University; Tidwell, *April '65: Confederate Covert Action in the American Civil War*, 45.

32. ROG European Diary, 19–20.

33. Ibid., 9.

34. U.S. Naval History Division, *Civil War Naval Chronology, 1861–1865* (Washington, D.C.: Government Printing Office, 1971).

35. Frank Vandiver, *Confederate Blockade Running Through Bermuda* (Austin: University of Texas Press, 1947); G. G. Gibson Letter to J. M. Sexias, August 28, 1863, G. W. Blunt White Library, MSM.

36. ROG European Diary, 27.

Chapter 30: The Messenger: London, 1863

1. John Bennett, "Chelsea Link with the Confederacy," accessible at www.americancivilwar.org.uk/ articles/linkchelsea.htm.

2. ROG European Diary, 55.

3. ROG to Boteler, February 17, 1864, M. J. Solomon Scrapbook, Rose O'Neal Greenhow Papers, Digital Scriptorium Special Collections Library, Duke University.

4. Letter from James Murray Mason, September 21, 1863, published in *The Times* (London), September 25, 1863, British National Archives, Kew, London. Mason's instructions to give up his quest for official status and leave London were contained in a letter from Secretary of State Judah P. Benjamin dated August 4, 1863, the day before Rose left for England. The letter she carried from Davis may have been the president's explanation for the order.

5. Schuyler Dean Hoslett, "Southern Expectation of British Intervention in the Civil War," *Tyler's Quarterly Magazine* 22 (1940–41), 76–95, 141–61.

6. ROG European Diary, 32–33. Spence's book, *The American Union,* had been widely quoted in *The Times* when it was published in 1862.

7. Contract between Rose Greenhow and Richard Bentley, September 19, 1863, British Library Collections, Add. 46617, Folio 334.

8. ROG, *My Imprisonment.*

9. The *Index,* December 3, 1863, 506. British Newspaper Library, London.

10. *The New York Times,* December 5, 1863.

11. ROG European Diary, 36.

12. ROG to Boteler, December 10, 1863, M. J. Solomon Scrapbook, Rose O'Neal Greenhow Papers, Digital Scriptorium Special Collections Library, Duke University.

13. Archivist H. G. Jones's note on original, dated December 8, 1966.

14. ROG European Diary, 38.

15. Alistair Horne, *The Seven Ages of Paris* (New York: Alfred A. Knopf, 2003), 230–45.

16. ROG European Diary, 39.

17. The convent, at the Hôtel Biron, 77 rue de Varenne, is now the Rodin Museum.

18. ROG European Diary, 44.

19. ROG to JD, January 2, 1864, Samuel W. Richey Confederate Collection, Walter Havighurst Special Collection, Miami University (Oxford, Ohio).

20. Letter from J. P. Benjamin to James M. Mason, January 18, 1864, in Virginia Mason, ed., *The Public Life and Diplomatic Correspondence of James M. Mason, with Some Personal History by His Daughter* (Roanoke, Va.: Stone Printing and Manufacturing Co., 1903), 469–72.

21. ROG to JD, January 2, 1864, Samuel W. Richey Confederate Collections, Walter Havighurst Special Collections, Miami University (Oxford, Ohio).

Chapter 31: An Imperial Welcome: Paris, 1864

1. ROG European Diary, 45.

2. Ibid., 46.

3. Ibid., 48.

4. Ibid., 49.

5. Ibid.

6. Ibid., 50.

7. Ibid.

8. ROG to Boteler, February 17, 1864, Rose O'Neal Greenhow Papers, Digital Scriptorium Special Collections Library, Duke University.

9. Horne, *The Seven Ages of Paris,* 241.

10. Poem by Georgiana Fullerton about Rose Greenhow, written after her death, which appeared in *Temple Bar Magazine,* published by Richard Bentley (London, 1870). Local Studies Library, Birmingham, England.

11. ROG European Diary, 52.

12. Ibid.

13. The *Index,* February 11, 1864; ROG to Boteler, February 17, 1864, M. J. Solomon Scrapbook, Rose O'Neal Greenhow Papers, Digital Scriptorium Special Collections Library, Duke University.

14. Westminster Rate Book, 1864, Westminster City Archives (London), C683, Box 2304.
15. Poem by Georgiana Fullerton, *Temple Bar Magazine*, 1870. Local Studies Library, Birmingham, England.
16. ROG European Diary, 58.
17. Ibid., 66, 72.
18. Ibid., 64.
19. Rose Greehow's European address book. Rose O'Neal Greenhow Papers, 1863–1864, P.C.1226.1, North Carolina State Archives. In Lady Wharncliffe's personal diary of 1863–1864, there is no mention of Rose Greenhow. The Provenance of the Address Book, 1981.45.28. In November 1942, Harper Brothers, publisher of *Harper's Magazine*, offered the address book and two photos of Mrs. Greenhow to the Cape Fear Chapter No. 3, UDC. They accepted the offer. In December, they were shown to the members and placed in the museum. That is where the phrase *loaned by Cape Fear Chapter No. 3, UDC* comes in. There is no information as to how *Harper's* came by it.
20. British National Archives, reference PRO 30/29/18/19.
21. Wharncliffe to ROG, September 5, 1864, Sheffield Archives, Wharncliffe Muniments M 461/8-10. Rose never received the letter.
22. ROG European Diary, 83.
23. Ibid., 65.
24. Gwin also had several audiences with Napoleon III promoting a Mexican venture that eventually failed.
25. ROG European Diary, 67–68. Garibaldi and one thousand Red Shirt volunteers had conquered the Two Sicilies and helped unify Italy under King Victor Emmanuel II. Rose may have known he lionized Lincoln for freeing the slaves in the secessionist states.
26. ROG European Diary, 79.
27. Ibid., 81. Charles Darwin's *Origin of Species* had been published in 1859.
28. ROG European Diary, 82.

Chapter 32: A Chance for Peace: London, 1864

1. ROG European Diary, 83.
2. Foote, *The Civil War*, 137.
3. ROG European Diary, 84.
4. Ibid., 86.
5. Ibid., 87.
6. Ibid., 90, for Rose's account. See also James M. Mason, Dispatches 8–11 (June 1 through July 8, 1864), in Mason, ed., *The Public Life and Diplomatic Correspondence of James M. Mason*. For travel, his reports of meeting with Palmerston, see James Morton Callahan, *Diplomatic History of the Southern Confederacy* (New York: Frederick Ungar Publishing Co., 1964), 231–33, and Robert W. Young, *Senator James Murray Mason: Defender of the Old South* (Knoxville: University of Tennessee Press, 1998), 161, 173, for sequence of events.
7. ROG European Diary, 93.
8. Ibid., 92.
9. Ibid., 95–96.
10. Ernest B. Furgurson, *Not War but Murder: Cold Harbor 1864* (New York: Alfred A. Knopf, 2000), xi.
11. ROG European Diary, 96.
12. Just before the war ended, Moore, a West Pointer, was promoted to brevet brigadier general for his wartime service. Historical Register and Dictionary of the U.S. Army, Biographical Register of the Officers and Graduates of the United States Military Academy and Brevet Brigadier Generals in Blue.
13. ROG European Diary, 104–6.
14. Ibid., 109.

15. Ibid., 111.
16. Young, *Senator James Murray Mason*, 175.
17. *The New York Times*, September 9, 1864; ROG European Diary, 112–15.
18. ROG European Diary, 119.
19. Ibid., 120.
20. Ibid., 123.
21. Ibid.
22. Ibid.
23. Ibid., 124.
24. Collie to ROG, August 9, 1864, James Barbee Papers, LOC. In 1875, Collie was charged with fraud and absconded. On August 10, 1875, *The Times* reported: "He has done his best to give the case its worst possible complexion."
25. Mason to Davis, August 6, 1864, James M. Mason Papers, Clements Library, University of Michigan (Ann Arbor).
26. ROG European Diary, 128.

Chapter 33: The *Condor*

1. Ship log of Steamer *Niphon*, October 1, 1864, May 13, 1864–December 1, 1864, in Records of the Department of Navy, Logs of U.S. Naval Ships, 1801–1915, E-118, pl. 123, volume 2, National Archives (Washington, D.C.).
2. Wise, *Lifeline of the Confederacy*, 294.
3. The report was relayed to Rear Admiral S. P. Lee aboard the North Atlantic Blockade Squadron flagship USS *Malvern*. *Official Records*, series 1, volume 10, 438, 468, 476, 484, 531, 552, 743, 781.
4. "The Southern Confederacy," *London Evening Mail*, November 4–7, 1864, British Library Newspaper Library (Colindale, London).
5. Various accounts list August Charles Hobart-Hampden, also a British officer and a colorful personality, as captain of the *Condor*. Hobart-Hampden, forty-one when he made captain in March 1863, used the pseudonyms "Captain Hewitt" and "Captain Roberts," as well as "Samuel S. Ridge," the same name used by William N. W. Hewett. Two letters in the Sheffield Archives in England from *Condor* owner Alexander Collie, dated August 6 and August 23, 1864, and one from James Spence, dated August 8, 1864, name Hewett as captain. In his last letter, Collie said Hewett was sailing under the assumed name of "Captain Wright," similar to one of his middle names. The transcripts of the letters became available a century after the *Condor*'s voyage. Colonel William Lamb, commander of Fort Fisher where the *Condor* went aground, wrote in his diary: "When the sea subsided, the Commander of the *Condor*, a Victoria Cross man and an officer of the British Navy, came ashore." Lamb identified him as Captain "Hewett." Sheffield Archives, Wharncliffe Muniments 460A/27, 28, and 30. U.S. consul M. M. Jackson, watching for South-bound ships in Halifax, also identified Hewett as the captain.
6. Welles to S. P. Lee, September 18, 1864, *Official Records*, North Atlantic Blockade Squadron, series 1, volume 10, 468.
7. The *Index*, November 1864, British Library Newspaper Library (Colindale, London).
8. Jackson to Seward, September 26, 1864, *Official Records*, series 1, volume 10, 484.
9. *Official Records*, series 1, volume 10, 475–76. The USS *Alabama* was not the same ship as the CSS *Alabama* sunk by the *Kearsarge* off Cherbourg.
10. Ship log of Steamer *Niphon*, October 1, 1864, National Archives (Washington, D.C.).
11. Taylor, *Running the Blockade*, 129.
12. Wise, *Lifeline of the Confederacy*, 197.
13. "But in the darkness, amid the deafening thunder of the breakers, nothing was seen or heard of poor Mrs. Greenhow." "The Southern Confederacy," datelined "Richmond, October 8," *London Evening Mail*, November 7, 1864; National Archives Record Group No. 94, AGO DOC file 1599620.

14. Ibid.
15. "Doc Conner and the Bag of Gold," in *Recollections and Records,* edited by Ann Courtney Ward Little for the Columbus County Bicentennial Commission, 1976, 164–65.
16. Author interview with Chris E. Fonvielle Jr. of the University of North Carolina, Wilmington, March 2, 2004.
17. Taylor, *Running the Blockade.*
18. Lamb, *The Life and Times of Colonel William Lamb,* 167.
19. Newspaper clipping, source unknown, Alexander Robinson Boteler Papers, Box 5 of 5, Special Collections Library, Duke University. The report reprints an account it attributes to the *Wilmington Sentinel.*
20. Eliza Jane De Rosset to son Louis Henry De Rosset, October 5, 1864, 214 De Rosset Family, Series 1.1.4, September–October 1862, Folder 62, Southern Historical Society, University of North Carolina (Chapel Hill, N.C.).
21. Newspaper clipping, probably *Wilmington Sentinel,* October 1, 1864, Alexander Robinson Boteler Papers, Box 5 of 5, Special Collections Library, Duke University.
22. Ibid.
23. Lamb, *The Life and Times of Colonel William Lamb,* 167.
24. St. Thomas Church Parish Records, #159, October 2, 1864.
25. Newspaper clipping, probably *Wilmington Sentinel,* October 1, 1864, Alexander Robinson Boteler Papers, Box 5 of 5, Special Collections Library, Duke University.
26. Ibid. The newspaper report erroneously inserted a middle initial "A." that was excised here to make the text conform to her name as she used it in the last years of her life.

Epilogue

1. New Hanover County Administrator's Bonds, Book A 1856–1865, 334. New Hanover County Library (Wilmington, N.C.).
2. Record Group 21, Records of the District Court of the United States for the District of Columbia, Entry 115, Old Series Administration Case Files, 1801–78, National Archives (Washington, D.C.).
3. Bill for Discovery and Relief, Fall Term, 1867, New Hanover Court of Pleas and Quarter Sessions, September 23, 1867, New Hanover County Library (Wilmington, N.C.).
4. STM to Major General E. D. Townsend, June 18, 1870, Book 84, Record Group 21, Records of the District Court of the United States for the District of Columbia, Entry 115, Old Series Administration Case Files, 1801–78, National Archives (Washington, D.C.).
5. Lettres annuelles de la Société du Sacré-Cœur de Jésus, 2de Partie, 1863–1866.
6. Sister Maryvonne Duclaux, RSCJ, Convent du Sacré Coeur, e-mail with author, October 3, 2003. The child made her first communion on May 25, 1865, which happened to be the day Sister Madeleine Sophie, foundress of the convent, died at the age of eighty-five. The Catholic nun always had very special and loving relationships with the primary school children, especially the ones preparing for First Communion who visited her regularly until three days before her death. "Little Rose was among the children who paid respects to her the next day," wrote Sister Maryvonne, who dug into convent archives for records of the child's life there.
7. *The New York Times* reported that Marié was well known and had a handsome estate called Brookdale, near Philadelphia. Lee and Louis had a son, Louis Jr., who followed his grandfather into military service as a U.S. Marine officer. Like his grandfather, he served in the Philippines, where he commanded the marine barracks at Subic Bay until his retirement as a colonel in 1930. Lee and Louis Sr. retired to San Diego and showed up in the 1930 census with the house with no radio. O'Neal Genealogy Association.
8. Clipping in the Wm. M. Reaves clipping file, North Carolina Room, New Hanover County Public Library (Wilmington, N.C.).
9. O'Neal Genealogy Association.
10. Ibid.

11. Geneology research by Darlene Ramey Freeman; the Oak Hill Cemetery, Washington, D.C.
12. *Harper's Monthly* 124 (December 1911–May 1912): New York and London, Harper & Brothers Publishers, 1912.

Appendix I: Assessing Rose's Spycraft

1. Tidwell, *April '65: Confederate Covert Action in the American Civil War.*
2. Fishel, *The Secret War for the Union,* 59.
3. The Rasmussen San Francisco Passenger List shows "R. Greenbow," most likely Greenhow, arriving in San Francisco via Panama aboard the *Golden Gate* on August 18, 1853. Rasmussen, San Francisco Ship Passenger Lists, volume 4, June 17, 1852, to January 6, 1853, 83–84. MSM.

Appendix II: Court Records of Black Washingtonians

1. Record Group 21, Records of the District Courts of the United States, District of Columbia, Circuit Court for the District of Columbia, Entry 6, Case Papers Containing Appearances, Trials, Imparlances, Judicials, etc., 1828–1850. Compiled by Robert Ellis, archivist, Old Military and Civil Branch, National Archives and Records Administration. (Partial list for this term.)
2. Ibid.
3. Ibid.
4. Ibid.
5. Ibid.
6. Ibid.

Index

ANN BLACKMAN is the author of *Seasons of Her Life: A Biography of Madeleine Korbel Albright* and co-author of *The Spy Next Door,* about the traitorous FBI Agent Robert Hanssen. In her long career as a news reporter with *Time* magazine and the Associated Press, Blackman covered American politics, social policy, and the powerful personalities that make up Washington society. She is married to Michael Putzel. They have two grown children and live in the nation's capital.

Visit the author's website at www.wildrosebook.com.